Educational Choice and Labor Markets in Japan

Mary Jean Bowman
with the collaboration of
Hideo Ikeda and
Yasumasa Tomoda

Educational Choice and Labor Markets in Japan

The University of Chicago Press
Chicago and London

MARY JEAN BOWMAN is professor emeritus in the Departments of Economics and Education at the University of Chicago.

HIDEO IKEDA is professor of education at Hiroshima University.

YASUMASA TOMODA is professor of education at Osaka University.

The University of Chicago Press, Chicago 60637
The University of Chicago Press, Ltd., London

88 87 86 85 84 83 82 81   5 4 3 2 1

Publication of this book has been made possible in part by a grant from the Ford Foundation.

Library of Congress Cataloging in Publication Data

Bowman, Mary Jean.
Educational choice and labor markets in Japan.

Bibliography: p.
Includes index.
1. Education—Economic aspects—Japan. 2. High school graduates—Employment—Japan. 3. College graduates—Employment—Japan. I. Ikeda, Hideo, 1930- II. Tomoda, Yasumasa. III. Title.
LC67.J3B68   331.7'02   80-25557
ISBN 0-226-06923-0

Contents

Preface

Indirectly, but unmistakably, this book has its origins early in the 1960s in a series of conversations with Herbert Passin and with Professor Michiya Shimbori during his year as a visitor to the Comparative Education Center at The University of Chicago. In the course of these conversations we came increasingly to appreciate the special value of collaborative research into educational choice and labor markets in Japan. Furthermore, Japan seemed an ideal choice of country in which to apply some of the new ideas that have been developing so rapidly about investment in human beings, both in the school years and in postschool careers. In addition, we saw an opportunity in such work to give more explicit attention to expectations, which are the heart of economic theories about educational choice. The formation of expectations and their relations to actual educational and career decisions had received little empirical attention from economists. (Expectations had been given somewhat more attention by sociologists, but in a different theoretical framework.)

During the first and most intensive phase of our ensuing collaboration, we developed the main features of the research design and carried out the fieldwork and initial analysis of the data. Our first report was completed in 1971. Then, in 1976, the work was taken up again in response to the interest and enthusiasm of American specialists on Japanese society. The original 1966-67 materials were reexamined in the light of subsequent events, more recent data from other sources were scrutinized, and results were incorporated in the present book.

Over the years of our recurrent collaboration we have accumulated debts to many people who have encouraged and supported our activities or who have shared in them.

For financial assistance we are indebted first to the United States Office of Education, which financed the project from its inception to completion of the analysis of results of the 1966-67 survey data for male students. We owe special thanks to Alice Scates, then of the vocational education section in the Office of Education, for her interest in our work. Also deserving of special mention is the help given us by Robert Leestma, then with the Department of State, in facilitating arrangements for work in Japan. The Social Science Research Council financed the work done in 1976 and 1977 to bring the present book to fruition.

Of the many people who have made important contributions to our work, we wish to single out Professor Michiya Shimbori of Hiroshima University. Professor Shimbori encouraged our endeavor from the beginning. He generously turned his office into our headquarters and helped us develop the questionnaires and work out sampling plans and procedures for data collection. At this initial stage we were also assisted by Tsuyoshi Ishida, who made valuable contributions in working out the questionnaires and research design.

Before selecting schools for the samples or printing the questionnaires, we met in Kyoto with the Japanese associates who would share responsibility for the fieldwork. The ready and efficient cooperation manifested at this conference and thereafter was of immeasurable value. Assistance was generous, despite the very modest budget for field costs and the lack of any obvious rewards for involvement.

Leading senior educational scholars and researchers who shared in plans at this stage were Professor Yoshihiro Shimizu, then of Tokyo University; Director Hisao Kamidera, then of the Osaka City Institute for Education; and Professor Shigeo Matsui of the Institute for Comparative Education at Kyushu University. Also among the senior men who participated in the Kyoto conference were Professor Motoo Kaji and Mr. Seikichi Ando. Professor Kaji's economic sophistication, superb command of English, and skill in cross-cultural communication have been of prime value. Mr. Ikuo Amano, then of the National Institute for Education in Tokyo, led the fieldwork in the Tokyo-Tochigi area--an exceptionally demanding task. We are also indebted for help at this time to Professor Haruo Matsubara of Tokyo University; Professor Takashi Yano of Kyushu University; and Mr. Tooru Umakoshi, then of Kyushu University.

Contributors to our work in Chicago included Ichiro Iwano and Bruce Harker. Mr. Iwano translated the final version of the questionnaires back into English, and he worked with Professor Bowman on the occupational coding system. Dr. Harker carried out a special analysis of combined tapes for farmer fathers and students.

Professor William Cummings, whose enthusiasm helped launch the second phase of the project, facilitated work in Japan during the ten weeks Professor Bowman spent there with Professors Ikeda and Tomoda in the late spring and early summer of 1976. He went over the penultimate version of the manuscript with great care. Solomon Levine was helpful in several ways both early and late in this work. Arnold Zellner gave helpful suggestions on chapter 2.

Among many Japanese specialists who facilitated the 1976 updating of our work, Mr. Sasuma Shibanuma of the Ministry of Education deserves special thanks. In addition to providing summary materials from both published and unpublished sources, he engaged us in many a challenging discussion. Professor Ikuo Arai of the Tokyo Institute of Technology gave us many leads and further valuable insights into the situation today. And Mrs. Reiko Imamura of the Research Bureau in the Ministry of Education assisted us generously on many fronts in 1976, as she had done in 1966.

The contributions of Mrs. Ikeda and Mrs. Tomoda to the success of this work went beyond just patience and moral support. Mrs. Tomoda worked side by side with the rest of us in shaping the successive revisions of questionnaires, she was the mainstay of the office in Hiroshima during the period when Mr. Tomoda was trying to supervise fieldwork in several places at once, and she kept things moving without error as the coding of schedules from the Tokyo, Hiroshima, and Fukuoka offices piled up. Mrs. Ikeda joined Professor Ikeda in Japan and then back in Chicago in combing the relevant literature in Japanese; she spent many hours pursuing evidence that would facilitate interpretation of the Japanese sources and related matters as we were preparing the 1971 report of our study.

Finally, we owe some special thanks to Professor C. Arnold Anderson, who encouraged us throughout and who went over the final manuscript with practiced skill and devoted care.

Mary Jean Bowman
Hideo Ikeda
Yasumasa Tomoda

Introduction

Over the past quarter century, in nation after nation, education has expanded at a pace heretofore unimagined. This phenomenon has precipitated problems and provoked questions with respect to social policy that are unprecedented in their scale and ramifications. It has also brought education to a new and central place within the behavioral sciences and within economics in particular.

Our research on education, careers, and labor markets in Japan, part of which is reported in this book, is in itself another manifestation of the growing concern with education in policy and social science. Analytically, the study had its origin in human-investment theories that have been progressively elaborated over the sixties and seventies. However, economists have given little empirical attention to the study of expectations, despite the important place expectations occupy in their theories of decision making and behavior. Sociologists have studied the role of schooling in social mobility or status preservation and, most recently, in sequential patterns of career development. Their work converges with that of economists, especially in the United States.

Among the educational issues that arise in all nations, none are more important than those bearing on the secondary schools. At both the entry and graduation stages the secondary schools are the strategic arena within which youth must make the decision to enter the labor market directly or to continue with their education, and to choose one sort of career or another. It is for this reason that we focused this part of our research on upper-secondary pupils. Our data come primarily from a special survey of seven thousand Japanese boys who were in their senior year in 1966-67.[1] Five major curricula are represented: the academic general course, the nonacademic general (usually terminal) course, commerce, agriculture, and technical courses. Questions look both backward to time of entry into the upper-secondary schools and forward to anticipated future education and adult activities. The data include information on family backgrounds and on pupils' perceptions of the way labor markets operate. Supplementary information is taken from questionnaires filled out by the students' fathers (keyed to the interview-questionnaires obtained from their sons) and from a variety of published sources and official documents.[2] Where most immediately pertinent, we have drawn a few results from our unpublished research on labor markets as well as from work by others in this field.

Decisions and the Future

This study is organized around the concept of investment in human beings. This means that it is centered in the study of decisions, which are inherently expectational. Much of our discussion focuses, accordingly, on pupils' plans and expectations with respect to future education and career options, including but not limited to the monetary aspect. We explore how far those perceptions are conditioned by family backgrounds and geographic location. We ask how perceptions affect and are affected by the type of upper-secondary curriculum in which a youth is enrolled and by related aspects of secondary-school experiences. So far as the data permit, we compare choices and expectations with "objective"evidence relating to their realization or their reasonableness.

To our knowledge, only two other studies have systematically included empirical data on expectations as part of an analysis of the economics of some aspect of investment career decisions,[3] although expectations have been included in some sociological investigations. One of the several reasons for this research gap is undoubtedly that, where the future is vaguely perceived or is seen as uncertain, conventional probability models may be unsatisfactory. Such models can be adapted for our purpose, however, as can Shackle's treatment of the attention-arresting possibilities in decision making under uncertainty.[4] The present study remains distinctive in its treatment of these questions.

Also distinctive is our inclusion of data relating fathers' attitudes concerning labor market structures and job opportunities to students' perceptions of how labor markets operate.[5] A comparison that turned out to be especially illuminating was that between sons of wage and salaried men and sons of independent entrepreneurs. Here the complex interplay of monetary and nonmonetary considerations and of family and individual determinants of choice is clearly revealed. The sons of independent entrepreneurs have special opportunities, but they also have special obligations to the family business. Their situation measurably alters perceived options, the relations between their preferences and their expectations, and their assessment in strictly economic terms of the value to them of schooling.

Japan as a Challenging Case

In Japan we see a nation leading in educational and economic development, poor in natural but rich in human resources, and outstanding for both continuity and flexibility in virtually every aspect of a modernization process that has been uniquely adapted to its own historical background. Japanese distinctiveness derives not only from the conformation of well-integrated traditions but also from a remarkably persistent and assiduous creative adaptation of foreign technologies and ideas. Some broad comparisons of Japan with the United States, with only incidental explicit reference to other countries, should suffice to suggest at least a few of the important reasons why Japanese schooling and labor market processes must be of great interest around the world.

To begin, there is the overwhelming scale of the educational enterprise and the voluminous flows of students through the schools and into the labor markets. Everywhere among the economically advanced nations education has been part and parcel of an economic-technological revolution in which the diffusion of schooling has been both cause and effect--no one has yet managed to separate out the one from the other. But until recently, only in Japan and the United States has the educational operation been truly massive; even Russia could not match this spread of schooling. At the same time education has been both a contributor and a reactor to its own internal dynamic. The sheer scale of education in Japan and the United States accelerates that dynamic, a socioeconomic power that can be awesome. Educators are experiencing rising frustration in the face of the increasingly complex and all-embracing tasks that men would put upon them. Meanwhile, whether events move at headlong speed or at a more moderate pace, time moves with inexorable irreversibility. Schools and educational systems are not toys that can be played around with as though they were structures made out of children's building blocks to be knocked over and put together again at will. Real problems and societal decisions relating to them must be understood against this tide, which, although it limits the real options, paradoxically may also give seemingly small changes a cumulative power far beyond our expectations. All of this Japan and the United States share.

Let us grant that Japan and the United States, and now some other industrial nations as well, share in the experience and problems arising from a massive educational momentum. What, more specifically, are the commonalities and the contrasts most relevant in looking to Japan for illumination of problems and issues in the interaction of education and labor markets?

Japan resembles the United States in the wide diffusion of secondary and (more recently) higher education. Both countries have put a high pragmatic value on education, but perhaps this runs deeper in Japan. The Japanese have a diversified school system with a large private sector and a full continuum of quality, or prestige, institutions on the higher and upper-secondary levels. The massive diffusion of schooling, the high pragmatic value put on education, and the wide range in quality together form a syndrome that cannot be regarded as accidental. Nor is the Japanese pattern a product merely of the American occupation following World War II. Educational pragmatism and open access have a long history in Japan, despite some seeming contradictions. Intergenerational mobility in education and in occupational status is and has been comparatively high in Japan, as in the United States. Indeed, without such mobility Japan's spectacular development would have been impossible. Finally, the Japanese have a large highly technological and modern sector in their economy, and this economy operates in an open market system overall, despite an alleged (and much belabored) "dualism." At no time, even in her most nationalist days, has Japan stood in opposition to the market system as a matter of principle.

Against this background of shared characteristics stand out some important contrasts. The Japanese economy and Japanese labor markets in particular have been distinctive, with no close parallel elsewhere. The contrast with the United States has centered in Japan's paternalism, with strong attachments of individuals to their patrons and through those patrons either directly or indirectly to their employers. The most widely cited element in this complex is the so-called life-commitment (*nenko*) system in large enterprises. This system arose in its present form only when Japan was well into the twentieth century, and it has probably been declining for some time; the associated dualism that characterized Japanese labor markets before 1960 definitely has been fading. Some of these changes may have been temporary adjustments to demographic and economic swings, but even if they prove more permanent, the effects of the past remain, still conditioning linkages between types and levels of schooling and career patterns. One interesting question today is how these labor markets or changes in them may influence career options and student perceptions of those options. Another question is how far the Japanese pattern may illuminate the implications of comprehensive seniority agreements in other countries, a pattern at once both similar and yet in sharp contrast to that in Japan.[6]

Other striking contrasts between the Japanese and the American situations are to be found in the structure and operation of their school systems. These contrasts reflect underlying societal differences and historical experiences of each educational system before (and during) World War II. Japan's history, along with a description of the present situation, will be discussed in some detail in chapter 1. Here we can be brief, stressing only a few relevant contrasts: (1) Although the Japanese educational system can be described as exceptionally open in some respects, for decades it has also been marked off by one examination after another, from the very earliest years (even at entry to first grade) on up to entry to college. This custom of frequent examinations clearly has militated against a completely open system, with important implications for selection as pupils have progressed through the system, and in the allocation of students among types, qualities, and levels of schooling. (2) Although in the international achievement test in mathematics Japanese 13-year-olds displayed a high variability in performance, as did those in the United States, the Japanese mean was the highest whereas the United States (and Sweden) were at the bottom of the list. (3) Japan has an extraordinarily low drop-out rate between entry to and completion of upper-secondary school, found nowhere else except where the upper-secondary schools admit only a tiny elite. (4) Before the American occupation, Japanese postelementary education was differentiated among types of curricula, with streaming and vocational specializations more like the German or French than the American pattern. This heritage influences debates over the implantation of the "comprehensive high school" on Japanese soil, an issue that has been revived in recent years. This pattern is reflected, of course, in the design of our research.

In sum, we face a series of seeming paradoxes. Japan's educational system is both elitist and massively popular, both flexible and streamed. Japanese labor markets are simultaneously dynamic and free, yet constrained by the patronage system.

The Structure of This Book

Any study of how educational choices and career expectations are interrelated, and of how they are affected by family backgrounds, local environments, and the characteristics of labor markets, must necessarily be seen in the wider context of educational and economic history. Such a study must also be rooted in a broad but systematic theoretical decision model. Part 1 lays the groundwork. Thus, chapter 1 summarizes the Japanese educational structure and the composition of the labor force as these have developed through time and as they stand at present. Chapter 2, which is theoretical and methodological, is fundamental in setting out the analytical bases of the ensuing chapters. (In later chapters aspects of the general theoretical framework are particularized according to the problem under consideration.)

Part 2 is concerned with what we have called the "Stage I decision", the decision at completion of lower-secondary school to enroll in one or another upper-secondary course, to register for shorter training, or to enter the labor market. We start in chapter 3 by exploring socioeconomic selectivity into upper-secondary schools and among types of courses. In this analysis we attempt to identify both differences in constraints on choice and differences in perceived future options associated with enrollment in one or another curriculum as those differences derive from parental and locational characteristics. Chapter 4 deals with course preferences, reasons for discrepancies between initial preferences and actual enrollments, and changes in preferences between entry and graduation. In chapter 5 we formulate a model for analysis of the Stage I decision; that model is used to bring together the findings reported in chapters 3 and 4 and to assess how far we have come in filling in empirically the main components of the analytic framework. It is clear enough that in Japan as elsewhere there are systematically patterned constraints on individual choices with respect to secondary education, but also that Japan is a relatively open society. Equally clear is the economic reasonableness in the patterning of choices.

With part 3 we come to the "Stage II decision", the decision at completion of upper-secondary school to pursue higher education or enter the labor market. Chapter 6 introduces this part of the book with some brief descriptive data and a reformulation of the model laid out in chapter 5, but now in the perspective of the Stage II decision point. In chapter 7 we examine the effects of parental and community backgrounds and of occupational goals on the college decision. Economic constraints are examined in detail in chapter 8, and income expectations as related to the college decision are the subject of chapter 9. The principal findings are brought together in chapter 10, as a conclusion to part 3.

Too often the postschool years are collapsed into a single block in discussions of how education and the labor market interact, despite the fact that such simplifications are both far from reality and conducive to serious misinterpretations of the nature of such relationships. In part 4 we look at the postschool years as moving histories that extend forward into the future, an approach that mirrors the way students actually perceive the future. Because of the importance of making this a reasonable-sized volume, it has been necessary to cut this material back sharply from its original scope. This has meant the elimination of much of the evidence not directly linked to our student survey and of much of the detail from that survey. However, we have retained enough to provide the dynamic framework for the analysis, which is set forth in three chapters. The first, chapter 11, focuses on occupational expectations and sequences; in chapter 12 we present information on how the students and their parents perceive the labor markets; and in chapter 13 we concentrate on life earning paths, tying this anlysis back to chapter 9.

Individual decisions both reflect and affect societal institutions and changes in them, just as they set the stage for and respond to shifts in educational policies. Throughout this book we have sought to place our analysis of decisions of students and their fathers in the context of a stable, yet continuously changing society, as the conditioning environment of those decisions. Chapter 14 reverses this perspective, to draw selectively on our findings as manifestations of and indicators of societal developments in relationships between education and the labor markets; it gives special attention to educational policies and related issues and prospects for the shaping of Japanese life in the future.

Part 1

Points of Departure

1. Educational Expansion and the Japanese Labor Force

Education has deep roots in Japanese society, going back well into pre-Meiji times. Despite early elite readings of the Chinese classics, Japanese education has largely been economically and politically pragmatic, and marked by an ever-growing emphasis on the importance of schooling for all. The spread of education to progressively higher levels had been gathering momentum long before World War II. By the middle sixties the magnitude of the forward surge became awesome, fed not only by continuously rising aspirations but by the successive cohorts of the postwar baby-boom as they moved up the educational ladder. Today the demographic swell has diminished, but aspirations continue to grow. None of this has happened in isolation from the rest of society. The spread of schooling has both affected and responded to changes in the labor markets and in the Japanese economy generally. The interconnected changes in schooling and labor markets are not reversible, nor can they be understood as simple extensions from the past. On the contrary, signs of some fundamental future readjustments already are evident as recruitment, training, and promotion policies of big firms are modified in response to the slowdown in economic growth, to the wide diffusion of schooling, and to distortions in the age structure of the population. It is against such a dynamic background that we must seek to ascertain and to understand the hopes and fears, the actions, and sometimes the frustrations, of successive cohorts of Japanese youth.

But "education" is not a unidimensional process, and expansion in enrollments fans out in many directions. Individual decisions, and expectations, may be as concerned with differences in kind as with quantities or years of schooling. The patterns of the channels through which young people move and the growing magnitude of the movements are important to development and adjustment. In both these respects the upper-secondary schools occupy a central place. Above all, it is the curriculum differentiations in the upper-secondary schools that exercise the greatest influence on both patterns of career development for individuals (including the choice of entering or not entering college) and systems (formal or informal) of postschool development of human resources in the economy at large.

Japanese Education from 1872 to World War II

Since at least the beginning of the Meiji era Japanese education has undergone almost continuous reform, reflecting now one, now another, aspect of Western education while maintaining all the while a distinctive national character. The reform of the school system in an American image during the occupation years after World War II was less of a break with tradition than sometimes is supposed.

In 1872, as one of its first major actions, the Mieji government laid out the basic plans for a modern national system of education. These plans embraced all levels of schooling, from primary through middle and secondary levels and up to higher education. From the start a chief aim was to establish universal primary education and to build the system upward from that base. Japan had long possessed a widespread system of *terakoya*. or Confucian temple schools, in which use of the abacus and basic literacy were taught; those schools chiefly served children of the economically successful, notably the children of merchants. Important also was the education provided sons of the samurai, in feudal courts where Chinese literature and the martial arts were taught. The new plan provided for a transfer of these schools to a national system, extending their coverage to provide four years of compulsory, coeducational schooling for all. It was intended that the new educational system (as it was soon to become), by achieving equality among the four social classes, would serve two larger purposes: national unification and economic growth.

Governmental intentions were slow in realization, however. Despite government policy, many factors militated against early establishment of a nationally integrated system of primary schools. Among these were a shortage of school facilities, lack of teachers trained in technical fields, and frequent resistance among both feudal elites and the peasantry. Also important in the short run was government officials' ignorance of how to implement a national educational policy. Consequently, the temple-school pattern and Confucian predominance in centers of higher learning continued for some years with little interference from the government.

These difficulties and the emperor's commitment to economic modernization led the Meiji government to solicit the aid of Western educational experts--principally and at first, representatives of the common-school system of the United States. Under their influence the Japanese even went so far as to construct model schoolhouses, furnished with replicas of Western school desks and blackboards. But that early period of American influence in Japanese education was short, marked by experimentation with variations on the American theme of universal education. Japan was to find a more satisfactory model, better suited to her purposes, in the German school system. The guiding principles of Japanese education under the German influence were formally promulgated in the Imperial Rescript on Education, issued in 1890. This rescript ended the period of searching for Western answers and established education firmly in a nationalist context, where it was to remain with only minor modifications until the Japanese defeat in World War II.

The development of Japanese industry, already remarkably modernized by the time of the Sino-Japanese War in 1884, imposed new tasks of manpower training. While up to this time the Meiji government had been concerned chiefly with the establishment of universal primary education, now interest shifted to the development of vocational education in order to supply skilled workers. Vocational schools at the middle and secondary levels had been organized, but they served the lower white collar classes, not blue collar workers. Continuation schools introduced in 1893 provided vocational education for those seeking work after completing the four-year primary schools. These schools, attached to primary schools, multiplied thereafter.

During the first decade of the twentieth century, the educational system was elaborated to a multitrack structure that remained fundamentally unchanged up to 1947. There were separate post-elementary tracks for girls, and when compulsory elementary education was expanded (in 1908) from four to six years, only the first three years remained coeducational; this marked the formal beginning of special training in "female roles."

By 1910, most on-coming cohorts of Japanese children were completing at least the required six years of elementary school. At this critical point boys could (1) enter the academic middle schools; (2) enter one or another vocational middle-secondary school; (3) undertake two additional years of elementary education (which might be terminal or might lead to normal school or to a somewhat higher level of vocational school); or (4) seek immediate entry into the labor market. This last alternative might occasionally involve some informal or formal apprenticeship arrangement. For girls the main alternatives in 1910 were (1) to terminate schooling and formal training altogether; (2) to attend special classes in distinctively "female skills" outside the regular school system; (3) to enter one of the "girls' high schools." Although commonly translated this way, these "girls' high schools" were in fact at the level of boys' middle schools and for most girls were terminal courses; they were a distinctively Japanese institution, notwithstanding some superficial resemblance to British-American "finishing schools" for the making of gentlewomen.

Of special importance for boys in the prewar educational system were the academic middle and the vocational schools. At completion of his sixth year in school the Japanese boy of 1910 faced the first of the important examinations that would determine his future. The most fortunate or successful gained entrance directly to the academic middle schools, which constituted the main route to higher schools and thence to universities. About a tenth of the male cohort of 1910 attended these academic middle schools, with proportions rising to nearly a fifth over the next thirty years. Of these favored young men, a small minority advanced through academic higher schools to the imperial universities and another (growing) minority to other universities. The remaining youth who completed the academic or other middle schools either went directly into the labor market or entered higher normal schools and technical colleges or institutes. The latter have often been designated misleadingly as "junior colleges" in attempts to find their American equivalents. A closer parallel may be found in British terminal polytechnic education at completion of the O-level in contrast to entry to the British "sixth form," which is roughly comparably to the Japanese academic higher schools as preparatory for the universities.

In principle, the academic middle schools were open to all boys who passed qualifying examinations, and were free channels through which they could advance up the social ladder, although in fact their progress was indirectly affected by parental socioeconomic status. Few rural people could afford to send their children to boarding schools, even when prior training and abilities enabled a rural youth to score well on the examinations. Meanwhile, nevertheless, the numbers of candidates for continuation at each successive level of schooling were multiplying. Competition for entry became ever more severe, and schools at each level, even the elementary, derived differential prestige according to the success of their graduates in obtaining places at the prestigious institutions of the next higher level. A system of "first schools" evolved, along with the proliferation of examinations at all levels of the system. Typically, "first schools" for the more elementary students were associated with first schools for students at the next higher level, thus forming a closely articulated system of academic advancement. Despite both decentralization and democratization of the educational system in the wake of World War II, important elements of this system survive in Japan today, often in new manifestations. Examinations came to be used for selection from kindergarten into elite elementary schools. But probably more important at present is the extensive and expanding *juku* system of private individual and group tutorial sessions, often conducted in the homes of retired or moonlighting teachers after school hours, but in other, more formal settings as well.[1] Closely related is the pervasive *rōnin* system (from the word for "patron" or "protector"), whereby youth who fail to win entrance to the university of their choice come back to compete in the examinations again, and often yet again. Often they attend special schools called *yobiko* ("preparatory schools"), which differ from the *juku* in that the former are entirely exam-cramming programs for youth in grades 10 to 12 and for *rōnin*.

With the Vocational School Act of 1899, a system of vocational tracks resembling the German system but characteristically modified to suit Japanese perceptions and purposes was introduced. Vocational tracks for boys came to include four major curricula: agriculture, commerce, industrial or technical courses, and the merchant marine. Two years later fishery schools were added. Each has an approximate counterpart at the upper-secondary level today, though the fishery schools and merchant marine enroll very few students and have been excluded from our study. Some technical courses gave entry into "higher" schools of engineering;[2] these were comparable to British polytechnic institutes. Also, by the 1920s and 1930s other male graduates of elementary schools were being recruited directly into technical programs operated by large firms to produce skilled workers for their plants--programs that sometimes lasted three to five years. The "life-commitment" system under which most of these trainees were hired made such a position in a big firm highly attractive to the children of laboring families; with low quit rates, it also ensured a return to the employer on his training investments.

The formal incorporation of postelementary education for working youth into an integrated educational system came comparatively late, with the part-time "youth schools." These schools, which had been growing rapidly since 1935, were made compulsory in 1939 for boys not continuing on other (mainly full-time) educational paths. The youth schools of this period had been foreshadowed in part by the earlier continuation schools (introduced in 1893); in part they developed as an extension of upper-elementary education. They included not only courses of part-time instruction in lower-level vocational skills but also trade courses lasting as long as five years beyond termination of full-time study in the elementary grades. Formally established during the period of Japanese militaristic expansion on the continent of Asia, these schools were strongly nationalistic. By the time of the attack on Pearl Harbor the youth schools were enrolling a majority of all boys between the ages of 14 and 19 and were used primarily for pre-induction military training. With the increasing strains of World War II, the youth-school pattern of mixing work in shop and factory with part-time schooling and military training was temporarily extended to young people going through the regular upper-secondary and higher levels of the educational structure as well,[3] but this expedient ended with the cessation of hostilities, as did the formal youth school in its prewar and wartime nationalistic modes.

The Japanese Educational System after World War II

Among the first changes in the months immediately after the war was the withdrawal of the Imperial Rescript on Education and the drafting of new laws expressing a nonnationalist and democratic philosophy of education. Formerly regarded as the *duty* of every Japanese, in appropriate service to his emperor and his nation, schooling was recast as the *right* of every individual. The emphasis now was on equality of opportunity, the realization of individual potential, and the expression of individual interests and preferences. This American-style individualist-egalitarian philosophy provided not only a basis for further democratization of Japanese education but also the rationale for decentralization of control. Up to the 1960s, decentralization, democratization, and modernization were the rubrics most widely used in describing postwar changes in Japanese schooling. While the Japanese system of compulsory schooling remained a national one, certain important powers were given or returned to local school districts. Prefectural units were given the power of teacher certification and control of the entrance examinations for upper-secondary schools (grades 10 through 12). Local school boards and teachers were given independent authority to monitor and select textbooks and to modify optional portions of the compulsory-school curriculum. In 1966, however, the national government resumed its practice of selecting a short list of texts for each course, from which local boards can make their choices.

Obviously, it would be quite wrong to infer that Japanese education has become a replica of that in the United States. Such definitely has not been the case at any time; differences in cultural heritage are not wiped out by legal fiat or formal reorganization. But where American ways have met the desires or needs of the Japanese, those ways have been accepted and integrated into the Japanese system by the same process of discriminating and creative imitation that has long been the genius of Japan. It is always easier to accept the formalities than the substance of a foreign model.

The introduction of a 6-3-3-4 system (as a simplified version of the American structure) was easy to carry out at the elementary and secondary levels, and was in fact suggested by Japanese educators working with the first American mission after the war. There is thus in Japan today a six-year secondary-school sequence split between lower- (or junior-) and upper-secondary schools, the latter overlapping part of the old middle and part of the old higher schools. Readily adopted also was the extension of compulsory schooling to nine years, through lower-secondary school. Most young people had already been completing eight years in school. More important changes were the formal (though not mandatory) extension of coeducation throughout the national system and the elimination of the earliest tracking point in the prewar system.

Professor Shigeo Matsui has argued that the developments in lower-secondary education in Japan in the postwar years established an essentially "comprehensive" education at that level:

> The new lower secondary school of three years was a common school mainly aiming to provide a basic general education for the citizens of a democratic society, and also training for a future vocational career in the case of pupils not continuing on to the upper secondary school. Pupils of all abilities were required to learn under the same roof by the common curriculum with only a small number of elective subjects. In this sense it was a genuine comprehensive school. Remarkably enough, it was established all over the country as the sole school type for its age group, with its own principals and separate from the elementary as well as the upper secondary schools. (Matsui 1971, p. 31)

Efforts to extend comprehensive education to the upper-secondary level never went very far, but espousal of a more nearly comprehensive arrangement has been increasing again recently in proposals for reform of the general upper-secondary schools.

The fact remains, however, that "comprehensive upper-secondary schooling," whatever one means by this, has not been the Japanese pattern over the past three decades. It is true that academic and nonacademic general curricula have been included in the same school. Also, there are rural "combined schools" in some prefectures, where general and agricultural tracks or, less often, general and commerce tracks are offered within the same establishment. However, the postwar system of upper-secondary schools and curricula retains the sharp distinctions among types of courses that characterized prewar secondary-level education: the academic (and nonacademic) general course, technical courses, commerce, agriculture, and (for girls) domestic arts.

If one considers all courses together, the proportions of lower-secondary graduates of 1964 (the cohort of our sample) entering full-time upper-secondary schools was almost as high for girls as for boys (62.2 and 63.9 percent, respectively), but more boys entered part-time upper-secondary programs. There are virtually no dropouts from the full-time courses, which means that a substantial majority of our age cohort were included among the 1967 graduates of upper-secondary schools. Today 90 percent of a cohort graduate.

Upper-secondary-school course enrollments are shown in table 1.1 for all students in 1955, 1966, and 1974 and by sex in 1966 and 1974. These figures include part-time students, who made up just over a tenth of the 1966 total. (Proportions enrolled part-time have declined steadily, from over 20 percent in 1950 and 1955 to 10 percent in 1966 and 6 percent in 1974.) Part-time enrollment has been somewhat higher in agriculture and the technical courses than elsewhere. On the whole, distributions of students among curricula have been stable since 1966, although there has been a definite decline in the proportions of males taking commerce courses. Proportions in domestic arts have slowly but steadily diminished in spite of the rise in the proportion of upper-secondary students who are female. The other curriculum that has consistently lost relative ground is agriculture, a predictable trend given the decline of employment in that sector.

Typical curricula in the various upper-secondary courses are shown for 1966 in table 1.2. While there has been much discussion of curriculum reform, in fact there has been little change since 1966, and the General B and technical curricula especially are tightly

Table 1.1 Male and Female Upper-Secondary-School Enrollments

A. All Courses

	Number Enrolled (thousands)			Male % of Total Students	
	1955	1966	1974	1966	1974
Full-Time	2,037	4,480	3,997	51.1	49.7
Part-Time	535	507	267	63.6	52.2
Total	2,572	4,987	4,264	52.5	49.8

B. Course Percentage Distributions

	All			Male		Female	
	1955	1966	1974	1966	1974	1966	1974
General (B+A)	59.8	60.1	61.7	55.6	59.0	65.2	64.5
Agriculture[a]	7.9	5.3	5.1	7.9	7.3	2.6	3.1
Technical	9.2	11.6	12.2	22.3	23.8	.5	.9
Commerce	14.3	17.1	15.0	14.2	9.8	20.1	20.7
Deomestic arts	8.2	5.6	4.7	...	...	11.1	9.6
Other[b]	.6	.3	1.3	c	.1	.5	1.2
Total	100.0	100.0	100.0	100.0	100.0	100.0	100.0

Source. Mombushō, *Gakkō Kihon Chōsa* [Ministry of Education, Basic School Surveys] (Tokyo, 1955, 1966, 1974).

[a]Including fishery schools.

[b]Including nursing and related studies.

[c]Under .05%.

packed and very demanding. General B is the academic, university-orieted course, whereas General A is a nonacademic, all-round upper-secondary program. There are heavier mathematics and foreign language requirements in General B, a wider range of nonacademic electives in General A. In each of the vocational curricula approximately half of the course work could be classified as essentially "general." The technical-school curricula are comparatively high on mathematics, the commerce curricula on foreign languages. The broad picture in the vocational schools is a quite even mix of general and specialized training. There are, of course, variations of specialization within the technical schools.

Table 1.2 Examples of Upper-Secondary Full-Time Curricula

	General B	General A	Technical	Commerce	Agriculture
Japanese language	15	12	9	9	9
Social Studies	15	13	9	9	9
Mathematics	15	9	13	9	7
Science	15	12	6	6	9
Foreign languages	15	9	9	15	9
Domestic arts	4 girls	4 girls	...	4 girls	...
Health and physical education	11 boys 9 girls	11 boys 9 girls	9	9	9
Fine arts	4	6	1	1	1
Electives (subjects other than above)	...	15 boys 13 girls	...	...	...
Industrial subjects	...	...	52	...	...
Commercial subjects	...	...	...	41	...
Agricultural subjects	...	...	...	...	55
Special curricular activities	3	3	3	3	3
Credits applicable to any subject	9	12	...	...	...
Total	102 boys 104 girls	102 boys 102 girls	111	102 boys 106 girls	111

Source. Ministry of Education, *Education in Japan* (Tokyo, 1967), pp. 68-69.

Note. These figures show the number of credits to be earned before graduation. Required for one credit are thirty-five unit hours in one grade.

Also, the options available differ between rural and urban locations. Technical schools are located (virtually without exception in 1966) in areas with populations over fifty thousand, and

Table 1.3 Urban and Rural Student Enrollments (1966 percentage distributions)

	General B	General A	Agri-culture	Commerce	Technical	Total
Urban	39	3	3	21	33	99
Rural	46	32	19	3	0	100

Note. Sample adjusted to all-Japan distribution of students among course types. The split between academic (General B) and nonacademic (General A) is based on findings of our survey; that split, though very much emphasized in Japan and quite unambiguous to teachers and students, was not available in national statistics.

commerce courses in small towns and villages were few. Agriculture courses are offered mainly in rural areas, as we would expect, though a few have been established in big cities. Among the male students, many rural but few urban youth enrolled in the General A curriculum; this reflects the lack of rural options in technical and commerce schools, not a lack of places in General B (see table 1.3).

Other options taken by graduates of the compulsory nine-year sequence are shown in table 1.4, where we give figures for 1964 because that is the cohort to which the students in our interview sample belonged. The most important training or education options for working youth at this stage were the part-time courses in upper-secondary school, the public vocational-training centers, and the training programs within industry. Already in 1964 the "miscellaneous" schools, which were mainly a carry-over from prewar patterns, had virtually disappeared for boys and had dropped sharply to small enrollment proportions for girls.[4] Formal training within industry was (and is) relatively less important for graduates of the lower-secondary level than it had been in earlier decades, when few entrants to the labor market had gone beyond eight or nine years of schooling. Nevertheless, such training still was important for the youth involved, whose numbers are understated in the official tabulations because of erroneous specifications of "training". The public vocational-training centers, most of which were comparatively few in the 1960s, provided training primarily for employment in smaller plants rather than in the larger concerns within which most of the in-house training occurs.

Summing up the picture revealed by table 1.4, we find that among boys 64 percent entered full-time and 6 percent entered part-

Table 1.4 Destinations of Ninth-Grade Graduates (1964 percentage distributions)

Total Graduates (thousands)	All (2,327)	Male (1,204)	Female (1,123)
1. Full-time upper-secondary school or technical junior college	63.1	63.9	62.2
2. Part-time upper-secondary school	5.1	6.1	4.1
3. Correspondence, upper secondary	.7	.4	1.1
4. Special course, upper secondary	.1	.0	.1
5. Youth class	.4	.3	.5
6. Social correspondence courses	.2	.2	.3
7. Public vocational-training center	1.3	2.3	.3
8. Training within industry	2.4	3.1	1.7
9. Training, farm	.2	.3	.0
10. Miscellaneous schools	4.6	1.5	7.9
11. Two (or more) kinds of training	.7	.8	.7
12. Total with some form of education or training after compulsory school	78.8	78.9	78.9
13. No postcompulsory education or training	20.6	20.5	20.6
14. Nonresponse	.6	.6	.5
Total	100.0	100.0	100.0
15. Total receiving training within industry (item 8 above or in combination with others)	2.7	3.6	1.8
16. Total receiving training at public vocational-training centers (item 7 above or in combination with others)	1.4	2.4	.3

Source. Mombushō, *Gakkō Kihon Chōsa* [Ministry of Education, Basic School Survey] (Tokyo, 1964), table 4, p. 16.

time upper-secondary schooling.[5] Adding together all those reporting any sort of study or training, we account for four-fifths of the boys and girls coming out of the ninth grade. Or, alternatively, as of 1964 one-fifth reported no further training or schooling immediately after completion of the ninth grade, one-fifth were studying or receiving training part-time, usually while working, and three-fifths were continuing in full-time schooling. This last proportion continued to rise dramatically over the succeeding decade, with a corresponding sharp decline in the proportion with no training after lower-secondary school.

The next important transition point in an education-career sequence comes with the decision (or opportunity) to continue schooling beyond the upper-secondary level (the old middle schools of the prewar years). Before the war the decision to continue posed more educational alternatives than usually are considered now. For boys, favored options included not only pursuit of academic studies leading to a place in the more or less prestigeful universities but also, quite often, the direct undertaking of specialized professional training to become highly qualified technicians.

We have referred already to prewar routes to the imperial and other universities, by way of higher schools or other preparatory programs. Under the postwar system the transition from academic upper-secondary schools (now at completion of twelve grades) to universities is direct: there are no intervening schools as part of the regular sequence. As before, graduates of the General B course, joined by a few from other tracks, compete for entrance to the major universities at examinations set up by each institution. However, many youth (at the time of our study, roughly a third) spend a year or more as *rōnin* in further preparation for the university of their choice--usually with tutorial assistance or in special cram courses. This sort of supplementary university preparation is familiar in countries in which only a small minority of highly advantaged individuals complete upper-secondary school; Greece and Brazil are examples. But Japan is different, with the large and growing rates of enrollment in higher education. In Japan competition for entry to preferred institutions has reached a frenzy probably matched in no other part of the world.

A few of the private secondary schools have long shared with the schools affiliated with the national universities the distinction of placing more students in favored universities, and private channels of educational advance have been strengthened with the expansion of private universities. But if these developments have modified, they have not by any means reversed the prewar pattern of sequential examination routes to the academically elite institutions. Persisting also are close cliques of university graduates who influence mutual career development opportunities. Higher education has continued to be one of the most conservative sectors of Japanese society, with firmly entrenched patterns of personal patronage and seniority in academic employment and promotions.[6] And despite some exceptions, especially in the private sectors of the economy, the Japanese version of the "old school tie" has systematically segregated occupations and career lines for graduates of particular universities. This problem has become, once again, an issue in public policy and a prime topic of current investigation.

Frequently it is supposed that the first United States Educational Mission to Japan proposed from the start (in its 1946 report) to give all institutions of higher education the same formal (and four-year) status. In fact, such a recommendation was not included in the initial report of the Mission. It was adopted, however, in the School Education Law a year later with the support of Japanese educators working both within the commission on educational reform and outside it. What is not so clear is why proponents adopted this policy and what results they anticipated. Was the intent to homogenize higher education in Japan, reducing the heterogeneity of options among (rather than within) institutions?

Starting from their experience at home, the American advisers undoubtedly visualized almost the opposite of homogeneity so far as standards of quality were concerned. Furthermore, they came to Japan from a nation that had historically displayed little hesitation in adding unconventional, pragmatically oriented courses to the college curriculum. But conversion of the complex prewar Japanese system to a highly simplified 6-3-3-4 plan was in fact both more and less than a shift to the American way of doing things.

The majority of prewar colleges and institutes were transformed rapidly into four-year colleges and universities (*daigaku*) during the first years of American occupation. Already by the summer of 1949 this policy was being modified to allow the establishment of "junior colleges" (*tanki daigaku*); about a fourth of today's in-coming college freshmen are enrolling in a junior college. However, the older professional institutes at this level were not revived, and the new junior colleges were very different from the technical and commercial institutes of the prewar years. They became mainly schools for girls, and male junior-college enrollments dropped from three-fifths of the total in 1951 to only one-sixth in 1970. As of 1967, over half of the females (but only 5 percent of the males) entering college were attending these junior institutions. Meanwhile, the proposals on paper for establishment of postgraduate professional programs for M.A. and Ph.D. degrees had little effect. The custom of professor-student cliques in graduate studies continued, and so did the graduate-student seniority system of waiting in line for a doctorate and for posts obtained through the professorial patronage system. Queuing for degrees is less rigid today, but the pattern of exceptionally strong group affiliations centering around particular professors, while found in other countries as well, is characteristically Japanese.

The increasing demand for a college education has had an effect on the relative proportions of public and private institutions that is the reverse of what has happened in the United States. There has been a proliferation particularly of private colleges and universities offering training in the humanities and law, along with junior colleges for girls. Between 1950 and 1971 charters were granted for 170 new private institutions of higher education. Like the other public colleges and universities, the renowned imperial universities increased their enrollments, but to nothing like the extent that the private institutions increased theirs. Total enrollments in higher education (including junior colleges) had reached 300,000 by 1951 and 1.3 million by 1966. The increase in enrollments since 1966 has been comparatively small; this reflects the demographic cycle, as the numbers of college-age youth peaked in the mid-sixties and dropped sharply in the 1970s. The nevertheless substantial increase in rates of college attendance has strained resources in qualified faculty. Relatively little is demanded of most students once they have surmounted the examination hurdles. One of the strongest critics of Japan's universities today is Michio Nagai, former minister of education. According to Nagai, the first two undergraduate years of general courses "are conducted under circumstances that differ little from those in the 'sardine-packed' elementary school classrooms. Mass microphoned instruction of five hundred to six hundred students at a time is a common scene on almost all campuses. In the light of these conditions it is not an exaggeration to say that education designed to develop men who love learning and think for themselves has already been abandoned" (quoted in Cummings 1972). Nagai's views of this and other features of higher education in Japan today would not be universally accepted, of course, but he is expressing the same concern with the effects of mass education on scholarship and intellectual endeavor "for the love of it" that reverberates through many societies. Despite widespread concern, a far-reaching reform of university structures and of the examination system in Japan remains a challenge for the future.

What appeared at the time to be one of the first major moves back toward a more European (Germanic) rather than an American system was the creation in the 1960s of five-year technical institutions (originally municipally supported) embracing the upper-secondary and the first two college years. Since their graduates are comparable in years and quality of schooling to graduates of junior colleges, these schools have often been translated as "technical junior colleges." On the other hand, since at entry stage these institutions are at the same level as the upper-secondary schools, they are often called "technical institutes."

Examinations for entry to these institutes are difficult, and quite a few who fail them enter technical or even academic upper secondary courses. However, the curriculum of the five-year institutes is by and large terminal in that graduates from these schools can transfer into universities only with difficulty. Even the oldest of the nationally supported and controlled technical institutes were just turning out their first graduates in 1966, and whether these institutes would become firmly established and enlarge their place in the system was uncertain and a sensitive point politically at that time. There can be no doubt of the salience of this option in the thinking of many of the upper-secondary students. It appears from today's perspective, however, that these institutes were not destined to become quantitatively important in the Japanese educational system, despite high standards in course content and quality. Unquestionably one of the main reasons has been the conversion of older polytechnic institutions into four-year colleges and universities, with whose engineering graduates the students from the technical institutes have had to compete. Cane (1974) has summed up the discrepancy between expectations and outcomes as follows: "Originally established to take 15-year-olds and turn them into qualified technicians for Japanese industry," these institutes turn out graduates "caught half-way between downgrading to low level technical status or upgrading to university status." In 1969 there were sixty of these institutes enrolling 41,637 students; in 1973 there were sixty-three with a total enrollment of 48,288. The last word certainly has not been said on this, however, and it could be that this seemingly abortive development will take root in the future.

Occasional reference has already been made to the private versus the public sectors of the educational system, especially in higher education. It is time to look more directly at the role of private institutions in Japan. Kindergarten aside, in 1966 private schools accounted for small proportions of students until we reach the upper-secondary schools and, especially, the universities and the predominantly female junior colleges. As of 1966, only five out of a thousand elementary-level pupils attended private schools. Private institutions accounted for a third of the upper-secondary schools, teachers, and pupils in 1966, and there has been no subsequent change in those proportions.[7]

Private schools at the upper-secondary level are almost all in urban areas. They are extremely diverse in quality. There are renowned, highly elitist private schools--the Etons and Grotons of Japan. In contrast, in the 1960s some private upper-secondary schools were taking in urban pupils who had not succeeded in the competition for entry to public upper-secondary schools. The continued expansion of public, academically nonselective general upper-secondary schools since 1966 has diminished the role of private schools, however.

It is in higher education that private institutions have taken on the greatest share of the education load (over 70 percent of the students in 1966) and where they are regarded as posing the most serious "problem" and challenge to government reform of educational programs and finance.

Educational Composition of the Japanese Labor Force

There are two related, but nevertheless quite distinctive, ways of looking at expansion in the schooling of a population. One is to examine past and present enrollment and school-continuation rates among successive cohorts. The other is to analyze the educational composition of the labor force. The former will of course always lead the latter, since it is only as successive cohorts of better educated youth are hired and less educated persons retire that expansion of education comes to be reflected in the labor force.

We will look first at time paths in the educational attainments of the population as a whole, irrespective of participation in the labor force. Closely related is the record of increases in rates of entry to upper-secondary and higher institutions. Following these summaries for the general population, we look at what has happened and is happening to the educational composition of the labor force as a whole and of new entrants.

The Spread of Education

Japan has long been an educational leader. Even before the Meiji Restoration (1868) there had been a wide diffusion of literacy and skill with the abacus. According to the census, only a fourth of the male children born in the first years of the Meiji Restoration (and surviving to 1960) lacked at least an elementary education, and even among the oldest of those born in the twentieth century male literacy is virtually universal. It took another decade for female literacy to reach this point, but progress in primary education for the first generation of children of the Meiji Restoration was dramatic for both sexes. With the birth cohort of 1910 Japan attained essentially universal literacy, regardless of sex.

As we noted earlier, over the years elementary education was prolonged and a higher elementary level was added, at grades 7 and 8. The other main extension of common schooling occurred within "youth training" and related job-oriented short programs. For older cohorts these supplementary programs were of negligible importance, but with the "youth schools" of the 1930s they came to describe the educational attainment of half or more of the male and two-fifths of the female population born between 1915 and 1930.

For some years before the war, upper-elementary education had carried youth through grade 8. The new compulsory lower-secondary schooling that replaced the older upper-elementary school in the postwar reforms now comprised grades 7-9. Thus, it would not be a serious distortion to consider lower-secondary-school completion today as approximatley equivalent to completion of the upper-elementary-school program (often with added youth schooling) of the previous era.

Trying to link the earlier middle and later upper-secondary levels is more difficult. Most attempts to put these data together treat them as approximately equivalent, when in fact completion of the prewar academic middle schools usually meant completion of either ten or eleven (increasingly eleven) years of schooling, as compared with the twelve years of the postwar upper-secondary schools. However, the old middle schools commonly began at grade 7, as an alternative to entering the upper-elementary schools; so did most of the vocational schools. Even when one works from data collected by the Ministry of Education, it is not at all easy to interpret statistics on rates of entry to middle schools. Also, drop-out rates from various postelementary schools were probably higher some decades ago than they have been since the war, and there was greater diversity in the length of many of the curricula (notably the normal-school and vocational programs). These facts complicate interpretation of data for the earlier years on numbers of graduates. Finally, census data are very evidently biased upward in the proportions of respondents who report having received "middle education," although it is only from such adult counts that we can construct estimates of the prewar composition of the labor force. Given these many problems, we present in table 1.5 two sets of estimates of rates of entry to middle schools before the war. Estimates given in columns 2 and 3 are based on data from the records of the Ministry of Education. Columns 4 and 5 through 1960 are derived from the 1960 and 1970 censuses. Somewhat to our surprise, we find very little error for the oldest respondents, but the discrepancies grow over the decades of the twenties and thirties.

Table 1.5 Rates of Entry to Middle (old) or Upper-Secondary Schools (1895-1978) and to Higher Education (1905-78)

Year	Percentages Entering Middle or Upper-Secondary Schools[a]		Percentages Entering Middle or Upper-Secondary Schools[b]		Percentages Entering All Higher Institutions[c]		Percentages Entering Universities[c]	
	Male	Female	Male	Female	Male	Female	Male	Female
(1)	(2)	(3)	(4)	(5)	(6)	(7)	(8)	(9)
1895	5.1	1.3	...	...	...	...	...	...
1900	11.1	2.7	...	...	...	...	...	...
1905	12.4	4.2	13.2	6.4	5.5	.6	2.6	.1
1910	13.9	9.2	15.1	9.0	5.6	.6	2.6	.1
1915	10.8	5.0	17.4	11.7	7.2	1.0	3.4	.1
1920	19.7	11.5	21.7	16.4	8.3	1.9	3.9	.2
1925	19.8	14.1	26.3	21.4	9.0	1.8	4.0	.2
1930	21.1	15.5	28.8	24.2	9.8	1.9	4.3	.2
1935	20.4	16.5	32.4	27.9	13.8	2.6	5.7	.2
1940	28.0	22.0	38.1	35.4	14.8	3.5	7.8	.4
1950	48.0	36.7	48.0	36.7	13.9	4.3	11.7	1.3
1955	55.5	47.4	55.5	47.4	17.4	6.8	14.9	2.3
1960	59.6	55.9	59.6	55.9	19.8	9.9	17.1	3.5
1965	71.7	69.6	71.7	69.6	22.4	11.4	20.7	4.7
1970	81.6	82.7	81.6	82.7	29.3	17.7	27.3	6.5
1975	91.0	92.9	91.0	92.9	35.4	29.6	33.3	10.6
1978	92.7	94.4	92.7	94.4	35.8	33.4	33.4	12.4

[a] Estimates based on documents in the Ministry of Education.

[b] Figures prior to 1950 are estimated from census data by year of birth, assuming entry to middle school at age 15. The postwar entries are as in columns 2 and 3.

[c] Figures for 1960 and earlier are estimated from 1960 and 1970 census data, assuming college entry at age 18. This is slightly too young, and has the effect of moving all figures prior to 1965 up, but only slightly. Otherwise there is no bias in the pattern displayed. Adjustments to include delayed entry are not needed for estimates based on census data. Estimates based on figures from the Ministry of Education are adjusted for delayed entry by the coordination of two sets of annual surveys (of graduates from upper-secondary schools and of entrants to higher education). Delayed entrants accounted for a third of the entrants in most of the postwar years.

Fortunately, there is still quite a lot of information provided within the bounds set by these estimates.

Already at the beginning of the century, over a tenth of boys were entering middle schools, and that figure rose to a fifth in 1920. If we accept the Ministry of Education estimates, there was a long period of constancy in this respect, until the sudden jump at the end of the 1930s and again immediately after the war. The census data give us a picture of much steadier gains in the two prewar decades. There is a jump between 1940 and 1950, to be sure, but it is not out of line with the pace of advance before the war. With the postwar years, the figures are relatively unambiguous and more reliable. The high rates of continuation into upper-secondary school are impressive. Among boys, already in 1950 almost half were entering the new upper-secondary schools. By 1964, when the youth in our study were entering the upper-secondary schools, the rate of entry (including part-time students) was 70 percent, and it has now passed the 90 percent mark. Even taking full-time enrollees only, the entry rate into upper-secondary schools is now five-sixths or more for both sexes. Moreover, since in Japan entry into full-time upper-secondary education virtually assures completion of the course,[8] two-thirds of the cohort from which our sample is drawn (98 percent of 68 percent) were graduating from upper-secondary school in 1967. With negligible drop-out rates, Japan now surpasses the proportions graduating from twelfth grade even in the United States; as of 1970 no other country could match that rate.

Although there was a definite lag of female behind male rates of entry into middle schools in the early years, that lag was remarkably small compared with the one between girls and boys who were schooled at all or who entered upper-elementary classes. Whichever series of estimates we use for the two prewar decades, the gap between girls and boys in rates of entry to middle schools persisted at about the same absolute level. Immediately after World War II the male rates rose more rapidly than the female. However, rates of enrollment of girls then climbed rapidly, and since 1965 females have matched or surpassed males in proportions entering the upper-secondary schools.

What has happened over time in higher education is equally dramatic. For all male cohorts born before 1925, and hence educated before the war, numbers enrolling in higher-professional schools exceeded university entrants. The conversion of most of the prewar higher institutes and colleges into four-year programs sharply reduced the proportions of males at the junior-college level, but brought instead a sudden postwar increase in proportions reporting university education. According to responses in the population census, overall male rates of entry to the higher institutes and universities taken together were rising steadily from an early stage, and they jumped ahead with the emphasis on higher-technical/professional schooling in the 1930s. There was no sudden increase immediately after World War II, but rather the shift to four-year institutions already noted. The truly dramatic quantitative leaps are very recent ones, with a third of the male youth of today entering postsecondary institutions.[9] This is only in part attributable to an increase in the proportions of upper-secondary graduates going on; primarily it is a reflection of the rapid rise in rates of attendance at the upper-secondary level.

The Changing Educational Composition of the Labor Force

Developments over the past half century or more in the educational composition of the Japanese labor force are summarized in table 1.6. According to census reports, the proportions lacking any education dropped from 60 percent in 1910 to 20 percent in 1930 and to virtually none by 1960. Those who had completed middle schools or upper-secondary courses constituted only 5 percent of the 1930 labor force, but over a quarter of the labor force in 1960 and almost two-fifths in 1974. Proportions with higher education (at either junior-college or university level) rose slowly at first but jumped to almost 7 percent in 1960 and 15 percent in 1974, when the numerous and highly educated children of the early postwar baby-boom had become active workers.

As in other countries, there is of course a relative concentration of better educated people in the younger age brackets. This situation has been particularly important in Japan because of its coincidence with the seniority structure of the life-commitment system, together with the rapid pace of technological change and economic expansion. The associated youthfulness of a leadership working within the formal bounds of a strong seniority system is one of the important seeming paradoxes of contemporary economic development in Japan, especially with respect to the roles of university graduates in the labor force. But still more important may be the effects of the truly massive expansion of upper-secondary schooling both in supporting teamwork for adjustment to change and in altering relationships between a man's schooling and his opportunities for job training.

Table 1.6 Educational Composition of the Labor Force

	Both Sexes				Female	
	1910	1930	1960	1974	1960	1974
Total labor force (thousands)	23,639	27,991	43,279	51,341	16,835	19,020
Distribution by education (%)						
Total	100.0	100.0	100.0	100.0	38.9	37.0
Higher education[a]	.5	2.1	6.8	14.6	13.6	24.5
Old middle or upper secondary	1.3	5.2	26.8	38.5	38.6	37.6
Elementary, lower secondary	37.8	72.4	65.5	46.9	42.1	39.6
None	60.4	20.3	.9	...		

Source. 1910 and 1930: Tsunehiko Watanabe, "Economic Aspects of Dualism in the Industrial Development of Japan," *Economic Development and Cultural Change* 13, no. 3 (April 1965): 293-312. 1960: *1960 Population Census of Japan*, vol. 2, part 1, table 8, p. 236. 1974: Office of the Prime Minister, Bureau of Statistics, *1974 Employment Status Survey*, table 9, p. 60; table 10, p. 76.

[a]Universities, junior colleges, and old higher schools.

The change in the educational composition of the labor force is revealed in figure 1.1, in which we have plotted the educational level of male entrants to the labor force over the period 1940-74. The sharp drop in entrants directly from primary school after World War II reflects the enforcement of the new nine-year compulsory system through lower-secondary school. Also reflecting postwar reorganization of the educational system are the sudden decline after 1951 in numbers of males coming into the labor market from junior college and the rapidly rising numbers and proportions who have continued through four years or more of higher education before seeking full-time employment. After 1953 the pattern stabilized, with more gradual rates of increase in the ranks of upper-secondary and university graduates. Already by 1953 the number of new upper-secondary graduates approximated those entering the labor market with less schooling, and the latter proportion has continued to shrink. The decline in absolute numbers of those entering the labor force from upper-secondary schools since 1969 is primarily a reflection of the demographic population cycle, though increased rates of continuation into higher education are of course also involved. The cohort of our sample (graduating in 1967) was one of the largest. Absolute numbers in the relevant

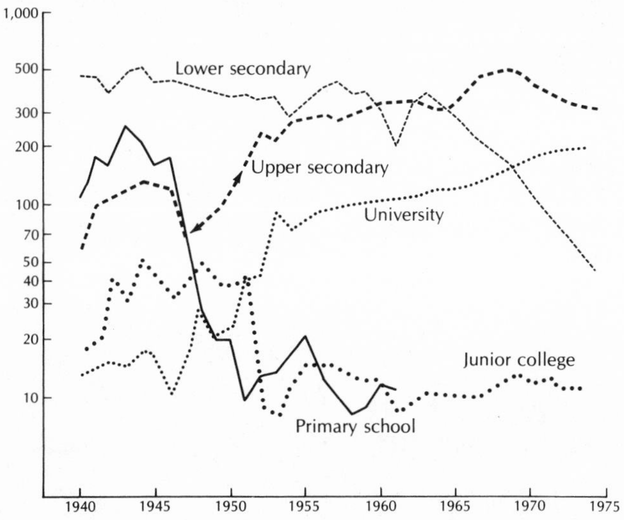

Figure 1.1 Estimated school completion levels of male entrants to the Japanese labor force, 1940-74.

cohorts dropped sharply thereafter, and numbers in upper-secondary schools fell to a low plateau in the early 1970s despite the rise to near-universal rates of entry to those schools. Even at those rates, the numbers enrolled in upper-secondary schools will reach the peak levels of 1965 only in 1985.

Both these demographic swings and the changes in rates of continuation into upper-secondary and higher education from the early 1950s affect the career prospects of youth with various amounts of schooling--and also, by the same token, the recruitment options and training and promotion policies of employers. These swings have also aggravated the intensity of examination competition to get into prestigeful higher institutions. Such are the bedrock facts on which any meaningful discussions of educational policies today must be built.

2. Key Decisions in Career Development

Let us stand imaginatively in some outer space and time to look down on Japan for a "moment" of, say, sixty years. We see a complex pattern of the movements of individuals from families and communities of origin through schools to labor markets and on along diverse career paths to career peaks and beyond. Although the flow is always moving from earlier to later in our sixty-year moment, we can nevertheless view the paths from two distinct perspectives. The first perspective traces individuals from their origins through successive branchings or "key decision points" in the chronologies of their lives. This perspective is the main orientation in both the economics of investment in human beings and the work by sociologists on status attainment, and will be the perspective used in most of this book. The second perspective looks back to the sources and paths through which those who have reached some particular destination have come. Entry to upper-secondary school or college might be such a destination; so might any particular sort of work activity or position in a firm or in a government hierarchy. This perspective is associated with manpower analysis--for example, when that analysis is carried back to sources of manpower supplies. In a societal context the two perspectives are of course two ways of looking at the same processes, and both perspectives are needed. We are in fact observing actions that reflect constrained choices--choices by those who provide education and by those who seek it, by those who employ workers or buy goods and services and by those who provide the services or seek the opportunities to do so. We can even study assortative mating in a similar double perspective.

"Key decisions" are always constrained decisions; there is no complete freedom of choice. But what has a key place in one perspective may not be central in another view. From the first perspective, the key decisions are those we make with an eye to the future. The important choices we make as individuals (or that are made for us) extend their reach well into the future; they affect our subsequent options and how we will see those options. However much or little conscious deliberation we put into a critical choice, any decision that strongly affects our future opportunities is a key decision. Some of the critical choices are obvious and common to many people; others are less easily identified, more varied in nature and timing, often more "personal." Only the former can be examined here. The decision to enter or not enter upper-secondary school and to pursue one curriculum rather than another is clearly a key decision for most Japanese youth. So also is the choice between continuing into higher education or starting full-time work after the completion of upper-secondary school.

Some constraints on options are so taken for granted that most people hardly notice them; we may "build castles in the air" but we do not take them seriously. Other constraints may be seen mainly as barriers to be circumvented or as societal injustices. Of greater interest here, however, are the constraints and the opportunities that follow from the prior key decisions we make in the course of our lives. Successive life experiences are neither fully predetermined nor sequentially independent. If choices were not real or, conversely, if they were completely random and unstructured, there could be little purpose in the present kind of study.

The main thread running through this book, accordingly, is the examination of sequentially conditioned choices that are marked off by key decision points common to many of the youth of Japan (and of other nations as well). Thus, our emphasis is primarily (but not solely) on the first perspective. Several distinctive types of models will be used; in this chapter we will briefly outline the nature and main sorts of applications of these models.

Models Grounded on Temporal Ordering

The models in which we are interested here entail "causal sequences" explicitly ordered in time; later events are conditioned by earlier ones. However crude or sophisticated their derivation, "laws" of some sort link the later with the earlier events. "Path models," by far the most common, work entirely with continuous variables for the intervening stages in a sequence, and usually for the final dependent variable as well. Where intervening variables cannot appropriately be expressed in continuous form (or where we want to give special attention to interactions in some of the causal relationships) we turn to sequential matrices and transitions between them.

Path Analyses of Status Attainment

The principal questions asked by sociologists in their analyses of the life histories of individuals are grounded in what we have designated as the first perspective: what happens to people who have different starting points in life as measured by family backgrounds and "ability"? Like much of the empirical economic work on investment in human beings, these studies treat the demand for labor of various kinds and levels as exogenously given. Unlike the economists in this field, sociologists have no explicit decision theory. Causal hypotheses are introduced, with greater or lesser analytical specification, in the initial diagraming of path models; in fact, one of the most important advantages of path analysis is that it has led to more explicit specifications of relationships predicted a priori.[1] The origin of the sociologists' work with path analysis goes back to biologically based explorations in genetic interpretations of differential accomplishments. In the hands of sociologists, the underlying causal hypotheses usually draw instead on theories relating to the differential impact of societal institutions or power structures on individuals born into one situation rather than another. However, with the development of more carefully specified path analyses and of better data for empirical testing, there has been a partial convergence in the theoretical foundations of the "status attainment" models used by sociologists and the economists' decision theory.[2]

A central feature of path analyses of status attainment has been the sorting out of the routes through which a father's occupational status, for example, may affect the occupational status of his sons. Effects may be in part "indirect," via the effect on the son's education; they may also be "direct," controlling for the son's education. Taken together, the direct and indirect effects so defined make up the "total effect." A simple path diagram for these variables would look like this:

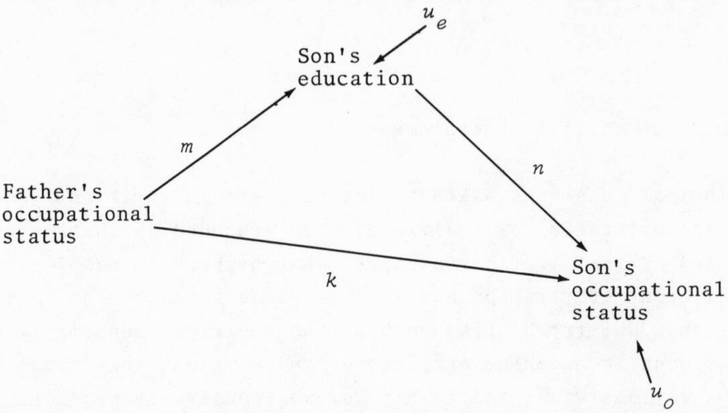

The path coefficient *m* is the standardized beta coefficient on the father's occupational status with the son's education as the dependent variable; *n* is the standardized beta coefficient on the son's education in an equation in which the son's occupational status is the dependent variable and the father's occupational status is included as an independent variable; *k* is the coefficient on the father's occupational status in that same equation, controlling for the son's education. The effects of the father's occupational status on that of his son are then

direct effect = k
indirect effect (through son's education = $m \cdot n$
total effect = $k + m \cdot n$

Notice that the total effect will not necessarily equal the zero-order correlation between the father's occupational status and that of his son.[3] The paths u_e and u_o refer to the effect of omitted variables; they are the square roots of the unexplained variance in a path model.

Few path models would be so simple; most would have additional variables at the beginning, along with the father's occupational status. Moreover, models that add earnings as the final dependent variable usually include the son's occupational status as an intervening variable; they thus provide estimates (for example) of how far education affects earnings indirectly, via its effects on occupation, and how far directly, controlling for occupation.

Path analysis also has severe limitations, and as it has become increasingly popular it has been increasingly misused. Three limitations are particularly relevant.

1. First and foremost is the fact that dichotomous "dummy" variables cannot be used at intermediate stages in a path sequence. For example, the yes-no variable "taking examinations for college" cannot be entered as a dependent variable at one stage (being "explained" by such things as family background and type of upper-secondary course) and then be used as one of the independent variables explaining occupation or earnings. When it is a dependent variable, taking examinations (or not) becomes a probability or likelihood, but at the next stage it is once more an observed event, expressed in certain (yes-or-no) terms. The same problem arises when there are several intermediate yes-no variables, as when type of upper-secondary course is treated as a likelihood in a first-stage analysis of the effects of parental traits, but then, at the next stage in the sequence, as a predictor of taking or not taking examinations for college.

2. A second limitation is the assumption, built into the methodology of path analysis, that there are no interactions among independent variables in their effects on the values of variables coming later in the path sequence. It is assumed, for example, that the effects of schooling in raising earnings will be the same for sons of university graduates or business executives as for sons of primary-school leavers or street sweepers.[4] (In fact the effects for the latter may often be greater even if their final earnings still do not match those of youth from more favored backgrounds.)

3. Finally, a limitation that is particularly serious for the present study is more substantive: this is the problem of how to treat expectations in a causal-chain framework. For example, can we properly designate college expectations as a dependent variable to be explained by type of secondary-school curriculum, or do those expectations explain the secondary-school course taken? This is in fact an example of a broader "identification" problem and is not confined to path analysis. This problem will confront us in the chapters that follow, where expectations are treated sometimes as independent, sometimes as dependent variables. Resolution of the problem through the use of simultaneous equations will be possible only in part and with the use of grouped observations.

The data of our survey of youth in Japanese upper-secondary schools, taken together with other sources of information concerning schooling and work in Japan, provide a rich basis for the analysis of educational decisions and career expectations. However, they are not longitudinal data such as would be best suited to path analysis in its fullest versions. Furthermore, interactions can be exceedingly important in the determination of key decisions and their sequels, and those decisions themselves often are best specified in categorical terms. We need a more flexible framework.

A Three-Period Sequential Activity Model

A simple, but flexible, basic model that we can use to help organize our analysis starts with three discrete periods and the transitions between them. For purposes of exposition we assume here that each individual engages in one, but only one, activity in each period.[5]

Let us start with a cohort of boys who have just completed ninth grade. We can classify them by their backgrounds, as specified for each of the n elements of the column vector V_B:

$$V_B = \begin{bmatrix} b_1 \\ b_2 \\ . \\ . \\ . \\ b_n \end{bmatrix} .$$

Each element in this vector could be defined as a compound set of characteristics. Thus b_1 might refer to only sons whose fathers were farmers who had completed elementary school only and who lived in western Shikoku. (We could subdivide cases further if we had data on ability as well.) In principle, the elements of V_B may be split up into as finely dissected a classification, cut on as many dimensions, as are relevant. But obviously, while the multiplication of dimensions avoids problems of dealing with multicollinearities in a regression analysis, too much detail can also clutter the picture--even assuming a sample size large enough to justify fine breakdowns. Such considerations apply equally to analysis using cross-tabulations or matrices and their sequential relationships. We must ask ourselves on what basis in any attempt at causal or predictive analysis we introduce one or another variable. Often simplification through selective combining of variables also will bring out more clearly the underlying factors at work.

For illustrative purposes we will specify here only whether or not a youth's father was a farmer, ignoring other parental traits (other aspects and categories of occupation, education, family size, and so on) and also community attributes. This gives us

$$V_B = \begin{bmatrix} b_1, \text{ father a farmer} \\ b_2, \text{ father not a farmer} \end{bmatrix}.$$

In this preliminary sketch, four mutually exclusive sets of activities are specified: full-time attendance at upper-secondary school, work, time as a *rōnin*, and attendance at higher institutions.

There are five main types of upper-secondary schools in Japan, and they are a focus of this research. We could categorize schools on other dimensions as well; examples could be distance in travel time to the nearest town of fifty thousand or frequency of public transportation per day to the nearest major metropolis or other community characteristics, elite reputation of the school, and so on. Some of these traits were considered in the sampling procedure, and some of them are introduced into one or another of our regression analyses. However, the key division on categorical variables is by type of course, and choice of one or another among the main types of upper-secondary schooling is among the alternatives more or less open to and preferred in varying degrees by the youth just out of ninth grade and entering what we designate here as period (1). We assume for present purposes that anyone who does not attend upper-secondary school in period (1) will not do so at a later date; movement from the labor market back into full-time secondary school is excluded in the model (and rarely occurs).

Activities that could be described primarily as work are myriad, and there are a number of ways in which we might classify them. Meaningful dimensions of jobs would include the amount of associated on-the-job training, which may differ with prior experience of the individual; but this is an attribute that we will have to consider chiefly in other ways. Other criteria of classification are more often used; none is free of problems. The meaningful categorization of elements of a work-activity vector on various dimensions is a problem that will be addressed at a number of points later in this book. For illustrative purposes we will use here a classification into just three broad types of future occupations: white collar work (and trade); technical and manual labor; and agriculture and related endeavors.

The *rōnin* and college activities become applicable only after completion of upper-secondary school. Kinds of colleges and universities and of courses within them are multiple; we simplify matters by ignoring these distinctions. However, it is important in the Japanese context to specify *rōnin* as a separate activity, which may be pursued in period (2).

With these simplified classifications we have a period (1) matrix in which two categories of father's occupation in the column vector V_B are cross-classified against eight elements of an activity row vector V_A (five types of curricula and three types of work). With our simplified specification, matrix G, as we shall call this, will have only sixteen cells. The cell counts for a random sample of ten thousand male ninth-grade graduates of 1964 will look approximately like the hypothetical entries shown in table 2.1. Each cell of this table (matrix G) refers to individuals in a particular parental background category and in a particular period (1) activity. The *rōnin* and higher-education options are not applicable at this stage in the life sequence.

Transitions into matrix G can be expressed as the proportions of youth from each background category who have moved into each activity after completing ninth grade (lower-secondary school). Those proportions constitute a transition matrix P_{bg}, shown in the lower half of table 2.1. They can be derived directly from an observed full G matrix--a familiar enough process in ordinary cross-tabulations in which percentage distributions are computed horizontally. Notice, nevertheless, that each of the entries in the transition matrix P_{bg} could be viewed as a crude empirical hypothesis, whereas no such generalizing value could attach to a single entry (taken independently of other entries) in the G matrix. The P_{bg} transition matrix can thus be viewed as a naive empirical or "objective" probability matrix. We would expect (as is in fact the case) that children of farmers are the most likely to enter agricultural curricula and that they are also more likely than other youth to go directly into agricultural activities without an intervening period in upper-secondary school.

Let us now move on to the close of period (1) and the opening of period (2). During period (1) some of our youth will have attended (and, by the constraints of the model, completed) upper-secondary school, and others will have had various work and on-the-job learning experiences outside the schools. Each is now entering period (2). No matter what his period (1) experience, there will be only a limited number of period (2) options conceivably open to a member of this cohort and a much more limited number of

Table 2.1 Period (1) Activities of Hypothetical Cohort of 10,000 Male Ninth-Grade Graduates of 1964

	Secondary-School Type or Course					Employment Category[a]			
	General B	General A	Agri-culture	Commerce	Technical	White Collar, Trade	Technical, Manual, Services	Agricul-ture and Related	Total
				G Matrix (numbers)					
b_1 (sons of farmers)	410	369	411	125	199	141	620	325	2,600
b_2 (other sons)	2,321	452	130	915	1,330	100	2,145	7	7,400
				P_{bg} Transition Matrix					
b_1 (sons of farmers)	.157	.142	.158	.048	.077	.054	.239	.125	1.000
b_2 (other sons)	.314	.061	.018	.124	.180	.014	.288	.001	1.000

[a]The distributions within this category are entirely arbitrary with respect to distinctions between farmers' sons and others just out of ninth grade.

interest to any one individual; but (as in path analysis) the period (2) options and how the individual youth perceives them will be affected by his period (1) experiences--as well as by his background characteristics and abilities, which have a continuing influence.

An empirical examination of the ways in which a cohort of youth have sorted themselves out and have been sorted out in the movement from background position through period (1) and into period (2) gives us a map of early-career stages, showing which paths are heavily traveled, which are most unusual, and (if we have more refined classifications) which are traveled not at all. Using our highly simplified sets of activities, we have set up in table 2.2 what we label the *H* matrix, to show what people who were in the various cells of matrix *G* are doing in period (2). The entire detail of matrix *G* presented in table 2.2 in column form defines the rows of matrix *H*, except that we have combined the three period (1) work activities, which reduces the number of rows in matrix *H* from sixteen (the cells of matrix *G*) to twelve. This consolidation eliminates the specification of flows from particular work activities in period (1) into the work activities of period (2).

The $P_{gh.b}$ transition matrix in the lower half of table 2.2 is again straightforward enough; it specifies the proportions of youth in each period (1) activity entering a given activity in period (2), controlling for parental occupation. The "control" in this specification is complete, since every background-activity cell of the *G* matrix is specified, consolidation of the period (1) labor-force cells aside. Notice that sons of farmers attending nonagricultural courses were less likely to enter farming than were sons of nonfarmers who studied agriculture. However, as the P_{bg} matrix (in table 2.1) showed, sons who were not from farm families rarely attended agricultural secondary schools.

If we want the full story of paths pursued by sons of farmers, for example, we must multiply the P_{bg} by the $P_{gh.b}$ matrix, and similarly for sons of nonfarmers. Summing across the period (1) activities, we consolidate again in another way, obtaining the period (2) distributions of sons of farmers and of all other youth. The rows labeled "actual" distributions in table 2.3 were derived in this way. The rows labeled "analog of indirect effects" are an approximation, in the sequential matrix form, of the indirect-effect estimates one would obtain in path analysis; they take no account of interactions among background and period (1) activities in their effects on activities in period

Table 2.2 Period (2) Activities of Hypothetical Cohort of 10,000 Male Ninth-Grade Graduates of 1964

		Period (2) Activity				
		Employment Category				
Period (1) Activity	Total Numbers (*G* matrix)	White Collar, Trade	Technical, Manual, Services	Agricul-ture and Related	*Rōnin*	College
		H Matrix (numbers)				
b_1 (sons of farmers):	2,600					
Education						
General B	410	67	22	3	70	248
General A	369	241	87	19	1	21
Agriculture	411	100	127	148	3	33
Commerce	125	80	21	1	2	21
Technical	199	59	112	2	6	20
Labor Force	1,086	181	616	289	...	...
b_2 (sons of non-farmers):	7,400					
Education						
General B	2,321	83	82	5	839	1,312
General A	452	177	216	2	5	52
Agriculture	130	32	70	15	1	12
Commerce	915	608	123	5	37	142
Technical	1,330	85	1,059	4	57	125
Labor force	2,252	120	2,127	5	...	...
		$P_{gh.b}$ Matrix (ratios)				
	Totals					
b_1 (sons of farmers):						
Education						
General B	1.000	.164	.054	.008	.170	.604
General A	1.000	.652	.237	.050	.003	.058
Agriculture	1.000	.244	.308	.360	.008	.080
Commerce	1.000	.644	.165	.004	.017	.170
Technical	1.000	.298	.562	.010	.030	.100
Labor force	1.000	.167	.567	.266	...	...
b_2 (sons of non-farmers):						
Education						
General B	1.000	.036	.035	.002	.361	.566
General A	1.000	.392	.478	.004	.011	.115
Agriculture	1.000	.246	.538	.115	.008	.093
Commerce	1.000	.666	.134	.005	.040	.155
Technical	1.000	.064	.796	.003	.043	.094
Labor force	1.000	.053	.945	.002	...	...

Table 2.3 Components of Differences between Sons of Farmers and Sons of Nonfarmers in Distributions of Period (2) Activities for a Hypothetical Cohort of 10,000 Male Ninth-Grade Graduates of 1964

	White Collar Trade	Technical, Manual, Services	Agriculture and Related	*Rōnin*	College
Actual distributions					
$\underline{b}_1$	.280	.379	.178	.032	.132
$\underline{b}_2$	.149	.497	.005	.126	.222
$\underline{b}_1 - \underline{b}_2$	.131	-.118	.173	-.094	-.090
Analog of indirect effects					
$\underline{b}_1$	.197	.525	.089	.059	.131
$\underline{b}_2$	.179	.443	.037	.119	.222
$\underline{b}_1 - \underline{b}_2$	.018	.082	.052	-.060	-.091
Direct and interaction effects					
$\underline{b}_1$	.083	-.146	.089	-.027	.001
$\underline{b}_2$	-.030	.054	-.032	.007	...
$\underline{b}_1 - \underline{b}_2$	.113	-.200	.121	-.034	.001

(2). These indirect-effect distributions were obtained by multiplying the P_{bg} matrix by the overall transitions from period (1) to period (2) activities *without* controls for parental backgrounds. The differences between the actual and the indirect-effect estimates combine interaction effects that elude measurement in path models and what would be called "direct effects" in path analysis.

A closer approach to path analysis is provided by the $b_1 - b_2$ rows of table 2.3, which give the differences between farmers' sons and other sons for the actual, indirect, and direct plus interaction effects of parental occupation on period (2) activity. That all of these sorts of effects are important in the distribution of labor market activities of sons of farmers compared with other sons is evident enough, but it is equally evident that the intervening type-of-course variables capture most of the difference in rates of college matriculation. Whether the significance of attendance in General B courses is properly regarded as a "cause" of going to college poses more difficult questions. Is the causation in fact the other way around in that individuals attend General B courses because they want to go on to college? Perhaps so, but General B education is nevertheless an important enabling factor in the pursuit of higher education, and it is the best single predictor of college attendance. This illustrates clearly enough the special sorts of problems concerning causation that often arise in the social or behavioral sciences but that are of no concern in the physical sciences, to which the motivations or purposes of human beings are usually irrelevant. We will come back to this sort of question from another angle, but first let us take a quick look at period (3) in our sequential matrix model.

With the transition from period (2) to period (3) we multiply the number of paths once again, since yet another period is added to the career sequences. Except for those who were delayed as *rōnin*, the entire cohort is by now in the labor market--some without any schooling after ninth grade, some with secondary schooling for another three years, and some with higher education. This last group has just entered the labor market, but the others have already had either one or two periods of labor-force participation, which may have significant effects on the work a man will be doing in period (3). There are good reasons, moreover, to expect temporal asymmetries in associations between one and another occupation or job over a man's lifetime; for example, a man is normally much more likely to move from a technical into a managerial activity than the reverse. Even with the simplified classifications we have used for illustrative purposes, an initial period (3) matrix, call it the *K* matrix, would have 240 cells: the four period (3) activities (three in the labor market and one for the delayed college students) multiplied by the 60 cells of the *H* matrix. Furthermore, period (3) as we have defined it is only an early stage in the postschool years; career development continues far beyond that stage and will occupy much of our attention in part 4 of this book.

It is obvious enough that a matrix with 240 cells, simplified though it is, is cumbersome, demanding with respect to sample size, and too detailed for effective interpretation. That, of course, is one of the reasons for the prevalence in empirical social science of regression models based on linearity assumptions. It is also one of the reasons for the preoccupation of many sociologists with the construction of "scales" built out of categorical variables, and with the expression of occupations in "status" terms on a quantitative index. But often the most critical variables will remain categorical in nature and cannot properly be combined and transformed into scalar variables. Furthermore, an indiscriminate multiplication of cardinal or scalar variables can confound as much as it illuminates. Most important, we will have to go behind the multiplicity of indicators to understand what determines observed path coefficients or the proportions specified in transition matrices, and how those coefficients and proportions may change.

Prediction, Preference, and Decision

The main emphasis in this section will be on expectations and preferences and their place in the analysis of career development. We will begin, however, with a few words about prediction and change, drawing on the hypothetical sample cohort used in the immediately preceding pages.

Prediction and Change

Let us suppose that there was no subsequent movement into or out of agricultural employment among youth who were in the labor force in period (2). We will assume also that of sons of farmers who continued into postsecondary education 10 percent eventually became farmers but that there were virtually no other college youth who did so. We will also (incorrectly) take "agriculture and related" employments to mean simply farming. With those assumptions we would find that a total of 19.2 percent of the sons of farmers would ultimately return to farming and .5 percent of other youth would become farmers. Of the 10,000 young men in our hypothetical sample $.192 \times 2{,}600 = 499$ farmers' sons and $.005 \times 7{,}400 = 37$ other youth would then become farmers. That would mean that only 536 out of the 10,000 (or 5.36 percent) would be farmers among the parents of the next generation--a decline to just over a fifth of the number of farmers among the parents of our cohort. This is not an unrealistic estimate, but there are reasons why the proportions of the Japanese population engaged in farming have declined and continue to decline sharply at the present time. Can we expect a repetition of such a rate of attrition from farming over long periods? The answer may be that we can indeed expect stability in the coefficients and the associated process of continuing decline in the agricultural labor force for a number of cohorts, but probably not into or beyond the generation of the sons of the cohort of ninth graders of 1964, for whom a mechanistic Markov chain analysis would predict only 1.5 percent employed in farming.

Two major generalizations are suggested by this small exploration. First, it is obvious enough that the stability of relations observed in empirical sequential analyses such as we have been discussing depend on the stability in associated aggregative patterns of change. To pursue analysis of long-term aggregative change is beyond the scope of this book. We are fortunate, however, in the availability of revealing data on occupational changes at the aggregative level in the recent past. Also, the wide swing of demographic cycles in Japan since World War II is in itself a predictor that can be used to identify bounds on the career decisions of forthcoming cohorts.

Second, our empirical observations reflect not only decisions of the members of a cohort whose career paths we are tracing but also decisions of those who provide the schooling and who seek the services of entrants to the labor force. However, to each individual the effects of the actions of many other individuals will appear as a given set of constraints and opportunities conditioning his own choices and behavior. Microanalysis approaches human investment and career decisions from just such a perspective. For present purposes this requires that we ask ourselves which factors are most likely to affect available options open to and constraints on the individual, and which parameters will presumably be most relevant for decisions made at a given stage of schooling and work career. A major concern in this book will be the empirical specification of more general concepts of decision theory; such an approach can give us much greater predictive power than is possible with a more casual empiricism.

The Place of Expectations in Path Models and in Decision Theory

As we remarked earlier, expectations are crucial in the economists' decision theory, but they have usually remained empirically in a "black box" between the "objectively"measured explanatory variables and observed behavior. A distinctive feature of the present study is its use of more explicit empirical indicators of expectations in a decision-theory framework. Attempts to specify expectations and aspirations (which are not the same thing) have been more frequent among sociologists. Like economists, the sociologists have been interested in determinants of expectations, but they have put greater emphasis on the empirical identification and explanation of differences in those expectations and on their associations with parental backgrounds in particular. In addition, there has been more explicit concern among sociologists than among most economists on two other matters. One of these is the psychosocial determinants of motivation or drive to achievement, with implications at both the microlevel (as people are sorted and sort themselves into one career path or another) and the macrolevel (as an entire society may reflect the prevalence or relative absence of the drive to achieve). We cannot address ourselves to this big topic within the bounds of the present research. The other matter that has received somewhat greater attention from sociologists, but must be of concern to us all, is the extent to which expectations are being frustrated or will be frustrated in the future, and how people accommodate to such disappointments. One can review events over recent decades in Japan for preliminary insights into these questions, and one can speculate about the magnitude and handling of such problems in Japan in the future; indeed, Japanese labor economists are already talking about the "crisis in Japanese labor markets" with the aging of the baby-boom cohorts--a problem that substantially alters the prospects for advancement in the postschool years, and that has had a major impact on the *nenko* system.

To emphasize the crucial place of expectations in decision theory is not at all the same thing as entering expectations in a temporally ordered model. We must distinguish between expectations that are simply a statement by the individual of what he intends to do in the near future and the conditional expectations relating to the perceived consequences of deciding one way rather than another on an immediate course of action. An example of a dubious use of expectations in path analysis is the entry in such a model of statements by seniors in upper-secondary school about their intentions to enter college in the following academic year. If this variable predicts well, are we saying anything more than that students themselves give accurate predictions about what they will be doing in a few months? And if with the incorporation of such expectations in a multiple regression the coefficients on other explanatory variables fade into insignificance, what do we learn beyond that when students say they will be entering college they know what they are talking about? The closer the correlations between expressed intentions and subsequent entry to college or the labor market, the more nearly do the "expectations" and the behavioral variables become substitute *dependent* variables. This is how college intentions will be used in the present study.

Although sociologists have studied occupational expectations and aspirations among secondary-school students in a number of countries, usually those variables have not been entered in path models, in part because the rationale of their time ordering is elusive. Nevertheless, when properly handled, occupational expectations do belong in an analysis of educational and related decisions. In testing decision theory by the use of expectational data it is necessary to specify how the individual perceives the consequences of deciding in one way rather than another. What differences does he perceive in the effects of one type of secondary-school course or another, or of college attendance, upon subsequent occupational opportunities and earnings? How are those perceptions related to parental or community traits? Taking such analysis a step further, are the perceptions reasonably realistic? How far can we identify associations between such expectations with respect to alternative futures and the decisions made today?

Preferences and "Potential Surprise"

No single individual will ever consider so wide a range of possibilities as we could observe in the actual flows of a fully specified (finely classified) transition matrix. Some possibilities simply do not interest him--he neither desires nor fears them--and of some options he is not yet aware. However vague his perceptions of the future may be, those perceptions will be focused on a limited range of options.

G. L. S. Shackle's early and continuing work on decision making under uncertainty is illuminating in an analysis of such perceptions.[6] Setting aside some of the more ésoteric and more complex elaborations of his theory, we may concentrate on its most relevant components for our purposes. One of these is the degree of attractiveness or unattractiveness of different futures. The other is the individual's assessment of the likelihood that desired futures could be realized and that undesired futures might unfortunately occur. Some futures are perceived as so unlikely that they would evoke a very high degree of "potential surprise." Particular conceivable careers with too great an element of potential surprise will be ignored. Attention will be focused on the most optimistic and the most pessimistic outlooks, relative to preferences, that do not exceed some potential-surprise limits. Perhaps when we ask individuals about plans and expectations for the more distant future, we often get responses toward the optimistic surprise limits; fears are less often expressed.[7] This consideration must always be kept in mind when interpreting data on expectations or aspirations. It is relevant also in any speculations in which we may be tempted to engage with respect to future frustrations and disappointments, and how people may express or react to them.

Decisions and Conditioned Future Options

Both in fact and in the perceptions of an individual, future options and anticipated choices are always in part dependent upon earlier decisions and opportunities; however, a key decision now can still leave a wide scope for future choices. The important question for the individual making a decision is which future options will be precluded, made more difficult, or opened up by what he does now. It is not necessary to anticipate in any precise way where he will go in the longer run. He needs only to be reasonably sure that the kinds of things he would most want to do later will remain open to him, and perhaps that he will be protected against the most unsatisfactory or painful eventualities. Some individuals may have more specific ultimate goals, but many young people will defer specific decisions until it becomes necessary to focus their choices more sharply. This, of course, is one of the reasons why youth in upper-secondary schools, when asked about their occupational aspirations or expectations, are so often vague or (when they are pressed to respond) conventional. Moreover, as an individual moves from one stage to another, two main kinds of changes in perceptions occur. First, the broad vista of options in fact remaining open will narrow; but second, knowledge and appreciation of the characteristics and range of available options will be enlarged.

Some Implications for Research Design

The preceding discussion is relevant to the designing of research on human investments and career paths. For the study of individual decision making and for the construction of expectation matrices, it points to the importance of selecting criteria for the classification of alternative activities that will be meaningful to the decision maker at a particular stage or stages of a schooling-career sequence. Also, what is relevant at each of these stages will depend upon the extent to which future options are affected by present choices. Criteria of relevance from the educational planner's point of view and from that of the individual decision maker will converge in this essential consideration, even though what kinds of options are regarded as in themselves important may differ.

Most of the attempts to identify how young people perceive their future careers have concentrated on occupational status. Yet, paradoxically, occupational status is the most difficult dimension of future career perceptions to identify through questionnaire or interview methods. First, even when a youth has in fact a fairly clear idea of the status level to which he aspires and which he believes he has a good possibility of attaining, it will be quite impossible to formulate a question that will enable him to articulate this hope directly. The extensive literature in sociology on the measurement or indexing of occupational status is itself sufficient evidence of this difficulty. Occupational status expectations, when they can be identified, are best identified indirectly, by asking what sorts of things the youth hopes or expects to be doing in his mature years. But second, many young people will not be specific enough in their occupational goals or clear enough in articulation of those goals to provide the basis for classification in status terms. Answers about occupational expectations often will be clear enough for categorization in other dimensions, however. Thus, in the present study we obtained high rates of response with reference to what we designated as "occupational types" rather than status, distinguishing, for example, among agriculture, trade, various service activities and a range of fabricating activities at one level of skill or another (all the way up to engineers). Youth also seem to have relatively clear preferences with respect to self-employment, work in government, or work in a large or a small firm. Even monetary expectations are not as elusive empirically as often as been supposed.

In short, even where answers are incomplete, critical dimensions of perceived occupational expectations, including expectations about earnings, may be identified. Even for individuals we may be able to specify the patterning of differences in expected earnings following from different decisions (as to go to college or directly to the labor market from upper-secondary school). It may be more difficult to specify the perceptions individuals may have of the range of occupational options open to them if they choose (or had chosen) one or another educational path. We can, however, build up expectation matrices from the distributions of responses among students in the various types of upper-secondary schools. These are not so much probability or transition matrices, however, as they are what might better be designated as "preference-possibility" matrices--the preferred among the options perceived as not too surprising.

Realistic or not, preference-possibility matrices (with their derived expectational transition matrices) are important to the analysis of decision making and of early-stage realized choices in a career sequence. They are important even when in the aggregate the distribution of preference-possibility expectation patterns is clearly at variance with reasonable aggregative projections of the distribution of future jobs among the members of a cohort. For correct or not, expectations and goal perceptions are parameters of decision making.

Human-Investment Models and Value Matrices

Every year millions of individuals (or households) in Japan, as elsewhere, are making human-investment decisions and acting upon them. The most obvious of these decisions, whether they are made with deliberation or by default, concern investment in schooling, but investments in people do not stop with the termination of formal schooling. Indeed, among the most important of human-investment decisions are choices at points of entry to the labor force between employments that may pay relatively well to start with but promise little advance in the future, as against those that may bring in less initially but provide learning and promotion opportunities with higher earnings later on. The scope for such choices, both at the entry point and later, will be in part a function of the individual's prior schooling and of labor market structures. That scope is very much affected also by ability, by sex, and often by race or ethnic affiliation. Furthermore, reasons for investments in people and the returns on those investments are not solely monetary. Such investments affect the kinds of jobs to which men will have access and associated satisfactions in their work, earnings aside. Economists discuss these nonmonetary returns in terms of "equalizing differences," where, for example, high wages compensate for especially dangerous work, or, conversely, low earnings go along with nonmonetary advantages. Investments in people may also have returns unrelated to participation in the labor market; for example, they may increase the capability of both men and women to provide a superior environment for their children and to further their children's educational achievements. The economic theory of investment in human beings has incorporated all of this and more.[8]

The power of economic models of investment in people reflects, nevertheless, the use of monetary measures, including--and this is very important--monetary valuations of uses of time. The concept of equalizing differences also finds empirical expression in monetary equivalents. However, such elaborations of the theory cannot be carried out in the present study. We will consider here only the simplest of the monetary models.

A Simple Monetary Human-Investment Model

Capital theory as applied to investments in human beings entails a model with three essential components: (1) the net life-income stream associated with the choice of alternative Y--let us say, for example, pursuing a four-year college education; (2) the life-income stream associated with the choice of alternative X, which we may take here to be direct entry into the labor market upon graduation from high school (in Japan, from upper-secondary school); and (3) some method of adjusting for the fact that one thousand dollars today is worth more than the promise of one thousand dollars (adjusted for inflation) ten years from now, and that the timing of incomes in the two streams may be quite different.

The most extensive empirical measurements of the effects of such human-investment decisions have used as their first approximation the average earnings of college men and high school graduates age by age from 18 (at high school graduation) to retirement (usually taken to be at age 65 for the United States). To bring them into conformity with cohort streams through time these cross-sectional data may be adjusted in various ways (for effects of economic growth on earnings, for example). Corrections have also been made for departures from assumed relevant homogeneities in the base populations (as race or "ability" differences associated with amount of schooling).

To start with, the income stream for men with college training includes a negative sum for direct outlays ($-D_t$) during the period of attendance at college; earnings, if any, during that period will of course be lower for young men still in school than for those in the labor market. In any year t the net earnings of college men may then be designated as $Y_t - D_t$, those of the high school traduates as X_t. If one of these streams were higher than the other in all years, there could be no question about which would be preferred. However, in the example we have just cited, the college men will have lower or even negative incomes over at least their first four years, when they are investing in schooling, but at some later date their earnings will doubtless rise above those of the secondary-school graduates. If timing made no difference, we could simply add up the incomes of the college stream (including its initial negative years) and compare them with the sum of incomes of the high school stream; normally, the summation for the college men would give the higher figure. But this does not necessarily mean that the college choice is economically preferable. Here is where the third element in the investment assessment comes in: discounting incomes according to the distance into the future before they can be realized. Take the subscript t to refer to the number of years into the future at which an income accrues, with $t = 0$ the year of high school completion and $t = n$ the last year of working life, and let the discount rate be i. The present values of the college stream and of the high school stream in the year t_0 (at completion of high school) are then found by the simple summations

$$Y_0^* = \sum_{t=1}^{n} \frac{Y_t - D_t}{(1 + i)^t} \tag{2.1}$$

$$X_0^* = \sum_{t=1}^{n} \frac{X_t}{(1 + i)^t} \quad . \tag{2.2}$$

The net benefit in choosing the college alternative will be

$$Y_0^* - X_0^* = \sum_{t=1}^{n} \frac{(Y_t - D_t) - X_t}{(1 + i)^t} \quad . \tag{2.3}$$

Because the Y stream is lower (and even negative) at first, reaching its peak later, interest rates will reduce the value of Y_0^* more than they reduce the value of X_0^*. At some discount rate, Y_0^* and X_0^* will be equal; this is the "internal rate of return." At still higher rates of interest, X_0^* will of course exceed Y_0^*, and the preferred choice will be to stop schooling with completion of high school and to enter the labor force. For some purposes it is preferable (or more convenient) to compare the internal rate of return with rates on other investments. For other purposes and in other situations there may be advantages in taking some external rate of interest judged to be appropriate and in comparing "present values" at that rate. For example, we will make use of the latter procedure in comparing life-income streams expected by upper-secondary students who are enrolled in different curricula.

Another way of working out these sums is to divide the sequence into two (or more) blocks of time. In our example (ignoring *rōnin*) we may take the period $t = 1$ to $t = 4$ as the college years. The undiscounted cost of the four years in college is then the simple sum of the direct costs and the foregone earnings involved in college attendance. Foregone earnings are what could have been earned by full participation in the labor force minus whatever the college student actually earns through part-time work during his four years of higher studies; for any year t this will be $X_t - Y_t$. Using the same discount rate as before but cumulating costs to the termination of the college years gives us the cost of the investment:

$$C = \sum_{t=1}^{4} (D_t + X_t - Y_t)(1 + i)^{4 - (t - 1)} \quad . \tag{2.4}$$

The returns to this investment in the ensuing years, discounted back to the date of college graduation, are then

$$R = \sum_{t=5}^{n} \frac{Y_t - X_t}{(1 + i)^{t - 4}} \quad . \tag{2.5}$$

The interest rate i will equal the internal rate of return when C equals R.

The model just described can be extended in two ways. We can consider the effects of differences among individuals in the interest cost of funds to finance schooling, including interest costs on the financing of subsistence while at school. Thus far, this sort of extension has been theoretical only. While we will contribute no direct empirical evidence, our data permit us to examine presumptively related variables, including father's income, in our analyses of the allocation of students among types of upper-secondary schools and of college plans. (For an explicit discussion with reference to higher education see chapter 8.)

The other most important theoretical extension has been to postschool investments in the acquisition of further human capital, primarily through choice of jobs with lower current pay but higher future potential, to which we referred earlier. Such investments are reflected in the time shapes of earning streams, from which inferences have been drawn about the timing and magnitude of investments. A critical aspect of such constructs is the assumption concerning the relative effects of the investments (on-the-job learning with foregone earnings) on the individual's subsequent ability (*a*) to learn and (*b*) to earn. The "neutrality hypothesis" in this connection specifies equal values of the "learning to learn" and "learning to earn"effects. It has not been possible to distinguish these effects empirically because skill obsolescence is a confounding factor. A further confounding factor is the effects of labor market institutions and the long-term contracts implicit in seniority systems or (for Japan) in the life-commitment practices of larger firms. Fortunately for our purposes, the empirical distinctions among aspects of human capital that have most concerned those attempting to estimate postschool investments are of relatively little concern. This is because we will be looking at how young people perceive entire alternative future earning profiles, whatever the investment and obsolescence elements in those profiles may be. In that broader view, we can include choices between jobs and occupations in which the effects of early-stage investments through foregone earnings may be as much to build up a reputation and clientele (for a business enterprise or for a man in independent professional practice) as to enhance one's capabilities.

Empirical implementation of the basic monetary human-investment model has been built on two types of data: census cross-tabulations of earnings against age-education categories of the population (and occasionally census tapes giving data for individuals), and longitudinal data on the schooling and earning careers of individuals. Each has its advantages and limitations.

The economic studies using longitudinal data have differed from the path analyses by sociologists primarily in the foci of interest, which are reflected in the statistical models used. For economists the first question has been, What effects does schooling have on earnings, and hence (allowing for costs) on rates of return to investments in schooling?[9] The dependent variable always is earnings. The economist then asks how much the regression coefficients on education are affected (usually reduced) when an equation that includes an ability indicator, for example, is compared with an equation in which only education is included among the independent variables. Where the data permit, he will ask further questions. Do the effects of schooling on earnings show up more markedly at some life stages (say, for a man in his forties) than at another stage (perhaps soon after he starts work)? Are the biases because of omitted background or ability variables greater for older than for younger men? To the first of these questions the answer is that education is a poor predictor of initial earnings and that in the United States, at least, it predicts best at about seven to ten years of labor-force experience.

Evidence on the second question is accumulating, and suggests that ability biases concealed in the crude measures are negligible for early ages but may be significant at more mature ages, although the extent of these biases is widely debated. A closely related question that has drawn increasing attention from economists is how interactions between ability (or family background) and schooling affect earnings: do men of greater measured ability gain more from college education over their careers than men of less measured ability? For the United States the answer seems to be in the affirmative. A recent contribution to this literature strongly suggests (for the United States, at least) that men who attend college would do less well with just secondary schooling than do men who do not go on; but that the former do much better economically after college than would be the case for the young people who go directly into the labor market, were they to continue to college (Rosen and Willis 1979). Whether a comparable situation characterizes Japan must remain for the present an open question. However, there is an advantage in using data on individual expectations with respect to the effects of alternative educational choices; namely, the results are controlled for personal attributes that bias results when we compare sets of people distinguished by whether they in fact chose this educational alternative or that one.

Up to the present, longitudinal studies have been plagued by sample biases in coverage of a population, or by too short a period between completion of schooling and the dates for which data on earnings are available.[10] Life profiles of earnings have been estimated more frequently from census publications and similar sources, most of which lack information on parental backgrounds or individual abilities. The starting point for studies using census publications is a quite simple matrix in which the rows refer to specified age-education categories (for a given sex) and the activities are defined not by what a person is doing but by how much he earns. Each column then specifies a limited range of earnings. This brings us to the relation between the sequential-matrix model and conventional economic studies of education as an investment.

Value Matrices and the Analysis of Investments in Human Beings

Instead of a matrix that specifies number of cases in each cell, we might construct a matrix that specifies a value (monetary or otherwise) per unit occurrence in each cell. That value, or per unit "price," could be an observed dollar or yen value stating, for period (2), for example, the amount the average youth coming directly into a manual job from completion of a General A course would earn. If we are in a situation in which a man's earnings depend not only on his schooling and what he does but also on what his father did, and if we have the data, we might want to set up a price matrix that distinguishes also by father's occupation. The price tags could refer to expected as well as (instead of) observed earnings.

The conventional economic analyses of investments in education have usually bypassed occupations, to go directly to matrices in which "work" activities are specified as earnings categories. Each row of the census matrix (let us call it matrix *Q*) refers to a particular sex, age, and schooling category of the population; hence, the numerical entries in each row give us a distribution of earnings for each sex-age-schooling category.[11] The next step is to estimate mean earnings for each of those categories. The steps in this procedure are obvious enough. One must construct a value matrix of the estimated mean earnings within each cell of the census table; let us call this the *Y* matrix. Clearly, the finer the initial income classes, the better defined will be the elements of *Y* and the smaller will be the (unmeasured) within-cell variance of earnings. To get the mean value of earnings for a given sex-age-schooling class, we simply weight the values in the *Y* matrix by the counts in the *Q* (quantity or numbers) matrix. For a given sex-schooling class we then have a set of estimates of mean earnings by age, or an age-earning profile; comparisons of those profiles for different schooling classes provide the preliminary estimates of net returns or benefits for benefit-cost or rate-of-return analysis.[12] Notice, however, that in constructing the mean life-earning profiles by sex and schooling, much of the information provided in the *Q* matrix is discarded. If we wish to know how much of the variance in earnings is explained by age (or experience) and schooling, we must make use of the full *Q* and *Y* matrices. It is better, where possible, to use detailed data for individuals, since only with the latter data do we capture the within-cell variance. The chief source of data for this latter type of analysis has been special computer tapes from the census instead of the published tabulations.

As we pointed out earlier, an advantage of setting the data up in matrix form is that no linearity constraints are imposed on the relations among variables, and interaction effects will be fully specified up to the degree of detail provided in the definitions of categories distinguished in the matrix.[13] Thus, even in the empirical human-investment analyses based on census tabulations there is a full specification of sex-age-schooling interaction effects. This is crucial for the economist's analysis. It is undoubtedly just as important when the center of interest is occupational status rather than earnings and when the "price tags" are occupational status index values instead of monetary earnings. However, if we wanted to specify for each sex the full interaction effects on earnings of age, schooling, and parental education (for example), we would have to multiply the total cells in the Q matrix by the number of categories of parental education being distiguished. With each added category the order (size) of the matrix is doubled. Once again we are challenged to discriminate in the selection of variables and of interactions to be tested.

The Viability of Monetary-Expectation Models

The most obvious sort of value matrix is one in which a monetary value is assigned to each cell, although other sorts of pricing are possible. One could "price" by value on an occupational status index, for example; but even if we set aside arguments over the meanings and construction of such indexes, we still have to face the fact that they are poor discriminators with respect to changes over the course of a career.[14] In principle it might be possible to "price" for job satisfaction, but identifying an indicator that is unambiguous and applicable across individuals is even more difficult. The simplest and most direct monetary measures have many advantages in both ex post facto observations and the analysis of expectations.

This last assertion calls for special comment. Expectations are central to economic decision theory, and economists are generally prone to measuring things in money terms or monetary-equivalent prices. Nevertheless, as we have remarked before, almost all economists dealing with human resource development have confined their work to ex post facto behavioral data. This has been as true of those who center their work in a theory of human-investment decisions as among those who bypass this approach. Indeed, while sociologists have been collecting data on all sorts of expectations (usually excepting the monetary), economists have tended to spurn such a procedure. Partly, economists have had more data at hand and have felt less need to go out and get their own. At the same time, the "revealed preferences" manifested in behavior have been regarded as more reliable indicators; this is tautologically true if one's purpose is to identify behavior, but otherwise it is an evasion. It has been argued also (in flat contradiction to the theory) that people really have no clear monetary expectations; if we still adhere to economic decision theory, this is to fall back on the weak position that people behave as if they had such expectations. Are we really in so vulnerable a position as that?

Our experience in this research, together with work by Myers (1967) and Wang (1975), suggests that monetary-expectation data are not so elusive as has been assumed, provided we set up our questions in a way that is relevant to the decision maker. Even theoretically, there is no reason for wanting to ask of a youth that he predict the particular kind of thing he will be doing in his mature years or exactly what he will be earning if he follows one path or another. We do find, however, that many young people have reasonably clear perceptions of the order of magnitude of the difference between what they might earn if they pursue one major direction rather than another--let us say, going to a university as compared with entering the labor market directly from upper-secondary school. Fortunately, much less weight will be put on perceptions for the later than for the earlier years of working life, since earnings anticipated for the more distant future will be the most heavily discounted in present decisions. The present study is unique, so far as we are aware, in attempting this sort of analysis for a sample of secondary-school youth.

Monetary measures have special advantages in making comparisons over time, which necessarily must be involved in key decisions whose effects may extend far into the future. As we have already shown, economists have handled the problem of comparing the more distant with the near future and the present by applying a discount rate to derive "present values" from an entire lifetime sequence of earnings associated with the pursuit of one early alternative (or sequence of early alternatives) versus another. Except that for any given positive interest rate the later dollars are discounted more heavily than the earlier ones, one dollar (or yen) is again treated as another. But what of more generalized preference matrices? Can they be handled by a similar method? Formally this can be done, and the parallel is much closer than most people have suspected; but there is one important difference.

At least potentially, there is freedom for the individual to trade future for present dollars and vice versa without changing the nature of present activities--even though there will be a price for such transactions in interest paid or received, according as one is the borrower or the lender. But work experience that constitutes part of the learning process whereby earning power comes to be embodied in an individual cannot be separated from the individual and shifted around in time with the same degree of freedom. This means that there are constraints on trading present against future nonmonetary values or satisfactions associated with one or another activity in period (1) or (3) or (x) or (z). We would be in considerably greater trouble if we tried to specify the parameters of individual decisions and the time trade-offs related to those decisions in terms of job satisfactions or even of occupational status. Whatever its limitations, the monetary model provides a testable hypothesis and a decision rationale that eludes measurement in the more generalized preference matrix.

Monetary measures have another advantage. Despite interesting developments on many fronts in studies of the social psychology of occupational choice, there is no other proposition with respect to preference orderings that can claim so nearly universal an acceptance as the proposition that, other things equal, men will prefer the job with more pay to that with less. This single proposition has permitted the development of empirically testable decision models that have extraordinary analytic power. No decision model focused on other variables has yet emerged that can compare with the monetary models in this respect. We must and will recognize, nonetheless, that what the monetary models can tell us is only part of the story, and in some situations it may be a small part.

Careers and Labor Markets

Earlier in this chapter we stressed that human investments do not cease with the termination of formal schooling and that human-investment decisions continue to be important after entry to the labor market. We have also referred repeatedly to occupational choices in a postschool career development context. However, we carried the initial formulation of our sequential-matrix model up to period (3) only, when all members of our cohort were in the labor market and some had been there for two prior periods. In fact it is necessary to take a longer view, and again to make selective simplifications. Here we turn briefly to two large topics: criteria in reducing the number of occupational categories distinguished, and the importance of labor market structures.

Treatment of Occupations in the Analysis of Investments in People

Earlier we remarked that sociologists, in their path models, had treated occupations as intervening variables between schooling and earnings. They were able to do this simply and conveniently because they first reduced complex data on occupations to a single dimension, with an occupational status index. However, there are other important ways of looking at occupations. Furthermore, average earnings of an occupation are usually incorporated in the construction of the status index in the first place. If it were not for the fact that there may be high variability of earnings within a given occupation (even at the level of refinement of the three-digit census codes), occupational status would be a stronger predictor of earnings than is in fact the case. Evidently there are some difficulties in interpreting the correlations that have been empirically observed. On the other hand, to retain a fine classification of occupations in a complex matrix with background characteristics, schooling, and finally earnings would be unmanageable and bewildering. This raises the difficult question of what an occupation really is and what criteria might best be used to reduce the observations to a more useful and limited set of categories. This is a huge topic, which we have already anticipated; our comments on it here will be brief.

One approach, pursued recently by Welch and Maclennan (1976), is to reduce occupational categories very deliberately to a classification that will maximize efficiency in the prediction of earnings from occupations. Using cluster analysis, Welch was able to condense occupations to only three or four major groupings; finer groupings added very little to the explanation of variance in earnings. For Welch this simplification was a step in the investigation of "equalizing differences" among occupations, to which we referred earlier. His experiments are well executed and interesting, but whether his categorizations are best for the study of relations among schooling, occupations, and earnings is not immediately obvious. What would happen, for example, if instead we had grouped occupations by a cluster analysis that maximized the efficiency with which schooling predicted occupation? It is obvious that Welch's analysis gives us a stronger occupation-earnings link but a weaker schooling-occupation link than would a similar analysis designed to maximize the latter.

A very different criterion has been used by some social statisticians and is also partially reflected in census rubrics, though very crudely. This is to group together as one occupation kinds of activities among which individuals move with comparative ease or frequency. This may be a useful approach in the study of career development provided we recognize the importance of asymmetry in such relationships. But we then come back to refinements that may be quite unimportant for most purposes. For example, we would have many distinct occupations among professional men; doctors do not become lawyers or engineers (or vice versa). These distinctions will be important in the perspective of manpower planning precisely because training is specialized and takes a long time, but they may not be what interests us most from other points of view. We have remarked before about the importance of jobs and employment situations that offer greater or lesser prospects for advance, with flatter or steeper profiles of earnings or changes in the scope of responsibilities. But this leads us immediately into aspects of work situations that may be poorly indexed in many cases by what we usually call occupations, however those occupations may be classified.

Obviously, there is no single best way to categorize employments, whether as groupings of occupations or of employment situations, or of combinations of these. Moreover, some kinds of categorization require major research for their derivation, including the collection of new data. In this book we will experiment with several alternatives.

The Firm, the Labor Market, and Investments in People

One of the main considerations that stimulated our work on the fathers of students in the upper-secondary and primary schools was an interest in the effects of labor market institutions and processes on relations between learning in school and human resource development and advancement at work. A priori observations suggested that Japanese labor market institutions and processes might have some distinctive and observable implications for roles of education in the economy and for the locus and timing of human resource development over the life span. Detailed analysis of Japanese labor markets is not within the scope of this book. However, to be meaningful, an examination of student preferences and expectations must take into account the relevant evidence on labor market situations and processes. Moreover, adjustment processes in the labor markets and changes in those adjustments reflect interactions of myriad small decisions.

Over the past fifteen years, two major strands of theoretical and empirical work have been oriented to just such questions. One of these has been of central importance in the theory of investments in human beings as initially set forth by Gary Becker. The other is the work on "internal labor markets," often associated with the names Doeringer and Piore (see Doeringer and Piore 1971). These are essentially complementary streams of work. In his seminal analysis of investments in human beings, Becker (1962, 1964) poses a basically simple dichotomization of on-the-job training and learning, as either "general" or "specific"; all other cases are viewed as mixtures ranging along a continuum from one of these extremes to the other. Training is general in this definition when what is learned will add as much to a man's productive potential, and hence (under conventional competitive assumptions) to his earning power, in other firms or agencies as in the one in which he receives the training. At the other extreme, training is specific in Becker's definition when what is learned has value only in the firm or agency in which the training is received.[15] It should be emphasized, however, that what makes a skill rapidly transferable to another setting or relatively (or completely) firm-specific may depend as much on the way activities are organized as on any distinctively firm-related competence. A member of a working team in the broadest sense may be far more valuable when he continues with that team than he could be for some time if he were to go elsewhere. Rosen (1972) has developed this theme succinctly in his analysis of what makes learning "Becker-specific" in an economy so large and diverse as that of the United States. His analysis is clearly an apt one with reference to the Japanese economy.

Whereas the individual who receives the training bears the full costs (in reduced wages) of Becker's general training and subsequently receives the full returns (in higher earnings) on his investment in himself, this will not be true for the Becker-specific components of his learning. On the contrary, a large, though indeterminate, share of the costs of fully specific training will be borne by the firm. The firm recoups on its human investments later, by paying the specifically trained workers less than their posttraining marginal products. It can do this even in a generally competitive economy precisely because the training has been specific to the firm, which introduces a noncompetitive posttraining element into the situation. Individuals so trained cannot be as productive in any other setting. But for this same reason, neither will individuals bear the full initial training costs by accepting correspondingly lower initial pay; or, more precisely, they would not do this in the generally competitive, year-after-year choice-making economy that Becker implicitly envisages.

If the amount of learning were the same, we should expect flatter life-income streams for those with specific training, steeper streams for those with general training. In Japan it may not be quite that way, however. Indeed, it is not quite that way in the United States, but the Japanese deviance is decidedly the greater. The reasons for this are closely linked to seniority systems in both countries, and to features of the Japanese life-commitment, or permanent employment, system in particular, which lengthen the time horizons implicit in employment contracts and customs. Questions that have often been raised in the literature on Japan have a much wider relevance than usually has been supposed.

Although Doeringer and Piore do not give us so powerful a basic theory of investments in people, they have examined in more detail some aspects of relations of informal training and learning through experience to seniority systems in large firms.

Clearly it is important for many reasons that we gain further understanding of how labor markets and their operations are perceived by those who have had one or another experience and those who are about to enter the labor force. We gave special attention, therefore, to the construction of a set of opinion questions for both students and their fathers, including fathers of pupils in elementary school. These questions were designed to elicit responses that would reveal perceptions of the life-commitment system and of penalties and gains (if any) of moving from one firm to another at the early stages of one's working life. There were questions relating to employment in large versus small firms, and in wage or independent work. Other questions were directed explicitly to perceptions of how employers view graduates of general versus technical courses and of higher institutions versus upper-secondary schools. Students' perceptions were compared with those of their fathers, individually matched and in summary distributions.

Wider implications aside, such an analysis has particular relevance to this study because perceptions of both fathers and students with respect to the labor markets will presumably have direct relevance to expectations, plans, and decisions among the options available to seniors in the upper-secondary schools. We will make our main use of this material in part 4, however, when attention is directed to views of early postschool experiences as an intervening variable between schooling and career-peak jobs, and where we ask what relations there may be between perceptions of labor markets and the course of expected earning streams.

The analytical heart of this book is in the analysis of sequential decisions for career development. As such it is built around an examination of expectations, options, and constraints on choice seen in the context of a dynamically evolving society. In this chapter we have sketched some of the theoretical constructs that underlie the present work, along with some implications for research design. We started with an emphasis on key decisions: decisions that strongly affect future options. These occur at stages in schooling and careers that are critical points for large numbers of people in Japan as in other societies. Decision theory is rationalistic in that it is essentially deductive in its most general, abstract formulation; but it also derives from empirical observations, whether formal or informal, and it encompasses a wide diversity of potential parameters of choice and constraints on choices.

In this chapter we have discussed four broad, interrelated aspects of analytical models and methods: (1) temporal ordering in path analysis and in a sequential-matrix model using categorical variables; (2) the treatment of preferences and expectations in the study of schooling and of anticipated postschool careers; (3) monetary and nonmonetary analysis of investments in human beings; and (4) preliminary ways of classifying occupations, and relationships between labor market structures and the associations between schooling and career development thereafter.

Under the first of these topics we have specified some of the potentials and the limitations of the two types of sequential models that are applied to the problems addressed in this book. A sequential-matrix analog of the direct and indirect effects analyzed in path models has been illustrated. We have found that a fundamental problem for the social sciences in contrast to the physical sciences is the handling of "causation." For example, are youth enrolled in the academic stream because they plan to go on to higher education, or does enrollment in an academic curriculum explain the much higher rates of entry to college and university --and what, in that case, do we mean by "explanation"? Questions of this sort are not trivial, and they recur at a number of points in the chapters that follow.

Under the general heading of "prediction, preference, and decision" we have treated a number of questions that are of importance for much of this book. We have drawn the distinction--essential for both path analysis (used only for grouped data in the present case) and decision theory generally--between expectations of a particular course of action, best interpreted as proxy variables for the action ("intentions"), and conditional expectations, which are at the heart of choices between alternative courses of action. We have drawn on theories of decision making under uncertainty applied to other topics (especially in work on decision making in business) to formulate models appropriate to the analysis of individual career decisions; especially important in this connection is the selective focusing of attention on certain alternatives and perceptions of outcomes from a much larger set. Pursuing Shackle's concept of attention focus and "potential surprise," we have distinguished preference-possibility matrices for analysis of expectations from "objective" transition-probability matrices. Complementing this approach are criteria for determining how far present choices (at any given decision point) constrain the options for choices in the future, and the nature of those constraints.

The third main section of the chapter has laid out the simple human-capital model in monetary terms and provided some indications of the breadth of applicability of monetary-equivalent indicators. That section has specified some of the special advantages and the feasibility of using monetary-expectation data. One of the advantages of monetary data is that they constitute a cardinal variable from the start, eliminating the necessity of constructing an index such as that for occupational status. The monetary figures provide a more discriminating life-cycle picture than we can obtain from indicators of occupational status, especially perhaps for college graduates. Monetary measures lend themselves better than other indicators to comparisons over time, including discounting of the more distant future; there are fewer constraints on trading present for future money income (as in spending now to build up future earning power) than in trading present for future nonmonetary satisfactions associated with one or another activity. (A well-known saying is appropriate here: "who steals my time steals what can never be returned." This is of course not at all the same thing as "investing" one's time. There is a limit to what we can measure in monetary equivalents.) Monetary measures have one further advantage: whatever people's preferences may be otherwise, most of us would prefer more to less money income, other things equal.

Finally, we have commented briefly on investments by individuals and firms in human resource development during the working years. This is a very preliminary introduction to topics of concern to many economists over the past two decades, some of which will occupy our attention in part 4 of this book.

Part 2

To Upper-Secondary School or the Labor Market: The Stage I Decision

3. Selection into Upper-Secondary Curricula

How does a youth's background affect the likelihood that he will attend upper-secondary school and the curriculum in which he will be enrolled? Alternatively, what is the mix of pupils in particular curricula, and how great is the variation in classroom composition among schools?

The first orientation (which we termed the "first perspective" in chapter 2) starts with how individuals' backgrounds affect their opportunities and choices. This perspective is associated with the economists' human-investment approach. Paradoxically, because the motivations of individuals with respect to schooling are complex and include "noneconomic" along with "economic" elements, the demands of private individuals for schooling have sometimes been designated as the "social demand" for education (see Bowman 1970). Family backgrounds condition both the realities an individual may anticipate and his perceptions of the benefits to be derived from continuance in school and from entry into one rather than another type of school. Backgrounds also affect both the realities and his perceptions of the chances of gaining entry to one or another upper-secondary school or course. Depending upon the particular society in question, youth may be highly differentiated in these respects or they may be comparatively homogeneous and show little selectivity of entry to upper-secondary school or to one course rather than another.

Variations in background within the classroom are no less important. This is not merely a matter of tracing back from a manpower starting point, to identify where youth with one or another type of schooling come from. It may make a considerable difference to the school experience of young people whether their associations are almost entirely with youth of similar backgrounds or whether their classmates are from diverse backgrounds. While this study cannot add anything to the work by educational researchers on how peer groups affect achievement, it can portray variations in classroom composition and relate that compoisition to student perceptions of the future and to pursuit of higher education in particular.

The plan of this chapter is simple. The first section picks up the "second perspective" of chapter 2, to examine social backgrounds of students in each type of secondary-school course and to consider variabilities in classroom composition within each course type. The second section examines social selectivity, first in zero-order relationships and then with the use of multiple regressions.

Distributions of Background Characteristics by Type of Course

Variations in the backgrounds of students enrolled in one or another type of course could be measured in several ways. Here we will look at the composition of student bodies according to father's type of occupation and occupational status and according to his education.

Occupations of Fathers

Two summary indicators relating to parental occupation suffice to give a good description of the composition of student bodies with respect to fathers' roles in the society. The first is a classification of occupations by type, the second a categorization by occupational status. We explain the latter indicator first.

Occupations were ranked by status in eight categories (the higher the number, the lower the status), using a modified version of the Duncan occupational status scale.[1] The break between categories 4 and 5 is an important one in that most white collar jobs are category 4 or above and most manual jobs are category 5 or lower, but there is some overlap. The lowest clerical positions fall in category 5, and trading occupations span almost the entire scale. Very highly skilled manual workers could rank as high as 4, and technicians and engineers are toward the top of the scale. The most difficult group to place were the farmers, most of whom were ranked 5; but a large minority were rated 6, and ordinary farm laborers, like common labor generally, are in category 8.

Several different classifications by type of occupation have been used in this study, but all are founded on a hypothesis concerning job-related differences in ways of thinking, perceiving, and behaving that are generally quite independent of position in a vertical status hierarchy. The resulting classification in its most abbreviated and simplified form distinguishes four broad types of occupations: (1) white collar, (2) processors (designated FAB, or fabricators, in our tabulations), (3) traders, and (4) farmers and others in primary industries (except mining). The white collar rubric ranges from business elites and the top echelons in the national government to the lowliest clerk; these jobs are similar in that virtually all are desk jobs and involve pushing paper. Most of the professions (for example, law, journalism) are included here. However, we classified professional engineers as processors. Category 2 thus covers the widest status range, from the top-level professional through the skilled craftsman to the semiskilled operative and the ordinary manual worker. The lowest common denominator in this category is an involvement in activities that entail three-dimensional perceptual comprehension and usually the handling of material objects. (Finer classifications controlling for status level uphold the validity of the distinction between type categories 1 and 2, as will become apparent at a number of points in this book.) Within category 3 can fall anyone from the street peddler and the small tobacconist to the head of a large department store chain, but the majority in this category are of course proprietors of small retail stores and salesmen. We included service workers (for example, barbers) and the proprietors and staff of inns and hotels in this category. Most of these jobs entail continual interaction at one level or another with the public. The distinctiveness of category 4--workers in agriculture, forestry, and fishing--hardly needs comment.

The occupational status and type characteristics of fathers of students in each of the five types of upper-secondary schools are summarized in table 3.1. In view of what has already been said about the kinds of schools found in rural and in urban areas and about the place of farmers on the occupational status scale, the distinctive distributions for agricultural schools and nonacademic General A curricula will be readily understood. Sons of workers in agriculture, forestry, and fishing account for three-fourths of the students enrolled in agriculture curricula, and the fact that farmers were rated 5 or, less often, 6 on the status scale accounts for the high concentrations of agriculture students in those status categories. The same facts account for the similar, but less extreme, pattern among students in General A courses; almost half of these students were sons of fathers engaged in agriculture or (much less often) fishing, and the bulk of the General A students came from families ranked 5 or 6 in occupational

Table 3.1 Relation between Son's Course Enrollment and Father's Type of Occupation and Occupational Status (percentage distributions)

Father's Occupation	General B	General A	Agri- culture	Commerce	Technical	Total (adjusted sample)[a]
Type of occupation[b]						
WC	43	19	10	24	22	29
FAB	25	22	11	37	48	31
RET	17	13	3	27	17	16
AG	15	45	76	12	13	24
Total	100	99	100	100	100	100
Occupational status						
1 (high)	3	1	1	2	2	5
2	7					
3	22	8	2	9	9	14
4	16	11	5	14	13	14
5	25	31	59	28	25	29
6	14	32	28	21	27	22
7,8	13	18	6	26	24	16
Total	100	101	101	100	100	100
Percentage not responding	10	11	6	8	12	11
Total number in sample	1,825	552	1,192	1,044	2,593	4,452

[a]In the adjusted sample the subsamples for all but the general curricula were reduced to conform to the 1966 distribution of students among course types in Japan. (The initial sample deliberately overrepresented vocational courses.)

[b]WC = white collar; FAB = technical, manual; RET = traders; AG = agriculture, forestry, fishing.

status. The table shows that considerable numbers of rural youth (15 percent) were enrolled in rural General B courses, and while a slight sample bias may have exaggerated this figure, the true value cannot have been far from one-seventh. Even in the commerce and technical schools, a sixth to a seventh of the students came from farming or fishing homes, but most of these youth were commuting from adjacent farm districts to schools in an urban, though not usually a metropolitan, place.

The occupational backgrounds of male pupils in the commerce and technical curricula were quite similar both with respect to status distribution and in proportions from white collar and farm homes. The main contrasts are what we might expect: sons of trading families were relatively more frequent among commerce students than among youth in other courses, and sons of fathers categorized as processors (FAB) were most frequent in the technical curricula, where they accounted for half the total. As we shall see, the more detailed job characteristics of the fathers in the broad category of processors were quite different for the commerce and technical schools.

Students in General B stood out for their distinctly higher representation of the upper occupational levels and of white collar parental backgrounds.[2] Indeed, almost a third of the General B students came from homes ranked 1 through 3 in status level, as against a maximum of an eighth from such homes among students who were in the commerce and technical streams (and under 3 percent in the agricultural schools). The excess proportions for General B in fact extended through level 4. Compared with all other types of curriculum, the academic general course was most dramatically underrepresented for status levels 5 and 6, rather than for the lowest levels. The spread of status among FAB fathers of General B students was extremely wide, from professional engineers to common laborers, but sons of skilled workers found their way into these courses far less often than into the technical streams.

Education of Fathers

The vast majority of Japanese men in the age range of fathers of students in the last year of upper-secondary school had been educated through eight years of the old compulsory system, and many had attended wartime youth schools but had gone no further; of all Japanese men aged 40-49 in 1966 the proportion with no regular schooling beyond the compulsory years was 72 percent. The reported proportions of such fathers in our sample were close to 70 percent in each of the curricula except the General B course, which had a smaller, though still a substantial, representation of fathers with compulsory schooling only (43 percent). The General B course had a correspondingly high proportion of students whose parents had gone beyond elementary school, but the contrast with other curricula is especially notable for youth whose fathers had proceeded into the higher schools (junior colleges) or universities. In an average classroom from our General B sample, a fourth of the youth would have come from homes in which the father had had at least some higher education, whereas the proportions from such backgrounds were only 8 percent in the technical schools (which rated second in this respect) and 4 percent in agriculture. This contrast between students in the academic general and other curricula was associated with rates of continuation from General B into college in complex ways, reflecting both why these students entered General B in the first place and how students' aspirations were affected by classroom composition.

Variations in Classroom Composition

Thus far, we have been comparing differences among courses in average classroom composition, but there are wide variations among schools of any given type. Those variations depend in part, but only in part, on whether the school is in an urban (fifty thousand or more) or a rural location. Thus, among students of our sample in rural general courses the proportions of fathers who were farmers ranged from 15 to 67 percent, the proportions who were white collar ranged from 8 to 37 percent, and the proportions who were skilled workers ranged from none to 18 percent. The corresponding figures for urban general schools were, respectively,0 to 11 percent, 15 to 42 percent, and 7 to 40 percent. Some of the urban general curricula had as many sons of technicians and skilled workers as the urban technical courses (from 25 to 44 percent). Even more striking are the variations in proportion of fathers with no more than compulsory levels of education. In our sample the lowest fraction, surprisingly, was in a rural agricultural school (11 percent); the highest was in an urban general school (84 percent). It is among the urban general courses, nevertheless, that one finds the classrooms with the highest proportions of fathers educated beyond secondary school. At the extreme, 80 percent of the 1966 students at an elite upper-secondary school in Tokyo (not in our sample) were sons of college men. Even when extremes are set aside, the wide ranges in classroom composition within each curriculum are important, as they reflect Japanese society and the variety of peer associations in educational experiences. Those variations will also serve, incidentally, to give us leverage in subsequent analyses of determinants of college decisions and career hopes.

Family Background and Destination at the Upper-Secondary-School Entry Stage

Turning our questions around, we now consider how things may look from the perspective of the individual (or his family) at the decision point of entry to upper-secondary school--the Stage I decision point of our sequential model.

Selectivity of Entry into Upper-Secondary School or the Labor Market

What are the chances that a young man with one as against another family background will enter upper-secondary school at all? Evidence already reported partially answers this question. As was stated in chapter 1, among the 1964 graduates of lower-secondary schools (the cohort of young people we are studying) two-thirds went on to full-time upper-secondary school. If in 1964 we had known nothing about a youth's background, we would have bet two to one that he would do so. (The odds are more like nine to one today.)

Knowing that his father did not go beyond elementary school would have reduced our estimate of a youth's chances somewhat, but not substantially, since (as previously remarked) roughly 72 percent of the general male population in the relevant age range for fathers had no full-time schooling beyond compulsory levels. In fact, using the data from our adjusted sample as a basis of estimation, we conclude that approximately half of the sons of men who had had only compulsory schooling entered upper-secondary schools in 1964, as compared with roughly 85 percent of the sons of men who had gone beyond that level. Sons of men who had been to upper-secondary schools were almost as likely to go on as sons of men with a university education.

Assuming no differences in the numbers of sons of upper-secondary age in the general population per thousand men aged 40-49 at each level of parental schooling, we computed "selectivity ratios" for the entire upper-secondary sample simply by dividing the distribution of fathers' schooling (in the adjusted sample) by that for all males aged 40-49. The ratios we obtained were

Sons of university men	1.52
Sons of men with "higher" (junior-college) schooling	1.43
Sons of men with middle (upper-secondary) schooling	1.41
Sons of men with no full-time schooling beyond compulsory levels	.83

Despite the limitations of our sample for such estimates, there is no reason to suspect any large error in these results. Selectivity of continuation into upper-secondary education clearly existed, but the extent of that selectivity was impressively moderate.

Matching the reported occupations of students' fathers to census reports of occupations in the general population is more difficult than for schooling. There are inherent problems in occupational reporting and coding, and in combining the detailed occupational data on fathers of our students into a manageable number of categories we used classifications that differ from the broad categories in the Japanese population census. After some preliminary trials, we decided to concentrate on evidence from our urban samples and to focus on representation of the two lowest occupational status groups only. A priori considerations as well as the evidence already cited concerning underrepresentation of sons of the least schooled men suggested that these lower occupations would be underrepresented among upper-secondary students. Comparisons made for the particular cities included in our study indicated an excess of base populations over students' fathers at status 7 and 8 ranging between 5 and 9 percentage points for each city except Fukuoka, where the difference was 17 points. In Hiroshima, where we drew the most representative secondary-school sample, 24 percent of the employed male population aged 40-49 were in statuses 7 and 8 as against 15 percent of the fathers of male upper-secondary students; the selectivity ratio of .63 was decidedly greater underrepresentation than the ratio .83 cited above for sons of the least educated parents. This is hardly surprising; in pushing down to status levels 7 and 8, we are focusing on a distinctly lower level of fathers than that singled out in taking all who lack regular schooling beyond compulsory grades. Even the Osaka ratio, which was biased upward, was just .80 for levels 7 and 8.

Effects of Parental Backgrounds on Courses Chosen: Some Simple Comparisons

Leaving out of our calculations those who enter none of the upper-secondary streams, we are now ready to ask how youth with various backgrounds sort themselves out among curricula.

If we regard each type of curriculum as indicative of a type of occupational predisposition, we can interpret the extent to which sons of men in one occupational category versus another attend kinds of upper-secondary schools that suggest "occupational inheritance" in the broad sense of a continuity in general type of

Table 3.2 Relation between Son's Course Enrollment and Father's Type of Occupation (percentage distributions)

Father's Occupational Type (FO-III)	General B	General A	Agriculture	Commerce	Technical	Total %	Total N	Index of Dissimilarity
1 White collar[a]	60	9	3	13	15	100	827	19
2 Higher technical (engineers and technicians)	50	6	2	13	30	101	331	16
3 Managerial in manufacturing and construction	61	6	1	13	19	100	328	21
4 Proprietors and managers in trade	41	10	1	26	22	100	651	10
5 Artisans	37	6	1	28	28	100	147	17
6 Skilled workers in heavy industry and construction	24	9	4	20	43	100	426	25
7 Other manual	28	11	3	22	36	100	311	20
8 Agriculture, forestry, and fishing	26	24	29	8	12	99	923	33
9 Miscellaneous	...	...	...	...	...	...	16	...
10 Nonresponse	41	12	5	13	29	100	492	6
Total	41	12	8	16	23	100	4452	...

Note. Adjusted sample (see footnote a, table 3.1).

[a]Professional, managerial, and office workers at all levels but exclusive of categories specified below.

interest or direction. Table 3.2 speaks to this question. The summary "indexes of dissimilarity" shown for each origin in the last column of the table specify the proportion of sons of a designated origin who would have to be shifted to match the distribution among courses for all sons.

Farmers' sons were the most clearly differentiated from all others, with an index of dissimilarity of 33 percent, attributable to their overrepresentation in the agricultural and General A curricula. As the other side of this coin, youth with nonagricultural backgrounds were substantially underrepresented among the agriculture students. Variations in the distribution of fathers' occupations in General A classes reflected primarily variations of occupational structures among localities.

Sons of men whose occupations were at once urban and high status--most notably sons of engineers, technicians, and managers in manufacturing enterprises--were the least likely to take nonacademic general courses of study in upper-secondary school, for fairly obvious reasons. Instead, sons of engineers and high-level technicians were found in somewhat more than their expected proportions just where inheritance of a mixture of status background and father's type of job would have led us to look for them--in the academic general and the technical curricula. But the dual effects of status and job type made the sons of engineers and technicians among the least differentiated in course distribution.

The closest approximation to the average, however, was the distribution of destinations of sons of proprietors and managers in trade and retail services, with an index of dissimilarity of only 10 percent. Sons of traders were overrepresented in the commerce courses, to be sure, but to a very moderate extent; despite their geographic spread from small towns to metropolises, the compensating underrepresentation for sons of this group was primarily in agriculture. In fact, the sons of small-scale artisans slightly exceeded the sons of retail proprietors and retail service workers in the proportions going into the commerce stream.

With the exception of the artisans (who sent exactly the same proportions into technical as into commerce streams), youth from each of the subcategories previously combined under FAB (including engineers, technicians, and all processing workers and manual labor) entered technical schools in substantially greater proportions than they went into any other course except (in some cases) the academic general. Two groups--the sons of skilled workers in heavy industry and construction, and the sons of semiskilled and unskilled ("other manual") workers--were decidedly underrepresented (along with the sons of farmers) in the General B curriculum. Particularly interesting is the decided preference among sons of skilled workers for the technical course; their overrepresentation in that course is an exceptionally clear instance of occupational inheritance in the broad sense. Among youth who continue into upper-secondary school, even sons of "other manual" workers enter the technical stream less often, other streams more often, than do the sons of skilled workers.

We had no way of estimating how a youth's chances of going to some, or any, sort of full-time upper-secondary school would have been affected by the death or illness of his father. Neither had we any direct evidence as to how secondary-school attendance would have been affected by parental unemployment or parental income, although occupational type and social status gave us clues on these points. However, for those who were enrolled we did have information concerning the incidence of nonemployment among fathers and on proportions of fathers who were deceased. Students in the technical course were the most disadvantaged on both counts: 12 percent of the fathers of those students were no longer living and over 4 percent were not working. The smallest proportion with fathers not living (5 percent) was among students in agriculture, and the smallest proportion with fathers not working was among students in commerce. (The low incidence of nonworking fathers among the students in commerce reflected the fact that more fathers of enrollees in that course were self-employed, and suffered neither periodic unemployment nor early automatic retirement.) The most interesting thing that these figures told us was that if a young man had lost his father and lived in an area in which technical schools were accessible, the likelihood that he would attend such a course rather than any other type of curriculum was substantially greater than if his father had been living. (Parental occupation as classified in all of the tables refers to a father's "principal occupation," and includes the last occupation of a father who was no longer living or was not working at the time of the interviews.)

Table 3.3 presents the course distributions for youth from different occupational status origins. There is a clear and consistent decline in the proportions of youth enrolled in the academic general course with decline in occupational status of the father; the range is from over nine-tenths in the small, top-status category to just over a fourth at status levels 6 through 8. Youth whose fathers were of middle status entered the academic courses more often than they entered any others, but there was a considerable shift between status categories 2 and 3, and then again

Table 3.3 Relation between Son's Course Enrollment and Father's Occupational Status (percentage distributions)

Father's Occupational Status	General B	General A	Agriculture	Commerce	Technical	Total
1 (high)	91	3	...	1	5	100
2	79	2	1	8	10	100
3	66	8	1	10	15	100
4	49	10	3	16	22	100
5	35	13	17	16	19	100
6	26	18	11	16	28	99
7,8	27	13	3	25	32	100

Note. Adjusted sample (see footnote a, table 3.1).

between 3 and 4 in the proportions who went into technical courses instead of the academic general streams. Rates of entry into technical courses were highest, nevertheless, for youth from homes in status levels 6 through 8. More surprising was the decided jump in the proportions of youth attending commerce schools from those in the three status levels 4, 5, and 6 (all around a sixth) to those in the lowest status groups (about a fourth).

As we saw earlier, the occupational status scale discriminated over a fuller range of parental socioeconomic status than did parental education, simply because the majority of Japanese men over forty had completed the compulsory schooling levels but had not gone further. Also, we found that differences in schooling among fathers who had gone beyond compulsory levels told us very little about their sons' rates of entry into upper-secondary school. However, those differences in parental education did relate systematically to the types of courses that sons would enter (table 3.4). Thus, as with occupational status, the proportions going into the General B streams were highest among sons of university men and declined progressively as we went down the scale of parental education. Among the sons of men who had attended middle or upper-secondary school, half went into the General B curriculum, the rest distributing themselves over the field, but especially into the technical streams. Only 30 percent of the sons of men without postcompulsory education went into General B. There was a progressive increase in the proportions entering each and all of the other types of courses as we moved down the scale of parental education, though that progression was somewhat less steep for the technical than for the other streams.

Table 3.4 Relation between Son's Course Enrollment and Father's Education (percentage distributions)

Father's Education	General B	General A	Agri- culture	Commerce	Technical	Total
		Level of Schooling				
University	77	3	a	5	14	99
Higher school (junior college)	65	7	3	8	16	99
Old middle (upper secondary)	50	10	7	13	20	100
Compulsory[b]	30	15	10	20	25	100
		Type of Secondary or Higher School Course				
Normal	73	11	3	5	7	99
Academic	67	2	1	11	19	100
Technical	57	7	1	8	27	100
Commerce	53	7	2	18	20	100
Agriculture	41	19	19	8	12	99

[a]Under .5%.

[b]See footnote a, table 3.1.

The lower part of table 3.4 introduces some distinctions not used before in types of schooling among fathers who attended middle and higher schools or institutes (upper secondary and junior college in modern terms); these types are arranged in declining order with respect to the proportions of sons enrolled in General B courses. The fact that sons of men who had attended normal schools were the most likely of all to go into General B courses, but least likely to enter commerce or technical streams, bespoke the influence of pedagogue fathers on the educational careers of their sons, an influence that might well prevail even when training at a normal school had not been followed by actual teaching. Once again, the inheritance factor came out with clarity not only for agriculture but also for attendance at commerce courses. Nevertheless, the distributions of students whose fathers attended agricultural secondary schools might suggest as much the effects of accessibility to alternative vocational curricula as transmission of interest in agriculture from father to son. The inheritance component at work in youth whose fathers had attended technical secondary schools or higher institutes was ambiguous, but so was the stronger pull of the academic general course.

Regression Analysis of Background Influences on Type of Course Taken

The effects of parental education and occupation on the likelihood that if a youth goes on to upper-secondary school he will enroll in a particular course have been analyzed in the preceding pages, taking one parental trait at a time. The simplest way of going beyond this, to the consideration of several influences jointly, is to use an ordinary linear multiple regression analysis. This we have done taking the likelihood of attending each type of course in turn as the dependent variable.[3] Thus, if the dependent variable is enrollment in an academic general course, for example, individuals in that course will be given a score of 1 on the dependent variable, those in other courses will be scored 0. Overall, the mean value of the dependent variable "academic general" should be equal to the proportion of all upper-secondary youth who are enrolled in that curriculum.[4] The mean values of the five dependent variables (which exhausts the types of courses) will add to 1.00.

Application of an ordinary linear model to analysis of these probabilities constitutes a crude (and inexpensive) approximation to a "maximum likelihood" estimation. It has the advantage of providing results that are comparatively easy to read and interpret, so long as the proportions predicted do not approach (or go outside) the bounds of 0 to 1. There are two important limitations, however. First, with a dichotomous dependent variable, the standard tests of significance are not valid. This limitation need not concern us too much, since our principal interest is in the regression coefficients as estimates of the magnitude of effects on probabilities, rather than in their statistical significance or the proportion of variance explained. Second, the form of relationships assumed in ordinary least-squares linear estimation will be inappropriate toward the upper and lower bounds of the dependent variable; at the extremes this can even lead to predictions that exceed a probability of 1.00 or that take on negative signs. Our results suggest that this second problem is not serious in the present case. However, when we come to the college decision (chapter 7), we will shift to probit analysis. Here, as in probit analysis later on, we make the simplifying assumption of independence (no interactions) in the effects of one and another set of independent variables, such as father's education and occupational status.

The independent variables have been treated as categorical throughout, even though some (as father's age) were cardinal numbers in their original form and others (as father's occupational status or level of education) could have been treated as if cardinal. The use of categories minimizes problems of the second type noted above. A further advantage is that nonresponse on a particular item can simply be treated as a distinct variable of a set.[5] Thus, we have five instead of four "dummy" variables in the set for father's level of schooling: elementary, secondary (or middle), higher (or junior-college), university, and (a variable in itself) "no response." To avoid overdetermination of the value of the dependent variable, one variable in each set among the independent variables is the "omitted dummy," which is in fact picked up in the intercept. The regression coefficients on all other dummy variables of a set are comparisons with those values of the dependent variable that are associated with the omitted dummy. Accordingly, we have chosen which variables to treat as omitted dummies to facilitate the interpretation of results. Thus, in all equations the omitted education dummy was elementary schooling (the most frequent among fathers), to which all other schooling categories were compared. In equations in which we used the father's occupational status, we selected level 5 as the dummy to be omitted. This status level was reasonably well represented in both rural and urban populations; it picked up a majority (but by no means all) of the farmers along with highly skilled manual workers and low-level clerical and sales personnel.

Both for its inherent interest and to serve as an introductory example that should elucidate the use of dummy variables and of a set of dependent variables whose sum equals 1.00, we present in table 3.5 the findings of a very simple regression in which we used only one set of independent variables--those for father's schooling (FLEVS)--with each of the five dependent variables. Since we used no independent variables other than father's schooling, the beta coefficients of this table provide the same information concerning percentage distributions among types of schools as that already shown in table 3.4, but in a different form. The intercepts in this case are the values for sons of men with elementary schooling only; these intercept values must add to 1.00 across the five types of schools. The other beta coefficients state by how much the proportions attending a given type of course exceeded or fell short of the proportions among sons of

Table 3.5 Regression Analysis of Effects of Father's Education on Type of Course Taken by Son (ordinary least-squares approximation to likelihoods)

	Beta Coefficients (metric)[a]					
	General B	General A	Agriculture	Commerce	Technical	Chi-square[c]
Intercept	.305	.146	.096	.198	.255	
Father's education (FLEVS)						
1,2 Lower school	b	b	b	b	b	
3 Old middle (upper secondary)	.195	-.043	-.026	-.070	-.056	124.62
4 Higher school (junior college)	.347	-.075	-.063	-.114	-.096	131.01
5 University	.467	-.114	-.092	-.147	-.113	154.64
0 Unclassified, nonresponse	.075	.002	.011	-.081	.003	26.18

[a]Because only one classificatory set of variables is included, these coefficients are easily derived from or translated into a simple cross-tabulation, in contrast to the use of multiple sets in tables 3.6 and 3.7.

[b]Omitted dummy; value is in the intercept.

[c]Chi-square values from a logistic maximum likelihood analysis using a simultaneous equation model in which one course is an omitted dependent variable. The total chi-square is 442.31, with 16 degrees of freedom. We have not shown the logit coefficients, since they are difficult to interpret directly and add nothing substantive to what can be read from this table. The logistic and probit functions and their use with dichotomous dependent variables are explained in chapter 7.

Table 3.6 Effects of Father's Type of Occupation and Education on Type of Course Taken by Son (ordinary least-squares approximation to likelihoods)

	Beta Coefficients (metric)					
	General B	General A	Agriculture	Commerce	Technical	Chi-square[a]
Intercept	.353	.114	.013	.290	.230	
Father's education (FLEVS)						
1,2 Lower school	b	b	b	b	b	
3 Old middle (upper secondary)	.133	-.028	.003	-.070	-.038	60.28
4 Higher school (junior college)	.263	-.048	-.018	-.115	-.082	76.10
5 University	.348	-.080	-.032	-.149	-.087	98.81
0 Unclassified, nonresponse	.050	.005	.017	-.076	.004	30.99
Father's occupational type, classification III (FO-III)						
1 White collar	.118	.005	.022	-.097	-.048	31.49
2 Higher technical (engineers and technicians)	.044	-.036	.007	-.111	.096	32.34
3 Managerial in manufacturing and construction	.126	-.028	.001	-.089	-.010	22.81
4 Proprietors and managers in trade	b	b	b	b	b	
5 Artisans	-.033	-.044	.001	.014	.061	9.36
6 Skilled workers in heavy industry and construction	-.148	-.016	.022	-.067	.209	71.27
7 Other manual	-.109	.004	.012	-.047	.141	36.15
8 Agriculture, forestry, and fishing	-.131	.137	.276	-.183	-.098	230.77
9 Miscellaneous	.016	-.086	-.005	-.043	.119	.52
10 Nonresponse	-.020	.024	.031	-.110	.075	33.40
Total chi-square	...	...	...	...	...	1,386.37

[a]Chi-square estimates from the logistic maximum likelihood analysis, for which the logit coefficients are not shown. (There are 52 degrees of freedom.)

[b]Omitted dummy.

elementary-school fathers who were enrolled in that course.[6] Thus, for sons of university graduates, table 3.5 tells us that the chances were .772 (that is, .305 + .467) for enrollment in an academic course, but only .051 (or .198 - .147) for enrollment in a commerce course.

With tables 3.6 and 3.7 we move on to the examination of

several sets of independent variables at the same time; the coefficients for each set are now controlling for the other sets included in the equation.

The variable set FO-III for father's occupational type specified in the row headings of table 3.6 (and used in table 3.2 also) was derived by computerizing a new combination of the original three-digit occupation codes. Although it has some "vertical" distinctions, as in the split between "higher technical" (code 2) and "skilled workers in heavy industry and construction" (code 6), it is still intended to be as far as possible a classification by kind with minimal overtones of status.[7] "Higher technical" occupations (engineers and technicians) are grouped together and again excluded from "white collar" on the hypothesis that the former kind of work calls distinctively for a sense of concrete objects, even when that awareness finds its expression on paper. The third category,"managerial in manufacturing and construction," is separated from "white collar" because production managers, again, are chiefly concerned with the processing side of things. The "white collar" group is of course large even after such deletions; it ranges from the lowliest clerical worker to the (rare) top-level bureaucrat or financier. The omitted dummy variable in this case is "proprietors and managers in trade," a category that appears in substantial numbers in both rural and urban settings.

As we should expect, the parental occupational category "agriculture, forestry, and fishing" (mainly farmers) carries generally high beta coefficients, positive or negative, across all course types, though sons of farmers differ less from sons of traders in their low propensities to attend technical school than in the likelihoods that they will enroll in commerce courses or General B. In the ordinary least-squares equation for General B, the positive effects of high-level white collar status come through, but not as strongly as when education is not included (a coefficient of .118 in table 3.6 as compared with 0.188 in equations lacking the variable set on father's education).

The most important findings in table 3.6 may be those relating to the commerce and technical courses. In view of the fact that the omitted dummy was for managers and proprietors in trade, it should come as no surprise that all the occupational-type coefficients except those on small-scale artisans carry negative signs in the equations for enrollment in the commerce courses. No sharp line distinguishes the small artisan from the trader; there is a much clearer distinction between the small-scale artisan and the skilled worker in the modern sectors of the economy. The other noteworthy feature of table 3.6 with respect to the commerce course is the systematically negative weights on parental schooling; there is a decided selection against entry into commerce courses among youth from better educated homes relative to youth whose fathers had lower schooling only.

The technical curriculum is notable for the very high positive coefficient among sons of skilled workers (rounding to .21 whether or not parental education was included in the regression), along with the decidedly significant coefficient at .14 (.15 in the equation without education) for sons of other manual workers. Also interesting is the appearance of a positive, though weak, coefficient for the higher technical workers. The controls (and negative values) of the regression coefficients for higher and university education tend to purify the "higher technical" category of its status elements. Indeed, this is generally the effect of introducing father's education along with occupational type on the classification used here, which makes this equation a particularly satisfactory one for all but the rural population.

In another equation (not shown) we included the set of dummy variables on father's age and that on family size. This had virtually no effect on the coefficients for education or for occupational type. Neither, for that matter, were the coefficients for father's age and for family size (SIB) sensitive to the sets of other variables in an equation including them. As we might expect, sons of very old men (and those whose fathers had died) were less likely to be enrolled in an academic general course with a view to going on to college or university than were sons of men in their peak productive years. The tendency of youth whose fathers were not living to enter technical secondary schools, noted previously in a zero-order comparison, was repeated clearly in this multiple regression, with father's schooling and occupation controlled. So far as family size was concerned, on the other hand, we found virtually no relationships. The only exception was a tendency for youth from large families to enroll slightly more often in the nonacademic general curricula, but this was largely if not wholly a reflection of the tendency for rural families to be larger.

A preliminary analysis of associations between father's occupational status (OSTAS) and son's course selection (along with career expectations) revealed that the supposed rank ordering by occupational status level was being confounded by the concentration of farmers in levels 5 and 6, and especially in level 5. No matter where farmers were located on an occupational status or prestige scale, they were out of place; we were dealing here with another dimension in attitudes, opportunities, and behavior. This problem was resolved quite neatly, however, by including a farm/nonfarm distinction in the regressions with OSTAS, not only for analysis of choice of type of course but in other contexts as well. Hypothesizing further that pressures to maintain the family farm or carry on the family business would be felt most keenly by first and/or only sons and taking into account the likely interaction effects between birth order and parental employment status on choice of course, we then went on to construct the independent variable set B-FSE as follows: (1) first or only son of a farmer; (2) other son of a farmer; (3) first or only son of a self-employed man (independent or family entrepreneur); (4) other son of a self-employed man; (5) son (order not specified) of a wage or salaried worker; and (6) others (including nonrespondents). Table 3.7 sets out for each type of course the results obtained using the variable sets FLEVS, OSTAS, and B-FSE.

So far as the agriculture course is concerned, it is immediately evident that most of the work was being done by the set B-FSE. That is, once we know whether a young man was the son of a farmer and, if so, whether he was a first (or only) son, we have learned about all that will be of any use to us in predicting the likelihood that he attended an agricultural school. Whereas the equation predicts that just over 5 percent of the sons of fathers who were employees in status 5 and completed only elementary school (the intercept) went into the agriculture course, 45 percent of the first sons of farmers did so (.054 + .395). Other sons of farmers were more likely than sons of men in other occupations to study agriculture to be sure, but in nothing like the striking proportions that characterized first sons. Furthermore, the beta coefficients on the OSTAS and the B-FSE sets for the agricultural course are highly stable no matter what other variables or sets of variables are added; neither father's schooling nor family size makes any difference.

The other type of course that draws disproportionately from the rural population and from sons of farmers in particular is the nonacademic general course (General A). But in this case the coefficients on first and on other sons of farmers are reversed: it is the other sons of farmers rather than first sons who are most likely to enroll in nonacademic general curricula.

Given the propensity of first sons of farmers to attend courses in agriculture together with the relative inaccessibility

Table 3.7 Effects of Father's Education and Occupational Status and of Son's Birth Order on Type of Course Taken by Son (ordinary least-squares approximation to likelihoods)

	Beta Coefficients (metric)				
	General B	General A	Agri-culture	Commerce	Technical
Intercept	.313	.062	.054	.230	.341
Father's education (FLEVS)					
1,2 Lower school	a	a	a	a	a
3 Old middle (upper secondary)	.120	-.025	-.008	-.058	-.030
4 Higher school (junior college)	.220	-.045	-.024	-.093	-.058
5 University	.265	-.069	-.035	-.116	-.045
0 Nonresponse	.051	.003	.010	-.071	.007
Father's occupational status (OSTAS)					
1 (high)	.373	.003	-.028	-.127	-.221
2	.274	-.011	-.011	-.091	-.161
3	.229	.027	-.026	-.082	-.149
4	.078	.041	-.009	-.015	-.095
5	a	a	a	a	a
6	-.072	.058	-.059	.002	.071
7	-.059	.087	-.022	.013	-.028
8	-.159	.087	-.010	.109	-.028
0 Nonresponse or unclassified	.016	.060	.001	-.069	.009
Birth order and father's employment status (B-FSE)					
1 First and/or only son of self-employed or family entrepreneur	.077	.021	-.017	.011	-.091
2 Other son of self-employed	.045	.027	-.013	.034	-.091
3 First and/or only son of farmer	-.087	.126	.395	-.152	-.281
4 Other son of farmer	-.018	.192	.119	-.109	-.183
5 Son of employee	a	a	a	a	a
6 All others (including nonresponse)	-.003	.045	.000	.018	-.060

[a]Omitted dummy.

of technical secondary schools to farm youth living at home, the strong negative coefficient for such youth in the technical course should hardly surprise us. First sons of farmers fell short of youth with the characteristics included in the intercept (fathers with only lower education, of occupational status 5, who were employees) by .281--leaving only 6 percent (as against a third for the intercept) who entered the technical courses. This exceeds the negative coefficient in the technical course even for sons of men in the highest occupational status.

The effects of a father's occupational status on his son's choice of course are blurred in the predominantly rural curricula and with respect to the technical course by some of the associations between a father's occupational type and status. However, there is a consistent modest monotonic relationship between likelihood of enrolling in a commerce course and father's occupational status: the higher his status, the less likely is enrollment of his son in that course. Conversely, and much more emphatically, there is a very nearly monotonic positive association between parental status and enrollment in General B. How far the inclusion of OSTAS and B-FSE in the equation reduces the coefficients on father's education is easily seen by a comparison of tables 3.5 and 3.7. Only for General B do the education coefficients remain important, and even there the inclusion of OSTAS cuts them back sharply. (By contrast, at occupational status levels below 5 the inclusion or exclusion of father's schooling made no difference, regardless of type of course.)

In sum, in Japan youth from every sort of background enter each sort of upper-secondary course. This is a fundamental characteristic of Japanese society and education today. Nevertheless, as study of both simple cross-tabulations and the regression coefficients has shown, there are distinct patterns in the choice of one sort of school and curriculum or another, patterns that reflect family backgrounds. Although many youth of humble background enter academic courses in the upper-secondary schools, the likelihood that the son of a well-educated man or of a man in a high-status occupation will do so is substantially greater. Youth whose fathers have manual or technical skills are more aware of and oriented toward training in technical skills, whatever their fathers' level of schooling. Indeed, youth with well-educated parents are more likely to enroll in the technical than in the commerce curriculum. The latter draws heavily from the trading population, as we should expect, but also from the lowest ranks of educational and occupational status. Finally, despite the density of farm settlement in Japan and the common stereotype of the Japanese farmer as a man geographically and culturally very close to the city, the profiles with respect to attendance at agricultural schools (and to a lesser extent nonacademic general courses) are distinctive. Agricultural schools draw primarily from the farming population, and being a farmer's first or only son increases very substantially the likelihood that a youth will go to an agricultural secondary school.

Whether we interpret these observations in the language of sociology or of modern microeconomic theory (including the economics of information) does not alter the facts. It is evident enough that costs and returns, even in a strictly monetary view that ignores "psychic satisfactions," are poorly specified if we fail to distinguish the particular sets of options available to youth as related to the communities in which they reside and the occupations and employment status of their fathers. We will have frequent occasion to return to this theme in later chapters.

4. Course Preferences, Realizations, and Frustrations

A priori, we should expect that the courses in which students are actually enrolled would reflect a number of influences that affect both their preferences and the extent to which they are in a position to realize these preferences. In fact we already introduced both of these aspects of allocation among course types when we considered occupational inheritance as a continuity in broad types of interests and career orientations on the one hand, and accessibility or inaccessibility of certain types of curricula on the other. In an attempt to break into the complex of influences involved, we asked students questions such as the following: (*a*) whether they were enrolled in the type of course and (separately) in the particular school that was their first preference at the time at which they entered upper-secondary school; (*b*) whether they had taken examinations for entry to any other type of course (and if so, which); (*c*) whether, looking back, they wished they had taken some other type of curriculum (and if so, which); and (*d*) for those who expressed other preferences, why they were enrolled in the course they had actually taken.

Even at the time of our survey, and indeed much earlier, many Japanese people were concerned with questions of equity and opportunity in education, and among the foci of such conern was access to various upper-secondary options and from these to higher education and alternative careers. Concern about equity, as well as efficiency, is more intense today, and has taken on greater political importance with the moods and events of the seventies. In part this reflects the rapid diffusion of upper-secondary education; in part it reflects developments that have been more international in scope--especially student unrest, manifest in all the more industrialized nations of the world. The demonstrations of 1968, which dramatized these changes, marked the arrival of a new era of heightened awareness, first at the university level but spreading to younger ages. Even as this chapter was being written, Japanese television was broadcasting news of a local demonstration of Hiroshima students in the last year of lower-secondary school; these students were facing the trials of examination for entrance to upper-secondary programs, with all that this could mean for their futures.

Course Preference Patterns

The preference patterns we will examine here have three components: initial preferences at entry to upper-secondary school, course types for which examinations were taken, and preferences at the end of the upper-secondary course. Each of these is compared with the others and with the course in which the student was in fact enrolled. This gives us information on the degrees of reciprocity in preferences between pairs of courses, the incidence of frustrations by types of course, and the degree of stability and focus in preference.

Preference Patterns, Frustrations, and Reciprocity

Table 4.1 summarizes the evidence on preference patterns by type of course the student actually pursued. It is clear that the students in the General B curriculum typically had wanted to be in that course (as they remembered) in the first place; only a fifth of the General B as against two-fifths to half of the students in other curricula indicated that they had entered a type of course that had *not* initially been their personal first choice. The same contrast between General B and all other students prevailed in the perspective of senior year, though the proportions who expressed preference for an alternative rose for all curricula. The amount of increase in dissatisfaction was minimal for the commerce stream (which had had the highest percentage of initially dissatisfied); students in the General A curriculum expressed both the greatest final rate of dissatisfaction and the greatest increase in that rate as between their (remembered) initial preferences at entry and their reassessments with approaching completion of upper-secondary school. When preferences with respect to specific *school* were taken into account, the General B students appeared in a very different light, however: more than a third (36 percent) of those who had initially wanted to be in that kind of course had not gained access to the school they had preferred. The parallel figures for other course types ranged from 6 to 17 percent. Adding the first two rows of table 4.1, we find that the percentages in other than preferred course and school were about the same for General B as for other curricula; in all cases proportions ran somewhat over half. Perhaps selection into the favored and academically elite schools, with its implications for subsequent allocations into and among universities, can be quite as important to the student as the processes whereby young people gain entry to one versus another type of curriculum.

A comparison of the proportions stating they initially preferred a course other than that in which they were enrolled with the proportions who took examinations for another course reveals that the most active in their efforts to gain entry to preferred alternatives were the disappointed students in the technical secondary and the commerce streams; but this does not mean that these technical-course students were typically disinterested in technical schooling. The disappointed technical-school students who had taken examinations for other courses were divided about equally between those who had sought entry to academic general courses and those who had sought entry to the five-year technical junior colleges. At the other extreme, only one in seven of the General A students expressing dissatisfaction from the start had taken examinations for entry to any other type of course. This does not imply that their expressed preferences were distorted, but rather (we suspect) that attendance in the preferred curriculum was precluded for one reason or another anyway, and hence there was no use in taking examinations. Also, among General A students dissatisfactions were more often vague initially: they had less focused perceptions of preferred alternatives at the time when they entered upper-secondary school.

Whether we look at the data on examinations taken or the preferred courses among those who in their senior year wished they had taken another course, the unrealized preferences were most frequently for either technical (including technical junior-college) or academic general curricula. This was strikingly the case with respect to examinations. Virtually all of the general course students who preferred something else and had taken examinations (including the General A students) had sought entry into a technical secondary school or a technical junior college. We have already commented on the even division of technical secondary students between examinations for academic general courses and for technical junior colleges. Students who had taken other examinations but were enrolled in agricultural courses had tried for

Table 4.1 Summary of Course Preference Patterns

		Course in Which Enrolled				
		General B	General A	Agri-culture	Commerce	Technical
1.	Percentage reporting they are <u>not</u> in the course initially preferred	19	46	43	51	41
2.	Percentage in initially preferred course but not in initially preferred school	36	17	10	6	11
3.	Total percentage initially in other than preferred situation (1 plus 2)	55	63	53	57	52
	Percentages Taking Examinations for Other Course Types[a]					
4.	Total	10	9	19	27	33
5.	For General B	b	1	6	19	16
6.	For General A	...	...	...	...	...
7.	For agriculture	...	...	...	...	...
8.	For commerce	...	1	3	b	2
9.	For technical secondary	3	3	9	5	b
10.	For technical junior college (five-year)	7	4	1	3	15
11.	Percentage of those in itially preferred course who had taken an examination for another course or school	9	7	15	17	31
12.	Percentage of those not in initially preferred course who had taken an examination for their preferred course	19	14	22	35	37
	Percentages Who in Retrospect Wished They Had Taken Another Course					
13.	Total	24	62	54	54	56
14.	General (B or A)	c	d	14	27	32
15.	Agriculture	1	3	b	1	2
16.	Commerce	3	14	7	b	5
17.	Technical secondary	8	26	19	11	b
18.	Technical junior college	7	15	10	9	14
19.	Other	4	4	4	6	3

[a] Only 1% took examinations for more than one other course; such cases are counted under both courses, which slightly exaggerates the totals.

[b] Inapplicable. (Examinations in the same course for another school are not included.)

[c] Reference is almost certainly to another *school* still in a General B stream.

[d] Under .5% (preferring General B).

technical secondary school more often than for any other type; fewer had attempted technical junior college. Only the commerce students leaned more heavily in their other examinations toward the general than the technical curricula.

The proportion in each curriculum who, after almost three years of upper-secondary school, expressed a wish that they had taken some other course was considerably greater than the proportion who in fact took examinations for other courses to start with. This in itself should result in a greater spread in types of courses for which at least a few respondents expressed a preference than in types for which they had taken examinations, but there were also some shifts in the patterns. Most of these shifts were the result of (*a*) the preference characteristic of those who saw no use in taking examinations for their preferred courses, and (*b*) changing perceptions of alternatives with widening experience and knowledge acquired during the years in upper-secondary school. Two modifications are of particular interest. First, the increase in the numbers of students in the technical upper-secondary schools preferring some other course in retrospect was in large part due to a belated interest in the general (and in fact the academic general) curriculum; the percentage wishing they might have secured entry to technical junior college was very nearly the same as the proportion who initially took examinations for entry into such courses. There was unquestionably a progressive raising of perceived possibilities and ambitions among the students going through the technical upper-secondary streams. Second, students in the General A stream expressed an increased interest especially in technical upper-secondary curricula, and there was a marked increase for this group in the proportion preferring commerce streams also. The data support the hypothesis posed earlier, that rural General A students (both from the start and as they approached completion of their upper-secondary schooling) commonly experience a special frustration associated with lack of accessibility to other than general and agriculture curricula, along with the general frustration associated with belated awareness of the possible implications of curriculum choice.

The patterning of preferences among types of upper-secondary courses is summarized diagrammatically in figure 4.1, which relates examination behavior and senior-year course preferences to the course in which the student was enrolled. Heavy lines are used for the strongest preferences within each section of the chart, dashed lines for the weakest of the preferences delineated there.

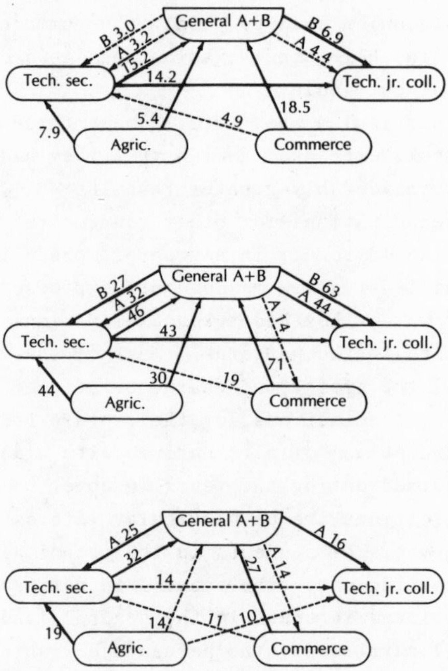

Figure 4.1 Intercourse associations in preference patterns. *Top*, percentage of enrollees in each type of course who took examinations for each other type of course (percentages under 3 excluded). *Middle*, percentages taking examinations for designated alternative courses among all in a course taking examinations for alternative courses (percentages under 10 excluded). *Bottom*, proportions of seniors in each course with "hindsight" preferences for designated other courses (percentages under 10 excluded).

The upper section of figure 4.1 shows the proportions of all students enrolled in a course (origins of the arrows) who had taken an examination for each other type of course (destinations of the arrows). Only linkages involving 3 percent or more of the students enrolled in a course are included in the diagram. This first diagram indicates that the proportions of students in the general curricula who reported taking examinations for <u>any</u> other course were very low, whereas proportions of those enrolled in technical secondary courses who had also taken examinations for general courses or for technical junior college were substantial.

The middle and lower diagrams show much more clearly the two-way preference between technical and general courses. Also, in the last diagram, the general drawing power of the technical secondary institutions as perceived by youth reaching the end of their upper-secondary schooling is conspicuous. On the other hand, whereas three-fourths of the technical students had initially preferred a technical course, either in the upper-secondary school or in a junior college, by the time they were seniors in the technical secondary schools the combined figure for these youth had dropped to 58 percent.

The fringe position of the agricultural schools is obvious in all three diagrams; students enrolled in other courses who reported initial or senior-year preferences for agriculture curricula were rare. This is hardly surprising, since youth initially wishing to attend agricultural schools typically can do so if they enter upper-secondary schools at all; other blockages aside, it is extremely unlikely that youth wanting agricultural schooling will find their preferences running counter to those of parents or teachers. Nor are students who in fact enter the agricultural schools any less (or more) satisfied than those enrolled in other courses, the academic general students aside. There is a distinctive limitation faced by rural students, nevertheless, in the comparative lack of locally available technical-school options, along with the difficulties of rural youth in qualifying for places in technical schools. This limitation on viable options among rural youth is reflected in the unrealized preferences for technical courses among seniors in the General A and to a lesser extent the agriculture courses. Students studying agriculture display remarkably little interest in general curricula.

Some Interpretations of Choices and Preferences

Seniors expressing preferences for courses other than those they had pursued were asked further questions about both why they were enrolled in their present courses and why they had other preferences. Table 4.2 records the main reason a student was attending a type of course other than what he would have regarded as most satisfactory if he could have chosen again without constraint.

The first row of the table refers explicitly to changes in information and knowledge that have altered perceptions of available alternatives and of their implications. Percentages in this row are of course minimum estimates of the importance of shifts in knowledge and preferences, since students who were pursuing their present course primarily as a result of parental or teacher

Table 4.2 Main Reasons for Enrollment in Nonpreferred Courses (percentage distributions)

	Course in Which Enrolled				
	General B	General A	Agri-culture	Commerce	Technical
1. Inadequate initial information or knowledge	16	12	7	12	20
2. Failure on examination for preferred course	16	12	12	12	18
3. Teacher influence or pressure	15	23	28	23	20
4. Parental pressure or preference	22	14	34	20	17
5. Less expensive than alternative preferred	4	5	5	5	5
6. Nearer home	11	25	8	7	3
7. Other	16	9	6	21	17
Total percent	100	100	100	100	100
Total number	350	291	534	495	1160

influence, for example, may also have changed their evaluations. Nevertheless, excepting agriculture students as many as an eighth to a fifth of the students who wished they had been enrolled elsewhere specified as the most important reason for the discrepancy between the course taken and hindsight preference their initially inadequate information or lack of more subtle knowledge concerning course options and their implications. Some of the General B and technical-school students went on to specify their lack of knowledge about technical junior colleges, and some of the technical-course students remarked on their prior limited awareness of the advantages of higher education and of the difficulties of getting into the universities from technical schools.

A wide variety of miscellaneous write-in responses aside, the other answers fell in three main clusters: first, failure to perform sufficiently well on examinations for entry to the preferred course (row 2); second, pressures and preferences of teachers and relatives (rows 3 and 4); and third, economic considerations, including nearness to home (rows 5 and 6).

Most of the general-course students (either B or A) who took examinations for other preferred courses failed to qualify on those examinations, as a comparison of row 2 of table 4.2 with row 12 of table 4.1 shows clearly. However, the situation was very different in other courses. Only half of the dissatisfied students in agriculture and in technical curricula who had taken examinations for other courses reported failure on those examinations, and among commerce students the corresponding fraction was only a third. The student selection and allocation processes were much more complex than stereotyped statements about the functioning of the examination system might have led us to believe--even after taking account of initial selection for taking examinations in the first place.

Advice and various degrees of pressure from parents and teachers together accounted for over a third of the answers in all types of schools, but came through with special force, to no one's particular surprise, among those enrolled in agriculture and, to a lesser degree, commerce.

A few special private institutions aside, the most important cost differences affecting type of course attended were associated with geographic location; expenses of commuting or of boarding away from home could prove prohibitive to many rural youth wishing to enroll in a type of secondary school not available locally. It was no accident that students in the General A curriculum were by far the most inclined to give nearness of their present school as their reason for attending it, despite contrary preferences. For the opposite reason, we found the lowest proportions giving this response among students in the technical secondary schools, which are the least widely accessible geographically. The low proportion of General A students specifying that these schools were less expensive than the preferred alternative might have been substantially increased had the students been cognizant of the true costs of attending school away from home.

The reasons given by those students who expressed senior-year preferences for other than the courses they had in fact taken (call them, for convenience, the "regretful" seniors) fell mainly in two categories (table 4.3). The first was Personal fit, in that another course was viewed as better suited to the youth's talent and abilities or in that it was believed some other curriculum would have been "more interesting" (46 percent of the regretful seniors in General B and 35 to 39 percent in each of the other curricula). The second comprised responses in terms of better preparation for a job or career. Students in General A and agriculture were the most likely to emphasize this reason (respectively, 52 and 45 percent of the regretful seniors). A fourth of the regretful commerce and technical-course seniors emphasized problems of access to college, but this response was rare among agriculture students. Overall, the pattern contains no surprises; it is exactly what we might expect given the cross-course preferences delineated in the immediately preceding pages.

Family Background and the Realization of Course Preferences

It might be expected that youth from higher status families would be more often enrolled in the type of course they prefer. However, the relationships among family background, type of course attended, and course preference are complex, and family backgrounds seem to have had only moderate effects on the extent to which the youth in our study realized their course preferences or experienced frustration. Table 4.4 provides a summary of these relationships for the initial preferences.

Overall the sons of higher status and better educated parents were the least dissatisfied at entry to upper-secondary school; they were the best satisfied of the students in General B. However, they were the most dissatisfied of those enrolled in agriculture or commerce. So far as failure to enter an initially preferred type of course is concerned, status made very little difference among the General A students. As we might expect, sons from status level 5 who were enrolled in agriculture (usually sons of farmers) were much less likely than other students in that

Table 4.3 Main Reasons for Hindsight Preference for Another Course (percentage distributions)

	Course in Which Enrolled				
	General B	General A	Agri-culture	Commerce	Technical
1. Better suited to talents or abilities; more interesting	46	35	39	38	36
2. Better preparation for career or job	35	52	45	22	23
3. Better chance for higher education	8	1	6	26	26
4. Other	11	12	10	14	15
Total percent	100	100	100	100	100
Total number	370	294	548	509	1287

course to have preferred something else initially. Sons of small traders and artisans in status level 6 (as compared with higher level traders, white collar workers or technicians, or low-level manual workers) were the best satisfied of the students in commerce and the most dissatisfied of those in technical schools.

By the time youth were nearing the end of their last upper-secondary year, larger proportions were inclined to express preferences for other courses, almost irrespective of family background. There were some interesting contrasts, however, in the extent to which the respondents' attitudes shifted (table 4.5). The General B students, most satisfied to start with, manifested very little change of mind, and the most thoroughly satisfied of all (with scarcely any increase in the numbers dissatisfied) were the General B students from status backgrounds 1, 2, and 3. Students taking agriculture were the most consistently inclined to view that course more dimly from their perspective as seniors than at the entry stage. Though sons of farmers experienced less disenchantment with the study of agriculture than did sons of white collar men, what was surprising was the lack of substantial difference by family background. The story with respect to shifts of attitude among students in General A curriculum was very different: here we observe a striking contrast between youth from farm homes or from status levels 5 and 6 generally compared with all others. The most distinctly rural General A students (those from farm backgrounds) seemed to have experienced a major change in perceptions of educational and career alternatives; these

Table 4.4 Students within Each Type of Course and Family-Background Category Who Were Enrolled in Other than Initially Preferred Course (percentage distributions)

Background Characteristics	Course in Which Enrolled: General B	General A	Agri-culture	Com-merce	Tech-nical	Total, all courses
Father's occupational status						
1,2,3	14	45	58	58	48	24
4	19	49	48	48	46	33
5	22	40	38	53	41	35
6	22	47	44	24	56	36
7,8	21	50	51	47	38	36
Father's type of occupation						
White collar and trade	18	43	58	50	45	31
Technical-manual (FAB)	21	48	54	49	39	36
Agriculture, etc.	21	47	39	59	37	37
Father's level of education						
University	12	41	50	62[a]	55	20
Higher school (junior college)	17			73	52	29
Old middle (upper-secondary)	17	46	42	50	43	31
Compulsory	22	47	44	49	39	37
Mother's level of education						
Higher and university	19	b	b	57[a]	48	26
Secondary (old girls' middle)	15	47	39	53	46	29
Compulsory	24	48	46	50	39	39

[a]*N* = 10 to 24 cases.

[b]2 out of 5 cases.

youth became increasingly oriented toward urban life and jobs. Finally, the marked shift among the sons of status 6 fathers who were attending commerce schools may have been significant, and for somewhat similar reasons: the data suggest, though they certainly cannot prove, an important change of perceptions and enlargement of horizons among the sons of the small artisans and traders during their years in commerce schools.

Table 4.5 Relation between Family Background and Hindsight Course Dissatisfaction

Background Characteristics	Present Minus Initial Percentages Reporting Dissatisfaction						Present Percentages, All Students
	General B	General A	Agriculture	Commerce	Technical	All Students	
Father's occupational status							
1,2,3	2	12	17	6	12	5	29
4	6	-1	18	15	15	10	43
5	7	24	14	5	12	12	47
6	7	21	13	25	-1	13	49
7,8	7	-7	17	1	16	7	43
Father's type of occupation							
White collar and trade	3	10	18	5	15	6	37
Technical-manual (FAB)	4	11	11	3	16	9	45
Agriculture, etc.	10	21	13	2	12	13	50
Father's level of education							
University	2	5	9	3	6	-8	12
Higher school (junior college)	10			-12	13	-13	16
Old middle (upper secondary)	5	17	11	3	17	9	40
Compulsory	7	17	14	5	15	11	48
Mother's level of education							
Higher and university	3	6	6	22	21	7	33
Secondary (old girls' middle)	6	15	14	2	12	10	39
Compulsory	4	18	13	3	17	9	48

Course Preferences and College Plans

For the purpose of relating the hindsight course preferences of upper-secondary students with their view of college and their college plans, we have distinguished four categories of response about higher education: (1) Day program. These students were taking entrance examinations for full-time day college or university (normally the latter). (2) Night program. These youth were taking examinations for admittance to night colleges and univeristies, usually part-time. (3) Yes/No. In this category we put students who said they would like to go on to higher education or wished that they could do so, but who were not taking any sort of entrance examinations. (4) No interest in college. In table 4.6 we display the distributions of hindsight course preferences among seniors in each curriculum for each college attitude-intention category.

It is remarkable that the college attitude-intention categories displayed a consistently monotonic relation with the proportions favoring general curricula in each case, but equally remarkable is the looseness of that relation. A third or more of both General B and General A students who stated explicitly that they had no interest in higher education nevertheless preferred a general upper-secondary curriculum. The corresponding proportions among students enrolled in other than the general courses were very much lower. By contrast, there was a surprising frequency of preference for the course actually taken among the enrollees in vocational (nongeneral) courses who looked forward to full-time college attendance. The proportion of such vocationally specialized preferences jumps sharply between the day-college group and those who were taking examinations for entry to night college, even setting aside those taking no examinations or not interested in college. Evidently the association between students' college aspirations and their attitudes toward various curricula in upper-secondary school is not nearly as tight as is often supposed, especially by the academics who write popular articles on the subject. The youth in our study saw and preferred a variety of paths into the future. It seems clear, furthermore, that in Japan there is at least a recent heritage of healthy respect for and appreciation of activities that generally are regarded as highly "practical." The theme of the Morrill Act of 1862, which laid the groundwork for the development of the land-grant institutions in the United States, should be well received by Japanese students: "If college is good for the doctor and the lawyer, it is good also for the

Table 4.6 Relation of College Aspirations to Hindsight Upper-Secondary Course Preferences

Senior Year (hindsight) Course Preference	College Attitude-Intention Categories			
	Day Program	Night Program	Yes/No	No Interest in College
Enrolled in General B				
General	80	58	38	35
Technical[a]	13	26	39	46
Commerce	2	9	13	14
Agriculture	1	2	3	...
Other	4	5	7	5
Total percent	100	100	100	100
Total number	1612	43	61	63
Enrolled in General A				
General	71	44	36	33
Technical[a]	19	56	43	43
Commerce	4	...	11	18
Agriculture	4	...	4	2
Other	2	...	6	4
Total percent	100	100	100	100
Total number	52	18	102	357
Enrolled in Agriculture				
General	42	29	22	10
Technical[a]	19	28	28	30
Commerce	6	...	9	8
Agriculture	29	36	36	48
Other	4	7	5	4
Total percent	100	100	100	100
Total number	109	14	197	814
Enrolled in Commerce				
General	57	25	35	13
Technical[a]	7	17	25	23
Commerce	29	44	33	58
Agriculture	3	2	1	1
Other	4	12	6	5
Total percent	100	100	100	100
Total number	184	48	248	551
Enrolled in Technical				
General	70	46	38	17
Technical[a]	25	46	52	72
Commerce	2	3	4	7
Agriculture	1	2	2	2
Other	2	3	4	2
Total percent	100	100	100	100
Total number	342	122	709	1271

[a]Including the five-year technical junior colleges or institutes.

farmer and the mechanic." This did not mean, obviously, that all <u>should</u> attend college, but rather that higher education should be widely available and not confined to a classical academic curriculum.

The ways in which parents, teachers, and young people perceive educational options at the upper-secondary level, the degrees and loci of dissatisfaction among young people with respect to the curricula in which they become enrolled, and the buildup of pressures for access to preferred courses are important facts of political, of social, and in the end of economic life. Several points deserve emphasis.

1. Already in the middle and late 1960s the pressures for access to academic upper-secondary school were building up, and those pressures have increased along with rising rates of continuation into higher education. Furthermore, there is unquestionably an association between parental education and occupational status and entry into the academic course; moreover, the old problem of "first schools" among the college-preparatory programs persists despite efforts of both national and local governments to modify this structure. Nevertheless, it is also a fact that associations between family background and secondary education of one kind or another are remarkably loose-knit. We are looking at an unusually open society educationally, and at a society that displays strong pragmatism with little of the traditionalist elitism that has characterized educational developments at secondary and higher levels in much of Europe, at least until recently.

2. An important element in the rapid change of the Japanese economic structure over the postwar decades has been the relative decline in the proportion of the population employed in agricultural activities. It is hardly surprising, in this context, that youth who attended the agriculture courses and those in the rural General A curricula experienced the greatest changes in their perceptions over the years of their secondary-school studies. These were not, in the main, shifts toward college ambitions. Rather, they manifested an increasing orientation toward urban life, urban jobs, and hence preparation for such jobs.

3. As we will show in chapter 12, the belief that vocational secondary schools (both technical and commerce) offered better career opportunities than the general curricula for students who

were not going to continue into higher education was widespread among both the secondary-school students in our study and their parents. There were variations in those perceptions, to be sure; the strongest support for this belief came from youth in the technical curricula who expected to go directly into the labor market. Uncertainties about the roles of general and vocational upper-secondary schools have become increasingly important with the expansion of secondary education to take in and graduate 90 percent of the on-coming cohorts. That expansion has given rise to new questions about the provision of preemployment or prevocational skills as part of the nonacademic general courses, thereby separating them more clearly from the academic general courses. This is associated, of course, with the perennial attraction and elusiveness of concepts of "comprehensive" education.

4. The strong strands of pragmatism and respect for technically oriented training and work that have stood Japan in such good stead are reflected in the responses of our students. In particular, the closest reciprocity with respect to curriculum preferences was that between youth enrolled in the technical and academic general courses. An important element in that reciprocity, however, was the then-new five-year technical institutes (technical junior colleges), which seemed attractive to quite a number of the youth in both the academic general and the technical secondary courses. We have also observed that many of the youth in the technical secondary curricula expressed concern about the difficulties of continuing with their technical training into higher institutions. Although the five-year technical institutes have expanded only slowly, subsequent events underline the fact that Japanese youth have not given up their interest in the continuous pursuit of technical studies from secondary on into higher levels of education. Stage I decisions are indeed viewed as part of a sequential process in which perceived Stage II options, whether through higher education or otherwise, play a central part.

5. A Formal Stage I Decision Model and the Evidence

Despite the considerable detail of the preceding analysis of relationships among family backgrounds, types of secondary schooling, and course preferences, the discussion has been unavoidably spotty and incomplete in its coverage of key elements of a rational decision model. It is necessary at this point to be more explicit and systematic in the specification of a full model and in showing where the preceding analysis fits into that model. In doing this we necessarily anticipate subsequent chapters in some measure since secondary-school decisions do indeed derive from expectations; those decisions are not some sort of nonrational propulsion or drag from family backgrounds and community environments. Moreover, from the start we must take future educational as well as job and earnings expectations into account.

The model we construct here will be simplified in four principal ways. First, its components will be presented in a generalized form; for example, we will speak of an entire vector of "job satisfactions" (or dissatisfactions), not of kinds of satisfactions or their associations with particular occupations or activities. Second, we will disregard immediate "consumption satisfactions" in the enjoyment (or pain) of attending one or another school or of pursuing higher education; we similarly will disregard future "consumption satisfactions" that might be anticipated as among the fruits of one sort and level of education or another. There is nothing in this study that would enable us to specify either realizations or anticipations of these sorts, and to include them would merely clutter the exposition. Third, we will simplify for the moment by designating an entire career (job or occupation and income sequence) as JY. Finally, we will make some strong assumptions about the ability of the decision maker to identify alternatives and to estimate probabilities.

Major Components of the Generalized Model

Under consideration is the decision at Stage I: whether, at the end of lower-secondary school, to enter one or another upper-secondary course or to seek immediate employment. Expressed in the most general terms, this decision is a matter of maximizing expected "utility." We all carry around in our heads very remarkable mechanisms for selecting the things on which we will focus attention and for putting these all together. But before we make a full synthesis we consider partial syntheses under selected conditions; thus, we can think of the final synthesis as an *optimum optimorum* U^*_{ki} in the choice an individual i makes among upper-secondary alternatives $k_1 \ldots k_n$ by comparison of the "best" or "optimal" solutions under particular conditions. In the present case we would have six alternatives: the choice among five course types plus the choice to not enter any of them. There are many ways in which we could choose the conditions to be distinguished. Here we will set up just two: (1) expectations of the net return associated with choosing any given upper-secondary course assuming the individual does not continue into higher education, and (2) expectations assuming he does continue. But each of the sets of expectations is bounded in greater or lesser degree by constraints, whatever the individual's preferences may be, even when costs are taken into account. These constraints must also be specified. We will use the following notation:

JY = a value matrix of job-satisfaction, earnings combinations (in utility units, or "utils").

JY_{kti} = a submatrix of JY that includes only combinations access to which would not evoke "potential surprise" in individual i if he terminated his schooling with upper-secondary alternative k. In this version of the model we do not distinguish degrees of probability of access to any nonsurprising combination.

JY_{kzi} = a submatrix of JY that includes only combinations access to which would be nonsurprising to individual i if he took upper-secondary course k and continued into higher-education option z.

C_{ki} = the cost (broadly defined) to individual i of attendance in upper-secondary course k.

C_{kzi} = the cost to individual i of attendance in higher-education option z after completion of upper-secondary course k.

We may then write the utility functions

$$U_{kti} = U_{kt}(JY_{kti} - C_{ki}), \tag{5.1}$$

$$U_{kzi} = U_{kz}(JY_{kzi} - C_{ki} - C_{kzi}), \tag{5.2}$$

where U_{kti} is a utility function associated with attending secondary course k and then entering the labor market, while U_{kzi} is a utility function of attending course k and then going on to higher-education option z. Notice that U_{kzi} is a much more complex function than U_{kti} and not only because of the inclusion of another cost vector. The comparisons of utilities within U_{kzi} include a set of z options for each of the k alternatives. Maximization of U_{kti} need not (and often would not) specify as optimal the same k alternative that would be optimal with maximization of U_{kzi}. For example, if an individual expected to go on to higher education, he might maximize his utility by attending General B; otherwise, by attending technical school.[1]

Before we can arrive at our final solution, we must introduce one further specification: constraints on access to the various educational alternatives. Expressing these in probability form, we may take

P_{kai} = the probability that individual i can gain access to upper-secondary option k,

P_{kzai} = the probability that individual i can gain access to higher-education option z assuming he has completed secondary course k.

These probabilities will depend on the individual's ability and the degree of ability selectivity into the various educational options. Constraints may also include difficulty in financing a particular educational choice. And P_{kzai} of course includes constraints on access to various higher-education alternatives associated with curriculum (and school) attended at the upper-secondary level.

We may now take the final step to arrive at U^*_{ki} . We have

$$U^*_{ki} = U^{\max}_{kti} \text{ if and only if } P_{kai}U^{\max}_{kti} > P_{kai}P_{kzai}U^{\max}_{kzi} . \tag{5.3}$$

In other words, individual i will select the course k that maximizes his net return when secondary education is viewed as terminal if, but only if, that course gives better prospects for earnings and job satisfaction (as he weights these) than another course that (taking access probabilities into account) would be best with continuation into higher education. Even if $P_{kai}.U^{max}_{kti}$ and $P_{kai}.P_{kzai}.U^{max}_{kzi}$ gave quite different utility values, it would still be entirely possible that students would give the same answer on choice of k, though with different answers at the Stage II decision point.

Before going further, let us fill in this model a bit with two observations from chapter 4. First, students in some courses had taken examinations for other courses as well. Quite a few hedged their bets on P_{kai} by taking examinations for a less desired course or school in case they did not realize their first choice. In fact, although those who did such hedging ended up in a second-choice alternative more often than not, the courses they entered as well as those they preferred were demanding ones. By contrast, students who reported that they did not get into the preferred course initially and did not even take examinations for the preferred alternative were more often in a relatively undemanding curriculum; presumably this group included many who assessed their chances of success on examinations for preferred schools and courses at a low probability. It included also rural youth who would have preferred courses not availably locally.

Second, we found a looser relationship than often has been assumed between upper-secondary course preferences and attitudes toward higher education. There is not necessarily anything irrational in those preference and decision patterns; there are many reasons why the k solution could be the same on U^{max}_{kti} and $P_{kzai}.U^{max}_{kzi}$ even when the k chosen has a significant effect on probabilities of access to many higher-education options.

A Further Specification of the Model and Its Empirical Counterparts

It is time that we look behind the generalized terms of our model to some of the observable factors that enter into the Stage I decision. Even though we cannot observe the utils or their sum in any direct way, we can deduce hypotheses that link observations to the models, and in some cases test them. An essential first step is to specify the determinants of J, Y, and C as these may manifest themselves.

It is of the first importance in doing this to remember that we are talking in the first instance about determinants of perceptions, and to distinguish in our thinking between determinants of the degree of knowledge or awareness of an option and determinants of preferences or perceived advantages given that awareness. The latter will commonly have clear enough objective counterparts.

We take it for granted here that schools and courses $k_1 \ldots k_n$ will differ in the ease of access they provide to higher education and in the extent to which they prepare youth for direct entry into particular occupations both in fact and in individual perceptions. (More direct evidence concerning those differences will be introduced in later chapters.) The job-satisfaction, earnings, and cost matrices or (in some instances) vectors may then be written themselves as functions, generalized as follows:

$$J_{kti} = J_{kt}(A_i, F_i, M_i, I_i) \; ; \qquad (5.4)$$

$$J_{kzi} = J_{kz}(A_i, F_i, M_i, I_i) \; ; \qquad (5.5)$$

$$Y_{kti} = Y_{kt}(A_i, F_i, M_i) \; ; \qquad (5.6)$$

$$Y_{kzi} = Y_{kz}(A_i, F_i, M_i) \; ; \qquad (5.7)$$

$$C_{ki} = C_k(D_k, L_{ki}, E_{ki}, W_i) \; , \qquad (5.8)$$

where E_{ki} is in turn a function of A_i as well as of k; and

$$C_{kzi} = C_{zk}(D_{zki}, L_{zki}, E_{zki}, W_i) \; , \qquad (5.9)$$

where D_{zki} and E_{zki} are in turn partially functions of A_i as well as of z and k. The variables introduced in the above functions and not already defined are as follows:

A_i = "ability" of individual i (including physical energy).

F_i = family-related career options and constraints (most obviously, places in a family business or the family farm).

M_i = location factors in the visibility of job and earnings opportunities in their relations to education options.

I_i = sets of other background, environmental, and personal traits affecting the individual's job preferences and perceptions.

W_i = an indicator of family wealth and access to low-interest financing.

D_{ki} = direct private costs of schooling k in fees, tuition, and so on.

L_{ki} = extra costs of schooling k due to lack of local accessibility.

E_{ki} = costs of entry to schooling k in examination fees, entry fees, tutoring costs to prepare for entry, and so on.

D_{zki} = direct costs of higher-education option z for individual i possessing secondary schooling k; these costs will differ both with the type of higher institution to which the youth gains access (itself affected by k) and with the extent of scholarship help he receives.

L_{zki} = effects of location and accessibility on costs of attending higher-education option z.

E_{zki} = costs of gaining access to higher-education option z from secondary schooling k; this includes the cost of being *rōnin*.

Where do we now stand? Even if we had been able to turn the clock back and interview our cohort at their entry to upper-secondary school, we could hardly have expected to elicit precise responses concerning job preferences or opportunities. Unquestionably at this stage parental (and teacher) perceptions of the range of options relevant to the individual youth play a major role. This fact was reflected incidentally in students' reports of the reasons they were enrolled in a course other than the one which, in their senior year, they preferred. It is evidenced also in some of the relations between course enrollments (and preferences) and "occupational inheritance" very broadly defined. Once again, we encounter the influence of parental views when we relate parental education to sons' enrollments and preferences, but with some exceptions (specified by F_i) this does not imply detail in expectations even on the part of parents. What it says, in effect, is that the future is anticipated for purposes of decision making only as such anticipations are deemed to be relevant to present decisions.[2] The J_{kti} and J_{kzi} matrices as seen from the Stage I decision point will not be finely specified; a few broad classifications are enough. Putting together information on parental backgrounds, courses attended, and course preferences gives us a good many hints and some clear facts on this score.

Our data on income expectations at the time of the Stage II decision allow comparisons of individual assessments for college and noncollege alternatives, given a particular (now past) upper-secondary schooling k. But clearly we do not have direct observations on Y_{kti} or Y_{kzi} matrices as seen from the Stage I point of decision, at entry to upper-secondary school; nor can we neatly sort out individual rankings of relative earnings prospects for various course or school alternatives even in the later perspective of the graduating seniors. Except in the broadest terms, perhaps the point of entry to upper-secondary school would be a bit too soon to ask young people anything more. But if so, perhaps we should ask ourselves about implications for educational policy.

We may pick up some of the more illuminating empirical threads by looking at the right-hand side of equations (5.4) through (5.9), and imagining as the dependent variable the type of school attended. In the language of the model and assuming rational decisions, the question is, Which k option gives us the maximum value U^*_{ki} for whom?

The role of ability is important and elusive. Does ability interact with education to enhance (or diminish) the perceived relative advantages of an academic, say, versus a technical course of training in upper-secondary school? Unfortunately we have no direct evidence on this important question. The only direct quasi-ability measure available to us is the self-ranking of respondents in relation to their classmates, which obviously cannot be used to analyze the role of ability in career or earnings perceptions and expectations of youth in one schooling category as compared with another--although how the internal rankings are related to occupational aspirations can be and will be examined in other contexts. We do have some other pieces of evidence, however. One of these concerns ability cutoff effects. Table 4.2 suggests a very large measure of self-elimination prior to attempting entry to courses where standards are high. The highest proportions of our sample reporting failure in examinations for a preferred course were among youth who nevertheless had found entry to the relatively demanding curricula: General B and technical. Their failures had been in attempts to reverse these choices or to gain entry to technical junior colleges. Also interesting are indirect indicators of "ability" in the broadest sense, as it is picked up by proxy variables such as parental education or occupational status. The difficulty here, however, is that we are simultaneously picking up indicators for what we have designated as I_i and W_i, especially insofar as orientations to the academic general course are concerned. However much measured achievement may correlate with parental status, achievement alone (which is already much more and other than "ability" more narrowly defined) can hardly account for the evidence (in table 3.3, for example) that sons of top-status fathers enter the General B curriculum in overwhelming proportions.

So far as direct costs (D_k) are concerned, differences in average costs among curricula are negligible, even though there are some high-cost private schools and there are substantial variations in amounts individual families spend on supplementary educational materials and activities. According to a special study of financial aid and continuation in schools, the 1960 direct "school expenses" borne personally averaged between 31,000 and 32,000 yen in the agriculture, commerce, and technical curricula, and there was another 3,000 yen or more in supplementary educational "home expenditures" for these youth. The average "school expenses" figure for the general schools was lower, at 28,000 yen, but higher average home expenses neutralized this cost saving among the general-school pupils as a whole.[3]

The costs of attending courses not available locally were reflected clearly enough in the fact that rural youth entered General B tracks as often as urban youth, but that those not entering General B or agriculture went into General A rather than commerce or technical courses. The technical, and even the commerce, courses were not generally accessible in the most rural locations. But here there is unquestionably an interactive effect with perceptions of options like those we designated by the variable M_i. referring to degrees of contact with and visibility of urban or metropolitan opportunities. M_i is measured in our data by several location attributes, but especially by FREQ-M, or number of times a day it was possible to travel from a locality to a metropolitan place of over a million people using public transportation.

The inclusion of the term W_i in a cost function requires special comment, since the more conventional economic decision models relating to education have normally distinguished ability to pay as a factor quite independent of costs. If we were looking at the schooling choice solely or primarily as a consumption choice rather than as an investment, the independence assumption would usually suffice. However, if the main thrust of these decisions with respect to schooling is viewed in terms of anticipated effects on subsequent job options and earnings relative to present costs--if the perspective, in other words, is that of an investment--then the important effect of differences in family wealth and income is primarily a matter of how readily the individual or his family may make a trade between present and future.[4] In a perfect capital market even a poor family could draw on anticipated future earnings. However, capital markets with respect to investments in education are far from perfect, and the interest rates paid directly or implicitly when poor families invest in education are likely to be much higher than among families economically better off (assuming that the poor families can get ahold of such resources at all). In addition, families used to living on small incomes, and thinking in correspondingly small money terms, may be more fearful of risking current capital commitments even where the options are open to them; if there is such a bias, it will impose an additional subjective risk on the interest costs of educational investments. As a reasonable approximation we might take interest costs to be an exponentially rising function of the funds needed from outside sources to finance an investment. The amount of such funds needed by individual i for secondary-education option k will depend not only upon any special costs for option k (included in D_{ki} and L_{ki}) but also upon how pressing are other demands on the family's resources, including the weight of the present sacrifice entailed in foregoing the youth's earnings while he is in any sort of upper-secondary school. Because such foregone earnings are common to all of the options, we did not include them directly in the decision model for choices among k.[5] However, these foregone earnings will affect not only whether a youth enters upper-secondary school at all but also his choices among the secondary options, through their relation to the effects of poverty (low W_i) on marginal interest rates associated with the more expensive k options. Furthermore, the kz options, which carry over into higher education, entail a further delay in the economic contributions of youth to their families; it may well be that the part played by W_i in the function C_{zki} is substantially greater than its effects on C_{ki}. As a first empirical step, in this chapter we make use of parental occupational status as a preliminary proxy variable for economic status; there is of course a problem of identification where low status is associated with other factors (as test performance or perceived career potentials) that are also at play.

We have pointed out that parental economic status was important in several contexts, but especially in (1) the effects of low economic status on entry to upper-secondary schools (of whatever kind), and (2) the effects of the anticipated costs of university education on choices among courses at the upper-secondary level. The fact that the 1964 selectivity ratio into upper-secondary schools (whatever the type of school) was as low as .63 for low-status youth in Hiroshima unquestionably reflects strong economic pressures, however much it may also be affected by test performance and damped career aspirations. At the same time, the strong representation of low-status youth in the technical relative to the other upper-secondary schools, taken together with their low representation in General A courses (table 3.3), strongly suggests an allocation process in which the initial considerations were pragmatically economic in several respects and quite unpolluted by ability distortions. Technical schools seem to have been seen by an important minority of the youth of 1964 (and by their parents) as promising both interesting and lucrative employment without incurring the future costs in working time (earnings foregone) and cash outlays that are involved in taking advantage of the college options associated with the General B curricula. There are unquestionably economic constraints at play in the associations between parental education or status and realization of course preferences. The cost of college attendance seems to be considerably more important than differences in costs among secondary schools in determining choices among upper-secondary curricula.

It may be of interest that the mean annual earnings of employee (wage and salaried) fathers of males enrolled in General B courses was 933,000 yen as compared with amounts ranging from 622,000 yen for employee fathers whose sons were enrolled in agriculture curricula to 715,000 yen for those with sons in technical schools. The net annual incomes of proprietors or operators of family business (nonfarm) concerns with sons in the General B and commerce courses were double those of similar fathers of students in other curricula.

This last observation points again to the factor in the earnings expectation functions that we designated as F_i, referring to special family-linked career opportunities (and constraints). Clearly the students in commerce schools are a mixed population, but there can be no doubt that linkage in curriculum choice exists. It is not always an income-maximizing choice from the strictly individual point of view, to be sure, but it can be important as a constraint even when not as a special opportunity. Economic obligations to one's family can and do weigh heavily. So can the unconscious conditioning of career perceptions. Thus as we showed in table 3.6 sons of white collar men and high-level executives go heavily into General B; we suggest that this is both a reflection of the effects of their backgrounds on perceived career preferences associated with continuing into higher education and a reflection of special family-linked opportunities to which higher education may give them access--the differential effects J_{kzi} over J_{kti} of I_i and F_i among these as compared with other youth. Sons of traders and artisans follow their fathers and families into commerce, and sons of farmers (and only their sons) take up agriculture.

Finally, there is clear evidence of the effects of limited perceptions of options at entry stage (the I_i and M_i dampening effects, in the terminology of the model) in the data of table 4.5 concerning attitude shifts over the years in upper-secondary school. It is the youth of low-status backgrounds in General A and commerce curricula who most often reported a change of view concerning course options between entry to upper-secondary school and graduation.

In sum, many odd bits and pieces of empirical information can be put together to demonstrate the systematic character of the decision processes whereby individuals respond to the economic options open to them. Even though it is not possible with the data at hand to round out the model empirically or to discriminate sharply between factors that are operating jointly to determine these choices, both the economic rationality of these behavior patterns and the operation of social constraints on individual choice come through clearly in a society that remains at once dynamic, open, and still cemented by traditional obligations.

Part 3

The College Option and the Stage II Decision

6. To Higher Education or the Labor Market: The Decision Model and Its Context

The transition from upper-secondary school to higher education or to the labor market is important everywhere. It has gained importance in Japan as the proportions of on-coming cohorts moving through the upper-secondary schools first passed 50 percent (in the late 1950s), rose to 70 percent (in the late 1960s), and reached 90 percent or more (in the late 1970s). A long time ago Japan passed the stage at which upper-secondary schooling was a privilege of the elite. Furthermore, that country has never suffered from what might be called the "hanging vine" syndrome so common in Europe, where often there has been concern that rising numbers of secondary-school graduates might not find places in universities. In this respect at least, Japan is more like the United States. But Japan is quite unlike the United States in its *rōnin* system. Before going on with the development of a decision model for Stage II, it should be useful to step back and look briefly at just where the students flowing out of Japanese upper-secondary schools have been going.

Destinations and Transition Processes

Of the 930,000 youth, male and female, who came out of Japanese fulltime general secondary schools in 1968, 36 percent entered some institution of higher education. Another 18 percent became *rōnin*, attending special tutorials and cram courses and studying for another year to take examinations once again in the hope of gaining entry to preferred institutions of higher education (or, in some cases, to any higher institution). Only 40 percent of the graduates of general upper-secondary schools took up full-time employment.

In the same year (1968) another 55,000 young people graduated from upper-secondary vocational (nongeneral) courses; most of these youth went directly into the labor market, and they accounted for 58 percent of the new labor market entrants from upper-secondary schools. Seven percent of the vocational graduates entered higher education, and 2 percent became *rōnin*. The proportion of vocational-school graduates entering higher institutions changed little from 1955 to 1970, but jumped dramatically in the 1970s. Changes over the period from 1955 to 1974 are shown by curriculum for the two sexes combined in table 6.1. The figures in the row following the totals for each course are for the successful applicants; those who did not succeed initially but were persisting are included in the figures given in the last row of each course grouping, but these cannot be distinguished on the basis of these data alone from young people (especially girls) who simply stayed at home. However, data collected by the Ministry of Education but not reported here showed quite steady proportions of applicants gaining admission to higher institutions despite the spread of applications, especially among youth from progressively less elite family backgrounds and from vocational as well as general courses. It is easy to understand in these circumstances why there is so much concern today about social pressures on young people and their implications for educational performance and policy. This concern is evident especially in (1) the increased desire of many parents to get their children into general courses and into the more prestigeful schools within the general curriculum, and (2) the situation of youth in technical curricula, which enroll a major share of the urban sons of fathers in blue collar occupations; more youth from the technical curricula than from any other vocational courses are actively seeking higher education, but the proportions among them who gain admission are far lower than in any other vocational curriculum--though close to the success rate among applicants from general curricula (at 69 and 72 percent, respectively, in 1974).

Another way of looking at the transition from upper-secondary to higher education or to the universities in particular is to ask not what secondary graduates do immediately after graduation but rather what routes have been followed by those who ultimately enter higher institutions. As of 1959, three-fifths of the students enrolled in day universities had entered directly from secondary schools, just over a third (36 percent) had been *rōnin*, and 4 percent had been in regular employment.[1] Over the decade of the 1960s the proportions of university entrants with *rōnin*

Table 6.1 Destinations of Graduates of Upper-Secondary-School Types (percentage distributions)

	1955	1965	1970	1974
All courses[a]	100	100	100	100
To higher education	18	26	24	32
To labor force	47	59	57	47
Other[b]	35	15	19	21
General courses	100	100	100	100
To higher education	25	38	36	45
To labor force	33	42	38	28
Other[b]	42	20	26	27
Agriculture	100	100	100	100
To higher education	5	5	5	10
To labor force	78	89	87	79
Other[b]	17	6	8	11
Commerce	100	100	100	100
To higher education	7	9	7	13
To labor force	75	87	86	78
Other[b]	18	4	7	9
Technical	100	100	100	100
To higher education	7	8	7	13
To labor force	77	85	87	77
Other[b]	16	7	6	10

Source. Mombushō, *Gakkō Kihon Chōsa* [Ministry of Education, Basic School Surveys] (Tokyo, 1955, 1965, 1970, 1974).

Note. These data refer to both sexes, as data by sex were not available.

[a]Including home economics.

[b]Including *rōnin*

experience declined somewhat; 31 percent of the successful applicants in 1967 had been *rōnin*. In medicine and dentistry the *rōnin* proportions were 50 percent, and among males entering junior colleges a surprising 40 percent had been *rōnin*.[2] The 31 percent figure matches quite closely the *rōnin* proportions among youth who had just graduated from upper-secondary schools in 1968 and were seeking postsecondary education. The overall 12 percent of all new upper-secondary graduates who became *rōnin* in 1968 constituted a third of the college-directed youth of that cohort. It does not follow that all *rōnin* will gain their objectives a year later, however. Of the *rōnin* upper-secondary graduates of 1963 through 1965, roughly two-thirds were admitted to college after their first *rōnin* year, and another fifth of the original *rōnin* persisted, to enter a higher institution of some sort after their second *rōnin* year. A few continued on and on as *rōnin*, with only occasional or part-time employment. The proportions of upper-secondary graduates becoming *rōnin* in the late 1970s were much the same as they had been a decade before, but they constituted a smaller proportion of the enlarged fraction of graduates who pursued full-time studies beyond upper-secondary school.

Most of the new upper-secondary graduates are coming out of public secondary institutions, which accounted in 1968 for two-thirds of the male upper-secondary graduates from both general and vocational curricula; public schools accounted for somewhat less than two-thirds of the female graduates. Despite their high visibility, the national general and vocational schools together turned out only four thousand of the million and a half upper-secondary graduates in the late 1960s, but almost all of their graduates either went on to higher education (59 percent in 1966) or became *rōnin* (36 percent in 1966). Both because of their sex composition and their orientation to private colleges and universities, the private upper-secondary schools produced fewer *rōnin*.

Private universities and colleges enrolled over half of all students who went directly into higher education and more than three-fourths of those going directly to day universities. Night schools claimed only a tiny fraction of the graduates of general curricula, public or private, though in 1968, 6 percent of the graduates of vocational courses entered night colleges and universities (mainly on a part-time basis). The combination of economic pressures and achievement orientations among these night-school youth was unmistakable.

A Stage II Decision Model for Higher Education

As a Japanese youth approaches graduation from upper-secondary school, he is facing a crucial choice, one already anticipated in varying measure at least three years earlier when he entered upper-secondary school. Whatever the determinants of and constraints on that earlier choice, it conditions the nature of the options now available. At the same time, the family and environmental background conditions that shaped the earlier perceptions and influences are still at play. But this is not all. The student has meanwhile grown three critical years older; his perceptions of educational and occupational career options have almost certainly become both more discriminative and more diversified. This diversification of perceived options will occur even if he has come to focus on a particular goal and has excluded more options on strictly preference grounds. (It is also possible that with enlarged horizons he will have become more uncertain rather than more definite about career anticipations.) Meanwhile, the kind of school he has attended, the courses he has taken, and the characteristics of his classmates will have contributed to the shaping and reshaping, the strengthening or weakening, of his orientations toward higher education in general and toward particular alternatives within higher education.

These commonsense generalizations can advantageously be systematized by use of a formal construct similar to the one we introduced in chapter 5. This time, however, we are laying out the model early in our analysis and will use it as a reference framework in subsequent discussions of empirical evidence relating to the "higher education decision". Most of the empirical analysis will be concerned with the simple distinction between taking or not taking examinations for college or university. However, we present the model in a generalized form that includes choices (and constraints on choices) among various types of higher education. The decision to become a *rōnin* is of course a derived choice, taken up only as it may be a necessary condition for entry to the preferred institution, or to any institution of higher learning; in other words, the *rōnin* option is part of the cost of entry to higher education.

A General Formulation

Following the mode of presentation used earlier, we may again set up an optimization problem, using a quasi-certainty model. Initially we will set this up in two parts.

The first problem is to choose the higher-education alternative z (excluding the noncollege options) that would maximize the individual's expected utility U_{zi} among postsecondary alternatives, subject to the constraint introduced before: the chances of gaining access to higher-education option z will differ with the individual's ability, the standards for admission to z, and the upper-secondary course and school already attended. Choice among z was in fact a suboptimization problem in the Stage I decision model as well, but the point from which expectations and preferences were taken and to which their "present values" were related was the upper-secondary entry point instead of the transition out of upper-secondary schools to further education or employment. Because the costs of upper-secondary schooling are now in the past, those costs will no longer be relevant for decisions. With a slight modification of the earlier format, we may then write

$$U_{zi} = U_z(JY_{zi} - C_{zi}) \ , \tag{6.1}$$

$$JY_{zi} = JY_z(A_i, F_i, M_i, I_i, G_{zjki}, G_{zyki}) \ , \tag{6.2}$$

$$C_{zi} = C_z(D_z, L_{zi}, E_{zi}, W_i) \ , \tag{6.3}$$

where E_{zi} is the cost of gaining access to option z. The important differences between these generalized functions and those presented for the Stage I decision are that the expectations (and the utility evluations of them) are in the perspective of Stage II, at completion of upper-secondary school. The effects of intervening experiences on opportunity perceptions are included, in the new terms G_{zjki} and G_{zyki} . The first of these, G_{zjki} , refers to the effects of the intervening experiences in option k on perceived occupational or job-career profiles and preferences associated with higher-education alternative z, income considerations aside. The term G_{zyki} refers to the effects of intervening experiences in option k on perceived future income profiles associated with higher-education alternative z. Subsequently we will distinguish between two major aspects of k as it operates through G_{zjki} and G_{zyki} : the curriculum effect, which we designate as S_k or simply S, and the classroom composition or peers effect, which we designate as H_k or simply H.

It must be evident that E_{zi} , the cost of gaining entry to a particular option in higher education, will depend upon an individual's success on examinations and on whether a year or more as a *rōnin* will be needed. But this will depend both on the individual's ability A_i and on how well his upper-secondary experience S_k prepared him for examinations. The chance that he will not succeed even after heavy investments as a *rōnin* is also pragmatically important, though we have not specified such probabilities in the model.

Letting $U_{zi}^{\max}$ represent the maximal value for U_{zi} among the various z options, we may then turn to the second half of our problem, which is to specify the optimal choice $U_{ti}^{\max}$ among the noncollege alternatives. Using the subscript t to denote alternatives with upper-secondary schooling as terminal, we may write

$$U_{ti} = U_t(JY_{ti}) \;, \tag{6.4}$$

where

$$JY_{ti} = JY_t(A_i, F_i, M_i, I_i, S_{ki}) \;. \tag{6.5}$$

Evidently college will be the preferred choice where $U_{zi}^{\max} > U_{ti}^{\max}$.

It is useful to express this another way, as the advantage (or disadvantage) of pursuing the best available college option versus the best available noncollege option. Define

$$\hat{U}_{zti} = U_{zi}^{\max} - U_{ti}^{\max} \;.$$

It is obvious that where $\hat{U}_{zti} > 0$ the college option will be the *optimum optimorum*, and where $\hat{U}_{zti} < 0$ the best choice will exclude college. This is of course tautological, but by setting it up this way we are now in a position to take another step toward operationalizing the model and specifying observable variables. Assuming cardinal utilities (as we have been doing all along) and designating with a tilde the particular *z* and the *t* options that maximize U_{zi} and U_{ti}, we may then write

$$\hat{U}_{zti} = \tilde{U}_{zjy}(JY_{zi}) - \tilde{U}_{tjy}(JY_{ti}) - \tilde{U}_{zc}(C_{zi}) \;. \tag{6.6}$$

(Notice that $\tilde{U}_{zc}$ is a measure of utility foregone.) In a full model the optimal *JY* combinations with and without higher education will be entire life streams of anticipated earnings and job satisfactions discounted back to the decision point. This formulation resolves, accordingly, into the human-investment model presented in chapter 2, but now generalized to include nonmonetary returns and costs. We can rewrite equation (6.6) to separate its monetary and nonmonetary components, which gives us

$$\hat{U}_{zti} = [\tilde{U}_{zy}(Y_{zi}) - \tilde{U}_{ty}(Y_{ti})] + [\tilde{U}_{zj}(J_{zi}) - \tilde{U}_{tj}(J_{ti})] - \tilde{U}_{zc}(C_{zi}) \;. \tag{6.7}$$

First Steps toward Operationalization of the Model

Certain reasonable empirical assumptions can be made about these utility functions and their relations. First of all, we may assume that, other things being equal, most people will prefer larger to smaller future earnings, and both U_{zy} and U_{ty} will be positive monotonic functions of anticipated earnings for any given date (with earnings for all other dates held constant). This same rather weak assumption allows us to specify that the larger the differences $Y_{zi} - Y_{ti}$ anticipated for years beyond the immediate future, the more attractive will be the college as against the noncollege option. Later (in chapter 9) we will introduce some direct observations on "peak-year" income expectations for college and noncollege men as those prospects are perceived and compared by the college-oriented and the terminal graduates of the upper-secondary schools. We will also introduce a preliminary statistical analysis of other determinants of those earnings expectations. More detailed examination of perceived future life earning profiles, and of how such profiles compare with constructions from published age cross-sectional data on earnings is deferred to chapter 13, however.

The second bracketed term of equation (6.7) is more problematic; even if we had a full matrix of job-preference-opportunity perceptions, there would be no obviously legitimate basis for translating such information into a form that would allow us to "add it up." What we will in fact do is to use expressions of selected dimensions of job preferences regardless of higher education along with observations on variables such as those specified in the model equations (6.2) and (6.5) to stand in for $[\tilde{U}_{zj}(J_{zi}) - \tilde{U}_{tj}(J_{ti})]$ in regression equations in which the dichotomy taking or not taking examinations is the dependent (likelihood) variable. The most important job dimensions (J_i) for the present purpose are the student's desired or expected ultimate occupational status, his preferred kind of employment situation, and special family-linked career options (F_i in our models). Other background characteristics such as parental education and occupation also are undoubtedly important in their effects on job perceptions and what sorts of activities have the most interest or appeal.

The cost factor C_{zi} is tidy enough in principle, though somewhat elusive in practice. The 1968 study by the Ministry of Education enables us to relate parental education and occupation to type of higher institution attended, but it is difficult with those data to distinguish among the various ways in which parental backgrounds come into play and how far they relate to the economics of the decision. However, the 1968 survey includes information on parental incomes by destination (see chapter 8); this gives us an indicator for family economic level W_i. Also, in our survey we obtained parental income data for employee fathers and for those who were self-employed (or operated family enterprises). While we have no direct measures of E_{zi}, we do have the students' statements on the matter of willingness to be *rōnin* if necessary to attain their goals. And we have locational measures, discussed earlier, that provide adequate indicators of L_{zi}. Taken together, the pieces for getting a picture of C_{zi} and its place in the college versus noncollege decision are reasonably satisfactory, despite limitations on the possibilities of fitting them together in neat mathematical fashion.

7. The College Decision: Location, Parental Traits, and Career Hopes

What effects do parental backgrounds and occupational goals have on decisions at the point of graduation from upper-secondary school? Do these influences operate primarily indirectly, through the upper-secondary curriculum attended, or also directly, within curricula? What are the effects of residence? Does classroom composition have an effect distinct from the characteristics of the individual's parents?

Socioeconomic Backgrounds, Occupational Expectations, and College Attendance

Interpretations of statistical associations between parental education or occupation and rates of college attendance (or active hope of going to college) in terms of investment decisions are confounded because these background variables operate in at least two distinct ways: they affect perceived sets of career options J_{zi} and J_{ti} and the utilities attached to those options on one hand, and they affect C_{zi} through costs of financing schooling on the other.[1] Help in sorting out some of these effects will come cumulatively from several directions, with the analysis of various aspects of the data collected in our samples. For a start, however, it will be useful to examine characteristics of students entering various types of higher institutions as reported in the 1968 study by the Japanese Ministry of Education.

Parental Backgrounds of Graduates Entering Higher Institutions and Labor Markets in 1968

On purely economic grounds we might expect a priori the following ordering in relative representation in postsecondary destinations (exclusive of *rōnin*) of youth from the lowest economic status groups: (1) directly to the labor market (especially among youth who live in locations inaccessible to night courses), (2) to night courses (usually with some work for pay or in a family business), (3) to national and public junior colleges and universities, (4) to private junior colleges and universities. The reasons for this a priori ordering, which disregards possible associations between either preferences or test scores and parental backgrounds, are simple enough. The first two options--directly to the labor market and to night school--take priority among the economically disadvantaged because of the importance of foregone earnings and the constraints on financing higher education wherever it is not feasible to earn all or a substantial part of one's living expenses. Private institutions would have the smallest representation because of their much higher tuition and fees. Poor youth unable to gain entry to the national or public institutions would be less likely to get higher education at all. In fact the data of table 7.1 validate the a priori ordering. This is readily seen by looking across the rows for sons and daughters of men with lower levels of schooling only, for children of men in agriculture and related pursuits, and for children of laborers. The big jumps, as we should expect, were between direct entry to the labor market and night schools, and then (excepting farmers' sons)[2] between night and day colleges and universities, regardless of whether they were national, public, or private. By contrast few sons of university men were entering the labor market and they were underrepresented among entrants to night courses in higher education.

Another feature of the occupation distributions is worth special notice: sons and daughters of managers and proprietors were decidedly overrepresented in the private universities and colleges relative to their representation elsewhere. This unquestionably is associated with differences in perceived career options and preferences that stem from family environments--the I_i and F_i factors of our models are clearly operative here, both as a sociological or communication phenomenon and in more narrowly economic terms.

Parental Education and the Two Decision Points

With table 7.2 we focus on the more limited question of taking examinations or not, regardless of the type of institution the

Table 7.1 Relation between Paternal Background and Destination of Graduates or Full-Time Upper-Secondary Courses (1968)

	Directly to Labor Market	To College or University (full-time)	Day University (full-time)			Day Junior College (full-time)		Night University Junior College (full-time)
			National	Public	Private	National, Public	Private	
Total numbers	836,500	376,000	49,500	7,100	195,000	6,800	107,200	10,400
Percentage Distributions								
Father's education								
1. College or university	3.9	26.4	27.6	25.6	27.3	21.1	25.7	12.5
2. Middle	27.8	39.5	34.4	38.3	39.5	37.7	42.8	33.4
3. Compulsory	59.3	29.0	31.8	31.0	28.4	36.0	26.7	45.6
4. Other and nonresponse	9.0	5.1	6.2	5.1	4.8	5.2	4.8	8.5
Total	100.0	100.0	100.0	100.0	100.0	100.0	100.0	100.0
Father's occupation								
1. Agriculture and related	31.2	12.1	14.3	10.5	10.5	17.7	13.0	20.2
2. Civil servants	11.1	21.8	26.9	23.4	20.7	24.8	21.9	14.6
3. White collar employees, private firms	23.5	27.9	29.9	32.5	28.6	29.7	25.7	25.4
4. Managers and proprietors	10.0	21.2	11.9	15.0	23.4	11.7	22.9	17.5
5. Shopkeepers, artisans, skilled and semi-skilled manual	11.4	9.2	8.3	9.6	9.1	8.2	9.6	11.0
6. Self-employed	1.6	3.3	2.5	3.5	3.7	2.5	3.2	2.1
7. Laborers	7.2	1.8	2.8	2.7	1.6	2.5	1.3	4.6
8. Other	4.0	2.7	3.4	2.8	2.4	2.9	2.4	4.6
Total	100.0	100.0	100.0	100.0	100.0	100.0	100.0	100.0

Source. Computed from data in Mombushō, *Kōtōgakkō Sotsugyōsha no Shinro Jōkyō ni kan suru Chōsa-Hōkokusho* [Ministry of Education, Survey Report on Courses Chosen by Senior High School Graduates] (Tokyo, 1969), pp. 27 and 29.

Note. The data are for both sexes.

Table 7.2 Effects of Father's Educaton on Son's Course Enrollment and Registration for College Examinations (percentage distributions)

	Father's Level of Education				
	Compulsory	Middle (secondary)	Higher (junior college)	University	All Cases
Percentage in General B	30.5	50.0	65.2	77.2	41.1
Percentage of General B students to college or university	84.7	93.2	96.3	99.0	90.4
Percentage in General A	14.6	10.2	7.1	3.2	12.4
Percentage of General A students to college or university	4.5	15.9	30.0	62.5	9.8
Percentage in agriculture course	9.6	7.1	3.4	0.4	8.1
Percentage of agriculture students to college or university	6.9	14.4	15.2	...	9.1
Percentage in commerce course	19.8	12.9	8.4	5.1	15.6
Percentage of commerce students to college or university	14.1	20.7	35.0	35.3	17.5
Percentage in technical course	25.5	19.8	15.9	14.2	22.9
Percentage of technical students to college or university	9.4	18.0	25.7	26.4	13.6
Total percentages taking exams	32.4	55.5	72.5	83.9	44.9
In General B	25.8	46.6	62.8	76.4	37.2
In General A	.7	1.6	2.1	2.0	1.2
In agriculture	.7	1.0	.5	...	.7
In commerce	2.8	2.7	3.0	1.8	2.7
In technical course	2.4	3.6	4.1	3.7	3.1
Total percentages not taking exams	67.7	44.5	27.5	15.9	55.2
In General B	4.7	3.4	2.4	.8	3.9
In General A	13.9	8.6	4.9	1.2	11.2
In agriculture	9.0	6.0	2.9	.4	7.4
In commerce	17.0	10.2	5.5	3.1	12.9
In technical course	23.1	16.3	11.8	10.4	19.8

youth hope to enter or of their success in doing so. However, these data (from our samples) allow us to treat males separately and to distinguish among types of vocational curricula in a two-stage matrix. Table 7.2 answers three questions: (1) What are the likelihoods (if he goes to upper-secondary school at all)[3] that the son of a man with each of the designated amounts of schooling will enroll in each of the five curricula? (2) If he enrolls in any curriculum S_k, what is the likelihood that a youth whose father had, say, middle-school education will take college examinations? (3) When we multiply these probability matrices, how do we come out on the likelihoods that the son of a man with, say, middle schooling will follow each sequential education path--such as to a commerce curriculum in upper-secondary school and thereafter to a college or university?

It must be evident from the start that the results shown in a tabulation such as we have presented here will be picking up several things at once. We are observing the more or less direct effects of parental education on perceived career options and preferences in association with education expectations (operating on J_{zi} and J_{ti} through I_i). We are observing also the influence of parental education on the valuation of immediate consumer returns to education. And we are also picking up indirect economic influences of other characteristics with which parental education is associated--in particular, geographic accessibility costs (through L_{zi} via rurality) and ability-to-pay, or interest, costs (through W_i). But if these associations are in some respects diffuse, the patterns are nevertheless clear and plausible.

The first-stage patterns are familiar enough from previous chapters. There is a strong positive monotonic relation between level of parental education and enrollment in the General B curriculum, whereas the relations are negative for all other courses, but especially for the agricultural course and General A. Once a youth has enrolled in a General B curriculum, the likelihood that he will try for higher education is extremely great; even among General B youth from the least educated homes almost 85 percent took examinations for entry to higher institutions. In no other curriculum did so many sons even of university graduates attempt the examinations. Though parental education operated in the expected directions within each of the various courses, the major within-course impact was the dramatic one for General A students. It is among the General A students of the least educated parents that we find the lowest college-going rates (with only 4.5 percent taking examinations) of any cell in the upper part of the table. Yet of General A youth whose fathers had been through universities, over three-fifths (62.5 percent) took examinations. This fact alone strongly argues that among many General A students there has been a deferral of the college (or noncollege) decision, that college-going options have remained viable, and that the direct and indirect effects of parental example and suasion have continued to operate to bring youth from educationally advantaged homes into accord with family expectations. In no other curriculum do we observe a comparable effect.

Overall, the highest frequencies in the lower half of table 7.2 are those for General B college-directed youth (regardless of parental education). The next highest frequencies are for noncollege youth of humble backgrounds attending courses other than General B and for technical-school youth entering the labor market (regardless of father's schooling). Despite the relatively large numbers of technical graduates entering the labor market, it is also notable that next to General B (though by a wide margin) these schools provided the largest share of college-oriented youth among sons of fathers in all but the lowest education category.

In sum, it seems evident that parental education is related to college-going plans and behavior both at Stage I, with selection among courses in upper-secondary schools, and later on, at graduation from those schools--especially among General A students. But the most important college effect of parental background is clearly the earlier one, in the choice between General B and other upper-secondary curricula.[4] Paradoxically, it may be all the more interesting and important to look into how other measures of family and community environment and/or job preferences and expectations may discriminate between college and noncollege destinations of graduates within each of the upper-secondary curricula.

Effects of Parental Traits on the Stage II Decision: A Multiple Regression Probit Analysis

In all studies relating parental background factors to educational decisions, we are in fact using indicators of influences (income aside) that we cannot measure directly or for which more direct measures are not available. Often they are poor indicators, though they are of interest in themselves. Fortunately, the effects of parental background on students' career perceptions and on access to resources for the financing of education (through I_i

and W_i of our model) tend usually to operate in the same direction, which enables us to specify the hypothesized directions of these effects. We have already taken a first step with table 7.2, which concentrated on paternal education. The empirical equations detailed in table 7.3 incorporate a more complex array of background indicators. (For the present we will ignore the location and the classroom composition variables at the bottom of the table.) As in tables 3.5, 3.6 and 3.7 we have a dichotomous dependent variable--in this case Yes or No on EXAM. The problem differs from the earlier analysis in two important respects, however: first, some of the proportions taking examinations are so high or so low that they could cause more serious distortions in simple use of ordinary least-squares functions; but second, there is no simultaneity constraint on a set of dependent variables comparable to the constraint on the summation of probabilities among types of course in chapter 3. The most convenient (and suitable) computer program in this case is a probit analysis, which gave us better estimators than did ordinary least squares.[5]

So far as parental education is concerned, the main results of the multiple regression probit analysis confirm the zero-order evidence from table 7.2. Within course types there is indeed a substantial difference between the lowest parental category (the omitted dummy in table 7.3) and all others. The most impressive and consistent monotonically rising effect of parental education on the proportions of students taking examinations is for the General A students and those in the technical course. In the commerce stream we observe a consistent rising probability of going to college from the sons of the least educated men up to junior-college level (FLEVS 4), but not at the next (university) step. Excepting agriculture, the patterns displayed in table 7.3 are very close to those in shorter equations that did not include the location and classroom-composition variables at the bottom of the table. However, for agriculture the coefficient on FLEVS 5 shown in table 7.3 is only half of that in the shorter equation (not shown). It must be remembered that there are relatively few sons of university men in either agriculture or commerce, and those few are definitely not randomly selected.

Similar influences, along with some that are quite distinctive, are reflected in the coefficients on parental occupational status. In all curricula the youth least likely to attend college were those whose fathers were unskilled (OSTAS 8), but there were considerable variations among courses otherwise. Thus, in General B the omitted status category 5 (relatively successful farmers, low-

Table 7.3 Within-Course Probit Analysis of Effects of Parental Background and Community Variables on Likelihood of Taking Examinations

	General B (N=1,825)[a]	General A (N=552)[a]	Agriculture (N=1,190)[a]	Commerce (N=1,044)[a]	Technical (N=2,593)[a]
Constant	.6419*	-1.8592**	-2.051**	-.1568	-1.2506
FLEVS					
1,2	b	b	b	b	b
3	.3841**	.5012**	.4325**	.1973*	.2609**
4	.3437*	.7471*	.4005	.7932**	.3510**
5	.5515*	1.7272**	.2223	.1993	.4398**
NR	.1106	.4763*	.1406	.5651**	.2446**
OSTAS					
1 (high)	3.2148	.1660	c	c	.3099
2	.9040*	4.4537	.1242	.2670	.2392
3	.3361*	.2661	.2410	.3858*	.1782
4	.0392	.6146*	.2911	.0264	-.0268
5	b	b	b	b	b
6	.3986*	.0807	.0419	-.2135	-.3067**
7	.0864	-.3523	.0166	-.0488	-.1223
8	-.0348	-2.9470	-2.3946	-.6811*	-.4760*
NR	.7766**	.6123*	.4291	-.1817	.1168
B-FSE					
SELF-1	.4241*	.2887	.5022	.0910	.2787**
SELF-2	.3504*	.1340	.3615	.1236	.0863
FARM-1	-.0029	.1272	.0294	-.6605	-.3524
FARM-2	-.0214	-.1049	-.0197	.4534*	.1184
EMPLOYEE	b	b	b	b	b
MISC, NR	-.0484*	-.0721	-.0734	-.1016	.1209
FW					
FULL	b	b	b	b	b
PT	-.4776	-.4140	.0580	.3906	-.6329*
NO	-.3594	-.4450	-.1532	-.2655	-.3964**
DEAD	-.3044	-.2732	-.0701	-.4699**	-.3418**
NR	-.5888	-5.6828	.1941	-.7791	-.4430
IQ (self-ranking)	-.0842**	-.1625**	-.1298**	-.0643*	-.0536**
FREQ-M	.0049**	.0093**	.0074	.0019	.0047**
SLOW-50	-.0101	.0290	-.0132**	-.0681*	-.0588
CLED-HI	.0216**	.0570**	.0670**	.0940**	.0322*
CLO-WH	.0069	-.0070	.1084**	-.0669**	-.0030

Note. Asymptotic t values significant at .05 are marked with a single asterisk (*); those significant at .01 are marked with double asterisks (**).

[a]Stratified sample.

[b]Omitted dummy.

[c]Under five cases.

level white collar men, highly skilled manual workers) was lower in probability of attending college than any other except status 8, and this is despite the fact that these equations include separate variables distinguishing farmers' sons. In the commerce and technical curricula, by contrast, it was only sons of men in status 3 or higher who exceeded the college-going probability of those from status 5 backgrounds. Indeed, among youth in General B there was a remarkably high college-going propensity of sons of men in status group 6, whereas in the technical course just such youth were particularly unlikely to seek higher education. For technical and commerce students the importance within OSTAS 6 of sons of small artisans and traders may help account for the comparatively large negative coefficients in both of these curricula. The really distinctive subgroup among the commerce youth, however, was the college-prone sons of relatively successful businessmen, who predominated in OSTAS categories 2 and 3 for the fathers of commerce students.

It was in the next set of parental background variables, the employment status set, that we picked up (in chapter 3) our best simple indicators of the incidence of special family-linked career options so far as the Stage I decision among upper-secondary curricula was concerned. Oldest sons of farmers in particular studied agriculture, and sons of independent businessmen (SELF 1 and SELF 2) were represented disproportionately among students enrolled in commerce curricula. However, once this Stage I allocation had occurred there was considerable ambiguity about any further (Stage II) effects of an F_i sort on the higher-education decision. We did observe marked negative effects of being the son of a farmer among the General B students in equations that did not include the location and classroom variables, though not in table 7.3. In the commerce course, the few first sons of farmers were decidedly not oriented toward college, but the other sons of farmers in that course were remarkably prone to continue into higher education. Paired with this was the least predictable finding in this set of independent variables--the marked contrast in agriculture between the negative coefficient on SELF 1 and the positive coefficient on SELF 2. These latter youth were decidedly the most college-oriented among the students of agriculture in our sample.

Economic constraints on investments in schooling should be picked up in the set of variables characterizing a youth's father as actively employed full-time whether for himself or another (FULL), as working part-time (PT), as not working (NO), or as deceased. With FULL as the omitted variable, coefficients are generally negative, as we should expect. They are most significantly negative in the commerce and technical-school samples for youth whose fathers were no longer living. These were the curricula that were most likely to attract such boys in the first place. The constraints of family income (effects of low W_i) for such young people are an unmistakable and persistent factor in educational and career prospects and realizations despite the openness of the Japanese system.

In every case, but most strikingly in agriculture, students' ratings of their own school performance make a substantial difference in likelihoods of seeking higher education.

Effects of Career Preferences and Aspirations on the Stage II Decision

Three sorts of preferences or expectation variables are introduced in the regressions of table 7.4. The first is a set relating to preferred employer or employment status in a permanent or peak-career situation. The second (EXPSTA) is the status code for the student's reported peak-job expectation. The third is a set of variables that specify occupational type on that expectation, paralleling the rubrics used for fathers on the set FO-III in table 3.6.

It might be supposed that upper-secondary youth preferring government jobs (GOV) would be especially prone to seek higher education. Such indeed was the case among students in agriculture and in technical schools. However, it was not the case among either General B or General A students, who more often took examinations when they preferred careers in large private corporations (BIG) or as independent entrepreneurs in business or professional practice (ME). Contrasts among curricula with respect to prospective employment in government aside, the least oriented toward college were generally those expressing a preference for wage or salaried employment in smaller enterprises (SMALL). These findings suggest some very important questions worth exploring with respect to characteristics of job-opportunity structures in Japan and the operation of communication or information fields in

Table 7.4 Within-Course Probit Analysis of Effects of Preferences and Expectations on Likelihood of Taking Examinations

	General B (N=1,825)[a]	General A (N=552)[a]	Agri-culture (N=1,190)[a]	Commerce (N=1,044)[a]	Technical (N=2,593)[a]
Intercept	1.542	-.552	-.170	-.245	-.100
PREF					
GOV	b	b	b	b	b
ME	.472**	.306	-.365**	.234	-.214*
BIG	.671**	.356	-.345*	-.327	-.129
SMALL	.118	-.094	-1.053**	-.126	-.386**
OTHER	.806*	-1.865	-.068	.116	-.133
EXPSTA	-.043	-.131**	-.010	-.071**	-.036*
EXP-OCC III					
1 White collar	b	b	b	b	b
2 Higher technical (engineers and technicians)	-.444**	-.041	-.712*	-.266	-.445**
3 Managerial in manufacturing and construction	-.410*	-.586*	-.580**	-.638**	-.640**
4 Proprietors and managers in trade	-.598*	.115	-1.070**	-.492**	-.574**
5,6,7 Manual (skilled and unskilled)	-.433	.116	-.677*	.236	-.470**
8 Agriculture, forestry, fishing	-.907**	-.183	-.904**	.135	-.057
9,10 Miscellaneous and nonresponse	-.155	.353	-.692**	.014	-.292*

Note. Asymptotic t values significant at .05 are marked with a single asterisk (*); those significant at .01 are marked with double asterisks (**).

[a]Stratified sample.

[b]Omitted dummy.

carrying messages related to career options.[6] In particular, how do what sorts of information and impressions feed back to secondary-school youth and to those who counsel them, not by formal but rather by informal communication networks? Such explorations would require research well beyond the scope of the present study, though we will take a few steps in this direction when we come, in later chapters, to look more intensively into labor market perceptions of upper-secondary graduates and their fathers.

In table 7.4 expected occupational status is treated in a simplified cardinal form, instead of as a set of categories such as we used with OSTAS in table 7.3. Since the highest EXPSTA are coded 1 and the lowest 8, the consistently negative coefficients on EXPSTA are as we should predict if we suppose that the higher a youth's status goal, the greater the likelihood that he will perceive higher education as a means to the realization of his hopes.

Associations between type of expected peak occupation and the higher-education decision were complex. In most curricula, likelihoods of going on to higher education were greatest among those with expectations of white collar and nontechnical professional employment, but there were exceptions in both agriculture and the commerce courses. The General A students excepted, youth oriented toward careers as proprietors in trade (code 4) were notably disinclined to continue into college, as were those who hoped to become proprietors or managers in processing or construction enterprises (code 3) and, especially in the General B and technical course, those hoping to become high-level technicians (code 2). Compared with their classmates, youth in agriculture and General B who looked forward to agricultural or related employments were distinctively unlikely to take examinations for entry to higher institutions.

In equations similar to those of table 7.4 but with the addition of a set of variables on course preference in upper-secondary schol, there was little effect on most of the coefficients shown in table 7.4. (The main exception was a reversal in the constant term in the commerce course, due primarily to the effect of taking preference for a general course as the omitted dummy in the preferred-course set.) In general, the coefficients on course preferences behaved very much as we should expect in the light of our analysis of correlates of course preferences in chapter 4. Student perceptions and broadly observable actual associations between schooling and occupations were reasonably compatible. Our evidence suggests that to this extent, at least, the Stage II decisions and behavior, with associated adaptations of expectations to external constraints on options, are well reasoned.

Location, Classroom Composition, and Curriculum

There is a growing and lively literature on peer-group influences (as distinct from background characteristics of individuals) on school achievement, and a few sociologists have looked at this topic in studying the determinants of continuation from secondary school into higher education in the United States. Meanwhile, we have from quite another source (mainly human geography) a rich literature on the spatial diffusion of new or growing practices. There are two quite distinct ways of examining such influences empirically. One approach (the one we have used thus far)is to take the individual as the unit of observation, estimating the effects of location and classroom composition on the likelihood that he will go on to higher education. The other approach is to treat the classroom as the unit of observation; the dependent variable is then the proportions of the youth in the class who will continue. We will start with the first of these approaches and then go on to the second.

Effects of Location and Classroom Composition on Individual Likelihoods of College Attendance

For this analysis we return to table 7.3, but draw also on analyses, not reproduced here, using various equations that include and exclude the location variables and those referring to socioeconomic composition of the student population. Whether those variables are added or excluded had only negligible effects on the coefficients on other variables included in either table 7.3 or 7.4. The location and classroom composition variables fit quite well into the M_i, the L_{zi}, and the H_k slots in our model.[7]

FREQ-M, which is the frequency per day of available public transportation to a metropolitan place of over a million,[8] is a good approximation for the concept of M_i in our model, the variable referring to locational factors in the visibility of higher level career options and their relations to college attendance. It is presumed, therefore, to operate positively through effects on both relative earnings expectations (Y_{zi} versus Y_{ti}) and perceived job options and preferences (J_{zi} and J_{ti}).

SLOW-50, which is transportation time by ordinary public conveyances to the nearest city of fifty thousand or more,[9] differentiates only among rural places and between rural and urban locations; it does not distinguish between larger and smaller urban centers. SLOW-50 is the best available indicator for L_{zi} of our model when we take z to refer to any and all varieties of higher institutions. Thus, SLOW-50 enters our models mainly on the cost side. Its M_i implications, which cannot be totally cleaned out, are diminished by inclusion in the same equation of FREQ-M and variables specifying farm fathers.

CLED-HI and CLO-WH are what we have designated in our models as H_k, variables describing classroom composition. CLED-HI is simply the percentage of students in a classroom whose fathers had attended postsecondary institutions (whether junior college or university). CLO-WH is the proportion of fathers who were in "white collar" employment, defined very broadly. Used in an equation that includes parental backgrounds of individuals as well, CLED-HI and CLO-WH should pick up class-environment effects on perceptions of career options and the role of education in realization of those options. They operate, in other words, through G_{zyki} and G_{zjki} of our model.

The different behaviors of the coefficients on CLED-HI and CLO-WH across school types is particularly interesting. The presence in the classroom of a comparatively large proportion of boys with highly educated fathers very generally raises college aspirations, even after the introduction of controls for the individual's own background (table 7.3) or for his preferences and expectations (not shown). This effect is weakest among those in the General B curriculum, where college orientation was pervasive from the start. This, of course, is what we should have expected. CLO-WH presents a more complex and even a confusing picture. Consistently significant positive coefficients on CLO-WH in agriculture and significant negative coefficients in the commerce course raise questions about the contrasting settings in which CLO-WH is being distinguished. In the agriculture course the implicit comparison is largely with proportions of students from farm homes (a majority of whom, in this course, expected careers in agriculture); a highly significant positive coefficient on CLO-WH under these circumstances is clearly indicated. However, significant negative coefficients on CLO-WH in the commerce curriculum have no such obvious explanation; we refrain here from ex post facto, ad hoc interpretation, observing only that problems of multicollinearity do not seem to be the explanation.

In all our tests FREQ-M came through strongly as a good M_i indicator precisely where we should expect it to be most discriminating, among General B and A students and in technical schools. FREQ-M does very little to distinguish among students of agriculture, where SLOW-50 picks up its greatest strength, with the expected negative sign. FREQ-M was somewhat less powerful in an equation that replaced parental background variables with expectation and attitude variables; this is what we should anticipate if FREQ-M is indeed operating as we implicitly hypothesized in specifying it as an index of M_i. The usually negative signs on SLOW-50, especially for the agriculture course, were as we hypothesized. The positive sign on SLOW-50 for General A students in table 7.3, which includes the family background variables, is a surprise, even when it is recognized that it is not statistically significant at a .05 level. This suggests that any L_{zi} cost effects may be neutralized in this equation because earlier constraints on options and inadequacies of information were particularly severe among those of the General A students who resided in the remoter communities. Such an interpretation is consistent with evidence concerning General A students presented in chapter 4 and with further evidence concerning their perceptions of the future and of labor markets in chapters 11 and 12. We will gain some further insights on the effects of relative remoteness in the immediately following pages.

A Path Analysis of Determinants of the Proportion of Students Taking Examinations

That decisions with respect to higher education and type of upper-secondary course are closely related is evident despite the fact that significant minorities of vocational-course students do in fact enter institutions of higher education and that a sixth of the General B students do not even take examinations. We have traced many of the ramifications of these interdependent decisions by analyzing first the associations between family background and types of courses in which youth enrolled, then going on to examine both overall and within-course patterns of association with the higher-education decision. By including classroom characteristics in some of the regressions, we were able also to identify in a first approximation the separate or marginal effects on continuation into higher education of peer association in the school environment. However, a number of awkward problems remain. One of these is the ambiguity in statistical interpretation of coefficients of determination and tests of significance when using a dichotomous dependent variable, as we did with EXAM. Another is the elusive question of how far in fact the higher-education decision is determined by course of study in the secondary years and how far choice of course type reflects initial university intentions. In its very nature, this identification problem cannot be fully resolved, but we can at least learn something by looking at the relationships for classroom units as well as for individuals as the units of observation. Furthermore, we conducted an experiment, reported in appendix C, in which we tested for single-equation bias in estimates of some key parameters by comparing them with estimates using simultaneous equations. We found no evidence of any upward bias in single-equation estimates of the effects of classroom composition on college intent. This enables us to proceed with a path analysis of the sequence location-classroom composition-curriculum content in their direct and indirect effects on the proportions of members of a class who were taking examinations for higher education.

The curriculum variable was translated from the category set type-of-course to a cardinal measure by taking a count of the number of hours of study in the core academic subjects; we designate this variable simply as *S*, omitting the *k* subscript of our theoretical model. For classroom composition we used the simple sum of the logit transform of CLEDHI (the percentage of parents with junior-college or university training) and the logit of proportions in the three top occupational status categories (OSTAS 1, 2, 3); we designate this variable as *H*. For the third variable, a location measure, we selected SLOW-50 because it proved the most promising for our purposes in the experimentation with simultaneous equations; here we designate it simply as *D* (distance in travel time to the nearest place of fifty thousand or more).

We estimated two path models, first omitting and then including *D*. The former is shown as model 1 of figure 7.1. In this, as in all path analyses, the first step is to take as a dependent variable an indicator that is hypothesized to occupy an intervening position in the explanation of the final dependent variable. In this case the intervening variable is *S* (curriculum content), and the final dependent variable is *Z* (the logit of proportions taking examinations).[10] The entry of .709 on the arrow from *H* to *S* is the standardized beta coefficient (the "path" coefficient) in the initial simple equation, with *S* as the dependent and *H* as the independent variable. The next step is an equation in which both *H* and *S* are independent variables, with *Z* as the dependent variable. The path coefficients on the arrows from *S* and from *H* to *Z* are thus the "direct effects" of each of these on *Z*, controlling for the other. The path values on "omitted variables" are simply the square roots of $(1 - R^2)$ in each case. Thus, the proportion of the variance in *S* that was explained statistically by *H* was .496, and the proportion of the variance in *Z* explained jointly by *H* and *S* was .814. All the paths in this first simple model are strong.

In the second model we introduced *D* (SLOW-50) at the beginning. The arrow from *D* to *H* carries a significant negative effect of degree of isolation on the proportion of highly educated, high-occupational-status fathers in the classroom population, as we would of course predict. The arrow from *D* to *S* tells us that once the effects of *D* on *H* are taken into account, a high degree of

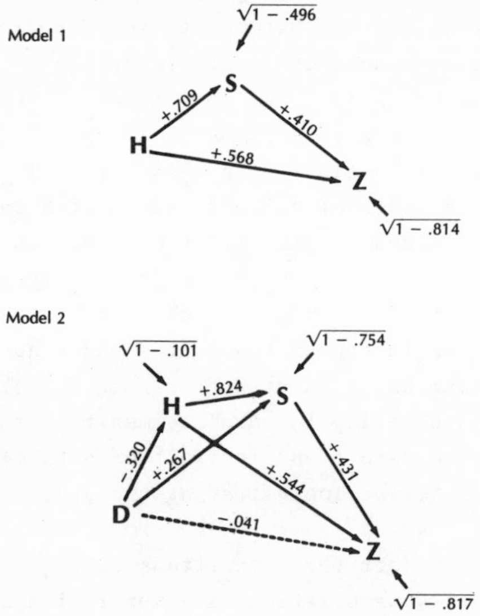

Figure 7.1 Path analysis of the effects of classroom composition and geographic remoteness on the proportions taking examinations.

isolation tends to increase the academic components of the curriculum. With *D* in the model, the estimated positive effect of *H* on *S* is increased; the "direct effects" of *H* and of *S* on *Z* are scarcely changed.

We have used the phrase "direct effects" several times in the last few sentences. It's time we spoke about "indirect effects", which often are more important. How, for example, does a father's education affect his son's occupational status? Does it exercise that effect primarily through its prior affect on the son's schooling, or is there something at work here in addition to the role of schooling? The former, indirect effect operates through schooling; the latter, direct effect is independent of schooling. In path analysis we measure the indirect effect by multiplying path coefficients on a given route from the initial explanatory variable through successive intervening variables. The two models in figures 7.1 are unusually simple in that we used only one initial variable (*H* in the first model, *D* in the second). Most path analyses start with several initial autonomous variables, and they generate a much more complex web of paths through successive intervening variables to the final dependent variable.

Another feature of path analysis is that we can specify what proportion of the "total effect"is indirect, what proportion direct; furthermore, we can divide up the indirect effects in terms of the intervening variables through which a path is traced. While "total effects" of a variable estimated in this way will usually be somewhat less than the zero-order correlation with the final dependent variable, this is not necessarily the case. In fact, entering *D* as an initial independent variable in our example raises slightly the "total effect" of *H* on *Z* , which is not at all surprising. Studies made earlier in the United States have shown, for example, that parental education has a greater effect on college attendance of American youth living in rural communities than on those dwelling in cities. The direct and indirect effects of *D* and *H* on *Z* are shown in table 7.5. We look first at the analysis of the effects of *H* on *Z*.

Does classroom composition affect the proportions taking examinations primarily through its association with curriculum or independently of that association? The answer we obtain is unambiguous and may seem surprising. With or without *D* in the equation, *H* exercises the major part of its very substantial effect on *Z* directly, and not through curriculum content.

Distinguishing among upper-secondary schools solely on the basis of time spent on subjects that are most closely oriented toward higher education, we do find that curriculum has a significant direct effect on the proportions taking examinations. Indeed, if this were not so, any significant indirect effect of *H* on *Z* via curriculum (*S*) would disappear. But the explanatory power of *H* is such that the direct path from *H* to *Z* exceeds that from *S* to *Z*. Inclusion of *D*, which operates in later stages of the model as a control variable, raises the proportion of the total effect on *Z* that is indirect, via curriculum, but still leaves the indirect effect just under two-fifths (39 percent) of the total effect of *H* on *Z*.

Striking as these results are, we must of course be cautious in their interpretation. Classroom composition reflects both an aggregation of the effects of individual background and the peer-group dynamics at work in the classroom environment. But however we interpret the individual and peer-group aspect of the variable *H*, the fact remains that the effects of curricula on rates of continuation into higher education may be less strong than is commonly supposed; family backgrounds and their mutual reinforcement may be more important than often has been assumed. If this was the situation in 1967, when 70 percent of the graduates of lower-secondary schools were entering the upper-secondary programs, perhaps it is equally important in relative terms today, with over 90 percent attending upper-secondary schools and increased proportions of young people in all curricula seeking entrance to institutions of higher education.

Presenting relationships in path form clarifies the way in which geographical remoteness (*D*) was operating in the determination of plans for higher education among the young men graduating in 1967. "Total effects" are negative, primarily because of the negative association of *D* with *H*, which makes indirect paths through

Table 7.5 Direct and Indirect Effects of Classroom Composition (*H*) and Remoteness (*D*) on Proportions Taking Examinations (*Z*)

	H	D
Equations Excluding D		
Effects of H on Z		
Indirect via S	+.291	...
Direct	+.568	...
Total	+.859	...
Proportion of total that is		
Indirect via S	34%	...
Direct	66%	...
Equations Including D		
Effects of H on Z		
Indirect via S	+.355	...
Direct	+.544	...
Total	+.899	...
Proportion of total that is		
Indirect via S	39%	...
Direct	61%	...
Effects of D on S		
Indirect via H	...	-.263
Direct	...	+.267
Total	...	+.004
Effects of D on Z		
Indirect		
D→H→Z	...	-.174 }
D→H→S→Z	...	-.113 } -.172
D→S→Z	...	+.115 }
Direct	...	-.041
Total	...	-.213
Proportion of total that is		
Indirect	...	91%
Direct	...	9%

Note. See text for specification of D, H, S, and Z.

H negative. When controls were introduced for classroom composition, *D* had a positive association with *S*, which is entirely reasonable when we look at it in the perspective of these recursive models and when we consider what lies back of the figures in terms of characteristics of the rural economy and the upper-secondary schools in rural locations. The negative direct effect of *D* on *Z* is so close to zero we could ignore it, though it does constitute about a fifth of the total very moderate negative effect of *D* on *Z*. The small size of the direct effects of rural remoteness (once other characteristics of the rural populations and their schools are taken into account) should not be forgotten in looking at simple summary data on geographical differentials in rates of enrollment in college and university.

8. Economic Constraints on College Attendance

The most important constraints on viable options in the higher-education (and *rōnin*) decisions are presumably of two main kinds. First is limited ability to perform satisfactorily on examinations, which goes back to the individual's genetic and social inheritance and to his upper-secondary experience. Second is the difficulty entailed in meeting direct monetary outlays required for higher education and in accommodating to the sacrifice in earnings foregone while continuing to study (including foregone contributions to the operation of a family business or farm). Both ability and financial constraints were considered to a limited extent in chapter 7, but with the aid of measures that were at best indirect. In this chapter we take another step toward specification of economic constraints on the higher-education decision.

Parental Income as Constraint and as Opportunity

If higher education were a homogeneous consumer good sold at a standard price, if there were no nonmonetary constraints rationing access to that good, if its acquisition did not entail major time costs (i.e., if this were not a time-intensive good from the point of view of the individual),[1] analysis of the effects of parental income on the higher-education decision would be simple. We would want to determine the highest, or saturation, rate of purchase of this good at top income levels and to see how far down the income scale from the top the saturation rate persisted at any given "price" for the higher-education commodity. Below that level we would ask how rapidly the rate of purchase fell off and at what income level, if at all, it approached zero. If we were ready to accept the hypothesis that tastes were independent of income and if the income variable was not standing in for other relevant attributes as well as ability to pay, this would tie up the package so far as income effects are concerned. Why the saturation rate was substantially less than 100 percent (if that were the case), along with what factors sorted out the takers from the nontakers, would be a separate, however interesting, question.

Evidently, however, higher education in Japan is not homogeneous, its price to the individual is not standardized or even closely associated with quality, there are nonmonetary constraints on access (some of which are perverse in their effects on lower income families), and education is most decidedly an intensively time-using good. It is also in major part an investment rather than an immediate consumption good, and returns to the investment may be functions of both ability and social background of the individual. The fact that a few comfortably situated families may indeed send their sons, or especially their daughters, to college with the idea that this is a luxury item does not alter the predominant career element in the motives of males for higher education.

Parental Income and the Interest Cost of Financing Education

As soon as we view education as an investment, we put time at the heart of the educational decision. First, it is there because of the intensity of use of personal time; whatever the purposes motivating a decision to seek further schooling, the individual can implement that decision only by becoming directly involved in the process himself. This immediately raises the question of the ability to forego earnings to continue with one's education. Second, even if education were not so immediately time-intensive in this personal sense, even if there were much wider scope for substitution of other factors than one's own time in education, another dimension of time would come to center stage in an educational decision, because the benefits flowing from education extend over so long a period into the future. This makes the rate of exchange (interest rate) in trading anticipated future for present purchasing power a critical factor in the financing of investment in education. The "durable good" aspect of the acquisition of human capital suggests that the purchase of education might be compared with the purchase of a house. However, the house can always be sold outright as a capital good, whereas only services but not the capital stock invested in a human being normally are treated as marketable property. This makes the timing of the education decision more critical, since to defer education will shorten the life span of returns flowing from it and the period over which the investment must be amortized. But there is another, more fundamental contrast between investments in housing and in people.

If education was regarded solely as an investment, we might raise the question whether a priori any parental-income effect at all should be expected, and if so, why? Suppose for the moment that family income per se has no effect on relationships between the flow of future benefits from higher education and the monetary outlays and foregone earnings entailed in acquiring that schooling; should parental income then make any difference? Presumably it would not (other fortuitous taste or ability factors empirically associated with income aside), if the society's institutions operated with perfect smoothness to provide credit facilities for investments in human beings.[2] But in fact in Japan, as elsewhere, there is ample evidence that the capital markets for such investments are rudimentary--if they can properly be said to exist at all in the sense of enabling a man to obtain credit, whether by loans or in an equity system, on the basis of his future earnings prospects. Under these circumstances, access to funds both for maintenance and for outlays on books, tuition, examination fees, and so on depends on the family's economic situation. This above all is why, with our initial presentation of the Stage I decision model (in chapter 5), we put W_i in the cost function and why we will be looking at family income first of all as a "constraint". It is also why we suggested earlier that in a reasonable approximation we might expect interest costs to rise exponentially with the funds needed from outside sources to finance education. Given such a relationship, we should predict systematic associations between family income on the one hand and both the decision for higher education in general and choices among higher-education alternatives (and *rōnin* investments) on the other--any "consumption" aspects of higher education aside.

These generalizations may be elucidated by visualizing the determination of the equilibrium point for investments in education for a particular individual viewed strictly in terms of monetary returns. To do this, we need two sorts of information: (1) rates of return to each incremental investment (in the terminology of economics, a schedule of "marginal rates of return," or "internal" rates); (2) a corresponding schedule of interest costs (external rates) associated with each incremental investment.[3] The former is the individual's demand curve for educational investments, the latter is his supply curve. We have drawn imaginary curves in figure 8.1. The demand curve *D* is drawn on the assumption, usually valid, that marginal internal rates of return to successive investments decline as the investments rise. (An explanation of the meaning of "internal rate of return," usually called simply "the rate of return," is given in chapter 2.)

The supply curve *S* depicts the interest cost to the individual or his family of successive increments of investments in education. As soon as a child reaches an age at which there may be a significant sacrifice of earnings associated with continuation in school, real cost will be incurred even if there are no direct costs of tuition, books, and so on. There will then be some interest cost, even if the interest is not paid out; there is always a foregone-interest cost when liquid resources are invested in schooling. This is the case even when those resources are not directly visible because they take the form of earnings foregone. Foregone interest is also incurred on direct outlays for education when the family gives up other investment possibilities to use its resources on a son's (or daughter's) education. But how much a family can finance in this way without borrowing will depend on its income and wealth. As the amount of the investment increases, the interest costs will rise, whether because progressively more lucrative alternative investments are foregone or because the family must have recourse to borrowing, and at progressively higher interest costs. If there are sharp breaks in the supply curve, it should be drawn as a stepped pattern, with flat segments and vertical shifts to successively higher levels, as in figure 8.2. (The demand, or marginal rate-of-return, curve might also have such discrete breaks.) The stronger the economic position of a family, the more it can invest without having to turn to more expensive sources of funds or encountering a complete barrier to further borrowing (the vertical line farthest to the right in figure 8.2).

Whether we take figure 8.1 or figure 8.2 as our model, the individual (or his family) will continue enlarging his investments in education so long as the rate of return to an additional investment (the *D* curve) exceeds the interest cost for that investment. Given curves D_1 and S, he will go to point Q_1 on these diagrams, but no farther. If the *S* curve has a final vertical limit, as we have drawn it in figure 8.2, he may run up against

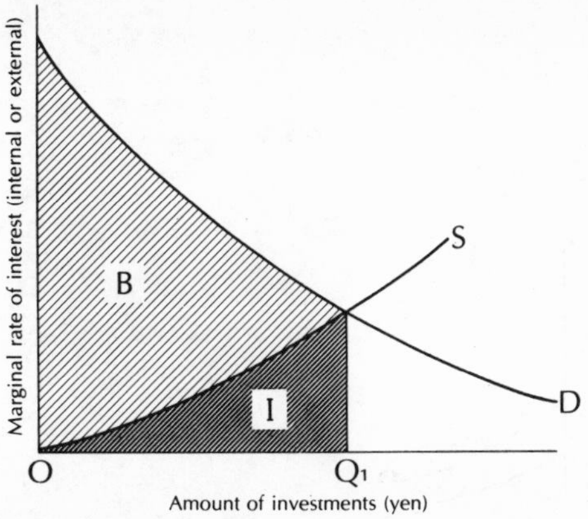

Figure 8.1 Individual demand and supply curves for investments in education.

that barrier even when the marginal rate of return is still high. This is what would happen with demand schedule D_7 in figure 8.2.

Thus far we have drawn our diagrams for one individual only, except for the introduction of a second demand curve in figure 8.2. To simplify the exposition of comparisons among individuals, we return to the use of smooth curves. In figure 8.3 we suppose that marginal rates of return to all individuals are the same, drawing a single D curve with no subscripts. However, some youth come from homes that are much more comfortably situated than others. The richest families can continue to make very substantial investments in the education of their children without encountering the necessity of taking recourse to more expensive (higher interest) sources of finance. Some, represented by S_1, do not face rising financing costs at all over the human-investment range shown. Members of the group S_2 face rising costs but do not hit an absolute barrier. The poorest families, represented by S_3, face a severely constrained situation in the financing of education for their children. We have drawn these S curves in a way that dramatizes the contrasts, but if we consider them to cover only the range of investments beyond completion of compulsory schooling, the impression they create may not be entirely unrealistic. (Fortunately, few in Japan today are as relatively disadvantaged as is suggested in curve S_3, though many may hit a barrier at a less restrictive level on the investment scale.)

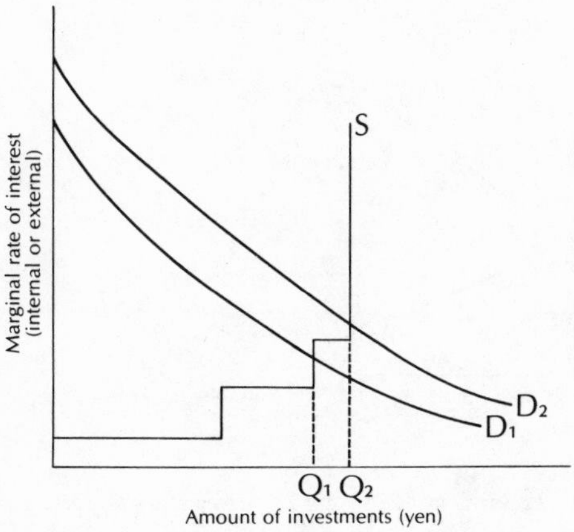

Figure 8.2 Stepped supply schedule with varied individual demand curves for investment in education.

A feature of this construct that does not concern us directly here is nevertheless worthy of comment. The sum of the two shaded (hatched) areas in figure 8.1 will equal the individual's later earnings (if we disregard postschool investments).[4] By shading in the appropriate areas on figure 8.3, we could get similar pictures for individuals with supply curves S_1, S_2, and S_3 and compare their earnings. A model such as this, which assumes all *D* curves to be identical, has been labeled by Becker the "inequity" model, implied by those who interpret inequalities in earnings as a result of inequity, or inequality of opportunity (due to economic situations). But there are also differences in the *D* curves; if these are attributed to positive interactions between ability and schooling in their effects on earnings, they contribute an "elitist" component to differences in earnings. At the extreme, if we assume all *S* curves to be identical but *D* curves to differ, we have Becker's pure "elitist" model of inequalities in earnings associated with schooling.[5]

Obviously, these models are grossly oversimplified, and not merely because they are confined to strictly economic motivations and economic "rationality." There are other constraints, and there are sharp contrasts in costs of education that are associated

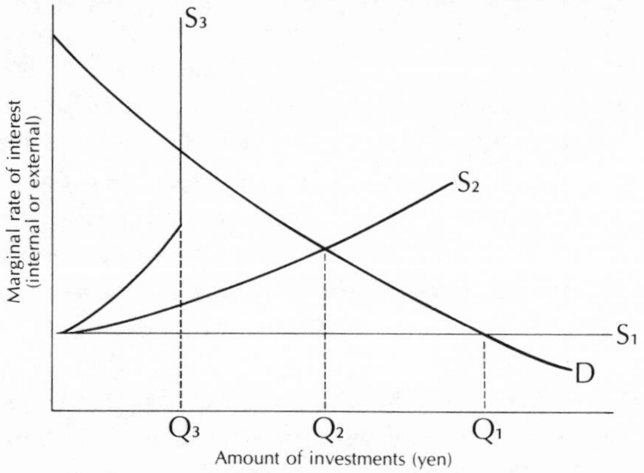

Figure 8.3 Uniform individual demand with varied individual supply curves for investment in education.

with those constraints. This fact is easily demonstrated in data on higher education in Japan, to which we will turn shortly. First, however, we discuss briefly in more general terms some interactive relations among parental incomes, examination performance, and the costs of higher education in Japan.

Parental Income and Performance on Examinations

Many factors besides innate ability affect performance on examinations. The education of parents is one of these factors: the better the parents' education, the more valuable the "inputs" they can contribute directly to enhance their children's education. Also, for any given level of income better educated parents may be prepared to make greater economic sacrifices to help their children prepare for examinations. But parental income is also a very important factor in examination preparation, especially perhaps in Japan. Moreover, the ability to pay for tutoring in various forms is of greater importance for children of the less educated parents. Unfortunately, it is just those parents who can least afford to buy for their children educational help outside of school hours. The large and rapidly growing *juku* system of tutorial schools for pupils in the elementary and middle grades

(1-9) undoubtedly raises the academic performance of many Japanese children. However, it also mganifies the effects of the parental economic situation on examination performance from an early age, and thereby on the upper-secondary schools and courses to which youth gain access. In the upper-secondary years parental income continues to affect performance on examinations for entry to universities. Economic problems for the poorest students in the upper-secondary schools are further exacerbated by family needs and associated demands on the time of sons in helping to meet those needs, which further discourages successful examination performance in an intensely competitive system. Unfortunately, places in the most prestigious universities, which also cost the least, are not available to youth whose examination performance is only moderately good. The remarkable fact is how many students from poor homes manage nevertheless to enter the gates of the national universities. But it is time to look at some figures.

Costs of Higher Education and Income-Selectivity of Enrollments: Some Evidence

Several surveys by the Ministry of Education provide benchmarks for the analysis of income-selectivity into higher education and into various types of institutions. The first of these compiled information on costs of attending national and private universities in 1959 and 1961 and on rates of entry to various sorts of higher institutions by family income class. The second, part of a special study of the upper-secondary graduates of 1968, included no cost data, but it gave information on the distributions of family incomes of entrants to higher education, again by type of higher institution. The fullest coverage of both costs and incomes was in a survey for 1974, when detailed data were also provided separately for males and females. We will look first at the early data.

Costs and Income-Selectivity to Higher Education around 1960

Higher education always entails private costs even where tuition is free, unless students are paid for attending; costs of foregone earnings are always involved, although they may be reduced by taking a two-year instead of a four-year course, or by enrolling in night courses that are not too demanding and leave the day free for work. We may expect that very low family incomes will operate as a constraint discouraging any sort of higher education. However, as we have already observed, there are also differences among institutions in tuition and fees, other school expenses, the availability of subsidized living quarters, and so on. In fact, wide variations in direct costs of higher education along with a lack of correlation between those costs and the advantages offered by particular institutions have been a matter of concern in Japan since well before the students in our sample were attending upper-secondary school. In 1974, as fifteen years earlier, direct outlays on educational expenses were twice as high in private as in national day colleges and universities, but there have been some modifications in that situation since 1974.

Drawing on special studies of the expenditures of university students,[6] along with our analysis (unpublished) of earnings and bonus payments in Japan in 1961, we estimated costs of higher education as a percentage of the average annual earnings of mature men with middle schooling:

	Students in National Day Universities	Students in Private Day Universities
School expenses for year (tuition, fees, books, etc.)	6%	12%
Commuting costs	2	2
Living expenses by residence:		
At home	7	10
Dormitory	14	19
Private lodging	20	25
Freshman entry fees	1	5

While subsistence normally will be less than the full cost of fore-gone earnings, direct money outlays are required to maintain a youth while studying, which places costs more directly and visibly on his (or her) family. Interpretation of estimates of student living expenses in the national and private universities are confounded, however, by the fact that those who have more spend more. Notice, in assessing these figures, that we took middle-school graduates as our base for comparison of expenses with presumptive fathers' incomes, even though in the cohorts of fathers of university students of 1961 the majority would not have gone that far in school.

Figure 8.4 shows rates of entry (for both sexes) to higher institutions by family income for the 1960 cohort. Both actual yen figures and their 1960 dollar equivalents are entered in the diagram to facilitate its interpretation. Looking first at the total length of the bars, disregarding their composition, we see that rates of college entry rise slowly at first; the poor boy faces many difficulties, and poor youth were underrepresented in the upper-secondary streams to start with. Nevertheless, 4 to 5 percent of these poorest young people entered institutions of higher education. The proportions increased at family incomes around $900 (in 1960 dollars) and reached 8 to 9 percent between $1,000 and $1,300. After that, the pace of increase accelerated, both because of increased rates of college attendance among males and because more females were coming into the picture. Above an annual family income of $2,500 we begin to witness the effects of three factors, each of which was manifested in higher rates of attendance at the private universities and the day junior colleges but not elsewhere. These are (1) an increased rate of college attendance among youth who were not particularly high in academic achievement but who saw higher education as important for their future career prospects, (2) probably an increased representation of young men with a wide range of competencies who conceived continuation in school partly as a consumer luxury, and (3) a quantitatively important increase in the rate of attendance among young women. The first two of these categories, but especially the first, are very clearly related to income, because at higher income levels families can pay for tutoring and other supportive features designed to get their sons into universities and allow them to continue at the relatively high-cost private institutions. The *rōnin* year or years is one of those costs.

Relative Costs and Distributions of Enrollments in Higher Institutions in 1974

The essential stability in cost rankings of the various types of higher institutions was noted earlier, as was the increased relative gap between costs in the national and the private day colleges and universities. The 1974 educational cost relationships are shown in some detail in table 8.1, along with enrollments by sex. For the moment we will disregard columns 9 and 10.

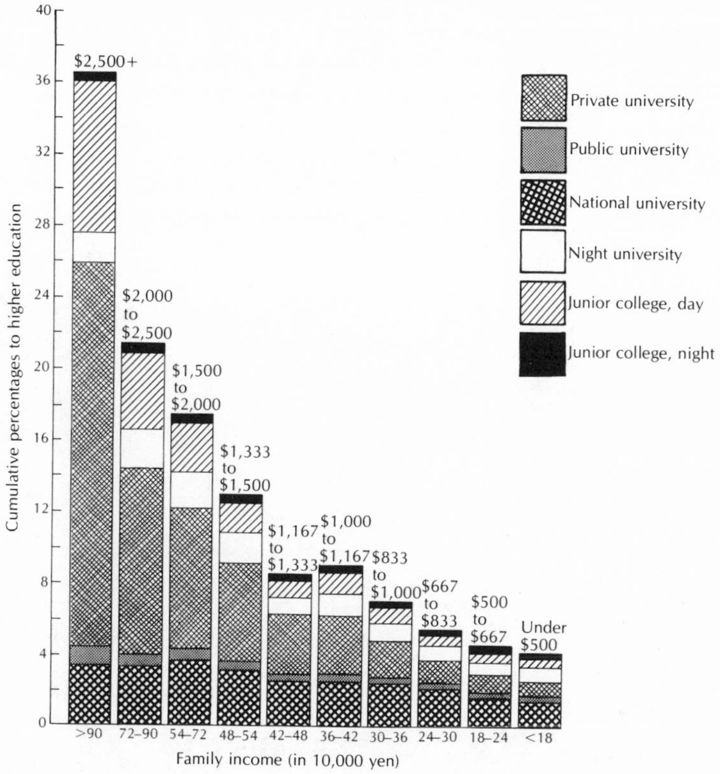

Figure 8.4 Percentage rates of entry to higher education in 1960 by family income classes. Source: Mombushō, *Shingaku to Ikuei Shōgaku* [Ministry of Education, Financial Aid and Continuation in School] (Tokyo, 1961).

The importance of the private universities in numbers enrolled is again obvious. So is female preponderance in the day junior colleges (although by 1974 there were slightly more females enrolled in universities than in junior colleges). Column 2 aside, the cost columns of table 8.1 can speak for themselves. It should be remembered, however, that the total costs of attending higher institutions will depend not only on direct outlays per year but also on the number of years of schooling and on how much is foregone in earnings each year. In comparing direct outlays, we would need

Table 8.1 Student Numbers, Mean Family Incomes, and Educational Expenses per Student in Higher Institutions (1974)

Type of Higher Institution (1)	Total Cost Group[a] (2)	Tuition and Fees[b,c] (3)	Other Educational Outlays[a,c] (4)	Total Educational Outlays[c] (5)	Number of Students: Male (6)	Number of Students: Female (7)	Percentage Female (8)	Mean Family Income (thousand yen): Male (9)	Mean Family Income (thousand yen): Female (10)
Day universities									
National	2	100	100	100	227,719	68,660	23.2	2,798	2,759
Public	2	107	108	107	28,695	12,746	30.8	3,089	3,310
Private	1	524	98	217	878,079	237,681	21.3	3,636	4,673
Night universities									
National	3	70	93	87	4,919	705	12.5	2,593	2,254
Public	3	59	73	69	2,621	671	20.4	2,754	3,357
Private	2	238	87	129	107,838	15,155	12.3	2,926	2,908
Day junior colleges									
National	4	97	80	85	342	1,315	79.4	2,201	2,722
Public	4	124	75	88	2,094	11,930	85.1	2,357	2,735
Private	2	589	84	224	19,597	253,176	92.6	3,315	3,895
Night junior colleges									
National	5	97	80	87	8,570	1,414	14.2	2,894	2,587
Public	5	54	83	80	1,643	1,577	49.0	2,615	2,408
Private	5	349	91	153	12,267	11,415	47.6	2,916	2,522

[a] For explanation, see text.

[b] Includes purchases of books and other study materials, student club fees, commuting expenses.

[c] Indexes: national day universities taken as 100.

Sources. Mombushō, *Gakusei Seikatsu Chōsa Kōhō* [Ministry of Education, University Life Survey] (Tokyo, 1974), pp. 4, 29-31, 48-51. Indexes are computed from data on p. 4.

Note. As of 1974, 10,000 yen was approximately $33.

to roughly double the university relative to the junior-college costs. With respect to earnings foregone (not shown at all in table 8.1), we would count day as more costly than night institutions per year of study. The total cost groupings entered in column 2 of the table take these considerations into account; groups run from decidedly the most costly (group 1, which is the private day universities) to the least costly (group 5, the national and public night junior colleges). The gaps between the groups are unambiguous and relatively persistent. This provides a basis for predicting contrasts across institutions in the distributions of parental incomes for male and for female students. We must be careful, however, when the available data do not distinguish by sex; the 1974 survey provides that information, but the 1968 study does not.

Income-Selectivity to Institutions of Higher Education in 1968 and 1974

Young people entering institutions of higher education in 1968 were just one year younger than the cohort of our study, which makes them of particular interest to us. The few students reported as entering night colleges and universities directly from upper-secondary institutions included the largest proportions from economically less advantaged homes (family incomes under about $2,800 in 1968 dollars). However, they were followed closely in this respect by the lower cost national and public colleges and universities. Little family income effect is evidenced in the distinction between the four-year and two-year (junior-college) programs, which show distinctions based on sex. The stronger economic position of youth entering private higher institutions is clear enough, but the proportion of those youth coming from families with very modest reported incomes is impressive nonetheless.

Part B of table 8.2 contrasts sharply with part A with respect to income-selectivity to national upper-secondary schools.[7] These prestige institutions clearly drew from the more privileged members of the community, and their graduates were the most likely to enter national or prestige private universities. However, the numbers of students in the national upper-secondary schools were few, and good performance on examinations by students in the public General B stream gave many young people of more modest background a chance to attend one of the national universities, sometimes with scholarship assistance.

Table 8.2 Family Incomes of First-Year College and University Students (1968)

A. By Type of Higher Institution

Type of Higher Institution	Group Rank in Annual Direct Costs, 1974	Total Cost Group, 1974	Number of Entrants to Higher Education, 1968	1968 Mean Family Income (thousand yen)	1968 Percentage of Families with Income: Under 1 Million Yen	1.5 Million Yen or More
Day universities						
National	3	2	47,600	1,190	52	17
Public	3	2	6,500	1,310	44	20
Private	1	1	182,400	1,630	33	33
Day junior colleges						
National or public	4	4	6,600	1,190	51	16
Private	1	2	101,700	1,610	33	33
Night university or junior college	2[a]	b	9,500[c]	1,160	59	16

B. By Type of Upper-Secondary School

Type of Upper-Secondary School	Number Entering Higher Institutions in 1968	1968 Mean Family Income (thousand yen)	1968 Percentage of Families with Income: Under 1 Million Yen	1.5 Million Yen or More	2 Million Yen or More
National	1,800	2,120	18	55	32
Public	220,100	1,350	43	22	9
Private	132,400	1,850	27	42	23

Source. Mombushō, *Kōtōgakkō Sotsugyōsha no Shinro Jōkyō ni kan suru Chōsa-Hōkokusho* [Ministry of Education, Survey Report on Courses Chosen by Senior High School Graduates] (Tokyo, 1969), p. 24.

[a]These are diverse, but predominantly private, which makes direct outlays per year relatively high (though less than at private day universities).

[b]Difficult to place because of diversity and the inclusion of four-year with two-year programs.

[c]This is an extremely low figure compared with 1974. It is not clear to what extent the contrast is in definitions for inclusion, to what extent it reflects a real contrast, but there can be no doubt that there has been an increase in night-program enrollments and a shift in their composition since 1968. Equally important, many who enroll in night programs after an intervening period of work are omitted in this 1968 study of immediate destinations of new graduates of upper-secondary schools.

Mean parental incomes of young men and women in the various institutions of higher education in 1974 are shown separately in columns 9 and 10 of table 8.1. In the day programs students in private institutions clearly came from higher income families; with the exception of the national universities, women in day programs were from higher income families than were men. Also, both men and women in day junior colleges were somewhat less advantaged economically than their counterparts in day universities under the same control. Relationships were more erratic in the night programs. Furthermore, there were considerable overlaps in these distributions of family incomes.

A better perspective on some of these relationships is provided by the cumulative distributions for certain of the main categories of institutions, shown for 1974 in figure 8.5. The steeper a curve on this probit chart, the less the dispersion of incomes; and the further to the right, the higher the family income at any given percentile. Thus, we can read the successively higher medians by following the 50 percentile line from left to right. We can do the same thing at the other percentiles, as the 25th and 75th percentiles, for example. The solid line, which is the distribution of males in the national day universities, is very closely approximated over most of its range by several other groups not shown on the chart, including females in national day universities (with somewhat fewer at the lowest incomes) and males in the private night universities (with somewhat more in the lowest income range). To match the median incomes of males and of females in the private day universities, we would have to move up in the distributions for students in the national day universities to the 33rd and the 20th percentiles, respectively. Notice that, though the numerous women in private day junior colleges were from less prosperous homes than the women in private day universities, they were generally somewhat better off than the men in private day universities. Equally important, the income overlapping in these distributions was substantial.

Cutoff levels at lower incomes are clearly displayed in figure 8.5. Less than 2 percent of the women in private day colleges and universities (and only 3 percent of the men in private day universities) came from families reporting annual incomes under a million yen (about $3,300 in 1974 dollars). Setting aside cases in which the student populations were very small (under 2,000), the group with the lowest average incomes and the least income dispersion was men in the public day junior colleges (the steepest line on the figure); the lowest incomes among male students were not (as we had anticipated) in national or public night junior colleges. The lowest income women were definitely those attending two-year night courses; that distribution, which also is shown in figure 8.5, lies consistently below the distribution for men in such institutions (not shown). This fact, together with the fact

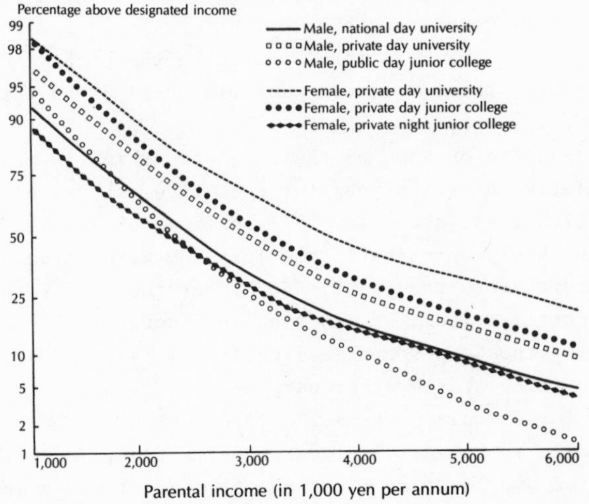

Figure 8.5 Distributions of parental incomes of students in institutions of higher education, 1974. Source: Computations from Mombushō, *Gakusei Seikatsu Chōsa Kōhō* [Ministry of Education, University Life Survey] (Tokyo, 1975), p. 10.

that almost as many women as men were enrolled in these private two-year night colleges, may be a more important pointer to the future with respect to women than usually is recognized.

Work among Day and Night Students

It is reasonable to suppose a priori that students attending night universities or night junior colleges will also frequently hold jobs, whereas youth attending day institutions will be much less likely to work. In fact data for 1959 support this supposition, in that the earnings of working night students were enough to fully cover their subsistence, whereas working day students averaged only a sixth or less of the earnings of the night students --whether in national, local public, or private institutions. While the proportions of night students working were higher in all cases (ranging from three-fourths in national to three-fifths in private night institutions), three-fifths even of the day students in national universities did some work for pay. The lowest proportion, for private day students, was a third.

Table 8.3 Assessments of Need of Male and Female Students at Least Partially Working Their Way through Day Universities and Junior Colleges (1974 percentage distributions)

Respondents' Judgment of Need	Day University			Day Junior College		
	National	Public	Private	National	Public	Private
Males						
Working						
Work though family help sufficient	26.0	33.7	43.6	30.3	42.4	45.3
Need modest supplement	36.6	36.9	29.5	37.9	24.4	24.4
Work necessary to continue	16.7	11.1	8.0	16.7	6.8	4.7
No family help	3.2	5.1	2.4	5.4	6.5	4.7
Total working	82.5	86.8	83.5	90.3	80.1	79.1
Not working	17.5	13.2	16.5	9.7	19.9	20.9
Total	100.0	100.0	100.0	100.0	100.0	100.0
Females						
Working						
Work though family help sufficient	32.9	45.1	52.7	50.0	58.8	53.9
Need modest supplement	34.2	31.2	17.6	29.0	17.2	12.2
Work necessary to continue	13.5	6.4	3.2	8.1	5.1	2.3
No family help	2.7	2.4	.6	2.9	.6	1.9
Total working	83.3	85.1	74.1	90.0	81.7	70.3
Not working	16.7	14.9	25.9	10.0	18.3	29.7
Total	100.0	100.0	100.0	100.0	100.0	100.0

Source. Mombushō, *Gakusei Seikatsu Chōsa Kōhō* [Ministry of Education, University Life Survey] (Tokyo, 1974), p. 44.

The 1974 survey gave information concerning work by students in day institutions only. The figures shown in table 8.3 suggest dramatic increases in the proportions of day students working part-time, with male proportions ranging from 78 to 90 percent, female proportions from 70 to 90 percent. However, for many this was no more than "pin money." In most cases the largest part of these earnings was spent on recreation, and large minorities of those who worked (even majorities among girls in day junior colleges) stated that family support was sufficient without supplementation. For some, however, earnings from work were essential.[8]

Family Economic Situation and the College Option: Seniors in Upper-Secondary Courses, 1966

There are a number of clues we can build on for analysis of the effects of economic constraints on attitudes and plans with respect to higher education among the male students in our sample. In addition to family income as reported by fathers, we have clues from reactions to a hypothetical windfall. Also, there are the more direct (though not on that account more reliable) reports of students on why they will not go on to higher education despite expressed desires to do so. Finally, there are attitudes toward becoming *rōnin*. It is the combination of these data, not any single clue, that gives us leverage in assessing the situation.

The Study Sample and Measures of Parental Income

Even under the best of circumstances there are problems in a proper accounting of incomes and in comparisons of income across broad categories of recipients such as wage and salaried men, men in independent business and professional practice, and farm operators. We made no attempt to merge estimates in a single continuum. Instead, we have treated sons of men in wage or salary employment and sons of men in independent or family enterprise as separate student (and father) samples. Sons of farmers are omitted in this analysis. As already stated, the income data were obtained on questionnaires from the fathers themselves.

In the case of employee fathers we derived annual earnings estimates from answers to questions concerning total monthly cash income (base pay plus a variety of other cash payments received by

Japanese employees) and information on bonuses received over the course of the year. The bonus payments run as high as a third or more of total annual earnings in some employment situations, and their inclusion was obviously essential. The most serious gap in the earnings figure is for payments in kind, of which there is a wide variety, especially in the big firms. However, the payments in kind are less important for our purposes than might at first be supposed. For one thing, company housing, which can be an extremely important component in the incomes of young workers (where it commonly may take the form of dormitory hostels), is of limited absolute and relative importance among the fringe benefits accruing to households of mature family men. Also, a good part of the larger payments in kind take an essentially luxury form. Such receipts are not substitutable for ordinary living expenses and are irrelevant in estimating real disposable income from which investments in education might be financed; for our purposes they are very properly excluded. However, such is not the case with respect to other sources of income, as from rents or securities or a share in returns to a family enterprise and so on. Lack of information on such income for employee fathers reduces our estimates of total family incomes. There is unquestionably a positive correlation between the errors of omission and the estimated earnings; and the use of the father's earnings to represent family income accordingly presents a distribution that has less variance and may have substantially less skewness than the true family income distribution. Exclusion of part at least of the "transitory" or windfall components in property incomes (positive or negative) may be an advantage, but this does not neutralize the fact that omission of the more stable, "permanent" component in income from other sources may reduce the predictive power of our income estimates; it will have that effect so long as the other incomes are only loosely correlated with earnings. On the other hand, to the extent that other income sources are positively associated with earnings, their omission will bias upward the estimates of metric regression coefficients, and hence of the marginal effects of family incomes on the predicted likelihood that a young man will take examinations for higher education; it could introduce such a bias even without affecting the coefficient of determination or its significance.

Income estimates for independent business and professional men and their families were taken from two summary questions asked of these fathers. The first referred simply to gross annual sales of the family enterprise, or of that part of it for which the respondent was responsible. The second was a net-income question, referring to what the family received after deducting the expenses of operating the enterprise. Although other data relating to the business were obtained, they were insufficient to allow a full accounting but were adequate for use as a check against the reported net family income. That data such as these will contain a very wide margin of error must be obvious. We may take some solace from the strong presumption in this case that reports of net family returns are tacitly corrected by the respondent to eliminate the effects of exceptionally bad or exceptionally good years; some part at least of the transitory component in these incomes has been purged from the estimates. However, the statistical "noise" created by both the remaining transitory components and sheer error is undoubtedly substantial, and we have no evidence concerning the existence or nonexistence of correlation between the reported values and the error terms.

Taking all students together, regardless of type of course, the mean incomes for entrepreneur fathers were double those for employee fathers, and differences in variance and skewness were also marked. Whereas the standard deviation of employee annual earnings was only 479,000 yen against a mean of 770,000 (a coefficient of variation of .62), the standard deviation of net family incomes among the independent entrepreneurs exceeded 4 million yen with a mean of 1.5 million (a coefficient of variation of 2.91). Reported incomes of employee fathers had some moderate positive skewness, and the skew (along with the mean) would unquestionably have been increased with a better measure of income, but hardly to an extent comparable with the tailing out into the upper reaches among the independent business and professional men.

Parental Incomes and College Attendance: Some Regressions

The strength or weakness of measured income as a factor in the likelihood that a youth would actively seek higher education--and how far the process operates through Stage I course allocations, how far within curricula thereafter--was explored in a complex set of regression equations with multiple control variables (not shown).

Among sons of employees, the effects of parental income on college attendance operated in part at initial selection or self-selection into General B (with a mean income 1.5 times that of fathers earning wages or salaries whose sons were enrolled in General A and agriculture). In particular, nonfarm wage workers whose sons were studying agriculture had low incomes with small variance, and only 5 percent of these youth reported any attempt to gain access to higher education; the pressure of economic constraints, along with other discouraging factors, precluded college attendance for most of these youth from the start.

Results with the net-family-income measures for fathers in independent and family business were quite different. Overall, their incomes as measured played very little part in determining college orientations. Nevertheless, at almost 2 million yen the mean income of fathers of youth in General B was double that of youth in General A and in agriculture and almost double that of youth in the technical curricula. On the other hand, the mean income of entrepreneur fathers of youth in the commerce course matched that of fathers of students in General B. It was in the commerce course that we found the most extreme skewness of parental incomes, with mean incomes 3 times the median. It was also within the commerce samples that the perceived value of college education for the family business came most clearly into play, and in association with the scale of that business. In this way, parental income did make a significant difference. Yet it was also among the sons of successful independent businessmen (whatever the curriculum) that the approach to college options could be most relaxed.

Parental Incomes and Stated Reasons for Noncontinuation despite Preferences

Reasons for not continuing into higher education given more directly by youth expressing a preference for higher education but not expecting or planning to go on are shown in summary form in table 8.4. It is important in reading the percentage distributions in this table to bear in mind that they apply to very different proportions of the total graduates of the various curricula (shown in the first row of the table).

With the partial exception of young men graduating from the agriculture courses, two responses dominate all others. First is inadequate scholarly ability as assessed by the individual himself (related to similar responses on secondary curricula in chapter 4). Second is the burden of direct costs in fees and tuition; it is notable that for the total sample, taking all curricula together,

Table 8.4 Principal Reasons Given for Not Going to College by Students Wishing but Not Expecting to Go On

	General B	General A	Agriculture	Commerce	Technical
Percentage giving yes/no responses on college plans[a]	3	19	17	24	29
Number giving principal reason	57	99	196	248	749
Percentage distribution of principal reason					
Total	100	100	100	100	100
Direct costs (tuition fees, etc.)	35	41	20	32	32
Family business	7	4	26	10	2
Parents opposed	...	4	2	1	1
Present course inappropriate	...	8	14	13	18
Inadequate scholarly ability	46	37	34	37	41
Other	12	6	4	7	6
Percentage of total giving economic reasons[b]	1.4	8.6	7.8	10.1	9.9

[a]Yes/no responses are responses of yes on college desires, but no on taking examinations.

[b]Counting as "economic" the responses "direct costs" and "family business."

a third gave tuition and related costs as their "principal reason" even though only 11 percent of the yes/no group specified that they would use lottery winnings to defray educational costs. These answers are not necessarily inconsistent, but there must be at least a suspicion of upward bias in the high proportions (according to table 8.4) specifying tuition and related costs as the principal barrier to further schooling.

The entries after "family business" reinforce observations made earlier with reference to family-linked options and family pressures in these matters among students of agriculture and commerce. It is the former, however, who most often experience

Table 8.5 Relation between Parental Income and Reason Given for Not Taking Examinations by Students Wishing but Not Expecting to Go On to College

	Nonfarm Fathers in Own or Family Enterprise: Net Incomes, 1966				Fathers in Wage and Salaried Employment: Annual Earnings (with bonus), 1966			
			Percentage with Incomes				Percentage with Incomes	
	Number Reporting	Median Income (thousand yen)	Under 500,000 Yen	Over 1.5 Million Yen	Number Reporting	Median Income (thousand yen)	Under 500,000 Yen	Over 1 Million Yen
All students[a]								
Entire sample	1,035	1,025	23.3	22.8	2,136	708	22.1	16.3
General B	304	1,200	15.7	35.4	628	827	9.9	28.9
General A	50	672	28.0	16.0	85	618	31.8	11.8
Agriculture	24	432	62.5	4.2	60	623	40.0	8.4
Commerce	244	619	24.2	20.8	335	673	23.6	10.2
Technical	398	725	25.8	15.8	993	661	27.5	11.0
Students giving yes/no responses on college plans[b]								
All students, by reason not going on								
All reasons	177	730	27.1	19.8	441	646	28.3	7.3
Cost burden	39	600	35.9	5.1	155	552	42.0	3.7
Family business	27	1,200	14.8	37.0	...	...	...	...
Course inappropriate	28	750	32.1	14.3	76	732	22.4	13.1
Poor scholar	72	950	25.0	23.6	175	677	19.4	7.5
Technical-school students by reason not going on								
All reasons	111	688	29.7	15.3	303	658	27.1	8.7
Cost burden	29	587	37.9	6.9	100	550	42.0	4.0
Family business	9	875	11.1	22.2	...	...	...	...
Course inappriate	21	812	28.6	9.6	59	741	20.3	15.7
Poor scholar	48	702	31.3	20.8	122	679	14.3	9.0

[a]For totals by course these samples include only students responding on the *rōnin* question.

[b]See footnote a, table 8.4.

Note. As of 1966, 1,000 yen exchanged for $2.80.

strong pressures to become involved directly in family economic ventures running counter to the individual's educational and career preferences.

For nonfarm youth, further evidence on some of these matters is provided in table 8.5, which presents summary data concerning parental income distributions within categories on the reasons respondents gave for not expecting to receive higher education, despite wishing that they might do so. Taking all students together, regardless of type of secondary curriculum, there are striking contrasts in economic background between the students who gave cost burdens as the principal reason and those specifying obligations to go directly into the family business. The former had the lowest median family incomes and the highest proportions under 500,000 yen a year; proportions in the upper relative income brackets were few. By contrast, those specifying family business as a reason were typically in a strong economic position, at least relative to other groups who wished to go to college but would not. They had by far the highest median incomes, the smallest proportions in low-income brackets, and strikingly high proportions in the upper income ranks. Among the sons of independent entrepreneurs, the closest in income patterns to those specifying cost burdens were students who indicated that their upper-secondary courses virtually precluded entrance to university, undoubtedly reflecting in part the effects of economic constraints in the earlier decision to enter presumptively terminal rather than college-preparatory curricula in upper-secondary school.

Two quite distinct forces are clearly operating as revealed in these data. Economic constraints are dampening or blocking access to higher education both immediately and as reflected in the earlier (Stage I) decision. At the same time, there is a special but important subcategory whose family-linked obligations and opportunities discourage college attendance. These are the sons of families conducting modestly successful enterprises seen as having first claim on the graduate's time and as providing an appropriate career for him in which neither he nor the family as a whole would benefit substantially from his further schooling. There are other successful independent and family entrepreneurs, as we have already seen, who make the other assessment, even as a family matter--judging that the youth would serve the family enterprise best by first continuing through higher education.

Amont the sons of wage and salaried men, family-linked enterprises were virtually (not quite) excluded almost by definition. But there were other differences from sons of independent and family entrepreneurs as well. Among the sons of employees the only important income contrasts in table 8.5 are between those specifying costs as the principal problem or impediment to college attendance as against all other response categories. Two-fifths of the employee fathers of young men specifying the cost barrier had annual earnings below 500,000 yen, and the median for this group was only 552,000 yen.[9]

The only course type with sufficient numbers of respondents in most or all of the response categories on "principal reasons" to justify internal comparison was the technical course. The distinctively low incomes of those specifying cost burden is again evident, both for sons of independent entrepreneurs and for sons of wage and salaried men.

Parental Incomes and the *Rōnin* Year

The importance of the *rōnin* phenomenon, its incidence with respect to upper-secondary schooling (attendance in national, public, or private general schools and vocational schools) and to higher-education goals, and its relation to school grade averages have all been mentioned in earlier discussions. Being a *rōnin* may in itself be expensive because of the delay in labor-force participation--though there is probably more incidental part-time wage work among *rōnin* than usually is remarked or recorded. But the matter is much more complex.

One of the items on our questionnaire asked about attitudes with respect to becoming *rōnin* if necessary to gain entry to the respondent's preferred institution or course. Translated from the Japanese, that question read:

> Will you seek to gain entry to your first choice of college or university even if you are not admitted this year and would have to spend a year or so as a *Rōnin*? Circle the answer that applies.
>
> 1. I won't go to university anyway
> 2. Yes, even if have to spend time as a *Rōnin*
> 3. No, would not spend time as a *Rōnin*
> 4. Not sure

Although conditional, "if" questions are always hazardous, this question is one that is inevitably very much in the minds of seniors in the upper-secondary institutions as they approach the time when they will take examinations for higher education. How well the responses to such a question predict what will happen when this contingency actually arises we do not know, but the degree of assurance in most of the yes and the no positions suggests that the correlation should be high.

When the various ramifications are taken into account, the decision to be a *rōnin* may not necessarily be the most costly alternative open to a given individual or family. Even if we exclude from consideration actual and perceived differences in the stream of future benefits accruing with enrollment in the preferred versus other institutions (the question of being a *rōnin* to gain admittance anywhere aside), it is still possible that to take up an available place in a private institution might be more costly than to take out a *rōnin* year during which a youth prepared successfully for entrance into a national university where, for the four ensuing years, his costs would be heavily subsidized. It is also possible that among many ambitious but poor youth education may be perceived as offering the only visible road to socioeconomic mobility. We might expect, other things equal, that relatively few of the sons of families under the most severe financial stress would seriously contemplate the *rōnin* route; but the questions are whether at such an economic level they would contemplate higher education at all, and once youth did look to higher education, would the *rōnin* path loom larger among those with low or those with high incomes?

An overview of attitudes toward being *rōnin* is presented by type of upper-secondary curriculum in table 8.6. The General B students are divided relatively evenly between the three attitude categories. Because 90 percent of the General B students were anticipating college, these figures imply that of all General B graduates 28 percent definitely would take a *rōnin* year if need be and three-fifths (62 percent) would or might do so. The predominantly rural youth in General A and agriculture rarely contemplate continuing to higher education, and among the small numbers taking examinations a smaller proportion express a definite commitment to taking the *rōnin* route if necessary to attain their educational goals. These students along with the college-directed commerce students are the most inclined to take a firm negative position on the *rōnin* question; they are also less likely than students from other courses to have focused their hopes on institutions of higher education that are among the most difficult of access, with swelling demands relative to places.

Particularly interesting are the responses among the college-directed technical-school graduates. A seventh of the technical students were taking examinations. Among that seventh we find a

Table 8.6 Attitudes toward Becoming *Rōnin*

	General B	General A	Agriculture	Commerce	Technical
Percentage taking exams	90	10	9	18	14
Percentage distribution of those taking exams by attitude on being *rōnin*					
Total	100	100	100	100	100
Yes, definitely	31	23	23	27	43
Uncertain	38	39	33	33	36
No	31	38	44	40	21
Percentage of all students who definitely would be *rōnin*	28	2	2	5	6
Percentage of all students who might or definitely would be *rōnin*	62	6	5	11	11

large proportion who are very determined about realizing their educational ambitions, not only for higher education generally but for a particular type and/or institution of higher education. Only a fifth of them state that they would not become *rōnin*. All in all, 11 percent of all the commerce and of all the technical-course graduates indicated that they definitely would or they might be *rōnin*. In a more detailed analysis (not reproduced here) we found differences in parental income distributions across *rōnin*-attitude groups among the college-directed youth to be negligible. An important exception was the strong emphasis on taking the *rōnin* route if necessary among the college-oriented sons of poor independent or family entrepreneurs in the commerce course.

In this chapter we have discussed (1) the theoretical effects of parental incomes on the costs and benefits of higher education; (2) the extent of income selectivity into various types of higher education as related to the differential costs in 1960 and 1974 (for the latter year we were able to distinguish family income distributions for each type of institution by sex); and (3) associations between family economic situation and college plans (taking examinations) of the upper-secondary seniors of 1966. In this last section we raised the question of how far the effects of parental income found expression primarily at the Stage I decision point, in allocations of youth among types of curricula, and how far the college decisions of youth within each type of course were associated with parental incomes. The ways in which family incomes affected college decisions differed markedly between the entrepreneurs and the sons of wage and salaried workers. A much more detailed sumamrization of the main findings of this chapter is incorporated in chapter 10 under the subheading "The College Decision and 'Ability to Pay.'"

9. Income-Opportunity Perceptions and the College Decision

The economic theory of investment in human beings takes as its starting point an economic rationality assumption which, when applied to the higher-education decision, stipulates that (other things equal) the individual will invest in higher education if, but only if, at the relevant criterion, or reservation, discount rate[1] the present value of the expected future income stream exceeds that associated with direct entry to the labor market from upper secondary school. The higher-education stream has negative values over the years of university study equal to direct outlays on schooling and schooling-related expenses (maintenance costs that would go on regardless of a man's activity are not included). "Foregone earnings" appear in the upper-secondary income stream; they are simply the early part of that earning stream that is missed by attending college or university.

The "other things equal" qualification takes account, for example, of the occupational preferences and nonmonetary satisfactions in the J_{zi} and J_{ti} vectors of our formal model (and also of direct consumer returns). Ideally we would price these satisfactions also and include them in the benefit-cost assessment. The criterion rate of discount is a function in part of family income and access to credit, as we have pointed out in preceding discussions. When the criterion, or "external," rate equals the "internal" rate of return, the individual will be indifferent between continuing school or entering the labor market directly; if the internal rate exceeds the criterion rate, college will be the route chosen, and conversely if the internal rate of return falls short of the criterion, or reservation, rate.[2] If this formulation is valid as a behavioral theory, it should be possible to find some supportive evidence in the perceptions and choices of persons at a critical decision point.

This chapter is divided in two parts. The first part uses observations on individuals to delineate patterns in student expectations of earnings with and without higher education. The second tests the economic theory of the Stage II decision with the use of grouped data.

Expected Peak Earnings and Their Distributions

It is essential in any empirical test of human-investment theory using expectational data to obtain an indicator of individual perceptions of future earnings with and without university education. In other words, the critical question is concerned with perceived differences between the university and nonuniversity earning streams, whatever their respective levels. But people are very hesitant to give direct answers to an open-ended question about their income expectations for the obvious reason that such expectations are never single-valued, and articulation of probabilities or surprise boundaries[3] may be almost as difficult as specification of the parameters of a driver's decision on when to pass a car on the highway. These difficulties are avoided in large measure by posing income expectation questions in a form that directs the respondent to select the most likely category from a set of income classes. This is the way in which we proceeded. Respondents were asked to check the income class best indicating their expectations for the first and fifth years in the labor market and for peak earnings; they did this twice, first assuming no further schooling and then assuming graduation from university. This gave us a set of six answers from each respondent. In analyzing the results, we retained the initial categorical classification for some purposes but in the main converted the data into cardinal variables by interpolating class midpoints from probit transforms for the first-year, fifth-year, and peak-year anticipations. The full analysis of expected life-income paths over the postschool years is deferred to chapter 13, however. Here we focus primarily on expected peak earnings.

Responses with respect to expected peak monthly earnings with and without university education are shown as cumulative distributions in figure 9.1 and summarized in table 9.1. In figure 9.1 the vertical axis is a probability or probit scale in which distances are marked off in standard deviation units on a normal distribution. The horizontal axis is in logarithmic form. The curves shown are cumulative percentages of students in each course type who responded with peak income expectations above the designated levels

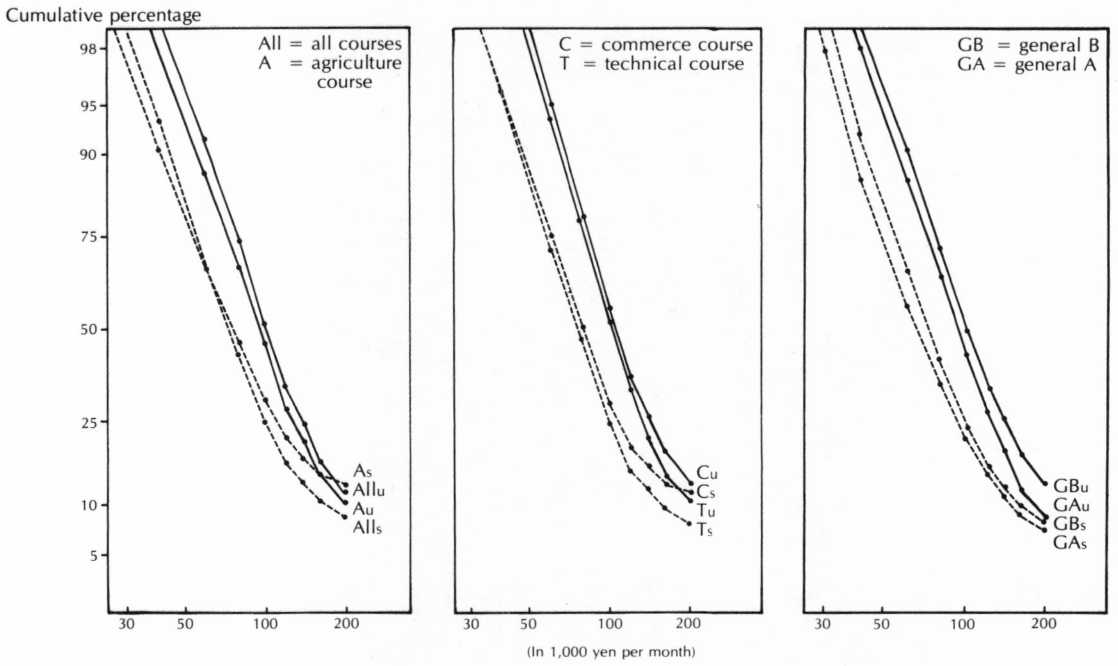

Figure 9.1 Cumulative distributions of predicted peak monthly incomes (percentages above designated levels). *Solid lines*, with university education (subscript *u*); *dashed lines*, with upper-secondary education only (subscript *s*).

Table 9.1 Predicted Peak Monthly Incomes (YL) with and without University Education

	General B	General A	Agriculture	Commerce	Technical	All Students[a]
YLU[b,c]						
Top 25th percentile	140	125	125	145	135	140
Median	98	92	97	107	103	103
75th percentile	77	70	73	85	83	80
YLS[b,c]						
Top 25th percentile	98	92	115	110	102	103
Median	72	65	76	82	77	74
75th percentile	53	47	55	61	59	55
YLU - YLS[c]						
At 25th percentile	42	33	13	35	33	37
At medians	26	27	21	25	26	29
At 75th percentile	24	23	19	24	24	25
YLU/YLS						
At 25th percentile	1.43	1.36	1.11	1.32	1.32	1.36
At medians	1.36	1.42	1.28	1.30	1.34	1.39
At 75th percentile	1.45	1.49	1.35	1.39	1.41	1.42
Percentages above 200,000 yen						
YLU	13	8	11	12	13	12
YLS	8	8	13	8	11	9
YLU - YLS	5	...	-2	4	2	3
Percentages below 50,000 yen						
YLU	4	6	7	2	11	3
YLS	20	28	20	14	15	19
YLU - YLS	-16	-22	-13	-12	-4	-16

assuming no further schooling (the dashed lines) and assuming university education (the solid lines). The "all" curve is from the adjusted sample, in which proportions in each type of curriculum match the actual distribution among curricula in Japan as of 1966. A straight line in these distributions would be a logarithmically normal distribution; the steeper the slope of that line, the less the dispersion in responses weighted logarithmically. We used

	General B	General A	Agriculture	Commerce	Technical	All Students[a]
Own peak income expectations[d]						
Arith. means[c]	115	87	102	100	94	103
Geom. means[c]	110	73	86	86	82	89
Coefficient of variation	1.86	1.50	1.56	1.62	1.73	1.72
Arith. mean/geom. mean	1.05	1.19	1.18	1.16	1.15	1.15

[a]Adjusted sample.

[b]YLU = prediction assuming university education. YLS = prediction assuming no education beyond secondary school.

[c]Thousand yen.

[d]Taking the responses on YLU or YLS according to whether the respondent is, respectively, taking or not taking examinations for higher education.

three panels simply because differences among course types were too small for visual readability on a single panel. Table 9.1 does part of the curve reading for us, by taking the median and quartile positions of all curves and laying them out in summary form.

Certain key features of these distributions are evident from even the most casual inspection of figure 9.1. First, differences between the expected college and noncollege peak earnings are generally much greater than differences among courses at all probit levels (or cumulative percentages) excepting the upper segments of the distributions. This is evident in comparisons of distances between the solid and between the dashed lines as compared with differences between a solid and its corresponding dashed curve. Second, in all cases the distributions closely approximate a lognormal form except, again, at the top, where some tail out (are distinctly skewed) even in logarithmic terms. That tailing or skewness is especially noticeable for the noncollege distributions among the students of agriculture and commerce. Also, as table 9.1 shows, the commerce and technical-course students were overall the most optimistic in their peak income assessments when those perceptions were specified for higher education. The most modest anticipations, with or without university education, were those expressed by students in General A and agriculture.

Differences between the university and nonuniversity income peaks anticipated by students in each curriculum are summarized in two ways in table 9.1: according to absolute differences at the medians and at the upper and lower quartiles, and according to income ratios at those same positions. In terms of the absolute differences, the students of agriculture generally distinguished much less between university and nonuniversity expected incomes than did students in other courses, and the General B students gave the university option the greatest edge in the upper 25th percentile of the distribution. Otherwise the patterns in absolute differences were very much the same from one curriculum to another, with differentials ranging from around 24,000 yen at the low quartile to around 34,000 yen at the upper quartile position. In ratio terms this is reversed (except for General B), the highest ratios in each case being at the lower ranges of the distributions--as is apparent also in figure 9.1.

The last block of entries in table 9.1 differs from all others in that it refers to the peak income estimate applicable to the individual in terms of his college expectations. Thus, if a youth was taking entrance examinations, the response used for him was his estimate for university men; if he was not taking examinations, the response was for noncollege men. This explains why the General B students were the highest in both arithmetic and geometric mean "own peak income expectations," even though commerce and technical students had higher medians for both the university and the noncollege estimates as given by all students regardless

Table 9.2 Students' Own Peak Monthly Income Expectations within Preferred Employment Status (geometric means in thousands of yen)

Preferred Peak Employment Status	General B	General A	Agriculture	Commerce	Technical	All[a]
Independent, family	113	87	98	104	93	100
Employee						
Government	79	64	72	78	73	74
Big corporation	106	77	78	83	85	91
Small firm	96	67	70	75	77	77

[a]Adjusted sample.

of their anticipations with respect to their own further education. General B students were the most spread out in their own peak income expectations if we measure relative dispersion by the coefficient of variation, but their distribution was also the one with the lowest skewness--as is shown by the low ratio of arithmetic to geometric mean. All the distributions were characterized by some positive skew.

Students' own expectations are shown in table 9.2 by curriculum and preferred peak employment status. In this table we have used geometric means. Several generalizations can be made from these data. First, within each preferred employment status the General B students had the highest income expectations, though among those preferring government employment commerce students had virtually the same expectations as General B students. Second, regardless of curriculum, youth expressing a preference for independent employment or employment in a family enterprise expected significantly higher peak earnings on the average than did those in any other category. Third, the next most lucrative sort of employment in the income predictions of these youths was in big private enterprise. Those looking forward to employment in government or in small private firms anticipated the lowest peak earnings.

On the average, students' perceived income peaks for the future were remarkably close to earnings reported by the wage and salaried men among their fathers. The 1966 incomes reported by employee fathers with university education averaged 1.27 million yen in Tokyo and Osaka and 1.2 million yen elsewhere in our samples. Dividing by twelve to put these figures on a monthly basis, we have 106,000 and 100,000 yen per month, as compared with median students' estimates of peak earnings for university graduates of 103,000 yen (shown in the last column of table 9.1). The correspondence for average incomes of fathers with upper-secondary education and students' median estimates of future peak incomes with upper-secondary schooling only was equally close.[4]

While it is clear enough that overall and in most curricula secondary-school seniors expected that earnings would be higher with than without university education, this says nothing about the effects of differences in those expectations on decisions to seek college education. Overall, we found highly significant correlations between perceived differentials and college intentions, but this was primarily a reflection of our relatively large samples; only minute fractions of the variance in the perceived earnings differentials could be explained statistically by the variable EXAM. Moreover, the associations looked quite different within different subsamples distinguished by type of curriculum--due in part, of course, to the fact that choice of curriculum in the first place reflected anticipations of going on to higher education or of not doing so. In any case, given the complex of nonlinear complicating factors in the college decision, we turned to aggregations of observations as a way of screening out some of the relatively idiosyncratic or unmeasured factors in observations on individuals.

Income Expectations and the Higher-Education Decision: An Analysis with Aggregated Data

Given our interest in comparisons among types of curricula as steps in career paths, along with the fact that our samples had been drawn by classrooms and schools, the most useful aggregation procedure for analysis of income expectations and the higher-education decision was to group individuals by classrooms. With such groupings we could analyze results for the entire sample, regardless of type of course, and we could also examine relationships separately, by curriculum. We treated as separate "classes" or "classrooms" all students in our sample for a particular school who reported that they were taking examinations and all those reporting that they were not. Thus, in most cases we had two "classrooms"per school, although some school samples provided only one "classroom" unit because the students reporting that they were (or that they were not) taking examinations were too few to justify use of a group mean.

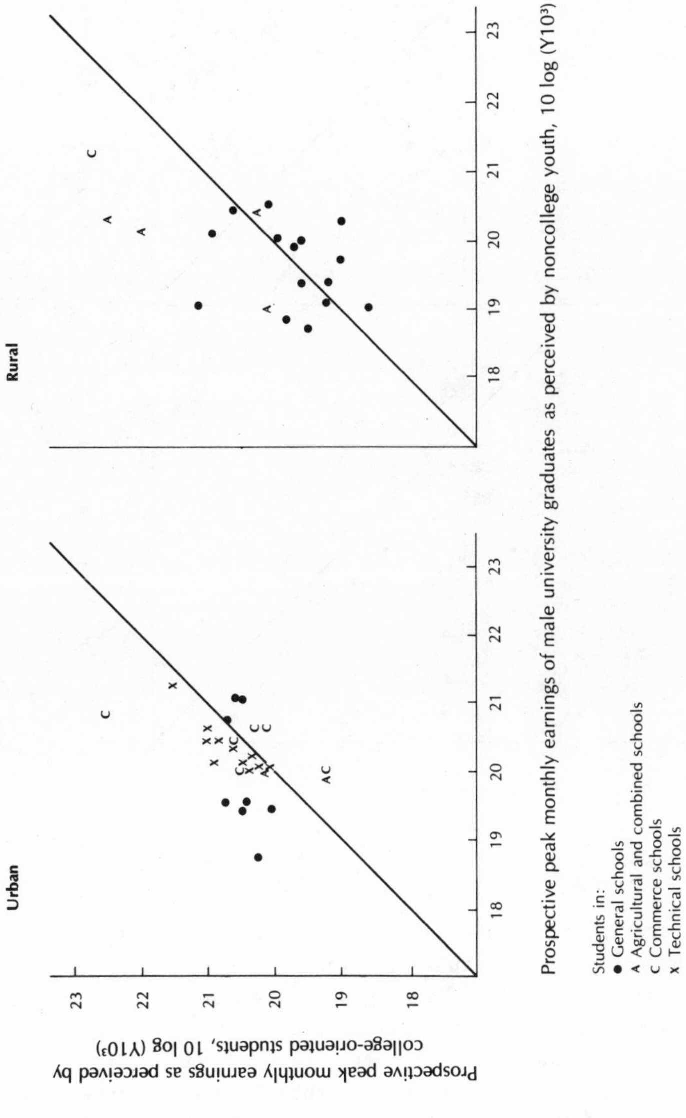

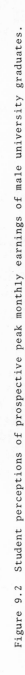

Figure 9.2 Student perceptions of prospective peak monthly earnings of male university graduates.

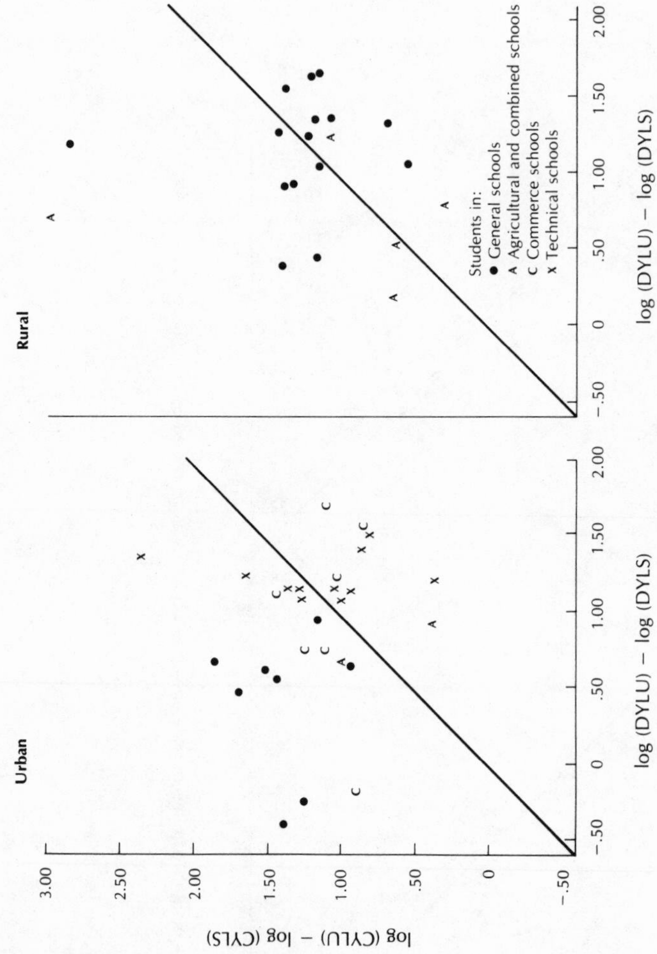

Figure 9.3 Student perceptions of college/noncollege differentials in prospective peak monthly earnings.

The scattergrams in figures 9.2 and 9.3 compare school by school the prospective peak monthly earnings of university men as perceived by those students taking examinations (on the vertical scale) and those not taking examinations (on the horizontal scale). Urban schools are shown at the left, rural at the right; and in both cases symbols indicate the type of school involved. Entries above (to the left) of the diagonal are those in which the college-directed students averaged higher than the noncollege students in their estimates of peak earnings of university men, and conversely for those below (to the right) of the diagonal. It is also easy to observe from these charts to what extent mean income expectations of these two categories of students within the same schools were associated. Generally the association was slight with the exception of the technical-school students, where a positive association was indicated. Among the urban general students (who were predominantly General B) there was very little relative variation among school means in the income anticipations of those expecting to continue with higher education, but a wide interschool variation in these estimates among students not taking examinations. In all cases the technical-school observations and in most cases those for the urban general schools lie where we might expect them, other things equal; that is, they are above the diagonal, the college-directed youth estimating higher peak incomes for university men than were estimated by their classmates who were not seeking further education. Among the commerce students, on the other hand, there is no relation of this sort, nor do we find any such pattern in the rural general schools. The one rural commerce course sample with enough students in both categories to include in this analysis, like one of the urban commerce schools, lies far above the diagonal even though it is also high on the horizontal axis. Also striking is the contrast between college-directed and other students in three of the five agricultural schools; but it must be remembered that the numbers and proportions of students in these schools taking examinations are small.

What these perceptions may mean for the expectational economics of the higher-education decision depends, among other things, on whether high estimates for peak earnings of university people are accompanied by correspondingly high estimates for peak earnings of men with upper-secondary schooling only, and vice versa. Figure 9.3 expresses these differences in relative terms, as the difference between the mean logarithm of estimated YLU and estimated YLS, where YLU is the estimated peak income of men with university education and YLS the estimated peak of men with upper-secondary schooling only. Again, the means for the perceptions of student groups taking examinations (designated *C*) are plotted on the vertical, those for noncollege groups (designated *D*) on the horizontal axis. Looking first at the panel to the left, we see two striking contrasts with figure 9.2. All general students are now above the diagonal line; without exception, the urban general students taking examinations averaged higher ratios of estimated university to secondary peak earning options than did students not taking examinations. On the other hand, the technical-school students spread out above and below the diagonal, with widely diverging ratios in the responses of those taking examinations but a narrow range of these relative assessments among students anticipating direct entry to the labor market. Commerce students reversed the pattern displayed by the technical-school students, in that the variations in relative assessments seemed to be greater across schools for those who were not taking examinations than for those who were doing so. These patterns are entirely consistent with both the complexities introduced by family enterprises, affecting the noncollege commerce students, and the kinds of job options visualized by technical as compared with general students (to which we will turn in chapters 11 and 13). Among the rural youth, on the other hand, there was no systematic pattern at all. If those rural youth who entertained ambitions for higher education differed from the rest of the rural students in their economic assessments of the implications of that choice, it must have been on account of other dimensions of the economic prospects than estimates of future peak incomes resulting from one option relative to the other.

Clearly one of these other considerations could be immediate earnings foregone, which are approximated by perceptions of what the youth might expect to earn at entry to the labor market from upper-secondary school. Responses on this point were tightly clustered, but with somewhat higher figures on foregone earnings perceived by the college-directed youth, both urban and rural. The differences were greatest in a few of the urban general schools, where the noncollege students averaged exceptionally low in their estimates of direct-entry wages, and in three rural agricultural schools, where the college-directed students specified exceptionally high estimates of potential earnings in a first job from upper-secondary school. The close clustering on estimates for job-entry wages compared with the spreads on estimates of career-peak earnings (even when we take school means rather than individual observations as the basis for our analysis) leaves patterns of net benefits much as those shown for peak earnings, albeit with the college/noncollege differences slightly damped.

We present overall averages in table 9.3 giving each group observa-

Table 9.3 Summary of Effects of Location and Type of Course on Assessments of Economic Advantage of Higher Education

	Urban Students		Rural Students	
	Taking Exams	Non-college	Taking Exams	Non-college
	$\bar{G}$ (YLU - YLS)[a]			
All students	27	20	28	12
Students in (school or course)				
General (B and A)	31	9	25	23
Commerce	25	14	34	28
Technical	27	26	...	...
Agriculture, independent	14	17	16	13
Agriculture, in combined school	...	...	38	20
	University-Advantage Indexes[b]			
All students	4.04	3.23	4.40	1.91
Students in (school or course)				
General (B and A)	4.49	1.48	3.88	3.57
Commerce	3.79	2.26	5.28	4.58
Technical	4.12	4.14	...	...
Agriculture, independent	2.12	2.76	2.19	1.89
Agriculture, in combined school	...	...	6.74	3.14

[a] Where $\bar{G}$ refers to the geometric means and YLU and YLS specify predicted peak monthly income respectively with and without university education.

[b] $10 \times \bar{G}$ (YLU - YLS)/(4xY1S), where Y1S refers to predicted monthly earnings at first job on direct entry to the labor market from upper-secondary school.

tion a weight of 1. The main findings are easily stated:

1. Overall, youth taking examinations perceived a greater income advantage in going to college than did those anticipating direct entry into the labor market. This contrast was strongest and most consistent among the rural students.

2. The most striking contrast was that between the college-going and other youth within the urban general schools. Contrasts were still noteworthy among the urban commerce students and among students in the rural agricultural combined schools.

3. The inclusion of perceived foregone earnings in the university-advantage indexes (in the lower part of the table) did not alter the evidence for a monetary economic rationale in

the rural combined-school samples. However, it had no predictive power among students in the technical curricula or in the independent agricultural secondary schools.

Taken together, these results are further evidence that whatever the perceptions of seniors in the various curricula may have been with respect to income prospects with and without higher education, it was earlier perceptions (of the students or their parents) that were most critical in the college decision. That decision was anticipated in considerable part (though not wholly) by the decision made at Stage I, with choice of upper-secondary curriculum.

10. The Higher-Education Decision Reviewed

In chapters 6 through 9 the basic decision models presented earlier were specified with respect to the higher-education decision. It was hypothesized that youth seek entry to institutions of higher education according to their perceptions (and their parents' perceptions) of the net benefits of such schooling with respect to career prospects. Those prospects are viewed in terms both of monetary rewards and of preferences relating to other aspects of career options associated with direct labor market entry or higher education. Young people make this decision subject to two main sorts of constraints: (*a*) individual ability and achievement levels in school, and (*b*) the ability to pay (in an imperfect capital market) for the financing of investments in one's self.

We hypothesized further that, controlling for parental background, information concerning and perceptions of the advantages of obtaining further education for career purposes would be a positive function of degree of metropolitanism; the more metropolitan areas presumably would make more visible both a wide range of career options and educational selectivity into those careers.

Finally, we anticipated that experience in the upper-secondary schools, including not only school activities and training per se but also peer-group traits and increased knowledge of the adult world geenerally, would modify students' initial perceptions of college options and of the subsequent implications of the higher-education decision. However, no explicit hypothesis concerning the nature or direction of shifts in perceptions or preferences was attempted. The findings concerning upper-secondary course preferences initially and in hindsight, discussed in chapter 4, already had indicated that substantial shifts do in fact occur, and that they are especially frequent precisely where the information is most limited and the direction of endeavor least defined--that is, among youth in the rural General A streams and nonfarm students of agriculture. Among the questions concerning educational decisions is indeed the extent to which Stage I and

Stage II decisions are interlocked, the Stage II decision being anticipated at Stage I.

Each of these elements in our analysis has many ramifications and points up a wide range of problems. However, we select out only a few strands from the empirical findings for this summary, grouping them under five broad headings.

Higher-Education Plans and Attendance by Type of Upper-Secondary Course

Among the important questions about relations between course type and continuation into higher education are not only the contrasts by course in the proportions taking examinations and gaining entrance to higher institutions but also whether the vocational-school youth with college aspirations hope to go more deeply into fields closely related to their specializations at the upper-secondary level or to shift to quite other fields of study. In the remarks that follow we draw both on our survey of the graduates of 1967 and on the special study made by the Ministry of Education in 1968, supplemented by some summary information for more recent years.

1. In Japan the choice of an academic general as against any other upper-secondary curriculum is for many youth simultaneously a decision (voluntary or otherwise) with respect to continuation into higher education, and is indeed so viewed by the students. But this is not by any means the whole story. There were minorities of General B students (in our male sample, 10 percent) who did not even take examinations for entry to institutions of higher education, and there are nonacademic general and vocational-school students who do continue.

Among the vocational-school youth in our 1966-67 sample, the proportions stipulating intent to take examinations ranged betweeen 10 and 20 percent; the lowest proportions were those studying agriculture (who also have the fewest hours in basic language, mathematics, and science courses); the highest proportions were found in some of the commerce schools, with the technical-school youth in between. As of 1968, graduates of vocational schools accounted for 10 to 11 percent of the upper-secondary graduates going directly into institutions of higher education without an interval as *rōnin*; they were of course a somewhat larger fraction (22 percent) of the very small group who entered night schools at the higher level. Despite the rapid spread of upper-secondary schooling to include 90 percent of the youth of 1975, the proportion of graduates of vocational upper-secondary schools taking examinations for further education has also been rising.

2. Most of those graduates of vocational upper-secondary schools who hope to continue into higher education are interested in pushing their studies more deeply and to higher levels in fields closely associated with their specialization at the upper-secondary level. We estimated these specialist proportions (using data from the ministry's 1968 survey) at between two-thirds and three-fourths for the (rare) college-oriented graduates of agricultural schools, between 70 and 80 percent among college-directed graduates of technical and commerce schools. Two-fifths of the 1968 commerce students who hoped to continue reported that they had intended to do so from the start.

Among the college-oriented youth in our sample of students in technical upper-secondary schools, many had initially had at least junior-college ambitions and had actually tried to get into the five-year technical junior colleges. But there had also been a further sorting out of ability within the technical streams, and youth who had been most successful there were setting their sights on full university education. Because they had proved themselves in an upper-secondary education that had relatively strong mathematical-theoretical underpinnings, they were also in most instances happy with and oriented toward pursuit of higher technical studies. The survival and re-creation of technical secondary education more nearly in a German-French than an American pattern undoubtedly contribute to the formation of this ambitious elite among the technical-school students. That effect might be greater if smoother paths into technical higher education were available.

3. Among the 1968 general and vocational-school graduates alike, a majority of those (male and female) who hoped to enter full four-year courses in higher education expressed a preference for the private universities, but this tendency was very much stronger for the vocational than the general graduates (85 percent and 55 percent, respectively). The actual figure among those going directly to college (for general- and vocational-school graduates combined) was 78 percent entering the private universities. However, of those aiming at entry to national and public universities very high proportions became *rōnin*--roughly half of those with such ambitions who had completed general courses and 60 percent of their counterparts from the vocational schools. On the other hand, more of the general-school graduates who tried for

entry to private universities became *rōnin* than their vocational-school counterparts (at 30 and 20 percent, respectively). These findings are confounded by the fact that there was no distinction by sex in the ministry's tabulations. Nevertheless, two facts seem reasonably clear: (*a*) The high proportions of vocational-school youth giving private institutions of higher education as their preference is associated with the ambition of many young men to make their careers in private enterprise and, quite frequently, as their own bosses some years hence; technical or commerce students, they are oriented to business. Evidence on this point is clear enough in the responses of the students in our male sample for 1966-67, as we will show in chapter 11. (*b*) It is much easier to get into the private than the public and national universities, as the *rōnin* figures attest; this fact is especially important for youth who take the vocational courses at the upper-secondary level. Expensive as they may be, the private universities may nevertheless make very good economic sense for those graduates of vocational schools who can find a way to finance four-year higher education, whatever the category of institutional control.

The College Decision and "Ability to Pay"

Indicators of "ability to pay" for higher education are both direct and indirect (among the indirect measures are parental education and occupational status). Under this heading, however, we will refer only to direct monetary measures of parental economic position.

Ability to pay depends upon both income and costs. For individuals, net costs will be affected by access to scholarships and by relative ease of borrowing (which is in turn related to family income). Costs depend also on the particular higher-education option. The chief differences so far as tuition and other specifically education-related outlays are concerned can be summed up briefly in two dimensions: (*a*) whether the institution is national or private (with a few of the non-national "public" institutions usually closer to the figure for the national colleges and universities), and (*b*) whether the student enters a day or a night college or university. Within these cells the annual costs do not differ much between the four-year institutions and the junior colleges, but the latter are of course less expensive in that they entail outlays for a shorter period of time. Night schools, and night junior colleges in particular, are decidedly the least costly, especially when we take into account the fact that comparatively little income is foregone and there is no need to have recourse to high-interest borrowing.

The ranking of day universities by costs of attending is relatively easy so long as we do not consider prior costs of gaining access to them. However, that caveat is an important one. For the brilliant student who passes examinations for entry to a national university without prior attendance at a prestige upper-secondary school or any supplementary tutoring or preparatory out-of-school investments, the national institution is unquestionably the least expensive. The cost situation is complicated, however, for those who must become *rōnin* and for those whose upper-secondary curriculum severely constrains the chances of acceptance in the national institutions.

Keeping in mind the differences in costs of attending one or another higher institution, we are now ready to look at the data relating parental incomes to college plans and attendance as a set of relations that reflect the influence of ability to pay. (It must be remembered that this is to look at only one side of the economics of the decision, however. The other side, the expected economic gains, will be considered in the next section, "Perceived Future Earning Differentials and College Plans.") We drew here on both published studies and our own survey data. The latter include incomes reported by fathers in wage and salaried employment and, separately, by entrepreneurs in their own or a family business.

1. The first effect of parental incomes is on whether young people attend upper-secondary school at all, and if so where. The poorest youth of 1964 had often been filtered out even before entry to any sort of upper-secondary school; the most favorably situated financially were the most likely to find their way into a university-preparatory stream provided they had the wish to do so. A majority of those in a favorable economic situation did seem to make the academic decision, anticipating the university options that would arise at Stage II. However, it is not clear how far this behavior was in fact a reflection of parental incomes and anticipated ability to pay for higher education, how far rather it may have been a reflection of particular career perceptions that were associated with high parental education and occupational status. Taking parental incomes as the measure, economically advantaged students also enrolled in significant numbers in the commerce courses, which sent more of their male graduates on to college than did any others except General B.

2. There is ample evidence that parental income is associated with the likelihood of attending some institution of higher education rather than entering the labor market directly from upper-secondary school. This evidence is repeated in public documents for 1960, 1965, and 1974 (and other years) in which family income distributions for the two major groups are compared. We were able to go further with our data in that we could control for parental education and occupation; even with such controls, parental income exercised a highly significant influence on the likelihood of taking examinations. For sons of entrepreneurs there is a special problem of interpretation of these findings, since among such youth parental income is likely to reflect not only ability to pay but also the existence of opportunities in a comparatively sophisticated family business. In any case, along with the significant positive correlations there is a large overlapping in the distributions of income among the college-bound and other young men. Whether we regard the evidence as indicating a "high" or a comparatively "low" degree of economic selectivity to higher education will of course depend in part on what sort of relation we expect and on how we interpret it. The association of going to college with parental economic status is clear enough, but it may be regarded as remarkable that so many from economically less advantaged homes nevertheless continue.

3. The influence of family income is systematically related to type of higher institution. In our sample, youth whose parents had the lowest incomes were the most likely to go directly to the labor market; the next economic level had the largest proportion taking examinations for night college or university (except in rural areas); the economically most advantaged were the most likely to take examinations for day colleges and universities. This pattern was found within course types as well as for the sample as a whole.

Data from the 1960, 1968, and 1974 surveys enabled us to take the next step, to distinguish among national, public, and private universities and colleges. The association between family income and the relatively more or less expensive higher-education options is evident in the findings, although the 1960 and 1968 data are contaminated by the lack of distinctions between the sexes. Sex breaks were available from the 1974 study, and it is safe to assume that the results have been relatively stable in pattern even if not in precise magnitudes. Whether the data are summarized with the use of means or medians or proportions from low- and from high-income families, the national universities consistently have the largest proportions of youth from comparatively low-income families; the private universities are at the opposite extreme; and the public universities are in between, but closer to the national than to the private institutions. This pattern applies to each sex, but with a steeper gradient for the women. The day junior colleges repeat this pattern, but in a moderated form. The associations for night junior colleges are less systematic, reflecting the fact that some of the public, but especially the private, night junior colleges have low costs; they are extremely diverse in both quality and curriculum content.

A number of factors combine to explain why as family incomes rise the rates of attendance at private universities go up more than do those at other higher institutions--and that this happens even though the private universities account for an even larger proportion of the college-bound youth from the vocational schools than of those from the general curricula. Especially important is the fact that examinations for entry are easier. Less able or more diligent youth who have strong economic backing can buy their way into many private institutions without facing such severe academic competition as they would face for the national and public universities, although a few private universities are exceptions. Interpersonal and related career-opportunity networks of those attending the private and the national or public institutions may also be different, especially when we contrast the business community and sons of comparatively successful businessmen with sons of men in the professions and of employees in government bureaucracies.

4. On the negative side, young men whose fathers are deceased appear to be the least likely to anticipate college attendance of any sort. This effect is especially marked among students in the technical and commerce curricula. This finding is all the more significant when we remember that sons of deceased fathers are more likely to enter those curricula in the first place, whatever the other components of their family backgrounds.

Perceived Future Earning Differentials and College Plans

In a very simple world in which "other things are equal" we could predict with reasonable assurance that the greater the difference between earnings anticipated with and those anticipated without higher education, the greater would be the likelihood that an individual would opt for entrance to college and would take examinations to that end. Indeed, we can apply this sort of reasoning in a very permissive decision model that gives wide scope also for nonmonetary preferences and for variations among individuals in those preferences. However, the various "other things," including interpersonal differences both in nonmonetary preferences and in real costs of further education, confound any simplistic use of anticipated income differentials for the prediction of which particular individuals will and will not elect to continue their education. The conventional model predicts only (*a*) that if you increase the anticipated earning differential for a given individual (which is automatically to hold "other things equal"), you increase the likelihood that he will opt for higher education, and (*b*) that if you do this for an entire group of individuals, you increase the proportion among that group who will make the college choice.

The tests we used in comparing groups of college-oriented with other students according to their perceptions of prospective earning differentials with and without university education are not by any means ideal, but they do provide rough approximations. The test is a strong one in that lack of positive results (or even, for some situations, negative results) could still be consistent with conventional theory. Negative findings can rule out only a rigid formulation of the theory that says the "other things" are either unimportant or invariant across the units of observation. It will be remembered that we used two indicators. One was the difference between projected incomes twenty to thirty years into the future if the individual received university education and if he did not. The other took those predictions and related them to perceptions of earnings that would be foregone while attending college. Results differed by type of course.

1. Taking all students across courses but for the urban and rural populations separately, those anticipating college projected greater economic advantages of college education than did the non-college men; this was especially striking among rural youth.

2. Results clearly supported the "economic," or investment, decision hypothesis among students in the urban general streams; in every school the anticipated differentials were greater among the students taking examinations than among those anticipating direct labor market entry. On the average, there was confirmation among the commerce students as well.

3. On the other hand, there was very little contrast between the responses of students taking examinations and those not taking

them in the technical courses, in the urban agricultural schools, and in the rural general schools. Other factors predominated in sorting these students out between college and labor market. By their own reports these factors included especially financial constraints, inadequate performance as a scholar, and pressures to terminate schooling to participate immediately in family undertakings.

Influences of Parental Education and Occupation

Parental education and occupational status exercise significant effects on the likelihood of taking university examinations. Some of the ways those influences may operate have been discussed at a number of points in previous chapters, but especially in chapter 7. We will not repeat any of those discussions, and our summary here will be brief.

1. These influences operate both via selection into the academic upper-secondary streams in the first place and then subsequently within whatever secondary course is taken. At an individual level, the effects via course selection are the more important, however.

2. The within-course effects of parental education operate mainly to distinguish sons from the least educated homes (with the smallest proportions taking university-entry examinations) from all others. The nonacademic general students were a dramatic exception; parental education differentiated very sharply among these youth in their examination behavior.

3. The within-course effects of a father's occupational status are limited, though relations are generally ordered in the expected direction among youth in the vocational curricula: the higher his father's occupational status, the greater the likelihood that a youth will seek university education; the lower his father's occupational status, the less the likelihood that he will do so.

4. There are multiple dimensions in the effects of paternal occupation on the ways in which students perceive future opportunities and on the nature of those opportunities (and related constraints). Paternal employment status and field of activity are striking examples. It is no accident that college-bound sons of proprietors and managers have been the most likely to attend private universities, and not solely on account of the ability to pay for places in those institutions. At the same time, next to

students in agriculture it was those in commerce who most often specified that they could not continue into higher education because of pressures to join immediately in a family enterprise. We found also, as we should expect, that first sons of farmers typically attend courses in agriculture, with their small allocation of time to the basic general academic subjects. Nor is it accidental that youth in some situations have much more definite views about their goals and how they hope to move toward those goals than do youth in other situations. Some of these matters will be pursued in part 4.

Classroom Composition, Rurality, and the College Decision

Most of the preceding remarks referred to observations on individuals, whatever the family backgrounds of their classmates, except as those backgrounds may have been reflected in the observed contrasts of college orientations by type of course. But peer influences can be important in addition to and independently of the course of study and the individual's own background. We looked into this queston in two ways. First, we predicted likelihoods that an individual would take examinations using equations (within each course type) in which variables measuring classroom composition were and were not included along with measures of the individual's own family characteristics. Second, we assessed the combined effects of location, classroom composition, and curriculum on the proportions of youth in the class who were taking examinations; in this analysis our units of observation were thus entire classrooms. The results are important, though we state them briefly.

1. Among youth in the commerce, technical, and General A curricula, classroom composition had a significant effect on the likelihood of college attendance, even when controls were included on the student's own background. This effect was especially strong among students in the commerce course, reflecting variations in the background characteristics and expectations of those students (some of which will become clearer in part 4).

2. In the analysis taking entire classrooms as the units of observation, we obtained very striking results. We conducted a test (appendix C) using simultaneous equation techniques to determine whether there was any single-equation bias of the coefficients on classroom composition in the explanations of the proportions taking examinations. We concluded that there was no such

bias. This justified the use of path analysis to estimate how far classroom composition affected the proportions taking examinations (*a*) *indirectly* (through its association with a cardinal measure of curriculum content), and (*b*) *directly* (with curriculum content held constant). Both the "direct effect" and the "indirect effect" were powerful, but to our surprise the direct effect was by far the greater, accounting for three-fifths or more of the total effect of classroom composition on the proportions taking examinations.

3. Taken by themselves, indicators of degrees of metropolitanism or of geographic isolation had remarkably little effect on the proportions of youth taking examinations, but this reflected a very complex interplay among types of courses available and their curriculum content, socioeconomic composition of the classroom, and time distance from urban centers. Geographic isolation as measured by our SLOW-50 index (time by ordinary train or bus to the nearest place of fifty thousand or more) had negative indirect effects on the proportions taking examinations through its negative effects on classroom composition. However, controlling for classroom composition, relative geographic isolation had positive direct effects on curriculum and through this it had associated indirect positive effects on the proportions taking examinations. Controlling for both classroom composition and curriculum content, the direct effect of rurality on the proportions taking examinations was negligible. These findings along with those on classroom effects call for further investigations, going beyond what can be done with the data available to us.

Part 4

Careers in a Context of Change

11. Occupational Paths: Student Expectations and Cohort Experiences

Student Expectations and Cohort Experiences

Just as choice of type of upper-secondary school and decisions with respect to higher education condition the range of future career options most readily available or most difficult to attain, so also, at the point of entry into working life, people are making choices that will affect in greater or lesser degree the future courses of their lives. Japanese youth are aware of this fact, although they vary in the extent of that awareness and in their knowledge of what might lie ahead, as in their readiness to formulate their thoughts in relatively explicit terms. It must be recognized furthermore, in analyzing their responses, that initial postschool choices, like previous educational decisions, are made in a world of considerably less than full certainty. The expectations and the uncertainties are of two general kinds: those with respect to what will be happening in the economy and in labor markets in general, and those that refer to individuals in particular. These are merged in the individual's assessments of the alternatives.

It is to perceptions of future career development and to how those perceptions relate to what has been happening in the Japanese occupational structure that we now turn. We look first, in this chapter, at occupations. In chapter 12 we compare the ways in which students and their fathers perceive Japanese labor markets. Then, in chapter 13, we examine expected earning streams.

There are many dimensions in which we might view occupational paths. Here we examine three: (1) employment status (distinguishing between independent work and wage work and among wage employment in government, in large firms, and in small enterprises); (2) types of occupations; and (3) occupational status.

Employment Status: Facts and Preferences

Japan is today a leading industrial nation whose growth dynamic has been the envy of the world. Along with the high level of industrialization goes an occupational and employment structure more like those of Western Europe and the United States than those of the less developed nations. But the Japanese structure is also distinctive. As late as the early 1960s more than a fourth of the economically active population was still engaged in agriculture. Moreover, within each of the major nonagricultural sectors family workers were far more important than in the West: they made up 6 percent of those in manufacturing and of those in service industries, and a fifth of those engaged in trade. The drift in Japan since 1960 unquestionably has been toward the Western pattern: the decrease in family workers from a fourth of the Japanese labor force in 1960 to a sixth in 1970 (for males, down from 11 to 6 percent) was matched by almost equal increases in wage workers. However, this is almost entirely a reflection of shifts from farm to city. The trade and service industries have retained substantial numbers of small and family enterprises, and even in manufacturing family endeavor continues. At the other extreme, the relatively small proportions employed in government even among the highly educated is a striking feature of the Japanese economy (only a tenth of the employed males and 6 percent of the employed females). Japan, closely following the United States, has been a leader in the proportion of businessmen with higher education.

Among the nonfarm fathers of our students, the proportions who were proprietors or members of a family enterprise substantially exceeded the proportion recorded in the self-employed (independent) category in the 1960, 1965, and 1970 censuses. There are several reasons for these comparatively high figures, shown in the next-to-last row of table 11.1. First, the definitions are not comparable, since the census count excluded but we included men running a family business who formally received salaries as family employees. Second, the age factor is important: in Japan, as elsewhere, over the course of their lives men are more likely to move into independent enterprise and proprietor status from wage employment than vice versa. Moreover, long-term trends probably are against independent and own-account employment relative to wage work. The fact that of nonfarm sons the highest proportions with fathers in independent employment were in the General A and commerce curricula is to be expected. Small entrepreneurs and own-account workers are relatively more frequent in the rural areas from which General A students come. Furthermore, whether they are rural or urban, fathers in small independent businesses are the most inclined to urge their sons to acquire commercial skills at upper-secondary school.

Table 11.1 Relation between Son's Preferred Employment Status, His Upper-Secondary Course Enrollment, and His Father's Occupational Category (percentage distributions)

	General B	General A	Agriculture	Commerce	Technical
Sons of Wage and Salaried Men					
Number of cases	620	82	58	336	987
Preferred employment status					
Independent (ME)	34.8	23.2	31.0	36.9	34.0
Government (GOV)	17.6	26.8	29.3	11.9	10.2
Big private (BIG)	37.4	18.3	15.5	27.7	26.2
Small private (SMALL)	8.2	31.7	24.1	22.9	27.9
Other, nonresponse	1.9	...	...	.6	1.6
Total	99.9	100.0	99.9	100.0	99.9
Sons of Men in Nonfarm Independent and Family Enterprise					
Number of cases	300	49	26	242	389
Preferred employment status					
Independent (ME)	55.3	49.0	34.6	63.2	47.8
Government (GOV)	10.0	20.4	26.9	4.6	6.7
Big private (BIG)	25.0	10.2	23.1	15.7	22.6
Small private (SMALL)	8.3	20.4	11.5	15.3	21.1
Other, nonresponse	1.3	...	3.9	1.2	1.8
Total	99.9	100.0	100.0	100.0	100.0
All Nonfarm Fathers					
Percentage in independent and family enterprise	33	37	31	42	28
Percentage of sons preferring independence	33	33	29	38	38

It is risky to draw inference about a society from the casual observations of members of academic communities. In Japan in particular, a common academic presupposition seems to be that virtually "everyone" would rather work for a big company, or for the government, than for a small firm, and that independent status offers relatively little promise. However, many seniors in Japan's upper-secondary schools had other ideas, as table 11.1 shows. Realistic or not, sizable minorities in all cases saw independence in their own enterprises or professional activities as a goal for their mature years.[1] Among the sons of men in nonfarm independent and family enterprises, a majority of those in General B and in commerce had such hopes, as did roughly half of those in General A and in technical courses. We estimated the proportion of youth in each curriculum who would be independent if they realized their preferences; the results, given in the last row of the table, are easily compared with the associated percentages of fathers who are independent. There would be little slippage into wage employment in any of the courses with the partial exception of General A. There would be a net increase of independent entrepreneurs (over their fathers) among men in the commerce course and a marked increase among those in the technical curriculum. Especially among youth in the technical curricula, these ambitions are associated with hopes of higher occupational attainment with or, often, without higher education. Such hopes may be somewhat less unrealistic than they appear at first glance, for there seems to be a rising tendency among some of the larger Japanese firms to set up skilled manual employees as independent suppliers, initially on contracts to the parent company.

The small proportions interested in government employment are remarkable; only in General A and agriculture did these minorities become sizable. The students in General A were in many ways the vaguest, and almost certainly among the least informed, about career possibilities; government offers opportunity and refuge for such youth in many societies. The fact that table 11.1 excludes sons of farmers is one of the reasons for the relatively high proportions studying agriculture who expressed an interest in government. Readers can examine table 11.1 at their leisure. Perhaps they, too, will find the proportion of wage-earners' sons who prefer to be employed by small rather than big private firms something to provoke further thought.

Types of Occupations

Frequent use has been made in previous chapters of one or another classification of occupations by types. Here we will again make use of very broad categorizations of types of occupations, along with classifications that are more refined. First, however, we look briefly at the shifting Japanese occupational structure and how successive cohorts of Japanese men have been moving through that changing structure in the course of their working lives. Attention will be focused on selected occupations rather than on the overall, broad categories.

Cohort Experiences and the Changing Occupational Structure

If nothing really changed from decade to decade or from generation to generation, a simple charting of relations between age and occupation would tell us the broad story of what men experience in occupational shifts from their early years in the labor force on through the cycle of their working lives. Such data would delineate the distributional patterns that would be realized, whatever the expectations of youth in each successive cohort might be. Cross-sectional data have often been interpreted in this way as a first approximation.

Just how misleading this procedure may be is easily illustrated from the Japanese data on farming. At any given date the older the age-group, the larger the proportions in farming; yet individuals rarely move from other activities into farming as their years go by. Figure 11.1 shows exactly what was in fact going on between 1955 and 1970 in this respect. For each calendar year the age curves slope upward. However, if we follow any particular cohort from one year to the next, the curves (dotted lines) all slope downward. Fewer people were entering farming to start with, as we can immediately observe from the fact that curves for later years all start lower than those for prior years. But in addition, men of all ages were leaving agriculture. The rates of departure were greater among younger men, but there were departures even among men in their 50s. The only exception (the rising dotted line) was the slight net movement into farming of the teenagers of 1965, but this was entirely a reflection of the fact that by 1965 many of the youth who would enter farming deferred that step until completion of upper-secondary school.

The opposite pattern is manifested in figure 11.2, for managers and officials. These are indeed positions men rarely attain in their twenties, but that is not all. Proportions of men in such employments have risen steadily since 1960, and for the older men since 1955. One of the results is that the age cross sections understate the steepness of the advance into administrative

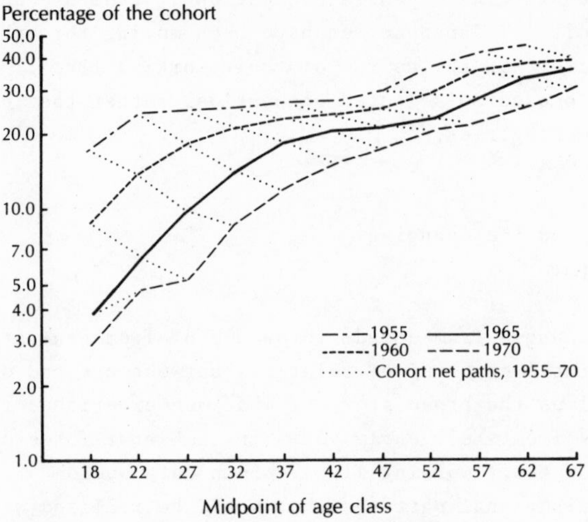

Figure 11.1 Male occupational paths and age cross sections, 1955-70; agriculture, forestry, and fishing.

positions. Moreover, this process continues long after the age curves for each year have turned down. Net movements out of managerial or official positions have occurred only when we reach an age of retirement well beyond the 55- or the 60-year limits commonly used in wage employment. We cannot tell from these observations the extent of turnover of individuals in managerial positions. Only longitudinal data on individuals would provide an answer to that question. But whatever the turnovers may be, it is important to remember the continuously rising cohort paths displayed in figure 11.2 (together with the associated upward shifts in the age profiles from one census year to the next) when we consider the career-development anticipations of the youth in our study and also their perceptions of labor market characteristics.

Many of the developments in other occupations could be viewed as a reflection of the sharp decline in both the proportions and the numbers in agriculture, but this would say nothing about causation. In fact, the fifties and early sixties saw a dramatic increase of productivity in agriculture. At the same time, capital investments in a technologically innovative industrial sector were proceeding at a rapid pace that brought cries of labor shortage from manufacturers. There was still a low-wage pattern with respect to utilization of labor in trade and services, but by 1960 the process of urbanization was in full swing and an

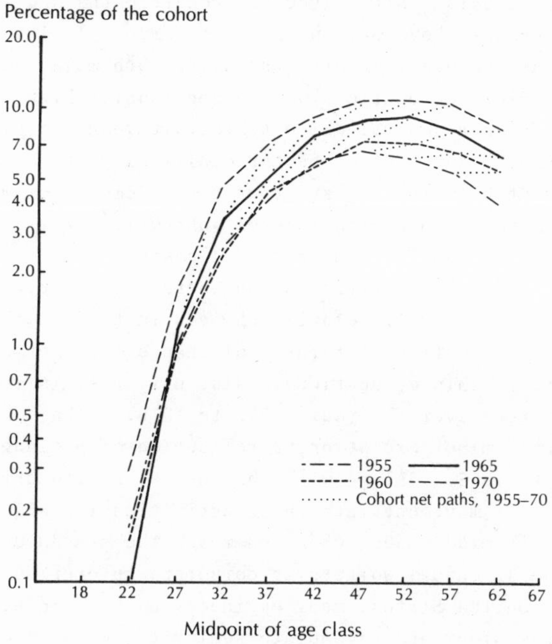

Figure 11.2 Male occupational paths and age cross sections, 1955-70; managers and officials.

affluent consumer society was in the making. In the midst of all this came a peaking of the demographic cycle, with a surge of new recruits to the labor markets.

Comparisons across nations in the early 1960s showed Japan to be an extreme in the large proportions of college and university graduates in clerical jobs. Those figures included women, but even when we look at men only, the clerical proportions among graduates from higher institutions were and are high. This raises the question whether clerical jobs may be mainly a stage on a path toward managerial or professional posts. A comparison between the 1955 and 1960 age profiles suggested that for the male clerical population in general this was not the case; the net paths for the 1955-60 period were rising or horizontal for all cohorts up to their late 50s, when retirements began to affect the percentages. However, these upward net cohort paths between 1955 and 1960 were evidently the result of a sharp increase in the demand for clerical workers that was not met by a sufficient flow of new graduates from the upper-secondary schools. After 1960 the cohort paths declined for men in all age-groups above 30, but not for women. In 1965 the proportions of new upper-secondary graduates, both male and female, entering clerical occupations were exceptionally high. There seems to have been a general drive to recruit young people for clerical work as the supplies of better qualified youth became available. But recent history suggests that net movements of men out of clerical employment into higher level jobs will persist, while women will continue to fill the clerical posts.

Craftsmen and production workers in manufacturing constitute a large category, and even small relative changes in their number can be important in implications for rates of change in other occupational categories. This occupation consistently rose in importance across all ages over the years 1955 to 1970. (The youngest groups were a minor exception, a reflection of prolonged schooling relative to 1955.) Along with the general upward shift, there has been a slight movement into these activities for all age-groups up to their middle 50s, when men reach the standard retirement age for most manual workers in corporate enterprises. In Japan, as in the United States, many engineers become production managers as they grow older and accumulate seniority, while younger, newly trained men take their places in technical responsibilities.

The Early Postschool Years

What happens at entry to the labor market is a matter of considerable moment from at least two, very different perspectives. This is the critical point at which really major shifts in occupational structure are most easily brought about--as young men (and women) begin to work and older people retire. It is also the stage at which young people board the "career buses" that may take them in one direction or another, at greater or lesser speeds. This is not to say that the first job determines everything thereafter; there are shifts in the early years of working experience for many young people. Yet even the nature of those shifts and their sequential effects will be in part a function of the first regular or full-time job. These early years are the period in which the contacts and communication networks on which many future opportunities rest take their shape, and they are the critical years for selective learning on the job--and for where that learning, if it is substantial, can lead.

Here we will comment first on evidence in official statistics and surveys concerning new entrants to the labor force in the 1960s and more recently. We will then turn to the students in our study, their perceptions of job opportunities at direct entry from upper-secondary school or after further education, and some of the relations of those perceptions to family backgrounds and curriculum.

Both the progressive diffusion of education among the Japanese population and the demographic cycle that brought the number of entrants to the labor force from upper-secondary school to a peak in the late 1960s were discussed briefly in chapter 1. What we were observing there (in figure 1.1) and what we will observe shortly with respect to entry jobs are the net effects of several connected factors: (1) the high birthrates of the immediate postwar years and the subsequent decline in births; (2) the rapid diffusion of upper-secondary and then of higher education; (3) the rapid and long-sustained pace of technological change in the Japanese economy, with associated shifts in the occupational structure; and (4) the economic slowdown with the world recession in 1974. The strong educational base of the Japanese labor force even before the war was a starting point, but the decades after the war saw a continuous flow of well-educated and well-disciplined youth into the labor markets. Without such a flow the Japanese "miracle" growth rates could not have been attained. But the rapid pace of growth, carried forward by high levels of investment in new capital, was also a source of sustained demand for the graduates of upper-secondary and higher education. What employers required in this dynamic economy was people who could adapt easily and learn rapidly on the (changing) job. The strong demand for better educated youth in turn supported the rising demand of young people and their families for more education. But the diffusion of schooling is only in a very limited degree (if at all) reversible; in Japan this progressive rise in schooling has continued despite the slowdown in economic growth.

Fortunately, perhaps, a demographic trough in the cohorts of young people coming through the upper-secondary schools coincided with the slackening economic pace. Not until the middle 1990s will the demographic cycle reach a secondary peak reflecting the large population now around 30, and that will be a much damped peak.[2] Consequently, the large proportions of present and future cohorts completing upper-secondary education are nevertheless smaller in numbers relative to the total labor force than they were a decade ago. Meanwhile, the richer educational composition of new recruits encourages continuing redesign of production.

Table 11.2 Occupations of New Graduates of Upper-Secondary School (percentage distributions)

Year of Graduation by Course[a]	Type of Occupation							
	Clerical	Sales	Sum of Clerical and Sales	Technical, Manual[b]	Agriculture, Fishing	Other[c]	Total	Percent Not Responding
General courses								
1965A	26.6	20.3	46.9	41.0	2.6	9.6	100.1	...
1970A	20.9	15.6	36.5	53.6	1.1	8.8	100.0	...
1967E	...	...	46.2	47.3	5.4	1.1	100.0	42.6
Agriculture								
1965A	9.3	10.0	19.3	40.2	33.2	7.3	100.0	...
1970A	11.9	10.9	22.8	49.3	19.1	8.8	100.0	...
1967E	...	...	15.3	33.1	51.4	.3	100.1	30.9
	...	...	(19.1)	(41.2)	(39.3)	(.4)	100.1	...
Commerce								
1965A	47.4	31.7	79.1	17.1	.6	3.2	100.0	...
1970A	38.2	26.3	64.5	28.1	.7	6.7	100.0	...
1967E	...	...	75.2	21.4	.8	2.6	100.0	37.0
Technical								
1965A	2.2	4.8	7.0	88.6	.3	4.1	100.0	...
1970A	4.7	5.8	10.5	84.2	.6	4.7	100.0	...
1967E	...	...	10.6	88.5	.2	.7	100.0	20.4

Source for 1965 and 1970. Mombushō, *Sotsugyōsha go no Jōkyō Chō* [Ministry of Education, Surveys of the Situation of School Graduates] (Tokyo). These surveys do not distinguish between the academic and nonacademic general course.

[a] A = actual job distributions of male graduates. E = expected job distributions of male noncollege students.

[b] Technicians, operatives in transport and communication, craftsmen, and production workers. The technician numbers (not shown separately) were small; the expected 1967 figures tended to be slightly under actual 1965 and 1970 figures except in the technical course, where expected slightly exceeded both actual 1965 and actual 1970.

[c] Includes service workers and unskilled manual. In the 1965 and 1970 data it also includes those not yet employed.

The experiences of youth entering the labor force from upper-secondary school depend on the courses they have taken as well as on the broader demographic and economic context within which they find their jobs. Percentage distributions of occupations of the 1965 and 1970 male graduates of upper-secondary school and of the expectations of the prospective graduates of 1967 are shown by type of course in table 11.2. Among the general and commerce students, but especially the latter, the importance of clerical jobs is obvious, along with some decline in clerical proportions between 1965 and 1970. (The clerical proportions among the rising numbers of female commerce students meanwhile rose.)

Employment in agriculture has declined steadily among the only group of young people who have ever entered agriculture in substantial proportions from upper-secondary school: graduates of the agriculture course. The compensating increases for the agriculture graduates have been in both clerical and sales occupations and manual jobs.

The dominance of technical and manual employment (often highly skilled) among youth entering the labor markets from the technical schools is evident, but so also is the decline in that proportion, a decline that continued into the 1970s. A more detailed classification than that shown in table 11.2 indicates that a main element in this decline, at least to 1973, was the drop in the proportions taking jobs as operatives in transportation or communication, a drop that occurred in all curricula. The proportions of technical-course graduates who became technicians rose slightly between 1965 and the mid-seventies. In all courses, so also did the proportions, still small, who took jobs as unskilled manual workers, reflecting the sharp decline in the numbers of young people entering the labor market without upper-secondary schooling.

How close were the distributions of expected first jobs among upper-secondary youth entering the labor market in 1967 to the actual distributions? We lack actual distributions for 1967, but there are some advantages in any case in making comparisons with 1965 and 1970; we are then asking how far the students' expectations reflected experiences of the cohorts just ahead of them and how far they foreshadowed those just behind. We may at the same time impose a crude "realism" test, assuming the actual 1967 distribution to have been between that for 1965 and 1970.

There are a number of reasons why expected proportions derived from student responses may not meet this test, however, even supposing the test itself to be a good approximation. There may be systematic biases, year after year, in what youth expect in first jobs relative to what actually happens. There may be systematic biases in some of our samples. Finally, and most important, there may be systematic biases in the subsamples of those who respond on entry-job expectations with sufficient clarity for accurate coding. The net effects of errors and biases in responses of the terminal upper-secondary students can be seen in table 11.2. (The category "other" is not comparable, since it includes for 1965 and 1970 youth who were not yet employed.)

On the whole the expected values are reasonably consistent with actual distributions except among the agriculture students, who expected to go into agriculture in far larger proportions than was in fact the case. That discrepancy is narrowed substantially if we assume (as seems plausible) that none of those who gave no explicit first-job expectation contemplated agriculture--the assumption involved in the entries in parentheses for agriculture. Even that adjustment still leaves substantial underestimates among the students of agriculture for technical and manual jobs. Youth in the technical courses had the clearest ideas of likely entry jobs, and their 1967 expectations were in line with actual distributions. None of the results are surprising, but they do give us insights into the process of decision, the precision or vagueness of students' expectations, and how far students are likely to meet with labor market situations contrary to those expectations.

Grouping occupations in only three major categories--white collar (including trade), technical and manual, and agricultural--provides a convenient basis for comparing entry jobs with and without higher education, and for examining relations between parental occupations and types of entry-stage work activity. This is done in table 11.3, where the figures refer to perceptions by all respondents, regardless of their college expectations.[3] Looking first at the summary figures by type of course, we immediately see that the chief contrast between perceived broad types of entry jobs with and without higher education is in the substantially higher proportions of agriculture and technical-course students who specified for university graduation white collar employments rather than their immediate vocational specializations. Nevertheless, two-fifths of the agriculture students gave some form of employment in agriculture for the first job out of university, and two-thirds of the technical-school students saw technical-professional or technician employments as the first job after university for themselves or classmates who pursued their education to that level. Among the General B and General A students there were no significant differences between perceptions of broad types of work on first jobs directly out of upper-secondary school and upon graduation from a university.

The lower part of table 11.3 takes all courses together but distinguishes by father's occupation. Occupational inheritance in this broad sense was strong, whether with reference to jobs

Table 11.3 Perceived Entry-Job Options with and without Higher Education (percentage distributions)

	From Upper-Secondary School				From University			
	White Collar	Tech-nical, Manual	Agri-culture	Total	White Collar	Tech-nical, Manual	Agri-culture	Total
Type of course								
General B	60	36	4	100	62	35	3	100
General A	55	40	5	100	58	39	3	100
Agriculture	18	31	51	100	32	27	41	100
Commerce	83	16	1	100	84	15	1	100
Technical	14	85	1	100	33	66	1	100
Father's oc-cupation								
White collar	49	49	2	100	59	40	2	101
Tech., manual	33	66	1	100	46	53	1	100
Agriculture	29	39	33	101	41	34	24	99

directly from upper-secondary school or after completion of college (with chi-square significance levels at .000 in both cases). Within curricula, the closest associations with paternal occupation (not shown) were attributable primarily, though by no means exclusively, to occupational inheritance among the sons of farmers. Otherwise, the effects of parental occupation on the students' job expectations were channeled in the main through curriculum.

Occupational Goals

The student questionnnaire asked two main questions concerning ultimate career hopes or goals. The first referred to dreams, or "castles in the air"; the students were encouraged to set down such thoughts, however unrealistic. A second question asked them to specify more realistic expectations.

Truncated distributions of students' occupational expectations ("realistic" hopes for 20 to 30 years hence) are shown by broad occupational type and type of course for sons of wage and salaried men and for sons of independent entrepreneurs in table 11.4. Most responses were adequate for such classification, with agriculture students of nonfarm origin the vaguest. Among sons of wage and salaried men responses were somewhat less complete than among sons of entrepreneurs, but even the former ranged from 85

Table 11.4 Relation between Son's Occupational Expectation, His Upper-Secondary Course Enrollment, and His Father's Occupational Category (percentage distributions)

Expected Occupation (ONEX)	General B	General A	Agriculture	Commerce	Technical
Sons of Wage and Salaried Men					
White collar[a]	71.9	53.7	48.3	42.0	40.4
Trade, service	2.9	6.1	1.7	8.3	5.6
Technical, manual	13.7	19.5	31.0	36.6	40.7
Agriculture	.2	7.3	3.5	1.8	.4
Nonresponse	11.3	13.4	15.5	11.3	12.9
Total	100.0	100.0	100.0	100.0	100.0
Sons of Men in Nonfarm Independent and Family Enterprises					
White collar[a]	31.3	18.4	3.9	16.9	14.9
Trade, service	43.0	34.7	61.5	55.4	33.7
Technical, manual	20.3	24.5	15.4	22.3	41.1
Agriculture	.1	18.4	7.7	2.1	2.3
Nonresponse	5.3	4.1	11.5	3.3	8.0
Total	100.0	100.1	100.0	100.0	100.0

[a]Includes nontechnical professionals, managers and proprietors (except in trade), clerical workers.

to 89 percent adequate. This is easily seen by reading across the "nonresponse" rows.

Since the sons of farmers are excluded from table 11.4, it should hardly surprise us that relatively few even of the agriculture students express a preference for or expectation of going into agriculture as a life career; if there is a surprise here, it is the sizable minority of General A students looking in that direction.

One of the most striking contrasts in table 11.4 is that between sons of wage and salaried men and sons of independent entrepreneurs in the proportions expecting to engage in nontechnical white collar activities. Across school types the *lowest* proportion among the sons of wage and salaried men was 40 percent, in the technical curriculum, whereas the *highest* proportion among sons of independent entrepreneurs was only 30 percent, in General B. Sons of independent entrepreneurs hoped to run their own or family businesses in trade or service sectors or, especially among nonfarm sons studying agriculture, to work for pay in those sectors.

Substantial minorities in all curricula contemplated technical or manual employment, whatever the father's employment status. Factors most conductive to generating expectations of entering such occupations (which we designate by the acronym EXFAB, referring to processing or fabricating activities) were examined in a number of multiple regressions (not shown). The main expected associations showed up clearly enough: negative associations with the commerce course; positive associations with the technical course, with metropolitan residence, and with being the son of a technician or a skilled worker.

More detailed distributions by types of occupations are shown by course in table 11.5, which includes the sons of farmers. Comparisons between fathers' occupations and the types of occupations anticipated by sons in each course reveal some interesting relationships.

1. First, the shift out of agriculture is manifest in all curricula, but especially among students in the General A course. Quantitatively, however, the important drop was among youth studying agriculture: whereas 81 percent of the fathers were engaged in agriculture, only 58 percent of the sons anticipated continuation in such a life (even the 58 percent overstates substantially what in fact has happened).

2. Ambitions for nontechnical professional employment are important only among the General B students and a small minority of youth in the technical courses. Technical-school youth with such hopes or intentions are fighting against the odds, though a few may succeed; these are young men who wished they had been enrolled in an academic stream, and they ranked themselves relatively high academically among their classmates. We must remember in this connection that it is the General B and technical-course youth who have experienced the lowest relative initial admission rates to institutions of higher education, and it is they (especially the ambitious technical-course youth) who have been readiest to become *rōnin*. This reflects in part, at least, their more ambitious goals in selection of the institutions to which to apply. Although professional employment is rising in Japan, as elsewhere, the hopes of many of both the General B and the technical-course aspirants to nontechnical professions will not be realized.

3. The proportions of students expressing the hope or expectation of becoming government officials exceeded the proportions of

Table 11.5 Comparison of Fathers' Occupations and Sons' Long-Term Occupational Expectations (percentage distribution)

	All		General B		General A		Agriculture		Commerce		Technical	
	F	S	F	S	F	S	F	S	F	S	F	S
White collar (= Occ III 1 + 3):	24.6	46.6	44.1	64.1	19.4	55.9	6.2	23.9	24.3	62.4	21.0	36.5
Professional (nontechnical)	3.4	14.3	9.2	26.6	.6	2.2	...	2.5	2.5	3.4	1.2	7.5
Administrative (government)	3.2	5.9	5.2	7.4	4.3	11.8	3.2	7.8	1.6	4.3	2.4	3.0
Managers, proprietors (private)	12.4	22.6	23.1	26.0	8.8	34.5	1.5	11.4	13.1	44.2	10.8	25.1
Clerical	5.6	3.8	6.6	4.1	5.7	7.4	1.5	2.2	7.1	10.5	6.6	.9
Consumer-oriented (= Occ III 4,9):	14.9	10.3	15.4	6.6	13.6	18.2	3.3	5.3	29.3	27.7	14.7	6.3
Retail sales and related	13.3	8.6	14.0	5.3	12.7	15.5	2.9	4.8	24.5	22.6	12.8	5.1
Miscellaneous services	1.6	1.7	1.4	1.3	.9	2.7	.4	.5	4.8	5.1	1.9	1.2
Object-oriented (technical, manual):	33.2	29.8	25.6	24.6	20.8	17.8	9.4	12.4	36.6	7.7	51.1	54.7
Professional-technical } (= Occ III 2):	2.6	14.0	5.4	18.0	1.6	8.3	.5	2.0	.9	4.0	3.4	32.5
Other high technical } (= Occ III 2):	5.6	8.2	4.6	2.5	2.2	1.9	1.1	4.1	6.2	.9	7.7	8.8
Skilled (= Occ III5 + 6):	16.3	3.9	10.6	1.7	7.1	3.4	4.2	3.0	19.9	1.4	26.6	7.5
Semiskilled, unskilled (= Occ III7):	8.7	3.7	5.0	2.4	9.9	4.2	3.6	3.3	9.6	1.4	13.4	5.9
Agriculture, forestry, fishing (= Occ III 8):	26.9	11.6	14.4	2.1	46.2	6.4	81.1	57.5	9.3	.7	12.8	1.0
Protective services and n.e.c. (= Occ III 10):	.4	1.7	.5	2.6	...	1.7	.1	.9	.5	1.5	.4	1.5
Total	100.0	100.0	100.0	100.0	100.0	100.0	100.0	100.0	100.0	100.0	100.0	100.0
Managers and proprietors in processing[a]	7.6	20.3	13.7	15.2	5.1	29.7	.7	10.8	7.4	27.9	7.2	23.6
Maximum object-oriented[b]	40.8	50.1	39.3	39.8	25.9	47.5	10.1	23.2	44.0	35.6	58.3	78.3
Reduced white collar total[c]	17.6	26.3	30.4	48.9	18.3	26.2	5.5	13.1	16.9	34.5	13.8	12.9

Note. Adjusted sample. Columns headed F refer to fathers; those headed S refer to students' expectations.

[a]Included in the wider classification "managers, proprietors (private)" under "white collar." This is OCC III 3.

[b]"Object-oriented" + "managers and proprietors in processing" (= OCC 2, 3, 5, 6, 7).

[c]"White collar" - "managers and proprietors in processing" (= OCC III 1).

their fathers in such positions in all courses. Nevertheless, only a small minority expressed such aims. The greatest shifts toward government were in General A and agriculture with their predominantly rural clientele. The greater leaning of the rural youth toward government employment may have been in part a manifestation of a limited knowledge of alternatives, of the relative security of government employment, and of perceptions of such employment as a channel of mobility out of rural and farm life into an urbanized society. There is nothing unique to Japan in these results, unless it is the modest proportions of even the rural general-course youth who looked toward advancement in government as their best career opportunity.

4. Clerical employment had little career appeal to the young men in our sample. We have already discussed what has in fact been happening in this respect: the rising demand for clerical workers has been met primarily by women and by young men who then move on to other activities.

5. A striking feature of the evidence presented in table 11.5 is the high frequency of sons in all curricula except General B and agriculture relative to their fathers whose ambition it was to become business managers or proprietors. These managerial or proprietorial aspirations were selective, however; there was no rush into proprietorial roles in retail trade and services, although a substantial minority of commerce-course youth, like their fathers, expected to engage in sales and related activities. Common to upper-secondary seniors in all curricula (with the partial exception of General B) was a significant shift toward management or proprietorship in processing or related activities as a goal. Excessive optimism unquestionably is displayed in these figures. Nevertheless, they constitute part of a broad thrust in both student orientations and economic developments toward higher levels in the technical-manual domain.

6. Interest among these Japanese youth in technical and processing activities was impressive, whether they aimed at becoming specialists in wage or salaried employment or at becoming managers and proprietors. If we include those hoping to become independent processors later in their careers, half of the students looked forward to "object-oriented" activities as against two-fifths of their fathers in such activities. The only course in which the omnibus figure (in the next-to-last row of table 11.5) was lower for students than for fathers was commerce. This result is extremely important in what it tells us about the routes through which the young people hoped to advance--and also for what it says,

however indirectly, about the performance of Japanese industry. On the other hand, while technical-course students had high ambitions to enter technical-professional occupations, there was no evidence of a desire among the sons of unskilled men to become skilled workers. The shift in favor of object-oriented activities among the rural youth in General A and agriculture entailed less expertise; it was dominated by intentions to move out of farming, but often into small-scale artisan enterprises that called for only minimal managerial skills.

Occupational Goals and Educational Choices of Farmers' Sons

In Japan, as elsewhere, whether educated men shun agriculture or embrace it depends more on the economic attractiveness of options open to them in and outside agriculture than on the particular content of their schooling. However, in Japan those who are oriented toward a career in agriculture (whether as farmers or in other capacities) usually study agriculture in upper-secondary school even though only half of the agriculture graduates expect to pursue agricultural careers and even fewer do so. Only 28 percent of the sons of farmers in our sample studied agriculture. They were preponderantly first sons--their brothers went into general courses. We conducted a careful study of who enters agricultural pursuits and who goes into farming in particular, using both data from our surveys of upper-secondary students and of their fathers and unpublished material from other sources. Here, however, we take space for only a brief summary.

Economic rationality in choosing farming (and in a father's desire that his son should inherit and operate the farm) suggested certain conditions as favorable to that decision. We tested some of those conditions, with results that strongly confirmed our a priori assumptions. Conducive to taking up farming were: (*a*) a family farm that was well equipped and a going concern, (*b*) a good economic outlook for the future of farming in the area (as perceived by the farm father), and (*c*) that the youth involved was the son chosen (by birth order, or in some cases by inclination) to inherit. Controlling for these factors, residence in a remote area reduced the likelihood that a young man would look forward to taking over and operating the family farm. This finding contrasts with the findings of a 1973 study that showed agriculture students in the most remote areas to be the most likely to continue in agriculture, but the studies were very different in design; in particular, our observations were on farmers' sons, not just on youth studying agriculture (as in the 1973 study). One of the most interesting results of the 1973 study was the evidence that substantial fractions of graduates in agriculture expected to obtain further agricultural training, whether via short-term courses in agricultural institutes or degree work in a university. Taken together, 53 percent of the agriculture students expected to come directly or eventually to agriculture--a figure in the same general range as our findings, though slightly higher. These youth divided into three equal subgroups: those going directly into farming, those pursuing further agricultural training, and those taking other jobs but then coming back into farming.

Occupational Status Expectations

The basis for specifying occupational status level has been discussed in earlier chapters. As in the preceding discussion of occupational type goals, we will focus here on what students thought "realistically" they could or would attain at the peak of their careers, which we will call "expected status."

Uncertainties and Potential Surprise

Students in the last year of upper-secondary school had no difficulty in expressing preferences with respect to employment status.[4] Though not quite so complete, responses on expected ultimate types of occupations were generally precise enough to permit coding on that dimension. However, answers that would enable us to code for expected occupational status were a different matter. This was due not to any ambiguity in the details of the questionnaires or in their administration in the classroom. It was more fundamental. In fact the proportions of students who could state clearly at least the kind of job they preferred and expected to hold during their adult years (over 85 percent in all cases) were remarkably high. On the other hand, a third of the students gave answers inadequate for status identification on their dream aspirations and 42 percent gave answers inadequate for status coding on their more realistic status expectations. Relative to findings elsewhere, the two-fifths figure is not a particularly high one; indeed, Lipset, Bendix, and Malm (1962) found that close to half of a sample of high school seniors in the United States could give no specific job expectations at all.[5]

In the discussion of expectation matrices in chapter 2 we made several points that are pertinent here. Restating, we may list five.

1. At graduation from upper-secondary school the range of options is still wide, even for students completing a vocational course, and the key immediate decisions usually do not require specific visualization of ultimate destinations. Even when a young man has a good idea of the general status level he hopes and expects ultimately to attain, often he will be unable to specify an occupational destination the status of which we could readily code. Much more important for many students will be getting started in a direction that promises advancement in future years, whatever the particular activities may be to which this will lead. Keeping options open may be part of such a strategy, and it is crucial that a person give heed to the ways in which present decisions will condition or constrain those options. The decision to enter or not enter higher education obviously is important from this point of view.

2. At graduation from upper-secondary school many youth still have only a limited awareness of possible occupations and careers. This is especially true of rural youth who expect to go to the city, but it characterizes many urban young men as well. Those who will not go to college are just about to begin (or have just recently begun) to search for a job and are also learning from the recruiting activities of potential employers. But even when a young man has a fairly clear idea about entry jobs, and which job may be on a "career express" or a "slow bus," it does not follow that he can specify his expected status destination.

3. Where career-peak expectations (or hopes) are more definitely expressed, they will commonly reflect optimistic choices toward the more favorable potential-surprise limits of realistic expectations. What we see here is a process of focusing attention on the most interesting or attractive outcomes that seem realizable. There is inherently a strong upward bias for all youth who view their world as one of open opportunities and who have a good measure of motivation and self-confidence. To the extent to which we find young men expressing high occupational expectations we are looking at people who are career-motivated and probably at a society that does in fact give many a reasonable chance.

4. The most clearly visible attractive options that are readily specifiable on a status dimension are likely to be occupa-

tions for which higher education is requisite. We therefore expect clearer status anticipations from youth in the General B stream.

5. Finally, there are some situations that may automatically focus a youth's perceptions with respect to the future--for example, participation in a family business or inheritance of a productive farm. However, these are precisely the kinds of activities that are most difficult to code properly on a status scale.

Commonly, persons not responding on a questionnaire item are compared with respondents in order to get some idea of the "biases" that may be involved in analyzing the responses. It is not at all clear that such a question about "bias" is meaningful in connection with expectational data such as these, however, for nonresponse is a distinct type of response. What factors are associated with focus, what with vagueness, in the formulation of occupational expectations? Without suggesting that expectations are good predictors, it is relevant to ask whether differences between respondents and nonrespondents might suggest that youth with the clearest foci are also those more likely to attain a high-level occupation.

Percentages with inadequate responses on occupational status expectations are shown for sons of wage and salaried men and of nonfarm independent and family entrepreneurs in the first two rows of table 11.6. (For the moment we ignore the rest of the table.) Except in the technical course, over 40 percent of the sons of men in independent and family enterprises gave responses that we were unable to code on status. However, these high figures were probably due in part, at least, to the fact that large proportions of these youth anticipated careers as entrepreneurs, and such activities are always the most difficult to code on a status scale. This more than neutralizes the fact that some of these same youth may nevertheless have had clearer ideas of where they were headed than many sons of wage and salaried men. Setting this problem aside, the pattern of inadequate-response frequencies across courses was similar to that among the sons of wage and salaried men.

For the most part, the rest of table 11.6 speaks for itself, though two points may be worth special mention. First, the youth in the technical curriculum who gave responses that we could code on occupational status were the most prone of any except the General B students to project high-status attainments at the peak of their careers; this is almost certainly a selective subsample, of the more ambitious of the students in the technical curricula. Second, and quite predictably, the highest proportions giving responses we were not able to code by status level were among

Table 11.6 Relation between Son's Anticipated Occupational Status, His Upper-Secondary Course Enrollment, and His Father's Occupational Category (percentage distributions)

	General B	General A	Agri-culture	Commerce	Technical
Percentages giving inadequate responses on occupational status					
Sons of wage and salaried men	36.6	42.7	46.6	39.3	41.2
Sons of men in independent and family enterprises	42.7	53.1	65.4	45.0	39.1
Percentage distributions of expected occupational status (excluding nonrespondents)					
Sons of wage and salaried men					
EXPSTA 1,2,3	72.6	46.8	29.0	39.0	60.1
4	22.9	38.4	32.2	49.7	25.9
5,6	4.1	12.7	35.6	8.3	13.1
7,8	.4	2.1	3.2	3.0	.9
Total	100.0	100.0	100.0	100.0	100.0
Sons of men in independent and family enterprises					
EXPSTA 1,2,3	62.9	34.7	55.3	44.5	54.9
4	24.4	39.2	11.3	42.0	30.3
5,6	12.2	21.8	22.1	12.0	13.5
7,8	.5	4.3	11.3	1.5	1.3
Total	100.0	100.0	100.0	100.0	100.0

the nonfarm youth studying agriculture, followed, albeit at some distance, by students in the General A course.

Subdividing the population in each course by the curricula they preferred (not shown), we found that students' course preferences and their status expectations fit very tidily. At the top are General B students who were in the course they preferred, but not far behind are the technical-course youth who wished they had been in a General B curriculum and the General B youth who wished they had been enrolled in a technical course. Again, students in agriculture had the lowest aspirations, followed by General A students (whatever their course preferences) and by commerce youth who were where they wanted to be. Very generally, preference for the commerce curriculum goes along with relatively low status expectations. Adding parental traits in multiple regression analyses of the determinants of expected status modified the coefficients on course type and preference, reducing the differences somewhat, but it did not alter the rankings. There was little correlation between curriculum rankings on status expectations and on proportions looking toward technical-manual activities in their mature years.

Determinants of Students' Status Expectations

How closely are sons' status expectations associated with the occupational status of their fathers? As a first step in answering this question we depart from our status codes 1 to 8 as the value weights, shifting to modified weights used by Tomoda (1968*a*) in order to provide comparability with an American study. This was done by first converting the categories 1 to 8 back to the original Duncan values; we then turned the analysis around so that the highest possible mean score on this coding became 9, the lowest possible .5. Results are shown in table 11.7.

Students from the highest status backgrounds did have the highest status expectations for themselves, but otherwise the variations are small and not monotonic. The important contrasts are by rural or urban residence and by type of course, not by parental status. Figure 11.3 displays the overall pattern by father's status for the entire sample of Japanese youth and for a sample of high school seniors in the state of Washington, studied in 1955. The contrast between the generally rising curves of both expectations and dreams in the American sample, and the flat or *U*-shaped curves for Japan is unmistakable. Will this contrast persist--has it persisted--with the universalization of upper-secondary schooling and the economic slowdown in Japan? Speculation would be hazardous, but the question is an important one. The data reflect distinctive features of the two societies; although many of the "problems" of a social and educational nature are common to the two countries, the form and magnitude of such problems differ quite markedly between Japan and the United States.

Taking a wider view, we ran a number of multiple regressions, with expected status (EXPSTA) as the dependent variable. Even with many other variables on family backgrounds and location in the regressions, among the sons of wage and salaried men type of course remained by far the strongest predictor. However, among the sons of entrepreneurs type of course made little difference, whereas

Table 11.7 Relation between Father's Occupational Status and Son's Mean Expected Occupational-Status Score

A. By Urban or Rural Origin

Father's Status			Student's Mean					
					Students of Nonfarm Origin			
Duncan Scale	Weight Value	Eight-Point Scale	All[a] Score	N	Urban Score	N	Rural Score	N
80+	9.0	1	8.15	33	8.17	27	8.29	7
70-79	7.5	2	6.80	96	6.85	77	6.17	21
60-69	6.5	3	6.56	330	6.59	250	6.48	74
50-59	5.5	4	6.31	318	6.43	254	5.98	67
35-49	4.2	5	6.04	653	6.17	288	5.81	58
24-34	3.0	6	6.06	482	6.15	237	5.90	53
11-24	1.8	7	6.15	342	6.16	268	5.89	71
10 or less	.5	8	6.33	45	6.70	28	6.02	13

B. By Upper-Secondary Course Enrollment

Father's Status		Student's Mean Score				
Value Weight	Eight-Pt Scale	General B	General A	Agriculture	Commerce	Technical
9.0	1	8.36	...	...	b	b
7.5	2	6.82	b	b	6.77	6.67
6.5	3	6.71	5.78	5.72	6.23	6.42
5.5	4	6.68	5.50	4.88	6.04	6.05
4.2	5	6.30	5.38	4.42	5.68	6.17
3.0	6	6.32	5.66	4.72	5.86	6.14
1.8	7	6.51	5.53	5.01	5.63	6.29
.5	8	7.25	5.62	4.34	6.26	6.08

[a]Excluding students of agriculture.

[b]Less than 10 cases.

parental education came through strongly and consistently--the better educated the father, the higher the aspirations of the son. Also, whereas preference as to employment status had virtually no effect when we were looking at the sons of wage and salaried men, the preference for independent activity carried strong coefficients predicting lower status aspirations among the sons of entrepreneurs. Finally, whereas FREQ-M (the index of frequency of daily transportation to metropolitan places) was strong throughout for the sons of employees, it was of no importance in predicting the status expectations of the sons of independent and family entrepreneurs.

Turning some of these observations around, we may ask what were the distinguishing characteristics of the sons of employees and of nonfarm entrepreneurs who expected a relatively high

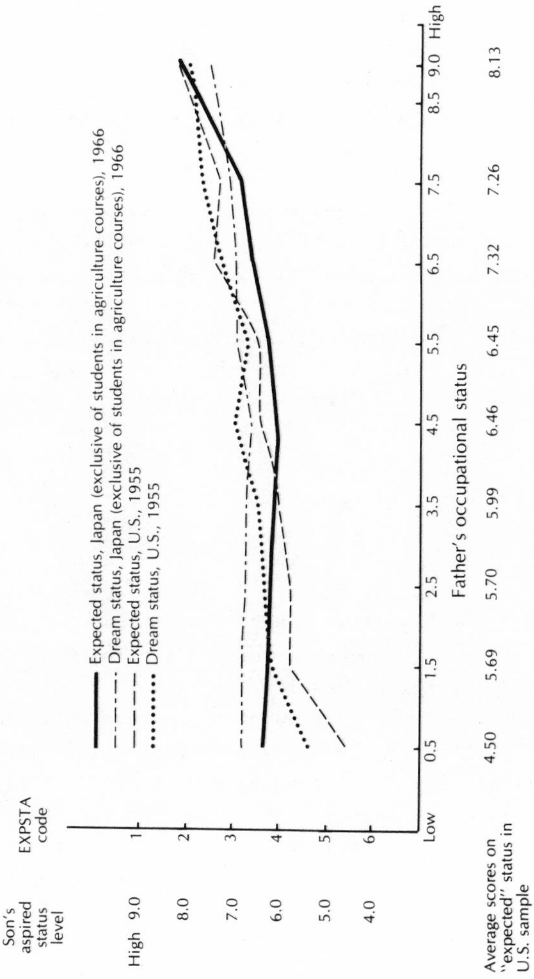

Figure 11.3 Relations between occupational status aspirations and father's status; male students in the final year of upper-secondary school in Japan and the northwestern United States.
Source: Yasumasa Tomoda, "Occupational Aspirations of Japanese High School Students," *International Journal of Education* 2 (1968): 217-25.

occupational status? Paternal education aside, within the general and technical curricula the important distinctions related to performance in school and to other aspects of career expectations and preferences, and even these were important primarily among the sons of entrepreneurs. Thus, the more ambitious or optimistic proprietors' sons tended to rank themselves high in their classes and preferred employee status in big private firms; they definitely did not prefer independence. The amibitious or optimistic proprietors' sons in General B and General A combined their high status expectations with high income expectations relative to other students in those courses, but there was no significant association between occupational status and peak income expectations among technical-course youth. The ambitious General A sons of entrepreneurs expected to attain relatively high earnings only at a later stage in their careers; they visualized high ratios of later to early earnings, whereas the optimistic General B youth expected relatively high earnings from the beginning of their working lives.

Among the commerce-course sons of wage and salaried men, amibition was associated with metropolitanism (high FREQ-M), with plans to attend university, and with a preference for employment in government--this last in marked contrast to the ambitious youth in all other curricula. Ambitious commerce students definitely did not look toward work in trade or service activities.

Student Perceptions of Career Development

A high degree of flexibility is built into both the educational system and the economic structure of Japan. There are remarkably open structures within the big firms, where there has been relatively little job analysis as such but much moving about of men and adaptive adjustments in both the organization of work and the reshaping of men to new tasks. These adaptations have included substantial shifts over time in the mixture of learning at work and in school, as technologies have changed and as supplies of better educated youth have increased. Nor is this all. Shifting between skilled work in a large Japanese corporation and management of a small enterprise that is set up initially as a supplier to that corporation may be a viable option. And there is still a substantial small-enterprise sector independent of such linkages.

Nevertheless, there are clear enough associations between upper-secondary curricula and types of jobs youth enter and to which they ultimately aspire. Furthermore, how men start their working lives as well as their initial skills and competencies may significantly affect the communication networks in which they come to participate, and thereby the ensuing range and direction of their activities. Many youth in the upper-secondary schools, especially in the urban schools, are alert to these processes and can state the broad directions in which they hope to move even when they cannot specify with any precision the nature of their ultimate goals or the status levels they expect to attain. This can be a wise decision process even if it does not always characterize the few men who reach top levels in economic or power status.

Of the several tables we created to study expected career paths, we present only one here (table 11.8), but we will draw again on information from tables not shown and regressions not presented, including data about expected ultimate status attainments as well as types of occupations and their relations to career starting points.

Anticipated paths to white collar employment, and the ultimate levels these young people expected to attain, differed greatly according to college expectations. Columns 2 to 4 of table 11.8 summarize these contrasts with respect to broad occupational types initially and at career peaks. Column 2 is of course dominated by General B students, few of whom expected to start in other than white collar work. If we divide the 24 percent not responding proportionally between the "from white collar" and "from other" categories, we get an upper limit of 16 percent as the proportion of university-bound youth who might be considered as expecting to start work in technical-manual and move on into white collar activities. Moreover, most of the college-bound youth expected to start work at quite high levels from the time they entered the labor force; very few imagined initial jobs below level 4, and a majority expected to start out at least at level 3. University-bound youth aiming for technical types of work were even less likely to imagine starting in any other sort of activity, and they were the more prone to assume that they would begin in their first jobs at level 3 or better.

Young people expecting to attend night colleges or universities were quite different. Many believed that night school would give them relatively quick access to higher white collar ranks, to be sure, but not in their first jobs. Others hoped through night school to obtain entry jobs in upper ranges of technical-manual activities, whatever their upper-secondary curricula. For some, higher education in night institutions seems to have been seen as simultaneously a way of gaining work experience and financing further education.

Virtually no one expected to start out directly from upper-secondary school into positions at level 3 or better in any sort of activity. The only exception was the 4 percent from technical courses who believed they could start out immediately in technician

Table 11.8 Relation between Persistence in Expected Major Type of Occupation, College Plans, and Upper-Secondary Course Enrollment

	Students in All Curricula							
Final Anticipated Occupational Type and First Job (1)	Taking Exams for Day University (2)	Taking Exams for Night University (3)	No College Intentions (4)	General B (5)	General A (6)	Agriculture (7)	Commerce (8)	Technical (9)
White collar final								
Percent from white collar	64	50	26	65	34	22	51	21
Percent from nonresponse	24	16	24	22	36	29	28	17
Percent from other	12	34	50	13	30	49	21	62
Total percent	100	100	100	100	100	100	100	100
Total number	919	84	1,130	727	168	167	450	621
Technical, manual final								
Percent from technical, manual	76	62	80	74	68	66	46	85
Percent from nonresponse	14	18	11	17	21	20	19	9
Percent from other	10	20	9	9	11	14	35	6
Total percent	100	100	100	100	100	100	100	100
Total number	424	68	1,063	308	66	107	112	962
Agriculture final								
Percent from agriculture	55	(14)	64	47	42	66	(50)	18
Percent from nonresponse	19	...	15	16	26	15	(17)	18
Percent from other	26	(86)	21	37	32	19	(33)	64
Total percent	100	100	100	100	100	100	100	100
Total number	69	7	447	32	19	449	6	17

positions described as at level 3. The General B youth who were not seeking entry to institutions of higher education were very like their General A brothers with two important exceptions. They were less vague about their expectations, and they were more inclined to look toward eventual high levels of attainment in technical-manual activities. The noncollege general-course students included a larger (though still small) minority than any others who looked ahead dismally to never rising beyond semiskilled manual work; it was the noncollege commerce youth who most often saw ahead only lowly types of clerical, sales, and related service activities.

Among both college and noncollege youth less than a tenth imagined career shifts from white collar (or agricultural) to technical-manual activities, whereas half of the noncollege young people who expected eventually to be in white collar jobs anticipated starting in other sorts of activities. This pattern was repeated across curricula with the exception of those young people in the commerce course who looked toward ultimate technical-manual types of employment (in all, a fifth of the commerce students, usually with modest status expectations). This is hardly surprising. It is much more difficult to move from modest white collar into higher level technical activities than to advance from technical to higher white collar.

The technical-course youth are especially interesting. Those who planned on higher education still aimed in much larger proportions than other college-oriented youth toward technical-manual positions. In fact, if we count all levels in technical-manual occupations, it turns out that they include 33 percent of the college-bound as compared with 38 percent of the noncollege graduates of technical curricula. The greatest contrast in this respect is the large proportion of the noncollege technical-course youth who specified technical-manual entry jobs but were vague about the future. On the other hand, as large a proportion of the many noncollege technical-course graduates as of the few college-bound graduates of that course expected ultimately to attain technical-manual positions at level 3 or better; many more of them hoped to move up through the technical-manual ranks from initially ambitious positions in those ranks. By the classification used in table 11.8, we included with white collar goals those who expected ultimately to attain managerial positions or to become independent entrepreneurs in processing activities; if we use the broader definition of "technical-manual" to include such management (with a correspondingly narrower definition of "white collar"), many of these responses would have been classified under "technical-manual final" (see table 11.5). But to say this is not to suggest that expectations for upward mobility were lacking; rather, it is to specify expectations of building realistically on prior skills and interests.

Although this chapter distinguished three main aspects of occupations--employment status, occupational types, and occupational status--the first of these three appeared repeatedly in discussions of the other two. This occurred both because of some interesting observed associations between expected employment status and other career perceptions and because of the importance in those perceptions of the distinction between sons of wage and salaried men and of nonfarm independent and family entrepreneurs (as, of course, of sons of farmers). Obviously, we cannot do justice to these complex patterns in a single chapter, let alone in a summary of it. These remarks are necessarily highly selective.

1. The large proportions of young people in General B, the commerce, and the technical courses who hoped or wished someday to become independent entrepreneurs, and the sizable minorities who "expected" to realize that goal, were impressive. While the proportions were higher among the sons of entrepreneurs, a third of the sons of wage and salaried men in those courses had such hopes. By contrast, it was only students in the predominantly rural General A and agricultural streams who commonly favored employment in government.

2. Expectations with respect to entry jobs among the noncollege youth of 1967 were on the whole consistent with actual distributions from the various curricula in 1965 and 1970, falling between the actual figures (some of which changed considerably in that interval). The major exception was the large overstatement of expected first jobs in agriculture, which fitted somewhat more nearly the experience of 1965 at a time when entry of secondary-school graduates into agricultural employment was falling precipitously. Expectations with respect to clerical employment were fully consistent with trends toward the increasing role of women relative to men in such jobs.

3. There were highly significant associations between a father's type of occupation, broadly defined, and his son's ori-

entation for both entry and ultimate expected types of work. This was reflected in choices of curricula. Detailed analyses not reproduced showed that even the sons of highly qualified engineers were more likely to attend technical upper-secondary schools than were sons of comparably educated men in other sorts of activities.

4. The importance of recognizing explicitly the wide variations among upper-secondary seniors in awareness of and information about career options, and in the degree of focus they have attained in looking to the future, came out most clearly in comparisons between the General A and agriculture students and all others. This problem is to be distinguished from the quite different proposition that in the face of uncertainties, always around us, we may expect a focus of attention on attractive favorable outcomes within a range of possibilities that would not evoke too great an element of potential surprise. It is to be distinguished also from an economy in decision making that considers only how present courses of action will condition the main options available in the future.

5. While there were statistically significant associations between type of curriculum and expectations of ultimate occupational status, there was little correlation between curriculum rankings on that variable and on proportions looking toward technical-manual activities in their mature years. Nor were ambitious youth as measured by status goals confined to the academic General B course or to youth taking examinations for higher education. Results differed substantially, however, according to whether a youth's father was in wage or salaried employment or was running his own or a family business. Among sons of wage and salaried men, type of course remained by far the strongest predictor of status expectations and little additional information emerged in within-course regressions; the exception was the commerce course, in which the more ambitious sons of wage and salaried men were distinctive in their drive to enter college and their goal of employment in government--a sharp contrast with all other curricula. Among sons of entrepreneurs there were some important within-course associations with high status goals: father's education, ranking one's self in the top fifth of the class, and the hope and intention of pursuing a career in a big corporation.

6. Among youth who looked forward ultimately to white collar jobs (at whatever level), those who were going on to college generally expected to start in such activities, whereas at least half of the noncollege youth hoped in some way to get into such jobs after first doing other things. By contrast, few of either the

college or the noncollege youth looking ultimately to technical or manual employments contemplated starting in white collar work. However, a third of the university-bound youth looked forward to technical types of jobs after their higher studies.

7. Students in the technical curriculum who aimed at eventual independent employment status seemed to be highly realistic in the routes by which they proposed reaching that goal, routes often bypassing further education. For the most part they looked forward to becoming managers or proprietors in one or another processing activity.

12. How Students and Their Fathers Perceive Labor Markets

The experiences of young people when they enter the labor market and in the years that follow, the postschool learning options open to them, the investments made in them by their employers and their explicit and implicit postschool investments in themselves--all of these are conditioned in significant ways by the structures of labor markets and by how labor markets are perceived by students and their employer and employee parents. Meanwhile, those structures are changing, even as they present persistent features around which the changes occur.

With the rapid increase in the proportions of younger cohorts completing upper-secondary education, young people now start work with different capabilities in a setting often demanding the rapid acquisition of new skills and quick adaptation to changing situations. Meanwhile, technology continues to shift at a rapid pace, supported in part by an able labor force and ensuring a continued demand for educated people with abilities to cope with change. The individual faces an altered set of postschool career options reflecting changes in labor market situations as well as his own range of competencies at entry to that market. Under these evolving circumstances, how experienced men and how their sons perceive the operations of the labor market with reference to the relative advantages of one postschool path versus another will reflect both differing perspectives associated with the position of youth and age in the system and changes over time in that system. These various perceptions are part of the climate in which early career decisions (including educational decisions) are made. Accordingly, we developed an opinionnaire dealing with aspects of the labor market and with relations between schooling and labor market opportunities that should be particularly relevant for early career decisions and experiences. Some of the questions test for the prevalence in a wider population of stereotypical views commonly asserted in planners' chambers or in the halls of academe.

The opinionnaire was administered not only to the upper-secondary students (as part of the larger questionnaire reproduced as appendix A) but also to their nonfarm fathers and (for a younger set of adults) to fathers of children in the second year of elementary school.

Distributions of Labor Market Perceptions: Students and their Fathers

The proportions of students, of their fathers, and of fathers of second-grade children who expressed agreement (strongly or mildly) on each item are shown in table 12.1.[1] The order of items has been rearranged to group them for readier preliminary interpretation. However, these crude groupings ignore some of the more subtle meanings and cross-relations brought out later in a principal components analysis.

Big Firms, Small Firms, and Independence

One of the prevalent stereotypes among the educated salaried men in academic and government posts who are most likely to write about such things--and to come in contact with their counterparts abroad--has been the notion that a job in a big firm is intrinsically preferable to a job in a small one. Wage statistics prior to the 1960s seemed to confirm this stereotype; within each education category, wage profiles of men employed in the big firms were consistently higher than those of men in smaller firms, and at all ages. However, there had already been some important changes in this respect by 1961, and by 1966 the age-earning profiles in the large and small enterprises were intersecting. Frequently the younger men earned less in the big firms than in the small ones, but the older men earned substantially more in the big firms. If labor markets were operating smoothly and if the young people hired by the large firms were not systematically superior in ability (within any given education category) to those in the small enterprises, the 1966 pattern would be the one an economist would predict. In the search for first jobs such a market would offer a reasonable choice: higher pay now but less increase in earnings in the future, as against lower pay now but better earnings prospects for later years. What is the reason for the change in relations between earning profiles in the big and the smaller firms? Our informed guess is that two forces were operating. First, over this period there was a squeeze on many of the smaller enterprises that could not compete in a situation of rapidly changing technology; the forcing out of the weakest of these left a different average wage profile for the smaller firms that remained. In common economic jargon, this involved a sharp reduction in the "dualism" of the economy and hence of labor markets as well. Second, at the same time the large firms were becoming less able to cream off the most able of the young people entering the labor market from upper-secondary school. Their diminished relative advantage in this respect reflected both government policies to discourage recruitment months in advance of graduation and a rising quality of entrepreneurship through much of the economy, with associated competition for able youth in the face of a general "shortage of labor". These two explanations are to some degree interrelated.

Whether these assessments are correct or not, neither the "bigness" stereotype nor its statistical underpinnings (in life-earning profiles and in survival histories of the smaller as compared with the larger enterprises) are in themselves evidence that attitudes indiscriminately favoring the big concern are pervasive. Furthermore, we were interested in identifying which situations and experiences might be associated with deviance in greater or lesser degree from the view that "big is good" in a career perspective. Two statements on the opinionnaire approached this point quite directly. Item *a* put it in reverse, stipulating better chances of getting ahead in the small concern as a part of the hypothetical available option. Item *g*, listed second in table 12.1, asserted the superiority of the big corporation as a place in which to work even if pay at entry, at least, was higher in the small firm.

Given these specifications, substantial majorities of students, regardless of type of course, expressed agreement with the first statement and disagreement with the second, though the General B students were less ready to be swayed toward the smaller enterprise. The parents of our students were not nearly so sanguine with respect to the appeal of the small firm even under the best of circumstances, and neither were fathers of the second graders. Contrasts between fathers in wage or salaried employment and those in independent enterprise were in the direction to be expected, the former being more inclined toward the big firms; however, these differences were small.

Answers on item *a* tended to be associated with those on item *l*, favoring a career as an independent entrepreneur. The students were

Table 12.1 Percentages of Students, Their Fathers, and Fathers of Second-Grade Children Agreeing with Labor Market Opinionnaire Statements

Opinionnaire Item	Students by Type of Course					Fathers of Upper-Secondary Youth		Fathers of Second-Graders	
	General B	General A	Agri-culture	Com-merce	Tech-nical	Wage and Salary Workers	Entrepreneurs	Wage and Salary Workers	Entrepreneurs
a) It is better to work at a company where there is promise of promotion and pay increase even though it is a small company rather than to work at a big corporation where there is slight chance of recognition	65	76	73	74	70	49	57	45	50
g) It is foolish to take a job in a small company even at a higher initial salary when one can get a job in a big corporation	30	22	27	27	23	47	34	45	33
ℓ) A man will lead a more fruitful life if he operates an independent business rather than being employed by others	62	66	78	72	63	*	61	*	14
m) If a man has his own business, he has too many worries and troubles. Therefore, it might be better to be employed by a stable company if possible.	18	20	16	13	14	*	14	*	14
b) Prospective employers look with suspicion on a man who has made frequent job changes as lacking in qualities of loyalty	51	54	61	51	53	71	68	66	63
f) Those who often change their place of employment must start anew each time. Therefore it is disadvantageous.	53	64	68	52	56	77	82	75	79
e) It is desirable to expand one's experience by working in various									

companies and government organizations when one is young	30	34	35	32	29	21	27	19	28
i) If one receives education in a company school, etc. it is difficult for him to change his job even though there is a profitable one, since he feels a moral obligation to the company.	34	36	38	33	35	57	71	46	69
h) Those who graduate from the general course can be trained to the need of a company. Therefore, the large corporation gives priority to those who graduate from the general course rather than those from occupational courses.	19	23	10	12	10	19	20	14	14
d) Among people who take a job directly after graduation from high school, career prospects will be better for those who have finished a technical than for those who have finished a general course.	55	50	63	45	67	61	61	58	53
c) Since the number of high school graduates has become so large recently, the advantages of being a high school graduate are going down.	37	36	38	31	40	43	31	39	31
j) With the number of college graduates increasing so much, it is difficult for even the college graduate to find a job. Therefore the value of going to university and paying the high cost will be going down.	18	24	25	19	23	15	13	12	10
k) With so many high school graduates now, a man will feel small unless he has at least graduated from high school.	46	48	45	48	43	76	59	73	52

*Unfortunately, these items were not included on the opinionnaire for employee fathers.

more inclined than even the "independent" fathers to regard running an independent business as leading to a "more fruitful life" than that to which being employed by others would lead. This attitude came through especially strongly among youth in agriculture. Among the General B and General A students the idea that independence could be too worrisome and thus employment by a stable company would be better appealed to a slightly larger minority than among the technical and commerce students.

Obviously, it would be a mistake to interpret the contrasts between student and father responses on either scale of enterprise (in employee status) or independent entrepreneurship as indicative of a trend in attitudes from earlier cohorts of men to more recent ones. No such pattern is evidenced in the comparison between the fathers of upper-secondary-school youth and those of primary-school children; in fact the latter showed less enthusiasm on the average for independent activities. Neither did we find any rising enthusiasm for independence at younger ages when we examined age patterns more directly (not shown here). We seem to be observing mainly the age-experience gap between full adulthood and adolescence. Moreover, many students who agreed on item *l* had in fact no expectation of attaining independent status, although there were also many who did have such hopes, as we saw in chapter 11, and who were apparently eager (in anticipation at least) to take on the associated risks and responsibilities.

The Life-Commitment Syndrome

A second major set of questions focused primarily on interfirm mobility and related facets of the life-commitment system. Before looking at the opinionnaire items on this topic, it is well to take note briefly of the distinction drawn by Becker (1962, 1964) between "general" and "specific" skills.[2] If a man who acquires a competency (human capital) in a particular agency or firm can readily apply the new skill elsewhere, that skill is "general." If on the contrary he can make effective use of his learning and hence command some sort of return to it only where it was acquired, it is "specific." Although this distinction usually is drawn in terms of the nature of the skill, that is not the crux of the matter. A skill might have extremely wide potential application; but if legal institutions or other forces require a man given training to serve an indenture to his "master" for an extended period in repayment, this human capital is "specific." The criterion is lack of the option of interfirm movement in carrying or selling an acquired skill.[3] Notice that if the skill is or can be made "specific," the firm will be more ready to invest in provision of that training, while the young man will be less willing to forego substantial earnings during the training period since he will not be able to reap the returns in employment elsewhere.[4] In fact most of us acquire mixtures of "general" and "specific" human capital as we go through life, and there are varying degrees on the continuum between fully "general" and entirely "specific" economic components in the formation of human resources.

To the extent that the life-commitment system tightens ties between employee and employer, learning on the job tends to be to a greater degree economically "specific." That institution has created implicit long-term contracts that assure "permanent" employees a future with the firm up to standard retirement ages. Given that assurance, the employee will be willing to accept relatively low pay at the start, provided he can expect a return on his investment in himself (in the form of foregone early earnings) later on. The firm meets those commitments not only as a way of making it worthwhile for older men to stay with the firm but also as a part of the implicit contract that keeps younger men committed to the firm and its fortunes. Thus, commitments by both employers and employees rest on their respective self-interests in a long-term association.[5] Whether these relationships are defined by strong "moral" obligations as well is another, much debated question.

Opinionnaire items that derived in our formulation primarily from questions relating to occupational mobility are *b*, *e*, *f*, and *i*. Statements *b* and *f* were phrased so that agreement implied that changing one's place of employment was on the whole a bad thing, and both of these questions drew agreement from at least small majorities of students in all curricula, with stronger agreement among the predominantly rural General A and agriculture youth than among those in other curricula. Fathers were much more emphatic, regardless of their age or employment status: three-fourths to four-fifths saw changes in place of employment as undercutting the prospects for advancement (item *f*). Item *e*, which suggested that it was a good idea to shop around a bit while young, proved to be weak bait to the majority of upper-secondary students; regardless of type of course, only about a third were ready to agree with this slanted statement. Even fewer of their parents agreed, especially among the wage and salaried men.

Most of the statements that were included in our opinionnaire primarily to obtain clues on how respondents perceived the life-commitment system were posed in terms of the self-interest of the individual in furthering his career. Even statement *b* had such an economically pragmatic connotation. Item *i*, which refers to the "moral obligation" to stay with a firm that has provided training, was included in an attempt to tap attitudes that might fit into the pattern of mutual obligations that often has been set forth as distinctively Japanese and an integral part of the life-commitment system. The fact that this sense of obligation may be far from pervasive has been suggested by some observers of employer-worker relations in Japan, and this has been one of the main themes in the attacks on Abegglen's (1958) famous model of the Japanese factory. Our findings display unambiguously the gap between attitudes of students as prospective employees and those of their fathers engaged in independent enterprise: only a third of the students in all curricula were ready to accept the idea of obligation even in principle, as against 70 percent of the enterpreneur fathers. Fathers in wage and salaried employment fell between thse extremes, with the younger among them closer to the students.

It must be emphasized that we posed item *i* in a way to elicit large percentages agreeing, since the stipulation was not of a general commitment to the firm but of one associated with prior receipt of training provided by the employer. Also, even those students and employee fathers who expressed agreement were doing so without being put to any real test. Agreement in principle is by no means the same thing as foregoing an attractive opportunity, for it costs nothing to express such sentiments. That a majority disagreed is all the more convincing evidence of the weakness of the "moral" aspect of employee commitment.[6]

Vocational versus General Schooling

The remaining questions were related in one way or another to level or type of schooling. Items *d* and *h* focused on the advantages of one or another sort of education as the route to good jobs with promising futures if one entered the labor market directly from upper-secondary school. Here we used statements of opposite positions, though they were not just mirror images of each other. The general leaning toward vocational curricula was unmistakable. It was revealed most clearly in the small proportions of either students or fathers who agreed that big corporations would prefer new graduates from general courses over those from vocational schools. Variations among students by type of curriculum and by curriculum preference were consistent. The only contrast among the four categories of fathers was the lower proportions favoring the technical curricula (item *d*) among the younger fathers of children in primary school when those fathers were independent entrepreneurs; even that contrast was small, with nothing like a reversal of majority positions. The independent and employee fathers of primary-school children especially were alike in their overwhelming disagreement with the view (statement *h*) that graduates of general curricula are preferred by corporate recruiters.

Overall it is clear that the leaning of all respondents, regardless of age or experience, was preponderantly toward vocational schooling for those who would enter the labor market directly after graduating from upper-secondary school. Whether they were right or wrong (or in between), the "vocational-school creed" stereotype was accepted by a majority in each of the subpopulations. This may have some poignant implications in view of the pressures among youth and their parents today to gain entry to general courses and through them to higher education, for many will not in fact go on.

Reactions to the Spread of Secondary and Higher Education

Repeatedly we have had occasion to refer to the rapid spread of upper-secondary and higher education in Japan, in progress long before 1964 when our students entered the upper-secondary schools. There has been little or no slackening of pace since that time; from a rate of entry to upper-secondary schools under 70 percent in 1964, the rate had risen to over 90 percent by 1980. Meanwhile, enrollments in higher education had climbed from half a million in 1964 to a million and a half (with over a third of the cohort). That the momentum of change would continue was evident enough even in 1966, although there has been a slight slackening of pace since the mid-1970s.

It was in an era of almost euphoric optimism and in the context of an extraordinary, sustained economic growth that we asked students and their fathers what might be happening to the value of education for the individual as schooling spread at all postcompulsory levels to larger and larger proportions of Japanese youth. Along with items *c* and *j*, which referred to secondary and higher education, respectively, we included an item that had a more psychological twist--the statement that with so many upper-secondary graduates a man would feel small if he had not gone at least that far in school (item *k*).

The broad picture revealed by table 12.1 is that sizable minorities of both students and adults saw the advantages of upper-secondary schooling diminishing with its rapid spread (item *c*). Considerably smaller, but still substantial, minorities took this view with respect to higher education (item *j*). Almost half of the students and substantial majorities of the fathers (especially those in wage and salaried employment) felt that whatever might be happening to the positive value of upper-secondary education, it just would not do for young people to be left behind in the wake of pervasive educational advance (item *k*).

Among course types, the most notable fact was the similarity rather than any contrasts in the distribution of students' responses. In all cases the fathers were less inclined than the students to expect declining returns to higher education. Independent entrepreneurs less often believed that the advantage of being a secondary-school graduate was declining (item *c*) than did those in wage or salaried employment. Fathers, and especially employee fathers, were much more emphatic than students in their agreement on item *k*; this strong response was as evident among fathers of primary-school youth as among fathers of young men who were just completing the upper-secondary course. Whatever lay behind these attitudes, they undoubtedly reinforced the rise in proportions of on-coming cohorts entering the upper-secondary schools.

The Patterning of Opinionnaire Responses

Thus far we have looked at just one statistical indicator: the proportions of respondents in each sample population agreeing with each assertion. Indirectly those figures are also partial, but only partial, indicators of the variability in responses within the various subpopulations. Furthermore, they tell us nothing about how closely responses on one item were associated with those on another.

Central Tendencies and Variation

As a summary, in table 12.2 we have combined our subsamples into just three categories: students (the adjusted sample), independent

Table 12.2 Mean Values and Standard Deviations of Responses to Statements on the Opinionnaire by Students, Wage and Salaried Fathers, and Fathers in Independent or Family Enterprise

Item[a]	100 × Mean[b]			100 × Standard Deviation		
		Fathers			Fathers	
	Students	Independent	Wage	Students	Independent	Wage
a	210	267	266	116	97	121
g	333	300	281	116	102	120
ℓ	216	244	...	120	109	...
m	368	354	...	105	98	...
b	266	243	232	131	108	117
f	260	228	213	126	103	110
e	320	318	350	121	89	109
i	317	245	280	113	113	108
d	246	269	244	129	92	116
h	364	323	341	98	78	93
c	311	310	303	130	98	124
j	355	341	370	118	91	96
k	296	250	224	127	98	113

[a]For specification of items see table 12.1.

[b]A neutral position would be 300; the most extreme disagreement would be 500; the most extreme agreement would be 100.

fathers, and employee fathers. Here the full distribution on each item is taken into account, not merely proportions agreeing (regardless of whether others disagreed or remained neutral, or of the strength of the agreements and disagreements). All entries in table 12.2 have been multiplied by 100 to avoid the need to use decimals; a mean score of 300 would imply a balancing of the agree and disagree responses weighted by their intensities; an entry below a mean of 300 indicates net leanings in favor of the statement, and conversely for mean scores above 300. The widest range between means of the three samples was for the two relatively personal sorts of statements, *i* and *k*; students were more disinclined than fathers to favor big enterprises.

The maximum possible standard deviation for any one item on a Lickert scale such as we are using would be 2.0 (or 200 in table 12.2), which is what we would obtain if half of the respondents "strongly agreed" and the other half "strongly disagreed". The entries in table 12.2 should be interpreted with this limitation in mind. We might regard a figure of 120 or more as indicative of high variability in the attitudes or perceptions expressed; it implies variation at 60 percent of the maximum possible figure in a symmetrical distribution around a mean of 300, or a higher percent of maximum possible variation around any other mean value.

In most cases the variability of responses was decidedly greater for students than for fathers; the only reversal of that ordering was for the two items referring to scale, where the standard deviations were greatest among the employee fathers. We may suspect that the high figures for employees were in part a reflection of the diversity in their life experiences. With the partial exception of item *i*, the entrepreneur responses were the least variable. Student variability in responses was especially striking on items *b* and *f* (the key items in the mobility, or life-commitment, set), and on *d*, *c*, and *k*. The high student variability on *d*, which referred to employer preferences in hiring graduates of technical versus general secondary curricula was associated with contrasts of student responses across curricula. High student variability on *c* and *k* had no simple cxplanation, nor did the high variability on *c* among employee fathers. Variability on *h* (roughly the opposite of *d*) was consistently low; taken together with the mean scores on that statement, this gives further evidence of the pervasiveness of what we termed the "vocational-school creed" applied to those who do not continue into higher education.

Correlations among Responses

An examination of zero-order correlations among responses for students, their employee fathers, and their entrepreneur fathers revealed looser structures for the students than for the adults. In general, the matrix for employees was more closely knit than for either students or entrepreneurs. For the independent and family entrepreneurs, correlations of statement *l* (favoring life as an entrepreneur) with other items on the opinionnaire were particularly conspicuous.

In all three groups there was a relatively close association between the two key interfirm mobility variables (*b* and *f*) and many of the other items on the opinionnaire. The relatively close association in responses on these items and on items referring to education had not been anticipated. On the other hand, associations among responses on *b*, *f*, and *e* were smaller than we had expected in view of the fact that all three of these statements referred to shifting among firms. The "moral obligation" variable *i* in the life-commitment set in fact found a firm place in that set only among wage and salaried men.

Responses on item *k* (respondents would feel "small" without at least an upper-secondary education) exhibited a surprisingly strong correlation with responses on most of the other statements. This pattern was especially striking for the wage and salaried men, but it appeared in the other groups as well. In every case responses on *k* were positively associated with those on *c*--strongly so for the students and the employee fathers. To anticipate a decline in the value of upper-secondary schooling was not by any means a sufficient reason to hold back from such education. On the contrary, respondents who were impressed by implications of the continuing rapid increases in rates of attendance in upper-secondary school saw this trend as simultaneously a reason for declining returns and a reason for not getting left behind. Item *e* excepted, the responses on *k* were positively associated with all variables we had grouped together a priori in the life-commitment set and with one or the other of the statements relating to size of firm. Among the entrepreneurs, the single strongest *k* relationship, however, was a positive one with enthusiasm for independence. Behind the zero-order association between *k* and other items was something very different from any clustering among other responses. This was evident enough from a careful examination of the zero-order matrices. It was unambiguously underlined in principal components analyses, whether for students, for one or another category of fathers, or in pooled matrices that combined some or all of these. Clearly, with statement *k* we were tapping personal attitudes that we should not expect to explain statistically from any economically grounded theoretical base.

Factor Analysis and Student Attitudes

We used principal components analysis for two related initial purposes: first, as a test of our initial hypotheses concerning interrelations that lay behind our construction of the opinionnaire in the first place; second, as the basis for the construction of a few attitude indexes that we could use as dependent variables in the investigation of factors that might explain variations in student responses.[7]

As is usually the case, the details of factors generated by the analysis depended in part on the number of factors allowed in programming the rotations. Two clusterings that turned up in a four-factor analysis but were not used for the construction of attitude indexes are worthy of comment. One of them, the second factor, carried high loadings for items *c*, *j*, *e*, and *d*, with other items far behind. All the loadings in this case were positive,[8] which implied disagreement with the suggestion that the spread of education was reducing its value, with the notion that it might make sense to gain some diversity of experience in different firms early in one's career, and with the statement that technical education gave better prospects than general education for those going directly into the labor market from upper-secondary school. A good label for this factor might be the "education-patron syndrome." The other factor pulled together those who defended terminal general curricula, who agreed that shopping around to try out various jobs when one was young was a good thing, and who disagreed with the "moral obligation" statement *i*. The counterpoint in these two clusters of traits is evident. These patterns broke apart in a five-factor rotation, however.

We have already anticipated results for item *k* in preceding remarks. No special theoretical foundation underlay inclusion of that item, which was added in its own right alone. The results surprised us in the closeness of zero-order correlations, but not in the fact that *k* carried little weight for any factor except the one it dominated entirely.

We constructed four attitude indexes on the basis of the components analyses, taking the weights in each case from associated factor scores but omitting variables that carried low values on the factor:

MOB: a clustering of attitudes relatively favorable to moving around rather than to the life-commitment system. The most important variables were *b* and *f* (toward the disagreement side); lower weights were attached to *e* and *i*.

BIG: relative preference for a big employer. This index carried a heavy weight on item *a*, and a slightly lower, reversed-sign weight on *g*.

VALED: faith in the continuing value of both upper-secondary and higher education (a simple average of responses on *c* and *j*).

GEN: support of general education as preparation for direct entry to the labor market. This index gave a weight of 7 to responses on *d* (concerning employer preferences for technical-school graduates) and a weight of 8 on the (reversed sign) responses to item *h*.

Each of these indexes can of course be read the other way. However, the directions indicated reflect the fact that principal components analysis is a method designed to pick out the latent variables that account for as much as possible of the total variance

Table 12.3 Univariate Statistics and Zero-Order Correlations between Attitude Scores of Students and Their Fathers

A. Mean Scores and Standard Deviations

	MOB	BIG	VALED	GEN
Mean scores[a]				
Students	2.772	2.362	3.363	2.405
Fathers	2.334	2.843	3.315	2.508
Standard deviations				
Students	.814	.816	.918	.852
Fathers	.706	.886	.828	.752

B. Correlations

Father's Score	Student's Score			
	MOB	BIG	VALED	GEN
MOB	.131	-.002	.024	.023
BIG	-.015	.101	-.015	-.015
VALED	.038	-.019	.152	.035
GEN	.013	.007	.023	.130

[a]Mean values would be 3.000 for an average position that was neutral. The values below 3.000 indicate leanings generally contrary to the MOB index (in conformity with the life-commitment syndrome), relative nonsupport of bigness, and more disagreement than agreement with GEN (favoring general curricula at labor market entry). The means in excess of 3.000 on VALED imply tendencies toward relative optimism on that subject.

in the matrix. That they often take the direction represented by a minority rather than a majority is not accidental.

The only variables referring to the individual's family that were associated with scores on any of the four attitude scales to a value of r = .100 or better (positive or negative) were fathers' scores on the same indexes, and even those results were modest, as table12.3 shows.[9] The only other associations worth mentioning all related to curriculum, to classroom composition, or to degree of metropolitanism or rurality.

Relations between student attitudes indexed by GEN and curriculum have already been noted. The only addition of any importance for students was the association of a predominance of white collar pupils in the classroom with relatively positive attitudes toward general curricula as routes of entry directly into the labor force. Fathers of students in technical courses and in classrooms in which a relatively large proportion of fathers were skilled manual workers were predictably negative on the GEN index. Among students there were no significant associations with VALED, despite consistent and predictable correlations on this index among fathers.

Especially interesting are the student results for the index MOB, which could be regarded as a measure of deviance from the life-commitment stereotype. It was the metropolitan youth who were most ready to express that independence, even though (as we saw in chapter 11) youth from the more rural schools showed a greater preference for independent employment status. Along with the positive association with metropolitanism was a negative association with membership in a classroom in which relatively large proportions of the fathers were farmers.

Taking together the evidence on distribution of responses, on how they cluster, and on the limited associations with other variables, we come out with a few major conclusions.

1. The stereotype of the life-commitment system was widely accepted as a specification of economically rational behavior. However, adherence to this syndrome was less firm and less pervasive among students than among older men.

2. Among students the strongest adherence to this stereotype was among the most traditional groups, and especially among students in the rural agricultural courses, relatively few of whom had had any opportunity to observe the operations of big industrial enterprises--even vicariously, through relatives and friends. The deviants tended to come from metropolitan areas.

3. Only a minority of the students, albeit a substantial minority, accepted the idea of moral commitment, even when the stipulation was linked to receipt of training at the expense of the firm. The younger of the employee fathers were also disinclined on the whole to accept the idea of moral obligation on the workers' side of a life-commitment, or "permanent employment," arrangement.

4. Bigness was not regarded by most students as good in itself--quite to the contrary. This was not merely that we slanted the opinionnaire items in ways that might have encouraged these responses; other evidence unrelated to the opinionnaire had brought out this same fact. Disinclination toward the big, preference

for the small, was associated with preferences for ultimate independence on the part of most young men. Fathers, even wage-earning fathers, were not devotees of bigness; under our stipulations they were evenly balanced on this assessment.

5. There was a pervasive believe among both parents and students that vocational schooling would be better than a general course in preparing youth to enter the labor markets directly from upper-secondary school. There were significant differences in both students' and fathers' responses associated with the type of course in which a youth was enrolled, but even among the General A students a clear majority shared this view.

6. A third to two-fifths of the students and their fathers believed that the value of upper-secondary schooling was declining as more young people attained that level. (The independent fathers were more optimistic.) However, realtively few thought this depreciation was operating with respect to higher education. At the same time, the vast majority of employee parents took a definite positive position on item *k*, agreeing that a man would "feel small" if he were left behind without upper-secondary schooling in modern society. This combination of responses tells us quite a lot about parental pressures with respect to education today, including the drive to get into schools that will facilitate entry to college. Considered in conjunction with the widespread acceptance of the "vocational-school creed" (correct or not), this poses problems for educational officials and policymakers. It is easy to see why, in this context, there is a new interest in including more of a vocational component in the general curriculum, and perhaps a greater general component in the technical courses and agriculture.

13. Expected Earning Paths and What They Imply

Analysis of the shapes of earning paths over the life cycle has evoked increasing interest since Becker (1962) and Mincer (1962) first extended applications of capital theory to include not only investments in schooling but also postschool investments in one's self and investments by firms in their employees. That work is theoretically grounded in decision theory and hence in the expectations on which decisions are based. However, as we indicated in chapter 2, with minor exceptions there has been no empirical attempt to apply these theoretical concepts using expectational data.[1] There are problems with any and all attempts to formulate empirical models in line with theoretical concepts. We argue, however, that it is time that expectational be added to the behavioral studies of these questions. We have in fact used both approaches with Japanese data, though we draw here only incidentally on our findings from more conventional types of analysis. The thrust of this chapter, as of most of the book, is on expectations and their correlates.

This chapter is divided into three sections. First, we briefly reconsider human-capital theory from the Japanese perspective. Second, we examine students' perceptions of future earnings and earning profiles. Finally, we look back of those projections to explore what factors may have been associated with how upper-secondary seniors perceived the paths of their future earnings.

Human Capital Theory and the Japanese Case

Two major applications of modern human capital theory call for special attention here: (1) the seeming paradox of unusually steep gradients in age-earning curves in Japan along with high firm-specific components in human capital, and (2) uses of the concept of the "overtake point" in analysis of the formation of human resources during the school and postschool years.

Postschool Investments, Earning Gradients, and the Life-Commitment System

The topic of postschool investments was approached briefly in chapter 12, but we need now to pursue it further. Let us sketch first the conventional argument. Suppose that a young man is choosing between two jobs, one of which will provide opportunities to increase his capabilities and thus his future earning power and the other of which will not. Most people will be more willing to accept lower initial pay on the first job than on the second. For the same reasons an employer who can offer such learning opportunities at work will be able to hire young men for less pay at first. Moreover, if the worker can take his newly acquired skills elsewhere, the employer will have no incentive to provide training unless the worker bears the cost in lower initial wages. Under these circumstances, in which we have assumed no restraints on interfirm mobility and hence on the formation of *general* human capital, we should then expect to see rising earnings such as commonly characterize age-earning profiles. In the earlier postschool years a young man invests in himself to the extent of the initial earnings he foregoes, thereby enlarging his future opportunities. Moreover, the greater those self-investments, the steeper we expect an age-income profile to be.

But now suppose that much of what a youth learns he can use only in the firm in which he acquires those capabilities. The situation will then be changed, since opportunities for the individual to gain from his new or enlarged skills will depend on the employer with whom he acquires them. We might expect then that he will be disinclined to invest in himself with large fractions of his initial earning potential. But the employer is also now in a different situation, since he will not merely be incurring the costs of training people who can take their skills to other firms that have not incurred such costs. Rational behavior on both sides will lead then to a sharing of the costs of investments in *specific* human capital and a corresponding sharing of returns on those investments. For any given sequence of total postschool investments in a man, we will expect flatter age-earning profiles when a large part of the human capital formed is firm-specific than when it is firm-general.

Does this theoretical construct fit the Japanese situation, and does it fit the life-commitment system in large firms in particular? We know that Japan has been characterized by unusually long-term associations between employer and employee, which means that statistically, at least, there is relatively low interfirm mobility of workers. This might suggest an exceptionally large relative importance of firm-specific components in human capital. On the other hand, far from displaying flatter age-earning profiles the mean earning gradients are relatively steep in Japan. Moreover, it is those with highest seniority in a firm relative to years out of school who have the most progressive earning experiences in most countries but perhaps especially in Japan. What then is going on? Three points may help resolve this seeming paradox.[2]

First, where the life-commitment system is strong, a substantial share of the investments in acquiring skills that are by their nature specific to the firm may be borne initially by the employees because they have the assurance of continuing work in the enterprise and at progressively rising pay. They see evidence of this in the firm's treatment of men ahead of them in age and career development. That assurance alters the parameters of individual job choices and undergirds anticipations of later rewards. Moreover, given incentives to build up seniority in the firm, we may find such attachments even where along with the specific human capital there are also large amounts of investment in more generally demanded capabilities.

Second, the assumptions on which the prediction of comparatively steep paths of earnings for Becker-general acquisition of human capital is based take no explicit account of technological change. But in a dynamic economy one of the chief things the employer may be looking for is the capacity to learn rapidly and to adapt readily to change. Furthermore, it will be the more dynamic firms to whom this is important, and by the very nature of their operations these will also be the firms that are likely to provide the greatest opportunities for acquiring new capabilities and further increasing the skill with which men adapt to change. Selection processes along such lines will tend to raise the earnings of those who are affiliated with the firm,[3] thereby increasing the age-earning gradients even with very little "opportunity-cost" (foregone earnings) investments in human resource formation by either employer or employee if we think of year by year decisions.[4] It will still be true that for given abilities there may be choices between entire earning streams; engineers, for example, might have higher initial earnings but experience slower rates of increase in those earnings than men in some other activities.

Third, as every experienced Japanese knows, one of the elements in firm-specific learning that is most highly valued is the acquisition of mutual understandings among members of a working team. The development of team cooperation has long been a focus of Japanese production organization, decision processes, and personnel policy. This is not just in identification with the firm but also in smaller groupings. Closely related, however, has been the characteristic enterprise unionism of Japan, which centers in the interests of the "permanent members of the firm."

Human-capital theory aside, it would be surprising if men attempting to build independent enterprises or to innovate and enlarge a family business did not anticipate relatively great increases in income between their point of entry to the labor force and their mature years. Sheer optimism with respect to business success would have this effect. But in addition, the savings and investment decisions are compounded of investments not only in one's self but also, very directly, in other aspects of the enterprise. Meanwhile, learning by the individual and learning by others about what he has to offer are inextricably entwined in the anticipated career experiences of independent entrepreneurs.

Postschool Investments and the "Overtake Point"

Whatever the underlying processes, individuals do pursue diverse learning-earning paths, and some categories of people pursue paths that involve greater postschool investments in themselves than do others. People do not come out of the schools as "finished products" whose earnings are fixed thereafter for the remainder of their lives. What Mincer (1974) has labeled the "overtake point" is the point of intersection between (*a*) a maximum possible horizontal life-earning path, in which no postschool income is foregone, and (*b*) a path of earnings that is lower than the maximum initially because of investments in opportunities (formal or informal) to build up one's human capital, but that then rises as returns on those investments begin to be realized. Mincer's conceptualization has an explicit theoretical base, but it can be used more loosely and pragmatically in many ways even when the specifications of the theory are not matched by the realities of the situation.[5]

Empirically, Mincer found (for American men) that schooling explained a much larger fraction of the variance in earnings at a given number of years of postschool experience than at a given age or at earlier or later periods in a man's working experience. He also showed that taking the internal rate of return to each increment of schooling and applying that rate to the incremental cost of the schooling gave an estimate of associated incremental earnings that coincided very well with observed mean earning paths at the years of experience that gave the highest correlation of schooling with earnings. In other words, we may estimate the maximum constant life-earning stream without postschool investment simply by multiplying the school investment by its rate of return.[6]

Figure 13.1 may help to elucidate these remarks. Here the curved path Y_m is an observed incremental mean earning path for individuals with schooling m. The horizontal line Y_m^* is the constant incremental earning stream attributable to schooling m from the date of completion of the schooling to the end of working life, at $t = T$. At first Y_m^* lies above Y_m because part of the potential incremental earnings are used (foregone) for postschool investments. We can nevertheless specify $A + B$, the rectangular area under Y_m^* from the origin to T, as the undiscounted lifetime gross rental value attributable to schooling. The difference ($J - A$) between that area and the total area under Y_m is the net rental value attributable to on-the-job learning and training.[7]

A number of assumptions underlie what we have been saying thus far, of which two are most important: (*a*) It is assumed that rates of return to investment in schooling m and to postschool investments after schooling m (over and above postschool investments associated with the next lower level of schooling) are all the same. (*b*) The exogenous effects of economic growth on earnings are disregarded. Assumption (*a*) is implicit in virtually all estimates of rates of return to schooling even though nothing is usually said about it. The whole separation between school and postschool returns would evaporate under the extreme assumption (the opposite of Mincer's) that postschool earning paths follow automatically from given schooling choices. People in such a world would still choose between flatter and steeper paths of earnings, but all would do so in an initial decision with fixed implications through to $t = T$. We still might be interested, nevertheless, in an analysis along the lines suggested by figure 13.1 using the undifferentiated rate of return to determine the path Y_m^* and the point at which the rental value of earnings would cut across Y_m^* so computed. This is a much looser interpretation and definition of "overtake" than the theoretical construct on which Mincer built.

Setting aside the effects of growth for the moment, we may find it useful to turn back to an early application of this type

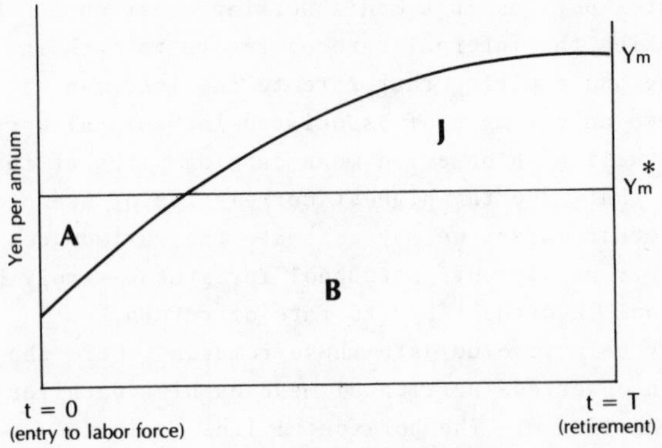

Figure 13.1 Hypothetical earning profiles and postschool investments.

of analysis. Notice that a high ratio $(J - A)/(B + A)$ tells us unambiguously that the curve of realized earnings rises compared with the average rate of return. If Mincer's assumptions are valid a relatively high ratio tells us further that postschool investments are large relative to the investment in schooling. Some years ago Bowman (1968) estimated such ratios for the four-year college increments in the United States and Japan. The ratio for urban native-white wage and salaried men as displayed in American age cross sections for 1939 was .70, that for all American males in 1949 was 1.33 (a year when entry wages were cyclically depressed), and that for all males in 1958 was .96. The figures for Japan referred to males working in firms with ten or more employees in 1961. Mean paths, which are the figures most comparable to those for the United States, gave a ratio of 1.50, which is higher than any of the figures for the United States. But the Japanese ratios depended very much on whether we followed through with men who, whatever their age in 1961, had only just joined the firm--those on the "minimum seniority path"--or men who had been with the firm ever since leaving school--those on the "maximum seniority path." The ratio for the former was 1.12, that for the latter was 4.64. Corrections to take the effects of growth into account would increase both the steepness of observed life-earning paths and average internal rates of return. But the effect on the ratios just cited would be negligible, and growth effects on those ratios could work in either direction.[8]

Expected Earning Paths

In chapter 9 we simplified our examination of associations between the college decision and expectations of earnings with and without higher education by concentrating attention almost exclusively on expectations for earnings in the mature years. We considered expected earnings on first jobs at entry to the labor force directly from upper-secondary school, but only because such earnings provided estimates of expected foregone earnings when continuing into higher education. We did not incorporate that analysis in an examination of how the secondary-school seniors perceived the paths their earnings might take from the near future on through their working lives. That we attempt to do here.

We have three dated responses on expected earnings (with and without university education): *Y1* = earnings expected on the first job, *Y5* = earnings expected after five years of experience, *YL*= earnings expected for the mature years. The various combinations in these responses give us a picture of levels of expected earnings and gradients in their expected growth, including the degree of concavity of the earning path.

Distributions of Expected Earnings at Specified Years of Experience: All Curricula

The depiction of anticipated paths of earnings is complex at best; we proceed by initial simplifications. Our first step is to merge students in all courses (using the adjusted sample) in order to look at distributions of earning expectations both with and without a college education for one year, five years, and twenty or more years of work. Those distributions are shown graphically in figures 13.2 and 13.3. Since the income scales are logarithmic, equal distances between curves imply equal ratios, not equal absolute values.

Several features of these distributions are readily apparent. First, at the medians the relative gains are slightly greater between the fifth and the mature dates than between the first and fifth years (best seen in figure 13.2). This is characteristic of both the sequence for labor market entry from upper-secondary school and that with university education. However, as figure 13.3 clearly shows, the expected annual rate of increase in earnings with age is less for the later than for the initial years. This is in accord with actual paths as observed from cross-sectional

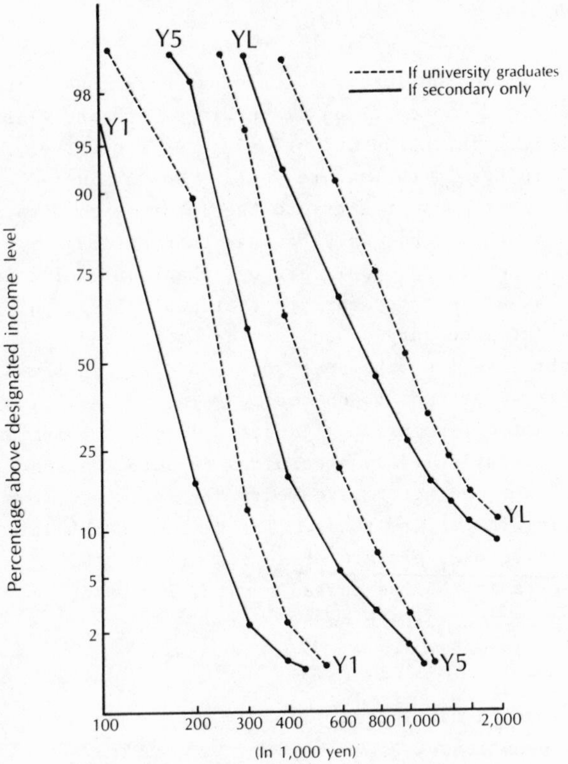

Figure 13.2 Distributions of expected future earnings at years one, five, and twenty following upper-secondary and university graduation (all students regardless of own expectations of further schooling).

age-earning data and also in such cohort data as we have been able to put together. It is also consistent with any plausible a priori expectation concerning the timing of postschool investments in learning at work, whether those investments are individual "opportunity-cost" investments or investments in its personnel by the business enterprise. As people grow older, the time period over which returns to investments in their human capital can be realized grows shorter. Moreover, time diverted from direct production activities becomes increasingly costly.

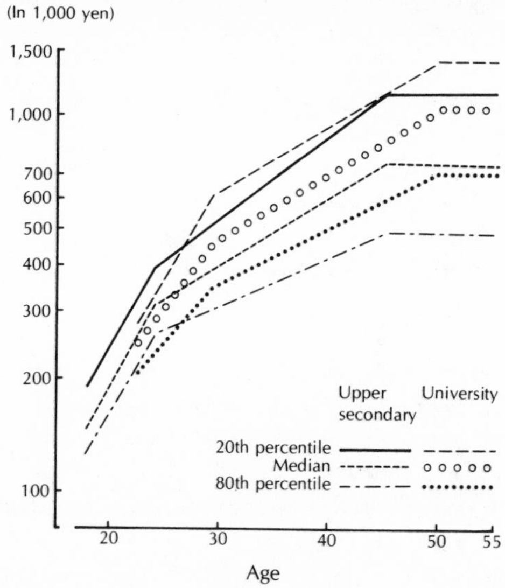

Figure 13.3 Expected life-earning paths at twentieth, fiftieth, and eightieth percentiles with and without higher education (all male students on each set regardless of own expectations of further schooling).

Second (figure 13.2), the upper tails of these distributions stretch out more for the secondary than for the university options at the five-year and the mature-year ages. This almost certainly reflects the disproportionate representation among the noncollege youth with the highest income anticipations of young men who look forward to making those high incomes in independent or family undertakings. It is no accident, of course, that this stretching out in the Pareto tails of the distributions for the secondary-school terminal group increases dramatically as we move from the first through the fifth to the mature years.

Third, in the vicinity of the tenth percentile from the bottom on these distributions the larger relative gain for the terminal upper-secondary option is between the first and fifth year out whereas this is not the case for the college option. The contrast is not sharp enough to build too much interpretation upon it, but it is consistent at least with observable patterns among wage and salaried men in private firms of thirty or more employees and in the government bureaucracies.

Fourth (figure 13.3), the incomes anticipated for the fifth year after entering the labor market from upper-secondary school generally exceed what these youth perceived as likely entry wages from completion of higher education, but shortly thereafter the curves intersect and those drawn assuming university graduation come to exceed those drawn assuming that the upper-secondary schooling was terminal. This is repeated at the twentieth percentile, the median, and the eightieth percentile, and is again in line with age cross-sectional data for wage and salaried employees in private enterprise.

Rates of return to investments in higher education (and net present values of such investments) depend upon relations between the absolute net benefit streams, beyond the point of intersection of the university and upper-secondary curves, and the net cost streams (plus direct educational outlays) to the left of that intersection. The relations at a zero discount rate can be read from figure 13.4 by a comparison of the relevant areas. In this case we have plotted the median stream for the higher-education option taking realization of "peak" earnings at two dates, the first matching the upper-secondary stream, at age 45, and the second deferring this peak five years, to age 50. Taking the earlier date increases the estimated internal rate of return considerably. Ignoring direct outlays on higher education (tuition payments and so on), which would of course cut back the internal rate of return, we obtain estimates for the internal rates implied by the two variants shown in figure 13.4 of 8 and 12 percent. These estimates are implicitly corrected for ability insofar as the students were in fact comparing options for themselves individually in stating their perceptions of those options. The rates are lower than university estimates made for 1966 from official age cross-sectional data on wage and salaried employees in the private sector, but they are of approximately the same order of magnitude after a modest correction for ability.[9]

Earning Expectation Patterns and Postsecondary Learning Options

Thus far we have viewed anticipated earning paths as though the rank orders among individuals in expectations for each of the three date points were identical, ignoring individual shifts in relative response positions. In actuality, of course, there were no such perfect rank-order correlations among the first-year expectations,

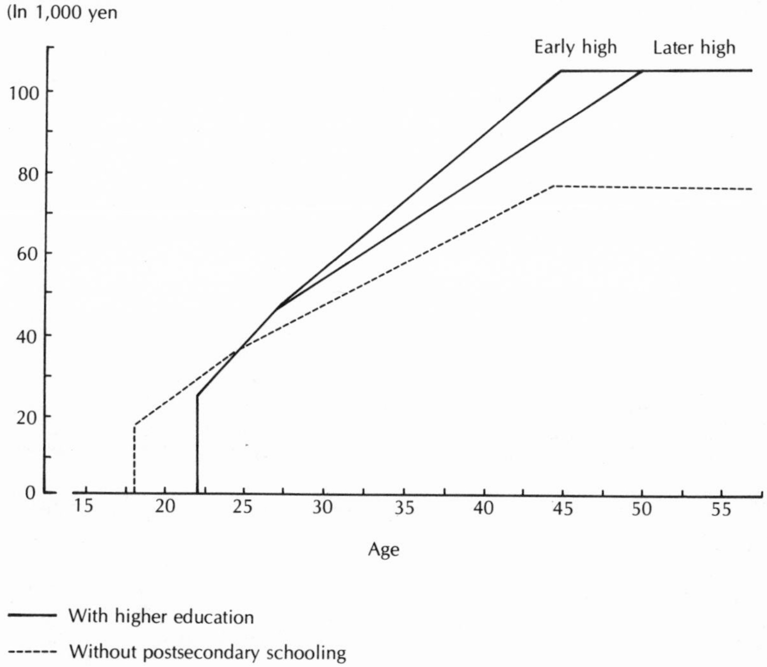

Figure 13.4 Median expected life-earning paths with and without higher education (all male students). Paths assume maximum anticipated earnings to be reached at age 45 for secondary-school and at 45 or 50 for university graduates.

those for the fifth year and those for twenty to thirty years hence. How these levels and the ratios between them were in fact related is summed up in table 13.1. Correlations between expected earnings at the first year and at career peak (*Y*1 and *YL*) are the lowest, as was to be expected. Those between *Y*1 and *Y*5 are considerably higher, though there is still room for substantial differences among individuals in relations between *Y*1 and *Y*5.

Two other measures refer directly to the shapes of the anticipated earning streams. These are the ratio of *YL* to *Y*1 and the proportion of the difference between *YL* and *Y*1 that is accounted for by gains between the first and fifth years of work. (Mean values for those ratios are shown at the top of the table.)

Table 13.1 Correlation among Indicators of Expected Earning Paths

	All Students	General B	General A	Agri-culture	Commerce	Technical
			Mean Values of Ratios			
YL/Y1		5.11	5.48	6.38	5.99	5.58
Y5/Y1		1.95	2.14	2.21	2.12	2.08
(Y5-Y1)/(YL-Y1)		.29	.33	.32	.28	.29
			Zero-Order Correlations			
Y1 with YL	.286	.282	.299	.200	.327	.247
Y1 with Y5	.679	.718	.583	.594	.655	.569
Y1 with YL/Y1	-.168	-.183	-.155	-.284	-.140	-.122
Y5 with Y1/Y1	.132	.099	.290	.158	.186	.203
Y1 with YL/Y1	.760	.708	.786	.719	.797	.839
Y1 with (Y5-Y1)/(YL-Y1)	-.042	-.504	.078	-.025	.017	-.069
Y5 with (Y5-Y1)/(YL-Y1)	.132	.277	.334	.162	.260	.235
YL with (Y5-Y1)/(YL-Y1)	-.415	-.384	-.472	-.548	-.549	-.567
EXAM-DAY with Y1	.345	.054	.360	.281	.533	.352
EXAM-DAY with Y5	.334	.176	.222	.215	.417	.372
EXAM-DAY with log YL	.295	.193	.237	.144	.277	.272
EXAM-DAY with YL/Y1	-.083	-.032	-.000	-.081	-.018	-.007
PART-U with Y1	-.101	.000	-.014	-.076	-.237	-.047
PART-U with log YL	-.030	-.030	-.170	.021	-.144	-.044
PART-U with YL/Y1	.019	.002	-.144	.081	-.021	.004
FIRM-T with Y1	.071	.014	.024	.079	.136	.083
FIRM-T with log YL	.089	.030	.012	.183	.117	.085
FIRM-T with YL-Y1	.065	.039	.062	.146	.100	.086

Note. For the all-student sample the correlation between YL and log YL was .958. The PART-U and FIRM-T indexes refer to expectations of and attitudes toward the options of part-time university study or education and training in the firm (see appendix D).

The ratio $YL/Y1$ is dominated by YL, which has much greater variance than $Y1$. The very low correlations between $Y1$ and the ratio $YL/Y1$, despite some inevitable built-in spurious associations, reflect the high degree of independence between anticipated first-year and later earnings even when we include in the same correlation youth expecting to attend college and responding in those terms and youth expecting to start work almost immediately. Associations between the level of *YL* and the proportion of the differences between *Y*1 and *YL* accounted for by the early gains (*Y*5 - *Y*1) are quite strongly negative; only expectations of sustained growth in earnings lead to the highest predicted peak, or mature-age, earning levels. An interesting feature of these observations is the fact that correlations of *YL* with (*Y*5 - *Y*1)/(*YL* - *Y*1) are lower among students in the general courses, especially General B, than among those in the three vocational courses.

Some of the associations between patterns of a youth's income expectations and whether or not he was taking examinations for college were reported earlier. Except for General B (and in part General A) students, we found that EXAM was more closely associated with expected earnings for the first and fifth years than for later stages in the career. We might have supposed that EXAM would be associated--for General B youth, at least--with anticipations of a larger relative gain in earnings through time (larger *YL*/*Y*1), but this did not emerge. The anticipated absolute differences between *YL* and *Y*1 are indeed larger among the college-bound students, but so are their expectations with respect to earnings on the first job, and across individuals the latter go up at least in proportion to the rise in expectations with respect to earnings in the more distant future. There is nothing here to suggest that youth expecting to go on to college anticipated yet further choices of careers with comparatively low initial incomes and high future returns as against higher initial earnings but lower gradients in accruals to income over the years thereafter--or that they did the opposite.

There was little association between income expectations and PART-U (part-time higher education) or FIRM-T (training in the firm) expectation-attitude indexes. Nevertheless, some of these findings are worthy of comment. It must be remembered that these indexes read so that the high scores imply disinterest, the low scores interest in the education option. Thus, the negative signs on the PART-U and the positive signs on the FIRM-T indexes in table 13.1 imply that a response favoring the taking of night university courses went along with higher earning expectations, whereas interest in training in a firm went with comparatively modest expectations for earnings at any stage of the life cycle. These latter results are due in large measure to narrow interpretations among our respondents of what was meant by training in a firm; they are related also to contrasts between earning expectations among those anticipating wage and salaried jobs and those looking forward to independent entrepreneurship. Across curricula, it is those with relatively poor options otherwise, especially among the students of commerce and agriculture, who expressed the most interest in training in a firm.

Expected Earning Paths and Upper-Secondary Investment Alternatives

How, when we add it all up, do students in the various courses differ in their expected earning paths, and what sort of an investment does each of these options involve in comparison with alternative types of upper-secondary schooling? Before we can go on to these questions it is necessary to look once again at the nature of the Stage I decision, with its implications for the future. Since we are looking at expected monetary returns only, we can specify the components of that decision in a simpler form than we used for our more generalized formal model in chapter 5.

The decision to engage in one or another type of upper-secondary study is also a decision to gain greater or lesser chances of entry to higher education. It will be useful to state this more formally, as two components of returns to the investment in upper-secondary education of one type or another. First is the return on the assumption that the secondary-school course will be terminatal. We can write this very simply:

$$V_{k0} = \sum_{t=1}^{T} \frac{(Y_k - Y_j)_t}{(1 + i)^t} , \qquad 13.1$$

where the subscript k refers to curriculum k and the subscript $k0$ specifies the case when curriculum k_0 is terminal. Y_k and Y_j are the earnings in each year t for men with upper-secondary schooling k and with lower-secondary schooling, respectively, up to the end of working life, in year T. For the years of attendance in upper-secondary school, Y_k can be taken as approaching 0, and the net values of $Y_k - Y_j$ are of course negative. Later on, Y_k will normally exceed Y_j. All this is familiar enough and is specified in chapter 2.

The second component of returns to investment in upper-secondary education k is the value of the option when continuation into further education is contemplated. The value of that option is the probability that it will have a positive discounted net value multiplied by the expected mean value when the net is positive.[10] We can write the probability as P_{kz}. There is also the question whether entry to higher education might be blocked in any case for reasons such as low academic ability or family situations that would prevent entry into higher education whatever the anticipated returns. Rather than elaborating this and related points, we may simply define P_{kz} to take such constraints into account. (They will of course reduce the value of P_{kz}.) We may then write the higher-education option value of investing in upper-secondary schooling k as follows:

$$V_{kz} = P_{kz} \sum_{t=1}^{T} \frac{(Y_z - Y_k)_t}{(1 + i)^t} . \tag{13.2}$$

The total net present value of investment in secondary schooling k is then

$$V_k = \sum_{t=1}^{T} \frac{(Y_k - Y_j)_t}{(1 + i)^t} + P_{kz} \sum_{t=1}^{T} \frac{(Y_z - Y_k)_t}{(1 + i)^t} . \tag{13.3}$$

This same equation could be written in the form

$$V_k = (1 - P_{kz}) \sum_{t=1}^{T} \frac{(Y_k - Y_j)_t}{(1 + i)^t} + P_{kz} \sum_{t=1}^{T} \frac{(Y_z - Y_j)_t}{(1 + i)^t} . \tag{13.4}$$

Mean expected total earnings in any future year t for youth enrolled in upper-secondary curriculum k will be

$$Y_{k,t} = (1 - P_{kz})(Y_k - Y_j)_t + P_{kz} (Y_z - Y_j)_t + Y_{j,t} . \tag{13.5}$$

Such earning profiles are shown for each curriculum in figure 13.5, in which P_{kz} automatically becomes equal to the proportions of young men who expect to continue into higher education. (Actually, we could elaborate the equations to specify various higher-education options, and the means of the estimated expected earnings would automatically carry the correct weights for the student population of curriculum k.) The curve for General B shows a sharp break at the age of graduation from four-year college because there is such a small proportion who will not continue into college; since $1 - P_{kz}$ is so small for k = General B, the mean value of $Y_{k,t}$ for t = 4 to 8 will be very small. In all

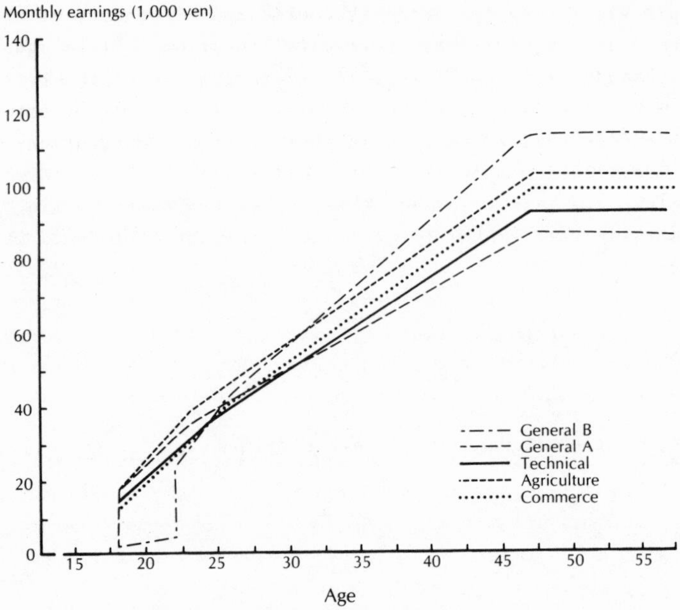

Figure 13.5 Mean expected male earning paths by type of course.

other curricula the value of P_{kz} is low and the gains in experience for terminal graduates bring their earnings up to (above) the expected entry wages for college graduates when they enter thelabor force four years later. The curves are therefore quite smooth but come down at the start to a point below the wage of new graduates because the factor 1 - P_{kz} is in all cases less than 1.

If we assume that the foregone earning stream Y_j is the same in all cases, we can use the expected paths of earnings shown in figure 13.5 as the basis for comparing present net values at any given discount rate of investment in one versus another type of upper-secondary education. General B intersects all the other curves because of the large percentage of General B students who will go on to higher education. The result is low initial but high later mean expected earnings. The technical and commerce courses cut across General A, which has the flattest curve of expected earnings.

That General B students predicted the highest earnings in their mature years was of course to be expected. Even setting any other advantages in their backgrounds and locations aside, these youth are taking the academic course and 90 percent of them expect to go on into full-day university education. It is equally clear that students in the General A curriculum are at the bottom, with the lowest levels of expected earnings. This contrast between General A and General B students in their earning expectations might be modified somewhat if we controlled for rurality. However, other factors are also involved. The contrast between earning expectations in the General B population as against students in the General A course is as much a function of which individuals elect to pursue the nonacademic route as it is of what that option may do to constrain expectations or ambitions. That a follow-up study would show the General B and General A youth at the extremes, as in figure 13.5, seems highly probable; this is not just an imagined contrast in the minds of students presently in their senior years. This picture falls in line with such follow-up evidence as is available to us by type of secondary curriculum in the United States, and for much the same reason. The terminal general secondary course has tended both here and in Japan to be negatively selective among urban children with respect to abilities and motivation and to pick up a disproportionate number of rural youth who have only the most nebulous or limited perceptions of where they may be going and who have the longest roads to travel into modern economic life.

The high levels of expected income among youth studying agriculture comes as a sharp contrast, and in some respects a surprising one. Indeed, if we took these curves at face value, we should conclude that economically, agriculture should be the favorite for all who did not wish to take on the high initial investment costs of the higher-education option that is so important for General B. These results dramatize the serious problems involved in comparisons across courses without regard to the fact that contrasts in the values of P_{kz} and in the mean sequence $(Y_k - Y_j)_t$ and $(Y_z - Y_k)_t$ reflect differences between students enrolled in one course rather than another, not just what the course does. In other words, the returns to investments in these courses are not independent of individual traits and family situations.

Behind the Expectations

We have shown that predicted earning profiles vary with college intention and with upper-secondary course. However, we have not pushed back of those observations to explore the effects of family backgrounds and community traits or to consider associations between expected earning paths and other dimensions of career expectations. We report here a few of our findings.

Backgrounds and Expected Peak Earnings

In multiple regressions taking YL and log YL as dependent variables, one of the fullest equations included (1) five categories of father's level of education, (2) the eight levels of father's occupational status as categorical variables, (3) a set of variables on father's employment status that distinguished at the same time between first and other sons of farmers and of nonfarm entrepreneurs, (4) the five categories of self-ranking by classroom ability quintile, (5) FREQ-M and SLOW-50, and (6) two indicators of socioeconomic classroom composition (CLED-HI and CLO-WC). The value of R in this equation was only .317, with an R^2 of .101, but some of the independent variables were highly significant as distinguishing traits. The main results, all statistically significant at the .01 level or better, were as follows:

1. Being the son of a father who had gone beyond compulsory schooling raised income expectations, but associations were not monotonic beyond the compulsory level.

2. Being the son of a man whose occupation was coded in any of the three highest status levels raised a sons' expected earnings significantly, but not to the same extent as having a father with more than compulsory schooling.

3. Sons of independent and family entrepreneurs had higher earning expectations than any others regardless of whether they were oldest sons. Closest to them were first sons of farmers. Lowest were sons of wage and salaried men and younger sons of farmers.

4. Youth who ranked themselves in the top quintile of ability among their classmates expected earnings substantially higher than any others, but otherwise self-ranking had no systematic effect.

5. The metropolitan indicator FREQ-M had the expected positive effect and the remoteness indicator SLOW-50 had the expected negative effect on expected earnings; however, the effects of SLOW-50 were small.

6. The proportion of classmates whose fathers had gone beyond secondary education was the strongest single predictor of expected earnings in this equation. Its inclusion damped slightly, but only slightly, the measured effect of parental

education, own father's occupational status, and SLOW-50; it had virtually no effect on any other coefficients.

Recent studies in both the United States and Sweden suggest that individual parental characteristics may have distinctive effects on the careers of sons in addition to their joint and common effects.[11] In particular, a father's occupational status seems to have a direct effect on his son's occupational status even after indirect effects via schooling and evidence concerning the son's ability are taken into account. Yet it makes comparatively little difference with respect to earnings. Conversely, parental income seems to carry through with effects on earnings in the next generation, over and above any indirect influence it may have via schooling or occupation.

We may expect related effects on sons' perceptions of their future earning potential. In pursuit of this question we divided our sample into sons of wage and salaried men (employees) and sons of independent and family entrepreneurs (entrepreneurs). For all courses considered together the association of expected with family income was modest in magnitude but highly significant among sons of employees, and for those in General B and technical courses even in equations that included multiple family traits back to the generation of the grandparents. Associations were relatively weak, however, for the subsample of sons of entrepreneurs; in part (but perhaps only in part) this may have been due to a downward bias in the regression coefficients due to greater errors in the estimates of parental income, even though those estimates were obtained directly from the parents themselves.

Career Expectations and Peak Expected Earnings

We experimented with a number of equations that included expected type of occupation and the set on preferred employment status, taking examinations for college, and in some equations type of secondary curriculum, but that omitted parental education and occupational status. Taking examinations came through strongly, as expected. Type of expected occupation had virtually no effect. There were two especially interesting results, however.

First, equations that included type of course but excluded the location variables (FREQ-M and SLOW-50) and those for classroom composition explained less of the variance (and with lower *F* values) than otherwise comparable equations that included location variables and classroom composition but omitted type of course. This result is clearly related to our findings in the path analysis of the proportions of youth in a classroom who were taking college examinations (chapter 9).

Second, those expecting the lowest incomes were definitely those who hoped for government jobs, and by a wide margin even over those who preferred employment in small firms, the employment category in which the next lowest incomes were anticipated. Standing out from all others, with by far the highest expected peak earnings, were those who wanted (and hoped or expected) ultimately to become independent entrepreneurs.

The Steepness of Expected Earnings

For the total adjusted sample the mean ratio of expected peak earnings to expected earnings on the first job was 5.50, ranging by curriculum from 5.11 in General B to 6.38 in agriculture (table 13.1). Among sons of independent and family entrepreneurs the ratios (not shown) were consistently higher, overall and in each curriculum, than among sons of wage and salaried men. Highest of all on the average was the expected rate of gain in earnings (YL/Y1) among commerce-course sons of entrepreneurs, at a ratio of 7.66. The most consistent relations in regressions taking YL/Y1 as the dependent variable were for PREF-ME (wish for the attainment of entrepreneurial status). That relation recurred for each course and for sons of both entrepreneurs and salaried men, but was strongest in its effects among the commerce and General A students. This is plausible enough. Students of agriculture were distinctive in both the high mean value of the expected YL/Y1 ratio and the strong positive effects of a farm background (which tended to work the other way in other curricula).

Partial correlations between parental income and YL/Y1 were higher than the zero-order coefficients for sons of employees generally, and especially for those in General B. For these youth the effects of parental income on expected earning gradients is thus seen more clearly when we control for the nonfinancial aspects of career hopes.

A by-product of our analyses of the determinants of expected earnings was the finding that among youth in both General B and General A, but not elsewhere, characteristics of the paternal grandfathers (specified by the fathers) were related to the steepness of the earning profiles predicted by the students when their fathers were engaged in an independent or family business. Once again, it is important to identify family entrepreneurship for understanding students' outlooks.

We have analyzed students' expectations with respect to earnings with and without college at three career points: at entry to the labor force, at the five-year point, and at career peak, constructing paths of expected earnings based on these responses. In all cases the paths of logarithms of expected earnings were concave, as is predicted by economic theory and confirmed in empirical observations. The upper tails stretched out more for secondary graduates who did not expect to continue into college than for those who were headed for higher education; this tailing out was much greater in the peak earning stage, relatively slight at that of entry to the labor force. Hopes and expectations for ultimate independent entrepreneurship were associated with the optimistic predictions of those who saw themselves in these upper tails of the expected income distributions.

When the steepness of earning curves for the full student sample was measured in terms of the ratio of expected peak-year to entry earnings, the lowest gradients were those predicted by students in General B and the highest were by those in agriculture, followed by commerce students (who had relatively low starting-income expectations). However, the association between expected peak-year earnings and the proportion of gains in earnings that took place in the first five years of work experience was strongly negative for all courses--especially among students in the vocational curricula.

We developed a model that incorporated option values and probabilities of continuing on to higher education in estimates of the mean expected life-earning streams for youth graduating from each of the five curricula. Although it started much lower (because of the many students who would be in college at first), the General B expected earning stream was ultimately the highest; General A was the lowest. The surprise in these results was the high level of earnings expected throughout by youth studying agriculture, which forces us back into more probing questions about what may be involved. A comparison across courses highlighted the problem that is involved when we try to interpret either earning expectations or what in fact happens over the postschool years as the effects of type of course, without also considering selection into and choice of one course rather than another in the first place.

A number of regressions were run to investigate factors determining earning expectations. In equations that included variables on family background, residence characteristics, classroom socioeconomic composition, and rank in class, the consistent strong predictors of relatively high peak earnings were FREQ-M (an index of nearness to metropolitan centers of over a million people), proportion of the fathers of classmates who had more than middle-level education, and self-ranking in the top fifth of the class. Neither individual nor classroom indicators of parental occupational status were as strong predictors. Other equations that emphasized primarily expectation and preference variables along with whether a youth was taking examinations for higher education revealed that the highest predicted peak earnings were among those taking examinations and among those expressing a preference for independence rather than wage or salaried employment. The lowest in most cases were among those with preferences for employment in government.

Again and again the importance of the distinctions among both parental and expected types of employment status has shown up in these data. Sons of entrepreneurs had the highest expected earning gradients (YL/Y1). Moreover, the most consistent positive relationship with YL/Y1 across courses and within each father's employment status was the positive association with preference for independence--a relationship that was especially marked among the youth in the General A and the commerce courses.

Part 5

Epilogue

14. Issues and Prospects

In 1960 Japanese children of the postwar baby-boom were in the lower schools. In 1970 the demographic swell was emerging from upper-secondary education into the labor market or higher institutions, but even then the proportions going on to college were around 15 percent for males and 8 percent for females. By 1980 almost two-fifths of the male and a third of the female graduates of upper-secondary schools were continuing further.

In 1960 a fourth of the economically active population in Japan were in agricultural pursuits; by 1980 that figure had dropped to less than a tenth. In place of farming as a life activity have come increases over a wide spectrum of wage employments characteristic of a dynamically modern, urban, industrial economy. Meanwhile, Japan has become an affluent society, which raises new problems even as it may resolve old ones.

Yet in a fundamental sense many of the challenges to educational policymakers have changed very little; many problems indeed are perennial and are common to most educationally and industrially advanced nations. Moreover, solutions to the problems of yesterday often spin off new sets of problems for tomorrow.

Viewed in a wide societal context this book has been modest in scope, and even when specifics were interpreted against a wider background, the focus has remained on determinants of the career decisions and career trajectories of individuals. Ultimately, however, our interests are societal in scope; even if great stress is placed on individual choices, the purpose of a social science investigation is societal understanding. Furthermore, that understanding requires that we focus on change, not merely on relationships and structures at a given moment in time. Accordingly, the first part of this chapter will bring together some observations about changes in occupational distributions and in earning profiles. We ask what those changes might mean for education and careers in the years ahead. The second section looks at educational choice and career perceptions of the variously situated youth who were graduating from upper-secondary school in 1967.

Occupations and Earnings through Time

Young people derive their career goals and their expectations of how education will affect them from what they see around them, from some casual awareness of recent changes, and from cues, however uncertain, to changes that may take place in the future. Each individual will be exposed in the first place to a particular configuration of activities and communications about education and the world of work, and each will retain what he perceives to be of interest. But in addition, the members of each successive cohort will experience in common those elements of the environment that are unique to that cohort. In a society as dynamic as Japan, there may be substantial changes in relevant aspects of the environment from one cohort of young people to the next, and in associated life time experiences. What has been happening? How have Japanese youth and their parents perceived these events? How are they related to educational decisions? And why do some people make decisions of one sort, some of another?

Jobs and Careers across Time

Job and career prospects for youth with any given level and type of schooling depend on what is happening both to aggregate supplies of variously educated people and to demands for their services. But supply is not independent of demand: young people make educational decisions in the light of what they perceive educationally related job opportunities to be. Furthermore, job structures develop over time, in part as an adaptation to the available supplies of variously educated people.

Japan has been fortunate. First, as in the United States, the idea of "suitable jobs" has been flexible--quite in contrast to viewpoints in most of Europe. Indeed, in the early 1960s the proportion of university graduates holding clerical positions was higher in Japan than in any other country for which data were available. Together with sales personnel, clerical workers accounted for 40 percent of the college and university graduates in the Japanese labor force, a higher proportion than even that in the United States, and this was not to be explained by the relative youthfulness of the college-educated members of the labor force. Second, the dynamism of the Japanese economy has provided a continuously rising demand for labor over most of the postwar years, and especially for qualified men with upper-secondary schooling or with higher professional competence. Only with world recession and the slowing down of the economy around 1974 did that demand slacken. Third, unlike some countries, Japan has remained free of pressures on the government to assure better-educated people of "appropriate" places. Assurances of that kind can strangle economic progress when the proportions of young graduates seeking government jobs are large and when the gates into higher education are wide open. Japan has never made such promises even implicitly, and it has been protected by a healthy private economy, a large private sector in its vast university system, and more personalized than formally organized communication networks and ways of solving problems. Fourth, there is still room for the viable independent firm in Japan, and an energetic, self-reliant population has been ready to take on such responsibilities. Furthermore, organizational inventiveness abounds, new arrangements seem continuously to be spun off to meet changing situations without undermining existing systems, and recently small enterprises seem to have been gaining strength under increasingly well qualified and relatively youthful leadership.[1]

Nevertheless, there is great unease in Japan today. In part this is centered around pressures for entry to higher education and the concern about the effects of the rapid increase in college and university enrollments since the mid-sixties. This is a late phase of the sweep into an advanced, sophisticated urban economy over two short decades. In part the worries reflect what the Japanese call the "aging" of the labor force, referring to career anxiety among the swollen cohorts of young people entering the labor force in the late sixties and early seventies. But this is not the first big change in labor market situations.

The days are not long past when forecasters of doom bewailed the impending disasters from rapid migration out of agriculture into the cities: would these people become an army of unemployed or marginally employed urban dwellers? The rural-urban migration was indeed dramatic; not only did the proportions of successive cohorts who entered agriculture drop by 50 percent in each five-year interval from 1955 to 1970; also, those initially starting in agriculture were moving out of it rapidly. But prophesies of doom failed to consider why people were moving; these migrations were less a push out of farming than they were a pull into the urban job market. The "problems" of the fifties and sixties insofar as these densely populated islands were concerned centered on "labor shortage" in an urbanized economy fired up to move forward rapidly, even as productivity in agriculture had risen with dramatic speed to provide the base for the urban advance.

Meanwhile, shifts in the types of first jobs new graduates were taking over the late 1960s and into the 1970s reflected, among other things, the replacement of lower-secondary by upper-secondary graduates, a swelling female component of all new recruits entering clerical employment, and a continuing strong demand for and increasing supplies of young technical and professional men possessing higher education.

Lifetime Profiles of Earnings in a Dynamic Society

The profile of what a man earns over his lifetime, age by age, will normally start relatively low, rise at a fairly rapid and then at a slowing rate, and then decline sharply or gradually when he reaches semi- or full retirement. This general pattern shows up in age cross-sectional data for a particular population category--for example, male graduates of upper-secondary school or (taking a more refined classification) male upper-secondary graduates employed in manufacturing. However, the cross-sectional earning profile will not rise as steeply as in a true cohort experience, and it may start to fall before retirement age even though the average member of a cohort suffers no reduction of income prior to retirement. The reason for the distortion in the cross-sectional picture taken to represent life experiences is of course that the income cross sections shift upward through time with the general raising of incomes and productivity in the economy as a whole. This contrast is depicted in figure 14.1, in which the cross-sectional curve (A_t) delineates earnings, by age, of, let us say, male upper-secondary graduates in the year t. Each point along this curve represents the intersection at time t with a particular cohort life path, the cohorts growing progressively older as we move to the right. The solid curve B_{35} represents the true past and future earnings, by age, of members of the cohort that was 35 years of age in the year t. Men who are now 25 (in year t) are earning more today than the members of the B_{35} cohort earned when they were 25, in the year t - 10, but normally the members of cohort B_{35} would earn more over the years ahead than is earned by older men today.

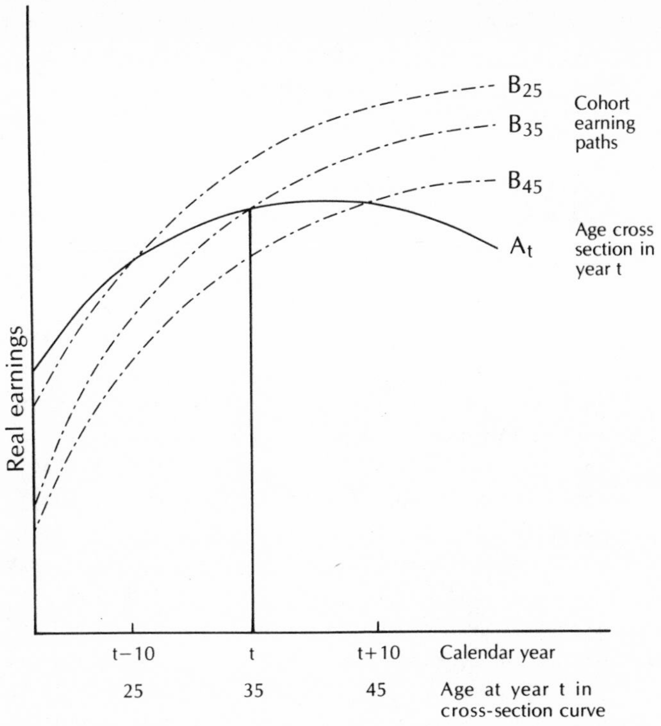

Figure 14.1 Prototype age cross-sectional and cohort earning profiles.

Slowing growth and the postwar baby-boom are altering those prospects, however.

These remarks have already introduced two dimensions of the life-earning profile. The first is its level for any given age; the second is its steepness. For any given cohort, the steepness of ascent will depend partly, but only partly, on the rate at which the age cross sections of earnings are rising through time. The faster the rate of economic progress, the steeper, other things equal, will be the cohort earning paths over a lifetime.

There is no such thing as a monolithic "Japanese system." Earning paths differ in both level and steepness with a man's education, with whether he is in independent or family business or in wage employment, and (if the latter) with whether he is in a big corporation or a small firm, in private or public employment. Life-income paths of independent entrepreneurs in a highly competitive economy diverge widely. Some men fail and disappear from the statistics, some hang on at low levels of survival; those who succeed build up their incomes by putting as much as they can back into the firm, and they enjoy the cumulative effects of a spreading reputation and multiplying connections and opportunities. We cannot say much about average earning paths of entrepreneurs in general.

More systematic are the contrasts in age-earning profiles of wage and salaried men with any given level of schooling between those employed in large private firms and those employed in smaller ones. Those contrasts have changed over time; some of the shifts in manufacturing from 1954 to 1961 to 1966 are illustrated in figure 14.2. The 1954 pattern depicts an unambiguous dualism in the labor markets; men who obtained jobs in the big firms were starting at higher wages and could expect greater increases in earnings than men of the same schooling who entered smaller firms. Under these circumstances, few would voluntarily choose employment in the smaller firms. But how could such a situation be explained? Unquestionably, labor was more productive in the big businesses, but why should those firms pay higher starting wages instead of simply pocketing a larger share of the profits? We suggest three explanations, all of which may have been involved at the same time. (*a*) The bigger firms may have creamed off the best graduates of any given level of schooling; these young men were worth more to start with. The trade-off between low earnings at an early stage and high earnings in the future is a trade-off for the same set of individuals, not between men of differing capabilities. (*b*) A comparatively generous wage policy may have been regarded as sound practice, if pocketing a somewhat smaller share of the immediate profits contributed to long-term efficiency and identification of the employees with the interests of the enterprise. The building of such attitudes has long been a major strategy in Japanese business, and is no doubt related to the predominance of enterprise unionism in Japan.[2] (*c*) The 1954 data for the smaller enterprises included many that were being squeezed out of existence. Those that survived were the most efficient, and they were those of the smaller firms that were most likely to compete with the big ones for well-qualified personnel. By 1961 the gap in starting wages between big and small enterrises had narrowed, and by 1966 the earning profiles in the big firms in some industries (clearly in manufacturing) intersected profiles in the smaller firms. Men with given qualifications might choose the flatter earning profile with a higher starting wage or the steeper profile but with a lower starting wage, as economists would predict for a smoothly functioning labor market.[3]

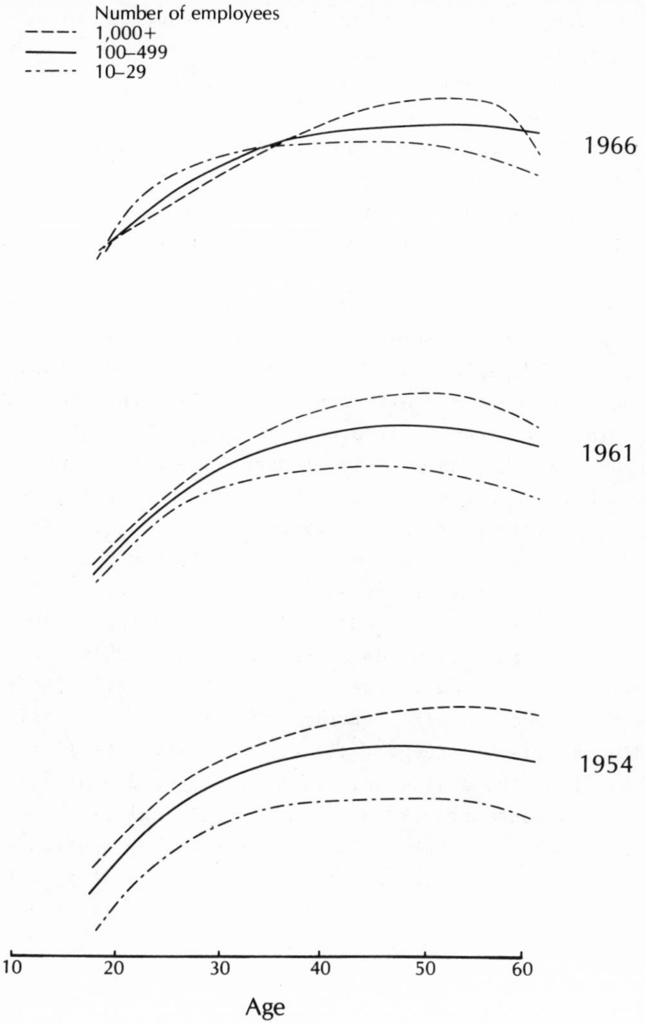

Figure 14.2 Age cross-sectional earning curves of male white collar employees in manufacturing, with middle or upper-secondary schooling; by size of firm (earnings in logarithms).

Still we have not really come to grips with why some earning paths are typically steeper than others among men in wage and salaried positions. It may be fruitful to approach the discussion of men obliquely, through some observations on women. We take women in the big private enterprises, where earning gradients tend to be steepest among men. Some years ago the situation for women was stated baldly to the senior author by one of Japan's leading businessmen. He said in effect: "We do not like to have women stay on up to or beyond five years; because we haven't invested in them, we don't want to have further commitments to them. Because we don't expect them to stay with us, we don't invest in them." Thus far, we are on common ground with what happens in the United States, though this situation has been changing dramatically in recent years among American firms. However, we then come to the next step with respect to Japan. Insofar as the life-commitment system is operating, continuation to or beyond five years entails acknowledgment of obligations by the employer to ensure permanent employment and to improve pay with seniority. But since less has been invested in the women, their productivity at the fifth year and expectations for what they could produce during the years ahead (without belated extensive investments in them) are less than for men. (This suggests nondiscrimination by sex in the definition of what would take place if the women stayed on, but discrimination in the future is ruled out by getting rid of the women in the present.) To add to all this, the routine nature of the jobs usually assigned to women discourages their voluntary continuance with the same employer--or in the labor market at all. The lesson with respect to men's earning profiles is straightforward: earning gradients will be steepest for those in whom the firm invests most heavily. The system for males is compounded of merit (performance assessment increases) and automatic seniority increases. It would be a mistake to underestimate the importance of performance. Not all those who start with a firm and stay with it are successful in the early sorting out of those who will ride the "career express" and those who will find themselves on the "slow bus."

These last remarks bring us to one other empirical observation. Earning gradients are much steeper for those who stay with a particular firm for long periods than for those who have less seniority relative to age. Again, two processes are at work: differences in ability and effort, and differences in the extent of postschool investments in their human capital. There has been a sifting process by both self-selection and employer selection in determining who will be groomed for more demanding responsibilities in the firm. Those who can look forward to a promising future in the enterprise have in turn greater reason to stay with it. The steeper gradient in earning profiles for men who accumulate seniority in a firm is not peculiar to Japan, but in Japan the seniority effect has been especially important.

The fantastic pace at which Japan moved forward over the decades following World War II could not be indefinitely sustained. The slowing up of the pace of growth has changed the situation considerably, for several reasons. We have already indicated that a rapid pace of economic growth tends to raise earnings at all ages, and in doing so it raises the steepness of cohort paths; a slowing up in the pace of growth damps this effect. But that general statement is too simple, even when we introduce caveats concerning the effects of job obsolescence. The relative coverage of workers by life-commitment arrangements has depended crucially on a firm's expectations of future expansion and on demographic swings in the numbers of entrants to the labor force. When a firm anticipates continuing expansion, it can promise permanent employment and regular pay raises to many newcomers, since high payouts to large numbers of men will occur only in a future in which the numbers of younger workers will have risen even more. However, cessation of expansion can entail an overloading with expensive, experienced personnel as the young men initially being received into life status and promised future rewards grow older and attain seniority. This problem is aggravated when the demographic waves of newcomers peak (as they did in the late 1960s and early 1970s).[4] These facts have been reflected clearly in more cautious policies of large enterprises over the past few years and in a shift toward greater reliance on contract labor and toward more subcontracting to suppliers. One result almost certainly will be reduced human investments by big enterprises because relatively fewer young men will be taken into full life-commitment status. Whether other channels of postschool learning at work will replace the lost human investments by large enterprises remains to be seen. Much depends on how far developments may go in the generation of independent or semiindependent enterprises in which men acquire rising competence through experience, with lesser or greater assistance from big enterprises or from other sources of programs for entrepreneurial education. Meanwhile, big or small, there has been and is no lack of organizational inventiveness in Japan.

Educational Choice and Career Perceptions

In our study of upper-secondary youth and their fathers we have shown again and again that a youth's socioeconomic background conditions the parameters of his decision making not only in some hierarchical sense, but in terms of both the general sweep of alternatives open to him and the extent to which special opportunities or constraints may condition his perceptions and his scope for choice in practice. The balance of costs and returns accruing to one as against another sort and level of education (even ignoring psychological satisfactions) is poorly indexed if we fail to distinguish particular options in relation to community of residence, father's type of occupation and employment status, and for some parental backgrounds birth order of the son. There are complex interactive effects among backgrounds, educational decisions, and career perceptions. Here we draw brief attention to a few of the relationships we have observed in this complex web.

Expected Life-earning Paths

Which of the upper-secondary-school seniors predicted relatively steep life-earning gradients? We looked first at comparisons on this point between those who were about to enter college and those who were headed directly for the labor force. Expected absolute increases in earnings per year were larger for the college-bound youth than for others, and for General B students than for youth in other courses. However, the ratios of expected peak-year to initial earnings were lower for the college-oriented youth because, as college graduates, they expected to start work at higher pay than would those seeking jobs directly out of upper-secondary school. Whatever the college expectations, the sons of independent and family entrepreneurs expected greater rates of increase in earnings over time than did the sons of wage and salaried men. Also, whatever their parental backgrounds, youth who looked forward to independent entrepreneurial positions expected steeper earning profiles than did their classmates. This is clearly what should be predicted for successful independent entrepreneurs, who must learn continuously on the job (and rapidly at first), who invest in themselves and in the business along the way, and who gain progressively more valuable reputations--or "goodwill"; young men who look forward to taking on such responsibilities will usually think in terms of success. Commerce-course sons of independent and family entrepreneurs predicted the greatest relative income gains over their working lives, followed by technical-course sons of entrepreneurs. These were the young men who often had the furthest to go to attain their goals, since their starting points (especially those of commerce students) often were low but their expectations for peak earnings were not correspondingly modest.

It is interesting in this connection to observe how students in various curricula compared with their employee and entrepreneur fathers in their perceptions of a cluster of attitudes and beliefs commonly associated with the life-commitment system. Information on this was obtained from analysis of some of the items included on an opinionnaire administered to the students and to their employee and entrepreneur fathers about a range of topics concerning how labor markets work and how schooling affects job opportunities. We constructed a simplified index based on a life-commitment factor that was identified by principal components analysis. On this index fathers were much more emphatic in their agreement with stereotypes of the life-commitment system and much more inclined to view conformity with its tenets as the road to economic advance over the life cycle than were their sons. Students in General A and agriculture were more conventional in their responses than students in the more urban curricula, who probably had more realistic perceptions of what was involved.

Career Outlooks and Educational Choice

Selectivity of enrollment in particular levels or types of education is not identical with selectivity of opportunity to pursue one course or another. Even if opportunity were the same for everyone, some young people would take up a particular educational option while others would choose differently, at both upper-secondary and higher levels. We must view selectivity from both perspectives--of constraints on available educational options (whether financial constraints, locational constraints, or constraints relating to academic performance) and of variations in viable and preferred careers.

Even in 1964, when the students in our survey were entering upper-secondary school, they represented 70 percent of their age cohort, and since then the rates of entry to upper-secondary school have risen to over 90 percent. The crucial selection relates to allocations among types of courses and among schools, and it was in these distributions that the effects of parental background were most clearly seen. Equally important, sizable proportions of youth in each curriculum wished they had enrolled elsewhere. The students in the academic general courses were the best satisfied with type of course, but often not with the school they were attending; students in this stream who had other initial course preferences had looked toward technical curricula, the preference of many of the dissatisfied agriculture and General A students as well. Large minorities of youth in the commerce course would have preferred being in a general curriculum. These preference patterns sharpened over the three years of upper-secondary school, as young men learned more about the world around them in general and more about the course in which they were enrolled, with some of its implications for future prospects. The students experiencing the greatest shifts in their perceptions of education and career alternatives between the freshman and senior year were those enrolled in agriculture (regardless of family background) and youth from low-status homes enrolled in the commerce course. The former revealed a clear growth in orientation toward urban life and jobs that may have had little to do with their school experiences except as the years opened awareness of new horizons. Something similar happened to the commerce-course sons of small artisans and traders, although the communication space in that case was less geographic and more social. However, the students who most often specified a lack of adequate information in their initial decision were in the technical curricula, and (the low-status commerce students aside) these were also the youth who had most raised their aspirations during their studies.

For most youth the higher-education decision is already anticipated in considerable measure in choice of upper-secondary course and in degree of prestige attached to the school to which admittance is gained. The latter, a problem that has caused much concern among educational policymakers in Japan, is exacerbated in its inegalitarian aspects by the *juku* and *yobiko* system, with expensive cram courses beyond the means of poorer people.[5] Nevertheless, rising minorities of highly motivated youth have been finding their way into higher institutions from all types of vocational curricula.

The extent to which decisions to take examinations for entry to higher institutions were related to the perceived effects of higher education on future earnings differed from one group of students to another. One of our approaches to this subject was the charting of cumulative distributions of expected peak-year earnings on lognormal paper, showing separately for each course the expectations with and without higher education. In every case differences between distributions of expected college and noncollege earnings were substantially greater than differences across courses within either college or noncollege groups, except at the upper tails. It does not follow, however, that those who perceived the greatest differentials were either desirous of continuing into higher education or able to do so. In pursuit of that question we found that college-bound rural youth consistently specified greater effects of higher education on earnings than did rural youth not continuing their education (in whatever curriculum), though the differences were small for young men in the general courses. Among urban youth in the general and commerce courses the contrasts between college-bound and noncollege students in their perceptions of the effects of higher education on earnings were substantial. Thus far, at least, the monetary behavior model is supported, even when ability to pay and academic performance are disregarded. However, among young people in the technical schools the college-bound youth estimated increases in earnings resulting from higher education that were very nearly the same as those estimated by the contingent expecting to go directly into the labor market.

Is curriculum responsible in large part for the different orientations to higher education, or do allocations among courses mainly reflect differences in initial goals, in classroom composition (in distributions of parental education and occupation), or in type of community? This question was attacked in several ways in chapter 7, with the use of both multiple regressions on observations of individuals and an analysis by classroom units. In the latter case we treated curriculum as a cardinal variable, constructed on the basis of credit hours in the subjects important in examinations for higher education; this enabled us to use a path analysis. Results were striking. With or without a location indicator, classroom composition exercised the major part of its effect on the proportions taking examinations directly, not through curriculum. The effects of rural remoteness were primarily indirect, through its effects on classroom composition (and associated informal communication networks). Classroom composition has two components: the simple aggregation of individual backgrounds and peer interactions. Further examination of regressions with individuals as the units of observation underlined the importance of the peer interaction effects.

Occupational inheritance very broadly defined was easily identified in associations between a father's education and occupation and the type of course in which his son had enrolled, even though there was nothing deterministic about these associations. Sons of professional men with higher education are of course disproportionately oriented to such careers. More interesting are the complex ways in which family situation and the success and prospects of a family business or farm relate to a youth's career expectations, including whether and how higher education fits into those plans. If the family business is a large one, the son is likely to attend a higher institution (usually a private one); if it is only moderately successful, investment in higher education may be judged not worth the costs in time and money. Successful farmers who are optimistic about the future of agriculture are the most likely to send first or only sons to agricultural secondary schools, but other sons are more likely to head for a university education and ultimate urban employment. Lacking any informally acquired knowledge of farming, youth who do not grow up on a farm start at a disadvantage; they rarely move into agricultural activities of any kind.

We found a remarkably strong interest in technical and processing activities among Japanese youth--though not at the lower skill levels. These orientations characterized many General B as well as technical-course students. When the latter expressed hopes of attaining either independent or managerial status, usually those aims were specified in terms of processing or construction activities on which careers could be built. Commerce youth were at the other extreme, with a focus almost exclusively on white collar and trading activities, at whatever level of responsibility. It is all too easy for academic people to misjudge how others see life and careers; some of the student responses are a refreshing corrective to widespread notions about preferences for big business as against independence, for example. Government ranked low on the scale for most students, but was clearly a channel for entry into an unfamiliar urban life among the General A youth in rural schools.

Also impressive in our view are the evidences of orientations of Japanese youth of 1966-67 to the longer future. They saw their society as one of opportunity, but opportunity that had to be earned. On the whole they were optimists in their ambitions, but remarkably realistic in their perceptions of possible routes to the realization of their goals. The optimism itself reflected realities of the 1960s. More recently, the economy has slowed and the baby-boom cohorts are blocking career progress for many of their own numbers and of those coming behind them--especially in the larger corporations. However, this does not necessarily mean that the decisions of individuals in the 1960s were misguided, or that the balance of benefits over costs in continuing into higher education is less favorable than before. In fact, the competitive incentives and the opportunities for higher education continued to grow in the 1970s despite some minor government efforts to check the expansion of higher institutions. Today changes in the pace of economic growth together with the long demographic waves and expanded formal education are bringing about changes in the associations between schooling and labor markets, and in the structures of the latter; these changes include innovative adaptations of career development and business policies to a continuously changing world.

Educational Policy and the Future

In all nations the making of educational policy takes place amid pulls and tugs of special interests and political maneuvers that affect which policies will emerge and which will be implemented, which options will be discarded or ignored. But the results are not the outcome of power games alone. Broad societal concerns underlie the making of public policies in education; whether they sharpen or help resolve disputes, basic societal values define the underlying directions of change. A convenient (though inaccurate) preliminary classification distinguishes between "economic" and "noneconomic" aims.

Growth is one of the "economic" goals most often cited. However, the relations between education and economic growth are little understood, and there has been a widespread tendency to disregard questions of what is best left to the schools, what part of education for growth is accomplished better elsewhere. Recent worldwide preoccupation with "deschooling" and "nonformal education" is a fad that does not come to grips with that question. As a goal, economic growth usually is more a verbal justification of decisions made on more limited grounds than a guide to those decisions. A first step is the assessment of labor market and career prospects associated with various kinds and levels of schooling. A further step is to compare those market assessments with societal costs (the sum of costs in time and money to individuals plus net subsidization by government or philanthropic agency); an economic-growth and a societal-allocative concern merge in such an analysis. Also in the category of "economic" concerns is the distribution of economic opportunities--opportunities for the formation of human capital and for the pursuit of a rewarding career. Most economists, though few laymen, would include as "economic" what women's education contributes to production in the home and to the formation of human capital in the rising generation.

Expressing the "noneconomic" goals in a positive way, we might sum them up as the contributions of education to the "quality of life," the forming of a "whole person," the enrichment of human experience. We might also classify as "noneconomic" societal concerns about women's "proper" roles and the adaptation of education to those roles.

There can be many problems in the reconciliation of societal goals the implementation of which is in part, at least, contradictory. However, there is very little contradiction between policies that would serve "economic" goals and those directed to what is sometimes described as more "human" ends. When the recent Japanese minister of education Nagai decried what had been happening in higher education and sought to redirect it toward the goal of "developing men who love learning and think for themselves," he was proposing an aim that is fully compatible with "economic" goals. Men who have learned to seek knowledge and to think for themselves will be the best qualified to cope with change and to contribute efficiently and creatively to economic development. The minister was standing also for an enlargement of the educational options available to individuals who seek from education something considerably more than access to jobs and careers (see Nagai 1971, 1979). Economists have a very unromantic name for this: the development of "human consumer capital," as distinguished from "human producer capital." But the distinction tends to melt away when we consider, for example, the subjective satisfactions men may find in their work.

These various underlying perspectives run through the debates and the decisions about Japanese policy with reference to both upper-secondary and higher levels of education. The emphasis differs with the level of schooling, however. It is in recommendations for reform of upper-secondary schools that "economic" concerns narrowly defined receive the most attention.

Flexibility and the Vocational-School Creed

Between 1960 and 1973 the proportions of graduates of general curricula applying for university places rose from 40 to 60 percent, and taking all vocational courses together the percentage of graduates of vocational schools who took examinations for higher institutions rose from under 6 to 14 percent. Also, the percentages of applicants who were admitted on the first try rose by 10 percent or more--to 1973 figures of 72 percent of the applicants from general courses, 69 percent of the applicants from technical curricula, and 86 percent or more of the applicants from other vocational courses.[6] These changes evince the popular drive for more and more education.[7] They are also evidence of the essential openness of the Japanese educational system despite the rigors of examination competition and the unambiguous separation of upper-secondary curricula.

Changes of this magnitude must inevitably give rise to many questions and problems. For example, there is concern about the effects of the intense pressures to get into the "prestige" universities and into schools that give the best chance for access to preferred higher institutions. But a majority of youth still go to work directly from upper-secondary school without seeking university education anywhere. And with the near-universalization of attendance at upper-secondary school has come concern about what may happen to the quality of education in many of those schools: What should be done to accommodate students of limited ability? Are terminal students from upper-secondary general curricula equipped for participation in the labor force?

Both the students in our survey and their fathers strongly supported the idea that, for young men entering the labor market from upper-secondary school, prospects were much better with technical (and to a lesser degree with commercial) training than with completion of a general course. There were exceptions, and those most supportive of general curricula even when not continuing to higher education were students in the general courses. But what we have termed the "vocational-school creed" was pervasive. To interpret these results, however, we must consider two things. First, even at that time (in 1966) the technical and commerce curricula allotted many hours to work in language and mathematics, with greater emphasis on mathematics in the technical courses and on foreign language in the commerce course. The foundations for the most fundamental contributions of education in a dynamic society--learning to learn and to acquire and interpret information--were not neglected. The weakest curriculum in these respects is and was agriculture. Second, to say that, if you are certain to go directly into the labor market upon graduation from upper-secondary school, you will do better in a vocational course is not to say that such a choice will be best if you want to keep open the option of going on to higher education. Furthermore, popular impressions that vocational education is appropriate as terminal upper-secondary schooling are not evidence of the facts of the situation.

In the face of an extremely complex set of problems, educational leaders in Japan seem to have been coming up with a new insistence on flexibility even as they also reaffirm the value of vocational studies in upper-secondary school. Graduates are not to be trained for narrowly defined occupational roles. Furthermore, counterposed against the worries about students of very little ability and the insistence that upper-secondary graduates be prepared to go out directly to *do* things is the democratic stress on access to higher education. The vocational schools must provide some curricular options that do not preclude entry to higher institutions.

But what is to be done about terminal students in general courses--usually in General A? Here there have been recommendations by some influential people for inclusion of short vocational courses, partly in response to the interest in such training expressed by small businessmen. Short courses that give young men some modicum of manual skills of general use in later life are easily justified. But that schools would prepare graduates for direct transfer into semiskilled jobs, in response to the stipulations of small businessmen, is something else. Complaints by businessmen that graduates of secondary schools are "not prepared to do anything" are common enough in other countries; they are not peculiar to Japan. Attempts to meet the specifications of prospective employers for short-course training conducted in the regular secondary schools have a poor record in the United States; one may at least question whether a Japanese experiment in this direction would yield different results. Are schools in fact the best place for such training? That the small businessman would ask for it is understandable enough; if you can get it done by the schools, why make such investments yourself? And if the school programs turn out to be of little value or excessively expensive, the businessman has not lost anything. Businesses may have a real problem that has wide societal import, nevertheless. There is little assurance (on either side) of continuity of the worker in the small enterprise, family attachments aside; when turnover is high, for whatever reason, even small investments in the training of new workers can be expensive. For modest skills, such as might be provided in short courses, there are two alternatives to placing responsibility on the regular schools or on the individual firm. One of these is the proprietary (private profit) school, which is likely to be more sensitive to the market for graduates than is possible in the more sluggishly adjusting general school system.[8] The other is a pooling arrangement among firms in the same industry, with or without some government assistance. Both of these alternatives have been tried in Japan, but in limited ways; we know too little even to speculate about what has been done and what might be done. However, the present surge of interest in adult education may promise more careful attention to these possibilities in the future.

When the various suggestions that are being made by Japanese educators with respect to upper-secondary vocational and General A curricula are put together, it might appear that these courses are converging, but this does not mean that a comprehensive solution is in sight. Furthermore, along with the emphasis on bringing more flexibility into the vocational courses, plans have been made to streamline curricula in General B and to concentrate on fewer areas of study for examinations. The question immediately arises. Will this increase or diminish the gap between the General B and the vocational students in the examination competition? Suggestions for revision of the academic upper-secondary course in fact stem from concerns very different from those that underlie recent decisions for vocational education, even though in both cases there is an attempt to relax pressures in order to free young people to develop as all-round human beings. The "whole person" of the General B curriculum seems to be visualized in an intellectually elitist mode, not as one who will be as at ease in building an addition to his house as in the study of philosophy. The suggestions for revision of the academic upper-secondary course are closely related to the problem of the "examination hell" and to the effects of that system along with the rapid expansion in university enrollments on quality in higher education.

Societal Decisions for Higher Education

Educational policies are made in a total societal context. In modern Japan, as in most of the West, this means inevitable tensions in the setting of priorities, the resolution of partially conflicting societal goals, the response to and containment of political pressures and dissent. All of these tensions come to a head in Japan in higher education, including the examination system.[9] To begin, we take our bearings with some very general statements of some basic problems. Then, for purposes of illustration, we examine these basic problems as they are revealed in the specific context of subsidy and tuition policymaking in Japanese higher education.

Far more often than most people realize it would be possible to find strategies that could resolve seeming contradictions in the goals of social policy; sometimes this happens and the contradictions are eliminated. However, in greater or lesser degree, at least three major sorts of compromise in the making of educational policy are probably inevitable. (1) There is the compromise between free choice by the individual or household and the collective good. We cannot even begin to understand the idea of optimal resource allocation without consideration of the relations and tensions between individual and collective--let alone central--choice. (2) There is the compromise between the realization of equity goals viewed in essentially egalitarian terms and the allocation of educational investments to maximize total societal returns (optimality in the allocation of resources). (3) In quite another vein, there is the compromise between quantity and quality. This specifies a more limited set of problems than does compromise (1) or (2), but it is not on that account any less important for an educational policy, or in the complex ramifications of associated educational strategies.

Even the most extreme advocates of laissez-faire admit the importance of government in the provision of "public goods" that benefit many people but that would not be produced privately because returns cannot be appropriated. Nor will most people see any conflict in principle between taking the preferences of individuals as the guiding factor in resource allocation and supporting government intervention in one way or another to assure that decisions made by individuals will not be seriously distorted because individuals do not incur the full costs or receive the full benefits of their actions. Air pollution (as the emission of smoke from factory chimneys and coal-burning residences) is an obvious example, and one that has been famous in the literature of economics since Pigou wrote of positive and negative "externalities" early in the present century.[10] Practical difficulties in working out solutions to such situations are many, but we are not dealing here with conflict of principle.

The view that individuals are less qualified to act in their own interests than is the state (or the persons taken as its standard-bearers) is another matter. No society goes all the way in assigning decision-making power solely to individuals or solely to a central authority. Collective judgments are imposed when the use of heroin is banned and when lower levels of schooling are made compulsory. Some modicum of individual freedom remains even in the most tightly controlled authoritarian state. The important question is where policymakers start their thinking. If they start with a presumption that in most matters individuals will decide for themselves better than a central agency can decide for them, public policy will reflect this view. If we presume that the state knows best, policy will be very different. Even the basic concept of "social benefits and costs" depends critically on whether first approximations in assessing social benefits derive from preferences revealed by individual choices or from detailed specifications of priorities laid out by a central authority. Efforts to develop socially responsible citizens for a harmonious and productive society are as self-conscious in Japan as anywhere. Building on that foundation, Japan emerges clearly as one of the societies in which the preferences and decisions of individuals and households are respected. The contrast with Sweden is striking, even setting more authoritarian societies aside.

Finally, there is a major problem that has been by-passed. How do people express preferences for changes in the institutions that condition their lives and in the range of choices open to them? The "university crisis" in Japan was a loud, disorderly confrontation over such large matters and a demand for a voice in large changes, not just for freedom of individual decisions within existing constraints. But for this very reason it may be especially interesting to ask how certain of the recent government decisions for higher education look in terms of goals of optimality in resource allocation and of equity. Has response to group pressures been in conformity with either of these societal goals, whether by accident or by intent, and in what balance of priorities?

In Japan, as elsewhere, costs per student in institutions of higher education have been rising at a rapid pace. To meet those costs, private institutions raised tuition as much as eightfold between 1950 and 1970; national universities maintained tuition unchanged, implying a big increase in government subsidy. Meanwhile, competition to enter the elite universities intensified and the quality of higher education declined--especially perhaps in some of the more economically pressed of the private institutions. A young man who secured entry to Todai had everything working for him in that his costs were minimal and his career prospects in public life were unmatched; but even there, all was not a garden of roses. Internally the universities were among the most status-ridden institutions, and an exaggerated version of the life-commitment system had reached exploitative dimensions in the treatment of graduate assistants; the medical students whose rebellion sparked major riots were an extreme example. Up and down the line there were issues of distorted resource allocation, of inequities in the distribution of rewards, and of quality decline following quantitative expansion. Many supposed remedies were espoused in

1971 by the Central Council on Education, including blueprints to reorganize the higher-education sector in a hierarchy of institutions each of which would have clearly delimited functions. Most of these recommendations have not been acted upon, which is fortunate since "reforms" of this sort impose unnecessary rigidities and could have generated more heated conflict than real reform from within.[11]

Two simple changes have been made, however. A law passed by the Diet in 1975 (in force until 1981) required the minister of education to refuse new applications for charters and for the expansion of already existing private institutions except to fulfill special needs. The other change concerns the financing of higher education. Government subsidization of private universities began in 1970, and the government share was raised until it constituted half of instructional costs by 1975. Meanwhile, tuition at the national universities was tripled. Both of these changes are reasoned responses not just to political pressures but to more fundamental questions. Let us elaborate.

a) It had been decided that higher education was expanding too rapidly to maintain quality. Correctly or not, some leaders felt that the narrowing in relative advantage of college over upper-secondary graduates in the labor markets was attributable to depreciation in the quality of higher education. But the desire to prevent quantitative overinvestment in education was given little weight; in fact the government subsidies to private universities must have stimulated rather than discouraged applications for entry to those institutions.

The decision temporarily to stop establishment of new institutions was not made in a seminar of economists, but perhaps it will not distort things too much if we try providing a rationale in economists' language. It could be argued that the social benefit-cost result of further expansion at this time (1975-81) would have been negative. This position could be posited on two arguments. The first assumes error (optimistic bias) in private benefit-cost anticipations among youth entering inferior institutions. The second argument is closer, we suspect, to the thinking of many in the Diet and of the Ministry of Education: by checking the increase in enrollments in presumptively inferior (newly established private) institutions, there would be more opportunity for the consolidation of efforts to improve quality elsehwere, which in turn would benefit future students. To put this another way, it could be argued that the *private* benefit-cost balance to individuals enrolling in the new institutions, had their establishment been permitted, would have been higher than the *social* benefit-cost balance because of the negative effect on the quality of education more generally, other social-private discrepancies aside. There was also an immediate obvious problem in the rising costs of subsidizing 50 percent of operating costs with an unconstrained multiplication of new private institutions.

b) Tuition (and subsidy) policy raises a somewhat different set of questions, however, complicated by the distinctions between the national and private institutions. In the past it has been assumed that the national institutions were providing a special service that redounded to the interests of the society as a whole and that students in those institutions should be subsidized on that account. But there is a flaw in this thinking even if we suppose that there is such a special contribution. Obviously there was no need for a special subsidy to attract able students to Todai or to Kyoto University; able young people were hammering at the gates. The private benefit-cost balance sufficed to draw greater numbers of the most able students than these institutions were willing to admit. The cutoff point on examinations was not chosen because all below that point were not good enough; it was a matter of rationing access to prevent a dysfunctional expansion in the size of a university. The special subsidization of the national universities on the original grounds was no longer possible.[12] Furthermore, by simultaneously raising tuition in the national universities and subsidizing it in the private institutions the government was bringing public and private universities into a more reasonable competitive relationship. This should reduce the cost to society of the queues for preferred places all along the line from primary to higher education. Again, we can conclude that the allocative effects of the movement toward equalization of subsidies within higher education must be unambiguously favorable.

But it does *not* follow that subsidy all around is the best answer from a resource-allocation point of view. Instead of increasing subsidy to private institutions, an alternative strategy could have been to reduce the subsidy to the national universities even more than in fact was done. In present-day Japan it would be extremely difficult to contend that the subsidy was needed to attract *enough* youth into the universities to meet social needs--that the *added* numbers who would enroll with subsidies (or with higher subsidies) but not without them would add more to the social product than the additional students would gain privately (in monetary and nonmonetary returns) from their university experience and diplomas. On allocative grounds, the subsidy decision for higher education as a whole (though not between its parts) was almost certainly perverse. Unfortunately, for the government to have followed the full economic allocation argument would have been very unpopular among just those (relatively privileged) young people who are most troublesome politically.

The political cries would almost surely have been phrased in noble language. It would be "inequitable" to raise tuition because such a policy would cut off the chances of the poor to receive a university education. Righteous indignation of this sort is a common phenomenon in many parts of the world today. But who are the families whose sons and daughters share in the public largesse for higher education? Who are those who must ultimately bear the cost? Even in Japan children of very poor families rarely enroll in universities, with or without scholarships. If we compare college and noncollege youth as groups, the distribution of public assistance in the form of higher learning is inconsistent with equity as well as with allocative criteria. Obviously, this does not end the argument, however. The cry comes, What about the able youth from poor homes who seek higher learning? Should there be equality of opportunity in access to such learning? Economists seeking answers to this dilemma have recommended (and invented) a variety of loan programs.[13] Perhaps it is time for a more systematic assessment of the distribution of the benefits and burdens of higher education in Japan and for fresh thinking about some of the ways to improve the situation in this respect. Higher public subsidies to all students through below-cost tuition is not a sound answer on either allocative or equity grounds.

"Certificitis" Japanese Style

Almost everyone who writes as much as a paragraph or two in English about education in Japan expounds on the examination system and the "examination hell." With this plethora of materials ranging from hard analysis to melodrama, we do best here to say little, but two main points call for explicit notice. (1) If reports from Japan are correct, that country seems to present an especially clear case of allocative distortion associated with an exaggerated role of "screening" relative to learning in higher institutions. (2) Meritocratic selection in education (sometimes called "degree-ocracy" in Japan) is a very elitist way of establishing "equity." We take up this second point first.

Normally the children of better educated parents, and of parents of relatively high economic status, tend to perform better on examinations than children from less favored backgrounds, although the overlaps in distributions of achievement between children from different sorts of backgrounds are substantial. Furthermore, even when they are not doing very well, children from relatively advantaged homes have access (and are subjected) to learning and cramming programs that may be too costly for those from more humble backgrounds. It is evident that meritocratic selection contains a very large component of selection by family environment and economic position, a clear departure from equity goals.[14] But that is not all. Whether "ability" is mainly genetic or mainly a matter of family environment, or a matter of interaction between these, it is the most valuable inheritance anyone could receive. Meritocratic selection is inevitably selection that is based in considerable measure on inherited human capital. Redefinitions of equity that specify equality of opportunity for men of equal ability evade the heart of the issue, as Dore has argued in his essay "The Future of Japan's Meritocracy" (1975). This brings us to what is probably the toughest dilemma of all: how can we select those who can best perform responsible tasks, of importance to the entire society, yet simultaneously provide genuine equality of opportunity to all people? There is no resolution of this profound and universal dilemma. What happens is one or another compromise and palliative action. Ultimately, we must decide what sort of society we want and how far we are prepared to go in one direction or another in a trade-off between competitive achievement and high productivity, on one hand, and a gentler if possibly less affluent future, on the other.

The term "certificitis," which was used by the senior author of this book in an earlier work (Bowman 1970*b*), is essentially what Dore (1976) has called the "diploma disease." That is, the certificate acquired with completion of a given level and type of schooling puts a stamp of approval on the individual though it is not a measure of what his educational experience has contributed to his capabilities. The intensively competitive examination system in Japan unquestionably motivates youth to work hard--even desperately and sometimes destructively hard--in the hope of doing well on the tests. Presumably there is considerable learning in this process, though how much it contributes to thinking and to personal development is not so clear--a problem recognized in the plans for reforming the General B schools to which we referred earlier. Finally, with or without a year or more as a *rōnin*, a young man gains entry to a university of greater or lesser prestige. By now he already knows fairly well what his chances will be when he has spent four years recovering from his examination ordeal and perhaps learning a little along the way. The misallocation of resources in this system must be immense, whether we think in terms of development of capabilities for productive and rewarding careers or of enrichment over the fuller spectrum of the students' future lives.

In Pursuit of Excellence

Japan has come into the postindustrial age as one of the greatest nations of the world by any conceivable criterion, in a position on the forefront economically and in education, with greater potentials for creative leadership. All this happened not by chance but as the accomplishment of a people who are simultaneously self-reliant and interdependent in an unusual degree. With all its defects, the Japanese examination system has nevertheless reflected a drive to achieve, both among individuals and collectively. Efforts to correct the excesses of that system are an expression of continuing self-criticism and of unremitting efforts to push ever upward on many fronts. However, the newest educational reforms are conservative, and the examination system emerges unscathed. Even allowing for attempts to break the hold of the prestige institutions in placement of men into the best careers, the steps taken thus far are not likely to bring either large or dramatic results.

Some years ago Professor Joseph Kitigawa remarked to the senior author that "Japan is run by young men," and the concept of "teams without heroes" may well be one of the secrets of Japan's economic success.[15] We do not have to take these aphorisms literally to start thinking about what they suggest for the future. Continuous adjustment and inventive adaptation is evident in the organization of business in the private economy, and some of the trends seem to favor a further diffusion of responsibility and creative opportunity. It is just possible that over the eighties and nineties there could be a new liberalization of education, that Japan may break the stranglehold of the examination system. The search for ways to reconcile support of motivation to work and to achieve, selection for responsibility, and wide diffusion of opportunities will certainly continue--whether through consensus or through conflict. Will the young in years and the young in heart find ways to bring Japan to a new unfolding of an old and unique cultural heritage? The world must watch with profound interest as Japan strives to find the answer to that question.

A. Male Student Questionnaire

1. In what course are you enrolled at present? Circle the one that applies.

    1. General (Preparing for higher education)
    2. General (Preparing directly for work)
    3. Agricultural
    4. Commercial
    5. Technical

I. Questions on Occupation and Education of Your Parents.

2. How old is your father?

    1. Less than 40.   2. 40-44   3. 45-49
    4. 50-54   5. 55-59.   6. 60 and over
    7. Not living

    If your father is dead, at what age did he die?

    1. Less than 30   2. 30-39   3. 40-49
    4. 50 and over

3. Is your father working at present?

    1. Yes, he has a fixed job.
    2. Yes. Although he has no fixed job status, he sometimes work.
    3. No, he is not working.
    4. Not living.

4. Next, here are three questions, A, B, C, concerning your father's occupation. If your father is dead or retired, please give your father's previous principal occupation.

    A. What is your father's principal occupation? If he has a regular position, please state it as exactly as possible: for example, farm operator, night watchman, foreman in a factory, section chief in administration, an independent shop keeper, teacher in a primary school, civil engineer, skipper of a deep-sea fishing boat, etc.

    ____

B. Where does your father engage in that job? Describe as exactly as possible: for example, municipal office, Department of Labor, National Railway, private railway, textile factory, shipyard, private high school, restaurant of a hotel, etc.

____

C. For what category of employer does he work?

1. Governmental agency.
2. Private corporation.
3. Farmer (self-employed).
4. In his own or family firm (in commerce and industry): no other employee than family.
5. In his own or a family firm: 1-9 employees other than family.
6. In his own or a family firm: 10 and over employees other than family.
7. Other (Specify:).

5. How many living brothers and sisters have you? Write the number in the [ ]

1. Older brothers [ ]
2. Older sisters [ ]
3. Younger brothers and sisters [ ]

6. If your family occupation is in independent employment--for example: independent farming, shopkeeping, factory proprietorship--will you be the inheritor? Circle the one that applies.

1. Family occupation is not of an independent type.
2. Yes, certainly.
3. Yes, probably.
4. No, probably not.
5. No, definitely not.

7. Do you expect to go into the same occupation as your father's? Circle the one that applies.

1. Yes, hope and expect to.
2. Would like to, but chances small.
3. Do not want to, but will have to.
4. No, do not want to and will not.

8. What is the last school that each of your parents attended? Circle the appropriate number in the column for your father and in that for your mother.

Father	Mother	
10	10	Ordinary Elementary
20	20	Upper Elementary, New Junior Secondary
26	26	Youth School
30	30	Middle School, Girls' High School, New Senior Secondary (General)

32	32	Normal School
33	33	Vocational Agriculture, Fishery, New and Old
34	34	Vocational Technical, Navigation, New and Old (include a school in corporation)
35	35	Vocational Commercial, New and Old
41	41	Higher School, Preparatory
42	42	Higher Normal School
43	43	Professional School, Agriculture and Forest, Fishery
44	44	Professional School, Technical, Navigation, Other Science College
45	45	Professional School, Commercial, Other Liberal Arts College
46	46	Military School at Secondary Level, Army and Navy
56	56	Military School at University Level, Army and Navy
57	57	University (include Graduate School)
58	58	Foreign University
99	99	Other

II. Questions about the Courses in Which You Are at Present Enrolled and How You Selected Them.

9. Is the type of course in which you are majoring the type you most wanted to follow at the time when you entered secondary school?

   1. Yes, it is the course I preferred.
   2. No, it is not the course I preferred.

10. Is the school you are attending the one you most wanted to attend at the time when you entered senior secondary school?

    1. Yes, it is the school I preferred.
    2. No, it is not the school I preferred.

11. Did you in fact take the examination for entrance to any other senior secondary school or technical junior college?

    1. Yes, I did.
    2. No, I did not.

    IF YES, please circle all the courses for which you took examinations, excluding the course in which you are at present.

    1. General
    2. Agricultural
    3. Commercial
    4. Technical
    5. Homemaking
    6. Technical Junior College
    7. Other (Specify:

12. If you were completely free to choose any course according to your own preference and were choosing again, which course would you choose? Circle only one response.

    1. The same course
    2. General
    3. Agricultural
    4. Commercial
    5. Technical
    6. Homemaking
    7. Technical Junior College
    8. Other (Specify:)

    If you circled a course other than your present one, answer A and B.

    A. What is the chief reason for the preference you expressed in questions 12? Circle ONE answer.

    1. It would have been nearer to my home
    2. It is the most interesting
    3. It is the best suited to my talents and abilities
    4. It gives the best chances for going on to higher education
    5. It gives the best preparation for the kind of career I would like to follow
    6. When you get through this kind of school you can be sure of a good job right away
    7. Other (Specify:)

    B. Why did you enter your present course, which you dislike? Circle the ONE answer that is most important.

    1. This school is nearer to my home
    2. My parents wanted me to go to this school and to take this course
    3. My teachers in junior secondary school wanted me to go to this school and take this course
    4. This school and course is less expensive
    5. I did not pass the entrance examinations for my preferred school and course
    6. I did not know enough about other schools and courses when I decided to go here
    7. Other (Specify:)

III. Questions about Entering Higher Institutions

13. If possible, would you like to continue with full time schooling after graduating from your present school?

    1. Yes, if possible
    2. No, I would not want to continue

14. Do you plan to take examinations for college or university next spring? Circle the one that applies.

    1. Yes, full-time university
    2. Yes, night university
    3. No

15. Answer only if you would like to continue your study but are unable to enter a college or university. What would be the single most important reason?

    1. Difficult to pay the tuition and fees
    2. My parents are against my going to college or university
    3. Have to help the family business as soon as possible
    4. The course that I am taking is not appropriate for the entrance examinations
    5. My scholastic ability may fail me in the examinations
    6. Other (Specify:)

16. Do you plan to go to your first choice of university, even if you should have to spend a year or so as a Rōnin to gain admission? Circle the one that applies.

    1. I won't go to university anyway
    2. Yes, even if I have to spend time as a Rōnin.
    3. No, I would not spend time as a Rōnin.
    4. Not sure

17. If you were to get a job right after your graduation from high school, which of the following kinds of occupational education would you want to receive? After each item, circle 1 if you have definite plans to take, 2 if you would like to take if possible, 3 if you would not be particularly interested, and 4 if you definitely would not want to take it.

	Have definite plan to take	Probably would take	Probably would not take	Definitely would not take
1. Night University	1	2	3	4
2. Other night school	1	2	3	4
3. Education and training program sponsored by firm	1	2	3	4
4. Correspondence Course	1	2	3	4
5. Other (Specify:)	1	2	3	4

IV. Finally, Questions about Your Views Concerning Occupations

18. After graduation from school, in which of the following places would you want to get a job?

    1. A farming or fishing village
    2. A medium or small-sized city
    3. A metropolis (Tokyo, Yokohama, Nagoya, Osaka, Kyoto, Kobe, Kitakyushu, or their suburbs)

19. Do you think you would like to remain in the prefecture where you live at present?

    1. Yes, definitely 2. Yes, if possible
    3. Prefer to move out 4. Not sure

20. When you select your occupation, to which of the following five conditions would you give most consideration?

    1. A secure job
    2. A job that carries respect
    3. A well paid job
    4. A job that promises rapid promotion
    5. A job that is interesting and enjoyable

21. Among the following four careers, which would you like best? Circle the one that you prefer.

    1. Self-employed job
    2. Work for the government
    3. Work for a big corporation
    4. Work for a medium or small-sized company

22. Suppose you are offered a chance to take any of the following six careers. Which would you select? Put 1 by your first choice, 2 by the second, and 3 by the third. Be sure to mark three.

    ______ 1. Farmer

    ______ 2. Independent shop keeper

    ______ 3. An office clerk in a big corporation

    ______ 4. An office clerk in the government

    ______ 5. A mechanic in a big corporation

    ______ 6. A skilled worker in a small corporation

23. Suppose you started your job as a salaried man, and the total sum of your earnings from the time you start until your retirement would be the same in each alternative. Which of the following would you choose? Assume that there would be no fluctuation of price.

    Circle 1 or 2

    1. As line A-A; a job that pays extremely well at first, but where pay increases thereafter are slight
    2. As line B-B; a job in which the initial pay is not so good, but the rate of increase in pay is good

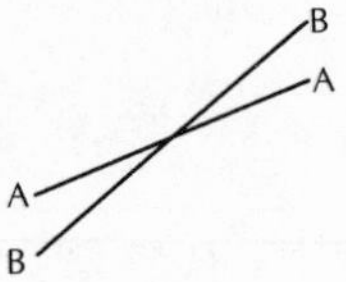

    Circle 1 or 2

    1. As curve C-C; a job for which pay is not so good over the first half of the period but becomes rapidly good in the second half
    2. As curve D-D; a job for which pay is extremely good in the first half of the period but not so good in the second half

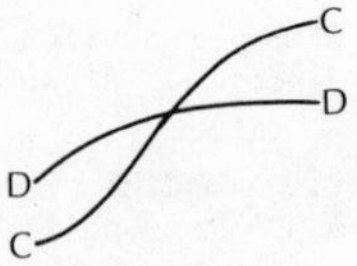

    Which of these four earnings curves, A-A, B-B, C-C, D-D, in the figures to the right above, do you think most desirable? Circle the one that you think best.

    A-A   B-B   C-C   D-D

Why did you choose it? Write your reason ________________

____

Among those four curves, circle the one that is most likely to be similar to your future earnings stream.

A-A B-B C-C D-D

24. Suppose you must get your job at one or the other of the following companies. Which company would you choose? Circle your preference.

1. A company that wants you to spend time for education even when you are off duty
2. A company that takes no interest in stimulating education but leaves you free except for your time on duty

25. Suppose you seek a job right after your graduation from high school. What is the best job you think you could get? If your job has been decided, write the place where you will work.

____

26. Has your job been decided already?

1. Yes, already 2. No, not yet

In case if has been decided, how did you find that job? Circle the one that applies.

1. Through personal connections
2. Introduction by your teacher or school
3. Public Employment Agency
4. Other (Specify:)

27. Suppose you are able to go to college or university. What is the best job you would be likely to be able to get? Explain as fully as possible.

____

____

____

28. If you were to (or expect to) start work right after graduating from high school, how much would you expect to receive per month? (If you will be in an independent, self-employed job, answer according to your best guess.) What do you think your monthly salary for the first year will be, what will it be after five years, and what at the highest you could reach in the future? Circle one answer for each period. Assume that prices do not change.

	First year	After 5 Years	At the highest in the future
a. Under 10,000 yen	1	1	1
b. 10,000-20,000 yen	2	2	2
c. 20,000-30,000 yen	3	3	3
d. 30,000-40,000 yen	4	4	4
e. 40,000-60,000 yen	5	5	5
f. 60,000-80,000 yen	6	6	6
g. 80,000-100,000 yen	7	7	7
h. 100,000-120,000 yen	8	8	8
i. 120,000-140,000 yen	9	9	9
j. 140,000-160,000 yen	10	10	10
k. 160,000-200,000 yen	11	11	11
l. 200,000-or more yen	12	12	12

29. Suppose you graduated from a 4-year university and took a job. How much do you think you could earn per month? Assuming prices do not change, circle the digit in each of the following columns that indicates your estimates for your first year of employment, after five years, and at the highest you can reach.

	First Year	After 5 years	At the highest
a. Under 10,000 yen	1	1	1
b. 10,000-20,000 yen	2	2	2
c. 20,000-30,000 yen	3	3	3
d. 30,000-40,000 yen	4	4	4
e. 40,000-60,000 yen	5	5	5
f. 60,000-80,000 yen	6	6	6
g. 80,000-100,000 yen	7	7	7
h. 100,000-120,000 yen	8	8	8
i. 120,000-140,000 yen	9	9	9
j. 140,000-160,000 yen	10	10	10
k. 160,000-200,000 yen	11	11	11
l. 200,000-or more yen	12	12	12

30. Suppose you were given a choice between a gift of 1 million yen now or each of the following sums assured after five years. Circle your choice in each set:

1.	a. Now	100 Manyen
	b. After 5 years	100 Manyen
2.	a. Now	100 Manyen
	b. After 5 years	125 Manyen
3.	a. Now	100 Manyen
	b. After 5 years	150 Manyen
4.	a. Now	100 Manyen
	b. After 5 years	175 Manyen
5.	a. Now	100 Manyen
	b. After 5 years	200 Manyen

31. Suppose you hit the jack-pot in a "Treasure Lottery" for 100 manyen. How would you use it? Circle one answer.

    1. Start my own business
    2. Save for the cost of going to university
    3. Save in a bank
    4. Travel in foreign countries
    5. Invest in land
    6. Other (Specify:)

32. What job would you imagine in your dreams for after you complete your formal schooling? Cite one job and describe your dream of it as fully as possible.

---

33. Looking ahead 20-30 years, what kind of work would you like to be doining and in what sort of organization or employment status? State what you think you are in fact most likely to be doing and describe it fully.

---

34. Here are some opinions and points of view about which people often disagree. What do you think about each of these opinions? If you agree strongly, circle the number 1 in the first column. If you agree mildly, circle 2 in the second column. If you disagree mildly, circle 3 in the third column, and if you disagree strongly, circle 4. If you cannot say, circle 5. There are no right or wrong answers. Mark exactly as you think yourself. Be sure to circle one of the numbers after each of the statements from a to m.

	Agree Strongly	Agree Mildly	Disagree Mildly	Disagree Strongly	Can't Say
a. It is better to work at a company where there is promise of promotion and pay increase even though it is a small company rather than to work at a big corporation here there is slight chance of recognition.	1	2	3	4	5
b. Prospective employers look with suspicion on a man who has made frequent job changes as lacking in qualities of loyalty.	1	2	3	4	5

	Agree Strongly	Agree Mildly	Disagree Mildly	Disagree Strongly	Can't Say
c. Since the number of high school graduates has become so large recently, the advantages of being a high school graduate are going down.	1	2	3	4	5
d. Among people who take a job directly after graduation from high school, career prospects will be better for those who have finished a technical than for those who have finished a general course.	1	2	3	4	5
e. It is desirable to expand one;s experience by working in various companies and governmental organizations when one is young.	1	2	3	4	5
f. Those who often change their place of employment must start anew each time. Therefore it is disadvantageous.	1	2	3	4	5
g. It is foolish to take a job in a small company even at a higher initial salary when one can get a job in a big corporation.	1	2	3	4	5
h. Those who graduate from the general course of high school can be trained to the need of a company. Therefore, the large corporation gives priority to those who graduate from the general course rather than those from the occupational courses.	1	2	3	4	5
i. If one receives education in a company school, etc., it is difficult for him to change his job (even though there is a profitable one) since he feels a moral obligation to the company.	1	2	3	4	5
j. With the number of college graduates increasing so much, it is difficult for even the college graduate to find a job. Therefore the value of going to university and paying the high cost will be going down.	1	2	3	4	5
k. With so many high school graduates now, a man will feel small unless he has at least graduated from high school.	1	2	3	4	5
l. A man will lead a more fruitful life if he operates an independent business rather than being employed by others.	1	2	3	4	5
m. If a man has his own business, he has too many worries and troubles. Therefore, it might be better to be employed by a stable company if possible.	1	2	3	4	5

35. When you divide your class into five groups, according go school achievement, what is your achivement ranking? Circle the one that fits.

Upper 1/5	Next Upper 1/5	Middle 1/5	Next Lower 1/5	Lowest 1/5

B. The 1966 Study Samples

It would have been desirable to sample a large enough number of schools to cover the entire spectrum of upper-secondary institutions in Japan. However, working on a very small budget and given the diversity among upper-secondary schools, it was necessary to be selective from the start. To sample students directly, including a few from each of a large number of schools, would have been almost as costly as full coverage of students in those same schools. This just was not feasible. The final sample of a hundred schools with eleven thousand students (male and female) and their fathers was systematically selective primarily in the exclusion of private institutions and in geographic coverage. It was stratified by type of curriculum. Other factors blocked our attempt to study technical junior colleges. The coverage and sampling methods are discussed here under two headings: types of schools and geographic representation.

Types of Schools

The first significant omission, the private upper-secondary schools, accounted for a third of all upper-secondary students in 1966. The problem in working with them on a small budget was their extreme heterogeneity in quality, size, and curriculum. Inclusion of a random sample from the private sector could have made our results wildly unreliable. It was more important to have adequate representation of the main types of curricula in upper-secondary education, and it was decided, therefore, to limit the sample to schools in the public system.

This left us with a set of critical dimensions in school types and student bodies that was still complex. What we did in fact was to select certain urban and rural areas (discussed below) within which we took stratified samples of general, technical, commerce, and agricultural (or "combined") schools. The stratification ensured adequate representation of schools and pupils in curricula other than the numerically preponderant general programs. Sample proportions in the academic and nonacademic general courses could not be predetermined, however; those proportions were calculated only after data had been collected from the general schools. Large samples were taken from the technical schools because of the greater diversity of their curricula compared with the other types of schools. We did not sample the small population of upper-secondary students in part-time programs.

Geographic Representation

Geographic areas were selected to ensure representation of students from communities differing in occupational makeup. The urban and rural areas sampled are shown in figure B.1.

Five urban areas were included. Tokyo, Osaka, and Fukuoka are metropolitan centers of over one million population; the least cosmopolitan is Fukuoka, which draws most of its working population from the surrounding agricultural and mining areas of northern Kyushu. The city of Hiroshima, the smallest of the major urban centers sampled in our study, had a population of approximately four hundred fifty thousand in 1966 and ranks as part of the second tier of industrial metropolitan areas in Japan; it is a major market center and the most important manufacturing city between the Osaka-Kobe conurbation and northern Kyushu. Tokushima is a prefectural capital and a local market town on the island of Shikoku; it is undistinguished as a manufacturing center and had a population in 1966 of just under two hundred thousand.

To encompass the full gamut from urbanism to maximal rurality, we should have included localities in the northern part of Honshu and in southern Kyushu, but were unable to do so. However, we were able to establish a basis for analyzing the effects of centrality versus comparative isolation by careful selection of rural areas from central and western Honshu and from Shikoku. Thus, Tochigi prefecture (north of Tokyo) and the southern half of Shikoku have little manufacturing, they were in the lowest quintile in rates of entry to upper-secondary school, and they have comparatively high proportions in agriculture. Hiroshima prefecture extends over a wide area, from the Inland Sea to the northern "shady side" of Honshu; we included locations back in the hills in our rural samples from that prefecture. These were the most remote communities in the study, despite the fact that Hiroshima prefecture as a whole has moderately high proportions engaged in

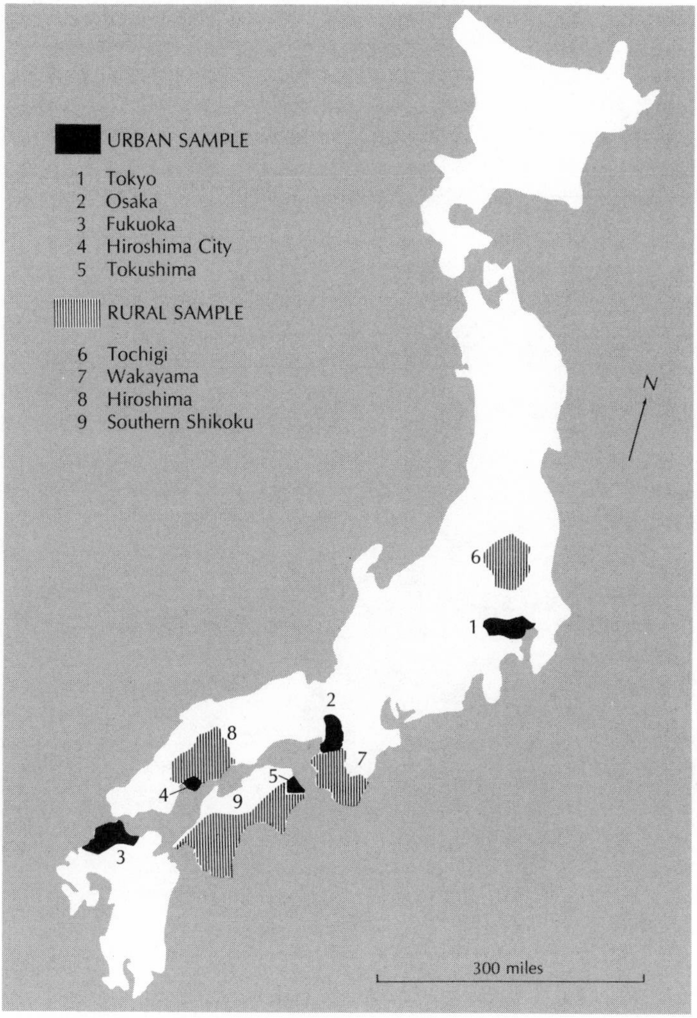

Figure B.1 Location of sample.

manufacturing (in the city of Hiroshima and in one or two smaller places on the shore of the Inland Sea). Wakayama prefecture, like Hiroshima, occupies an intermediate position on both the industrial and agricultural rankings; however, southern Wakayama remains distinctly rural both in occupational structure and in time distance from urban areas.

C. Simultaneity in the Stage I–Stage II Decisions: Tests for Bias in Single-Equation Models Using Grouped Data

There can be no doubt that selection of an upper-secondary course is influenced by goals and expectations for further education and later career opportunities. However, when the dependent variable takes a dichotomous form, as it does for the variable EXAM (taking examinations) in the Stage II decision, we are constrained in the methods available for testing single-equation biases. By using grouped data and logit transforms of proportions taking examinations and by converting the type-of-course variable into a cardinal index of course content, we can introduce such tests.

The primary purpose of this appendix is to make an assessment of (1) biases in the coefficients on class-composition variables explaining proportions taking examinations, and, conversely, (2) single-equation biases on variables explaining class composition. The results of this analysis, while incomplete, are firm on the most crucial question. This permitted us to go on with assurance in chapter 7 to examine "direct" and "indirect" effects (via curriculum) of classroom composition on the proportions taking examinations.

Throughout we use group variables in cardinal form. Those variables are as follows:

Curriculum Variable

S Credits in language, mathematics, and pure science, which are presumably most critical as preparation for university entrance examinations. It is hypothesized that the higher the value of *S*, the greater will be the proportion of students taking examinations. Values assigned to *S* by type of course in which the student was enrolled were General B, 75; General A, 55; technical, 48; commerce, 54; agriculture, 40. *S* varied among the general schools according to the proportion of students in the General B and General A streams or curricula.

Higher-Education Variable

Z Logit transform of the percentage of students taking examinations for entry into institutions of higher education.

Socioeconomic Background Variables

C Logit transform of CLED-HI (the percentage of parents with college or university education).

Q Logit transform of the percentage of parents in the top three occupational status categories (OSTAS 1, 2, 3).

H The sum *C* + *Q*

These three variables were treated initially as alternative measures. In the end the greatest use was made of *H*, which is unquestionably a better proxy for economic ability to pay than *C* or *Q* alone, and gives a broader index to socioeconomic status. These are also, of course, in part taste and in part information proxies.

Indicators of Rurality, Communications, and Accessibility

D SLOW-50, described in chapter 5 and used in numerous equations thereafter. Unfortunately, the implications of this measure shift drastically according to whether the dependent variable is *S* or one of the other endogenous variables.

M FREQ-M, also a variable used elsewhere in a number of equations. This variable is unambiguously an indicator (however imprecise) of information and perceived opportunity configurations favorable to higher education when entered in equations with individuals as units of observation. (A positive association with *Z* was hypothesized.)

K A classroom-rurality index. This is a modified logit transform of the percentage difference $P_{ag} - P_{tec}$, where P_{ag} refers to the proportion of parents engaged in agricultural and related pursuits and P_{tec} refers to the proportion of parents who are technicians or skilled manual workers.

The zero-order matrix for these variables is shown in table C.1. Table C.2 gives the set of equations used, with regression coefficients in standard deviation units to facilitate direct comparisons across variables with different initial units of count and variances. The intercept is thus, automatically, zero. *F* values for the standardized beta coefficients are shown in parentheses.

The structural equations (1.1*c*) and (1.1*h*) for *C* and *H*, respectively, were based on the hypothesis that children of better

Table C.1 Zero-Order Correlations among Variables Measuring Classroom Composition, Curriculum, College Intentions, and Location

	Curriculum	Socioeconomic Traits			Rurality and Metropolitanism			College Intentions
	S	*C*	*Q*	*H*	*K*	*D*	*M*	*Z*
S	...	.666	.663	.709	-.203	.046	.025	.813
C	.666	...	.758	.941	-.464	-.241	.219	.808
Q	.663	.758	...	.934	-.723	-.363	.327	.787
H	.709	.941	.934	...	-.629	-.320	.290	.851
K	-.203	-.464	-.723	-.629	...	.614	-.647	-.375
D	.046	-.241	-.363	-.320	.614	...	-.416	-.180
M	.025	.219	.327	.290	-.647	-.416	...	.145
Z	.813	.808	.787	.851	-.375	-.180	.145	...

educated and higher status parents would be drawn to and seek out not only academic courses but also schools reputed to send large proportions of their graduates on to college and/or that they would have advantages of entry into such schools. Hence, both *H* and *C* should be positive functions of *S* and *Z*. *H* and *C* are negative functions of *D* for the simple reason that the base population of the more isolated communities (high values on *D*) has relatively few men with higher education or high-status occupations. Even a greater relative selectivity into upper-secondary school in these areas is not sufficient to neutralize that factor. Equations (1.2*c*) and (1.2*h*) are similar to (1.1*c*) and (1.1*h*) except for the substitutions of *K* for *D*. The fact that the variable *K* comes through much more strongly than *D* in these equations was to be expected; *K* generalizes a relationship that is at once both a community characteristic (related to *D*)and a school-specific variable that tends to take on its highest values in the agricultural schools.

In both the structural equations and the zero-order relationships, *H* is more closely associated with both *K* and *D* than is *C*. This reflects the fact that the strongest association between *K* and *D* on one hand and any of the socioeconomic status variables on the other is with *Q*, which does more alone than in combination with *C*. In association with *Z*, the two components of *H* are more complementary or mutually supportive in their impact.

The existence of an identification problem in the structural equations for *C* and *H* is obvious. A school with large proportions of its graduates normally continuing into higher education may indeed attract relatively large proportions of high-status youth;

Table C.2 Equations for Analysis of Z, H, and C Treating S as Exogenous

A. Structural Equations

(1.1c) $C = .0923S + .7118Z - .1171D + u$
 $\quad\quad (.45) \quad\quad (25.96) \quad (2.07)$

$\quad\quad\quad\quad\quad\quad\quad\quad\quad\quad\quad\quad\quad R^2 = .665 \quad\quad F = 39.01$

(1.1h) $H = .1659S + .6790Z - .2057D + u$
 $\quad\quad (2.04) \quad\quad (33.17) \quad (8.97)$

$\quad\quad\quad\quad\quad\quad\quad\quad\quad\quad\quad\quad\quad R^2 = .761 \quad\quad F = 62.72$

(1.2c) $C = .0852S + .6648Z - .1973K + u$
 $\quad\quad (.44) \quad\quad (24.24) \quad (6.05)$

$\quad\quad\quad\quad\quad\quad\quad\quad\quad\quad\quad\quad\quad R^2 = .685 \quad\quad F = 42.83$

(1.2h) $H = .1636S + .5755Z - .3802K + u$
 $\quad\quad (3.32) \quad\quad (36.84) \quad (45.57)$

$\quad\quad\quad\quad\quad\quad\quad\quad\quad\quad\quad\quad\quad R^2 = .845 \quad\quad F = 107.07$

(2.1) $Z = .5012S + .4677C + .0301M + u$
 $\quad\quad (38.17) \quad (31.66) \quad (.23)$

$\quad\quad\quad\quad\quad\quad\quad\quad\quad\quad\quad\quad\quad R^2 = .790 \quad\quad F = 73.92$

(2.2) $Z = .4118S + .5676H - .0294M + u$
 $\quad\quad (24.83) \quad (43.26) \quad (.23)$

$\quad\quad\quad\quad\quad\quad\quad\quad\quad\quad\quad\quad\quad R^2 = .814 \quad\quad F = 85.89$

B. Reduced-Form Equations

(3.1h) $H = .7182S - .2907D + .1503M + u$
 $\quad\quad (85.52) \quad (11.59) \quad (3.10)$

$\quad\quad\quad\quad\quad\quad\quad\quad\quad\quad\quad\quad\quad R^2 = .646 \quad\quad F = 35.84$

(3.1z) $Z = .8215S - .2007D + .0410M + u$
 $\quad\quad (136.81) \quad (6.76) \quad (.28)$

$\quad\quad\quad\quad\quad\quad\quad\quad\quad\quad\quad\quad\quad R^2 = .710 \quad\quad F = 48.21$

(3.2c) $C = .5931S - .3630K - .0304M + u$
 $\quad\quad (43.97) \quad (9.59) \quad (.07)$

$\quad\quad\quad\quad\quad\quad\quad\quad\quad\quad\quad\quad\quad R^2 = .557 \quad\quad F = 24.68$

(3.2h) $H = .5928S - .5686K - .0933M + u$
 $\quad\quad (79.65) \quad (42.21) \quad (1.19)$

$\quad\quad\quad\quad\quad\quad\quad\quad\quad\quad\quad\quad\quad R^2 = .753 \quad\quad F = 59.92$

(3.2z) $Z = .7660S - .2370K + .0273M + u$
 $\quad\quad (111.33) \quad (6.20) \quad (.09)$

$\quad\quad\quad\quad\quad\quad\quad\quad\quad\quad\quad\quad\quad R^2 = .710 \quad\quad F = 36.10$

but it is also true that such youth in turn will tend collectively to sustain or raise the proportions of the school's graduates entering college. Thus, we have reversed the positions of Z and H (or C) in equations (2.1) and (2.2). Whereas S was relatively weak in the equations for C and H, in which it was swamped by Z, there is no comparable inverse dominance by C or H when Z is taken as a dependent variable. This is consistent with what should be expected a priori, in view of the fact that S measures those very aspects of the upper-secondary curriculum that are most deliberately and overtly linked to examinations.[1]

Coefficients on M, relating to degree of metropolitanism, fluctuated around zero, with the uninteresting exception of equation (3.1h). (The best we can say is that M does carry a positive sign in equations in which Z is the dependent variable and H is not included; inclusion of H switches the coefficient on M from an insignificant positive to an insignificant negative value.) The weakness of M precluded the tests we had initially planned for single-equation bias of coefficients on Z with C or H as the dependent variable, but these were not the most interesting or important coefficients. Fortunately, we found ourselves in a good position with respect to tests for single-equation biases in coefficients on C and H in equations (2.1) and (2.2).

Taking relations between H and Z and the equations using K rather than D as an example, we may find it helpful to express them first in algebraic form (omitting the error terms). From (1.2h) we have

$$H = s_1 S + z_1 Z + k_1 K.$$

From (2.2) we have

$$Z = s_2 S + h_2 H + m_2 M.$$

Solving these equations simultaneously gives

$$H = \frac{s_1 + z_1 s_2}{1 - z_1 h_2} S + \frac{k_1}{1 - z_1 h_2} K + \frac{z_1 m_2}{1 - z_1 h_2} M , \qquad (4.3h)$$

$$Z = \frac{s_2 + h_2 s_1}{1 - z_1 h_2} S + \frac{h_2 k_1}{1 - z_1 h_2} K + \frac{m_2}{1 - z_1 h_2} M . \qquad (4.4z)$$

Let the complex coefficients of equation (4.3h) be labeled to give $H = s_3 S + k_3 K + m_3 M$, and let those of equation (4.4z) be labeled to give $Z = s_4 S + k_4 K + m_4 M$. We now have the derived equalities

$$z_1 = m_3 / m_4 ,$$

$$h_2 = k_4 / k_3 .$$

These values may be compared with results from the reduced-form equations (3.2h) and (3.2z), which give direct estimates of m_3 and k_3 and of m_4 and k_4. However, the m coefficients are statistically insignificant throughout, which precludes inferring anything about single-equation bias in z_1 from a comparison with the ratio of reduced-form coefficients m_3/m_4. On the other hand, the coefficient on *K* in the structural equation (1.2*h*) was highly significant. (In fact, it is too high because it is too closely related to *H*, but let us set that aside for the moment.) Within the assumptions of the model we can then proceed to use this information to check for likely biases in the single-equation estimate of the coefficient on *H*, taking *Z* as the dependent variable --that is, in equation (2.2). We are in a position to do the same thing for the coefficient on *C* in equation (2.1) as well. Also open to us is the option of substituting equations using *D* for the reduced-form equations using *K* in testing the results on *H*. Always with *Z* as the dependent variable, the results are as follows:

	Coefficients on	
	C	*H*
Single-equation estimates (2.1) and (2.2)	.468	.568
Reduced-form estimates in equations with *K*		
(3.2*c* with 3.2*z*)	.653	...
(3.2*h*) with (3.2*z*)	...	.417
Reduced-form estimates in equations with *D*		
(3.1*h*) with (3.1*z*)	...	.687

The first test, using the reduced-form equation with *K* as an independent variable, actually indicated a downward bias in the single-equation estimate for the coefficient on *C*, but an upward bias in that on *H*. However, there is an inherent simultaneity problem within the reduced-form equation (3.2*h*) in the relation between *H* and *K*, and we have injected this distortion into the simultaneous equation estimate of the coefficient on *H*. Fortunately, that problem does not arise between *C* and *K*. With respect to *H* we can get rid of it by using *D* instead of *K* in the reduced-form equations. The result is the reduced-form estimate of .687, which is higher than the single-equation estimate of .568 (and virtually identical to the reduced-form estimate of *C* of .653 in the equations using *K* as the rurality variable).

D. Acronyms

The acronyms listed and defined in this appendix are used in more than one chapter. Those that are used in one discussion only are specified as they are introduced. We have grouped the acronyms by main topics in defining them. The preliminary alphabetical listis keyed to topic areas designated by letter and, where needed, by subsection number. Acronyms that are the defining part of sets of variables are shown on the alphabetical list with a dash but without the details of the set. Single asterisks (*) indicate acronyms that are used both as categorial sets and as quasi-cardinal variables; double asterisks (**) indicate that each variable within the grouping is cardinal.

Acronym	Topic Group
AGRIC	A.2
B-FSE	E
CLED-**	A.3
CLO-**	A.3
COMM	A.2
EMP	E
EXAM (alone and set)	B.3
EXPFAB	I.3
EXP-OCC III	I.3
EXPSTA-*	I.2
F-AGE	C
FARM (alone and set)	E
FIRM-T	B.4
FLEVF-*	D
FLEVS-*	D
F-REG	E
FO-III-	G
FREQ-M	A.1
FW-	E
FY-AG	H
FY-B	H
FY-N	H
GEN (GEN-B, GEN-A)	A.2
OCC III	G and I.3
ONEX-	I.3
OSTAF-*	F
OSTAS-*	F
PART-O	B.4
PART-U	B.4
PC-	B.1
POP	A.1
PREF-	I.1
RANK-*	B.2
SELF (alone and set)	E
SIB	C
SLOW-50	A.1
TECH	A.2
TJC	A.2
Y1 (Y1S, Y1U)	J
Y5	J
YL (YLS, YLU)	J

A. Community, School, and Classroom Characteristics

1. *Location and Size of Community*

FREQ-M	Number of train connections per day to cities of a million or more. Schools in such metropolises are coded 99.
POP	Logarithm of population of community in which the school is located.
SLOW-50	Time in minutes by regular public transportation (not superexpress) to nearest town of 50,000 population or more. Schools in towns of 50,000 or more are coded 1.

2. *Type of Upper-Secondary Course*

AGRIC	Agriculture
COMM	Commerce
GEN-B	Academic general
GEN-A	Nonacademic general
TECH	Technical secondary
TJC	Technical junior college (5-year course beginning at stage of entry to upper-secondary school)

3. *Classroom Composition*

CLED-HI	Proportion of fathers with education beyond old middle (new upper-secondary) school
CLED-LOW	Proportion of fathers with no postcompulsory schooling
CLO-WC	Proportion of fathers in clerical, managerial, and nontechnical professional occupations
CLO-RET	Proportion of fathers in retailing
CLO-SK	Proportion of fathers in skilled manual jobs
CLO-AG	Proportion of fathers in agriculture (farming and other)

B. Student's Course Preferences, Academic Performance, College Plans, and Attitudes toward Part-Time Study and Training on the Job

1. *Course Preferences*

PC-GEN	Prefers general curriculum (B or A)
PC-AGRIC	Prefers agriculture course
PC-COMM	Prefers commerce course
PC-TECH	Prefers technical secondary
PC-TJC	Prefers technical junior college
PC-OTHER	Prefers some other course, no response

2. *Self-Assessment of Rank in Class*

RANK	1 = top fifth, . . . , 5 = lowest fifth (used both in dummy sets and as a quasi-cardinal variable)

3. *College Expectations*

EXAM	Taking examinations for higher education
EXAM-DAY	Taking examinations for day college or university
EXAM-NIGHT	Taking examinations for night college or university
EXAM-NONE	Not taking any examinations

4. *Attitudes and Expectations for Postschool Study and Training*

FIRM-T	(from male student questionnaire, question 17, education and training program sponsored by firm)
PART-U	(from male student questionnaire, question 17, night college or university)
PART-O	(from male student questionnaire, question 17, other occupation-oriented training)

These indexes are scored as follows:

-1	Have definite plan to take
-2	Probably would take
-3	Uncertain, no response
-4	Probably would not take
-5	Definitely would not take

C. Father's Age and Family Size

F-AGE	Set of categorical variables on father's age, including father deceased 1. Under 40; 2. 40-54; 3. 55 and over; 4. deceased
SIB	Set of categories for number of siblings 1. Only child; 2. family of 2-3 children; 3. family of 4 children; 4. family of 5 or more children

D. Father's Education

FLEVF	Level of father's education as reported by father
FLEVS	Level of father's education as reported by son

Categories on FLEVF and on FLEVS are as follows:

-1	Elementary
-2	Higher elementary; lower secondary

-3	Old middle school, new upper secondary
-4	Junior-college equivalent (old "higher school")
-5	University

E. Father's Employment Status and Student's Position in Sibling Birth Order; Degree of Father's Economic Activity

SELF	Father an independent or family entrepreneur
SELF-S1	First son of an independent or family entrepreneur
SELF-S2	Other son of an independent or family entrepreneur
FARM	Father engaged in agriculture
FARM-S1	First or only son of a farmer
FARM-S2	Other son of a farmer
EMP	Father in wage or salaried employment
F-REG	Father in status of a "permanent" employee
B-FSE	Refers to set of categories: 1. SELF-S1; 2. SELF-S2; 3. FARM-S1; 4. FARM-S2; 5. EMP; 6. B-FSE other and no response
FW-FULL	Father working full-time (whatever employment status)
FW-PT	Father working part-time
FW-NO	Father not working
FW-DEAD	Father deceased
FW-0	No response

F. Father's Occupational Status

OSTAF	Father's occupational status coded on basis of father's report of his occupation
OSTAS	Father's occupational status coded on basis of student's report of father's occupation

OSTAF and OSTAS categories run from 1 (high) to 8 (low). For explanations see the second section of chapter 3, and chapter 11.

G. Father's Occupation Type

Several different classifications are used. Definitions used in the tabulations are specified as needed, with the exception of regressions in which the set FO-III is used.

FO-III	Father's occupation type, classification on OCC-III
-1	White collar, defined to include clerical, nontechnical professional, and administrative except as specified below
-2	Higher technical (professional engineers and technicians)
-3	Managers and proprietors in manufactures and construction
-4	Proprietors and managers in trade
-5	Artisans
-6	Skilled workers in heavy industry and construction
-7	Other manual
-8	Farmers and others in agriculture, forestry, fishing
-9	Miscellaneous other
-0	No response

H. Parental Income

FY-AG	Gross farm income
FY-B	Annual income of fathers in wage and salaried employment (including bonuses)
FY-N	Annual net personal income of fathers in independent and family enterprise

I. Students' Occupational Preferences and Expectations

1. *Preferred Employment Status*

PREF-ME	Prefer independence
PREF-GOV	Prefer government employment
PREF-BIG	Prefer employment in a big private firm
PREF-SMALL	Prefer employment in a small private firm
PREF-OT	Other preference, no response

2. *Expected Occupational Status*

EXPSTA	Expected occupational status from 1 (high) to 8 (low), as with OSTAF and OSTAS. In regressions this refers to expected career-peak status.

3. *Expected Type of Occupation*

EXP-OCC III	Expected career-peak type of occupation, classified on OCC-III as in FO-III for fathers.

ONEX	Set of expected career-peak occupation types
-1	White collar, including clerical, nontechnical professional, all managers and proprietors except in trade
-2	Trade and service occupations
-3	Technical, manual
-4	Agriculture and related
-0	No response
EXPFAB	Expectation of a technical or manual occupation at career peak. This is the same as ONEX-3 but is used alone.

J. Students' Income Expectations

Y1	Expected earnings on entry job
Y1S	Expected earnings on entry job directly from upper-secondary school
Y1U	Expected earnings on entry job from university
Y5	Expected earnings after 5 years of work experience
YL	Expected earnings in mature years (career-peak)
YLS	Expected career-peak earnings without further formal education
YLU	Expected career-peak earnings with university education

Notes

Introduction

1. Also studied were four thousand girls, but aside from incidental comments, our findings for girls will be reported separately. Except where indicated, tables refer to male students only.

2. In addition we studied fathers of pupils in the first two years of primary school. "Father" studies completed thus far using our data include an analysis of the effects of schooling on communication and innovation among farmers (Harker 1971) and an analysis of the effects of schooling and parental backgrounds on the behavior of small entrepreneurs (Koh 1977).

3. One of these analyzes expectational data and other variables bearing on decisions to stay in the United States or return to Peru among Peruvian students attending colleges and universities in the United States (Myers 1972). The other is a discussion of responses on a questionnaire sent to male college students in the Boston area and at the University of Massachusetts (Amherst) in 1966-67 (chapters 10 and 11 of Freeman 1971); Freeman did not obtain any information on parental traits.

4. His theory has been developed in a series of publications over the past twenty-five years. See especially Shackle (1955) and Bowman (1972).

5. Unfortunately, a sharply heightened sensitivity to anything that could be interpreted (rightly or not) by students to suggest a pejorative ranking of their fathers precluded any attempt to investigate parental attributes of the 1976-77 cohort of students in the final year of upper-secondary school. It is impossible, therefore, to compare relations between parental characteristics and student aspirations or expectations in the 1976-77 student cohort with the relations examined for the 1966-67 student sample. This situation is changing, however, and such a study might now be possible.

6. Evans (1975) has argued that the United States may become progressively more like Japan. For an earlier but more extensive comparison between the United States and Japan see Evans (1971). There is a large literature on this subject, to some of which we will refer specifically in later chapters.

Chapter 1

1. These *juku* activities serving children in grades 1 to 9, are not solely to cram for secondary-school entrance examinations. Some pupils who are falling behind are helped to catch up. Also, the *juku* provide a place for safe and constructive recreation for some of the younger urban children. The examination competition dominates in the purposes of *juku* for children in grades 7 to 9, however, and recently some are even serving a new sort of *rōnin*--

children who take an extra year of cramming to get into preferred upper-secondary schools. According to a 1976 Ministry of Education survey, a fifth of the boys and a sixth of the girls in grades 4,5, and 6 were attending the academic, exam-oriented *juku*, and proportions among students in grades 7, 8, and 9 who were enrolled in such *juku* were 45 percent for boys and 35 percent for girls. In Tokyo 40 percent of all fourth, fifth, and sixth graders and 53 percent of all seventh, eighth, and ninth graders were enrolled in academic *juku* and another 10 percent of the latter were working with a private tutor at home. These figures are estimated to be more than double and perhaps triple the rates for 1966. (See Rohlen 1980 for an illuminating discussion and interpretation of these developments.)

2. Not to be confused with the five-year "technical junior colleges" of the 1960s.

3. University students continued to be exempt from military service until the last stage of the war. However, neither they nor their professors were exempt from service in war industry, and as the war continued, it became common for university classes to meet in the industrial plants.

4. The rapidity of this latter change around the early 1960s is remarkable. In the 1962 cohort of girls completing lower-secondary school 56 percent entered full-time upper-secondary schools and 13 percent entered "miscellaneous" schools. Two years later, in the 1964 cohort, these proportions were 62 and 8 percent, respectively.

5. Of the latter, 2 percent were receiving training of other kinds as well.

6. These facts are well documented in the pathbreaking research by Shimbori (1965) and, more recently, by Azumi (1969).

7. There had been a substantial change from 1950, when 80 percent of the upper-secondary schools were public and 85 percent of the pupils at this level were in public institutions.

8. We estimated that of all students who entered upper-secondary schools in 1964, 97 percent of the males and 99 percent of the females graduated three years later, in 1967. (These estimates are based on data from Mombushō, *Gakko Kihon Chōsa* [Ministry of Education, Basic Statistics], which appears annually.)

9. An interesting assessment of more recent trends in university entrance is provided in Amano (1972, 1979) and Ushiogi (ed., 1979).

Chapter 2

1. For a selected list of references on relevant applications and the methodology of path analysis see the bibliography in Bowman (1976).

2. Use of arrow diagrams to describe the structures of analytical models has not been limited to sociologists or to models built on intertemporal relationships. A wider class of recursive, "causal-chain" models has been used by economists as well, though such models have not usually been used by economists working on relations between schooling and subsequent work and earning histories. For methodological discussions of causal-chain models in economics see Wold (1960) and Basmann (1963, 1965).

3. The total effects will usually be less than the zero-order associations, but they can sometimes be greater. For an illuminating example see Fägerlind (1975) and the discussion of his findings in Bowman (1976). Some applications of path analysis (along with other methods) are included in Cummings and Naoi (1974); see also their references to other related work, including Tominaga (1969).

4. Interaction terms can be introduced in the equation of a path analysis, but this may introduce ambiguities in interpreting the coefficients for direct and indirect effects (see Fägerlin, 1975).

5. The elements of an activity vector could easily be defined to specify separately combinations of activities, as part-time study and work, for example, in contrast to study only or work only. This would complicate exposition, however.

6. Obviously there will be differences among individuals in degrees of optimism and related behavior and in how these underlying attitudes are expressed.

7. For a discussion of applications of Shackle's model to human-investment decisions see Bowman (1972).

8. That theory has a long history, but modern developments have given it a new and more powerful content. See especially Schultz (1961) and Becker (1962, 1964) for seminal contributions to these developments.

9. Recently some sociologists have added statistical analyses appropriate to the economists' main question to their publications on career development (see Sewell and Hauser 1975).

10. The Swedish data analyzed by Fägerlind (1975) are a striking exception. He was able to construct detailed profiles of earnings at various short intervals to the age of 43. However, he did not consolidate these data in terms of discounted present values or of indicators of steepness in the age-earning profiles.

11. Typically in the United States the full set of age-schooling categories is set up separately by race also. Usually only level of schooling is known, but the sex-race-age-schooling categorization can be specified to distinguish types of curricula as well. In some special studies this has been done, but on limited subsamples of the population.

12. A rate-of-return analysis of investments in schooling should include not only earnings foregone while in school but also direct outlays on tuition and so forth (or, in "social rates of return," the costs of all resources used in providing the schooling). Foregone earnings while in college, for example, are already included in the earning streams for graduates of upper-secondary schools; direct costs are not.

13. One of the common ways of testing for interaction when all variables are expressed in cardinal or quasi-cardinal form is to create an interaction variable specified as the product of two independent variables. This method has sometimes been used for the study of interactions between years of schooling and ability (on various measures) in their effects on earnings. The extent to which interaction effects will in fact be revealed by such tests is of course constrained by the specification of the form of interaction in the model. Conflicting or ambiguous findings concerning interactions between schooling and ability in effects on earnings reflect not only differences in model specifications but also differences in the ability measures and in characteristics of the samples studied. The latter differ substantially even in the range of ability represented.

14. They make no distinction between the status of a professional man who has just begun his work and an older colleague who has gained (or failed to gain) a fine reputation. Furthermore, the poorest measurement of occupational status is for business proprietors and managers, who range widely over any plausible sort of prestige rating.

15. Becker's theory has been further developed with great brilliance by the young Japanese economist Kuratani (1973). The importance of the bonus system for wage flexibility, with adjustments of the bonus/earnings ratio to short-term changes in economic returns (monetary productivity), is analyzed by Hashimoto (1979).

Chapter 3

1. Some occupations listed in the Japanese census do not

appear in that for the United States. Furthermore, coding by Duncan scale is extremely crude for most businessmen and farmers because there is in fact such a wide range in both income and education (the Duncan criteria) within those census categories. We had available more detailed information about scale of operations and levels of responsibility in the activities of fathers of the students in our sample. Taking advantage of that information, we used a panel of judges working with a set of cards that included these extra specifications for the businessmen and farmers, along with examples of occupations that were less ambiguous in ratings. The results of this procedure were incorporated in the modified Duncan scale used in this research. For further details see the discussion in Tomoda (1968*a*).

2. On this point see the quite different, but consistent, assessments in Cummings and Naoi (1974).

3. In effect we are analyzing the partial transition matrix from the background vector V_b of chapter 2 into the various types of upper-secondary schools, but instead of elaborating the elements of V_b by multiple cross-classifications, we are imposing linearity constraints on the model. Note that while the individual case must be either 1 or 0 on the dependent variable for enrollment in a particular course, the predicted value treated as a probability is a continuous variable.

4. Since dropouts from upper-secondary courses before completion are negligible in Japan (3 percent among males nationally in the late 1960s, a little higher today), analysis of last-year students is virtually the same as analysis of the backgrounds of first-year entrants to this level of school. We are of course using the adjusted sample in this analysis; automatically this forces the mean values of the dependent variables for each course type to equal the proportion of all Japanese upper-secondary students enrolled in that type. An exception is the split between academic general and nonacademic general courses, which is taken from our sample.

5. A "dummy" or categorical variable is given a value of 1 where the particular categorization applies, 0 where it does not. Thus, the mean value of a dummy variable is the proportion of the sample population in that category. But dummy independent variables differ from categorical dependent variables in the regression analysis in that they are not probabilities and cannot be conceived as continuous in their values.

6. Reading across a row, the coefficients must sum to 0, thereby maintaining a sum of 1.00 when each is added to the value of the intercept for its curriculum.

7. When occupational type instead of occupational status is used, the problem of multicollinearity with father's schooling is greatly reduced. The interested reader can readily satisfy himself on this point so far as the education coefficients are concerned by comparing those shown in table 3.6 with the coefficients in tables 3.5 and 3.7.

Chapter 5

1. There will also be suboptimizing solutions on z for any given k and on k for any given z. Joint optimization on U_{kzi} specifies both z and k.

2. The concept of "conditional future parameters" as affected by current decisions was elaborated with respect to business decisions by Modigliani and Cohen, in Bowman (ed. 1958), and then more fully in their 1961 monograph. However, this concept has not yet to our knowledge been used in either theoretical or empirical studies of educational or job decisions of individuals.

3. Mombushō, *Shingaku to Ikuei Shogaku* [Ministry of Education, Financial Aid and Continuation in School] (Tokyo, 1961), table 12, p. 31.

4. The fact that education is by no means costless, even setting aside foregone earnings, is well understood in Japan. A report of student expenses in elementary and secondary schools in 1961-62 indicated that, including fees, textbooks, transportation, and other minor school expenses, the average private cost to the pupil in direct outlays was 9,400 yen in the elementary grades, 13,600 yen in lower-secondary school, 18,800 yen in upper-secondary night schools, and 33,000 yen in upper-secondary full day-time programs. These sums were roughly the equivalent of $10, $38, $52, and $92, and were not negligible sums in relation to Japanese incomes at that time. (See Ministry of Education, *Education in Japan* [Tokyo, 1964], p. 113.) Such direct costs relative to income continue to be high today, despite rising real incomes.

5. Once a modest income threshold was passed, there was virtually no association between parental income and the proportion of youth coming out of the ninth grade who continued into full day-time upper-secondary schools. While overall proportions rose substantially during the seventies, it is still relevant that as early as at least 1959 half of all youth continued into upper-secondary schools almost regardless of family income once the modest income level of about $440 to $600 a year was passed. Below that level only 30 percent were entering upper-secondary day schools. What did show up as a function of incomes in secondary education was the proportions attending night secondary schools, an option that both reduced cash outlays on education and gave more opportunity for the young person to earn part or more of his keep and even to contribute to the support and school expenses of younger siblings. Proportions going to night secondary schools ran at around 8 percent up to family incomes of $900 a year, then declined steadily to 1.4 percent in families with incomes of $2,500 or more a year. For further evidence relating to the early 1960s see Mombushō, *Shingaku to Ikuei Shōgaku* [Ministry of Education, Financial Aid and Continuation in School] (Tokyo, 1961).

Chapter 6

1. Among the small group attending night universities, the proportions were quite different: two-fifths had entered directly from secondary schools, two-fifths after a period of regular employment without postsecondary schooling, and one-fifth had been *rōnin*.

2. Central Council for Education, Ministry of Education, *Interim Report on Fundamental Policies for the Overall Expansion and Development of School Education in the Future* (30 June 1969).

Chapter 7

1. This is quite apart from the effects of income on the treatment of higher education as a consumer luxury.

2. This exception reflects in part the fact that night programs in higher institutions are relatively inaccessible to most rural residents.

3. Or, more precisely, if he goes to any of the five specified curricula. These are almost, but not completely, all-inclusive with respect to full-time upper-secondary schools for males.

4. It is important in this connection to remember that General B was indeed the curriculum most cited as the preferred one by students enrolled in other than their first choice of upper-secondary course; in other words, some who desired to take this option were unable, for one reason or another, to do so.

5. As we remarked in chapter 3, the use of ordinary least-squares regressions with a dichotomous dependent variable can create problems, especially in the upper and lower ranges of the distribution, where linear functions may predict probabilities exceeding 1 or below 0. A further estimation problem is that the error structure violates the assumptions of ordinary least squares, leading to biased estimates of t values. To avoid these problems, we may use a monotonic transform that converts the dependent variable into a function, the value of which can range from $-\infty$ to $+\infty$, with a value of 0 at a probability of .50. There are a number of functions that satisfy these specifications, the best known of which are the probit and logistic functions.

Probit analysis expresses probabilities in terms of a cumulative normal frequency distribution. Write $F(y)$ for the cumulated distribution of a standardized normal variate such that $F(y) = p$, where p is the probability of going to college. The probit transform y is then the inverse function $F^{-1}(p)$. If we write $p(x)$ as the conditional probability of going to college, dependent on some explanatory variable x, we may then write

$$p(x) = F(\beta_0 + \beta_x) = \frac{1}{\sqrt{2\pi}} \int_{-\infty}^{\beta_0 + \beta_x} e^{-\xi^2/2} \, d\xi$$

or, equivalently,

$$F^{-1}(p(x)) = \beta_0 + \beta x \,.$$

Expanding to include other variables, we get

$$p(x) = F(\beta_0 + \beta_1 x_1 + \beta_2 x_2 + \ldots + \beta_m x_m) \,.$$

Tests of significance of the regression coefficients are now asymptotic T values reached in the iteration process of finding the best estimates for a probit function.

The logistic function is similar. In its simplest formulation, using grouped data, the dependent variable is a *logit* which is the natural logarithm of the better's odds:

$$\ln \frac{p_\alpha}{1 - p_\alpha} = \beta_0 + \beta_\alpha x_\alpha ,$$

which can be similarly extended to include multiple independent variables. Solving the above equation for p_α gives us the logistic function

$$p_\alpha = \frac{1}{1 - e^{-\beta_0 - \beta \log x_\alpha}} = \frac{1}{1 + e^{-\beta_0} x_\alpha^{-\beta}} \,.$$

In chapter 3 we set this up as a simultaneous equation system with five dependent variables i (i = 1, 2, 3, 4, 5); to avoid overdetermination, one of the dependent variables (enrollment in General B) is then omitted and becomes the residual in the predicted distribution of enrollments among curricula.

6. On information fields see Hägerstrand (1965, 1968).

7. M_i is the effects of location factors on the visibility and perceptions of job and earning opportunities; L_{zi} is the effects of geographic accessibility on the costs of higher-education option z; H_k is classroom composition and peer-group influences in upper-secondary school.

8. Youth living in a metropolitan place of a million or more were arbitrarily coded 99. The frequencies otherwise ranged from 6 to 58 per day.

9. Those living in a place of fifty thousand or over were arbitrarily scored 1.

10. The logit is the natural logarithm of the better's odds. See note 5 above and appendix C.

Chapter 8

1. The classic paper on the theory of time allocation is that of Becker (1965). His analysis has been the basis of numerous studies of relationships among consumer behavior, schooling, labor market participation of women, and fertility. The earliest systematic elaboration of the economics of time in household decisions was that of Reid (1934). Treatments of time in microeconomics are becoming numerous and diverse despite common elements. Quite different from those most closely tied to Becker (1965) is Linder (1970).

2. So long as the internal rate of return on an additional educational investment exceeded the interest-rate costs to the individual (the criterion rate properly assessed), that investment would rationally be undertaken, but if the criterion rate exceeded the anticipated internal rate of return, this would not be the case. On this see especially Becker (1967) and Harvey (1967).

3. The following analysis is adapted from Becker (1967).

4. Applied to investments in schooling only, the diagrams abstract from the important matter of changes in earnings over time (discussed in chapter 13). Notice that the horizontal access refers to investments, not years in school, for example. Thus, Japanese families sending their children to private upper-secondary schools will normally be investing more than those whose children attend public upper-secondary schools.

5. The shaded area ($B + I$) under the D curve up to $Q = i$ is of course the integration of the marginal returns r_q. Thus,

$$B + I = \int_{Q=0}^{Q=i} r_q .$$

The shaded area I is the integration of interest costs, and B is the benefits net of interest costs. The sum $B + I$ equals earnings because we carried the investment axis back to zero. If we defined the diagram to refer only to investments beyond some specified level, the shaded area $B + I$ would represent the gross differential earnings beyond that starting point, and so on.

6. Primarily the Ministry of Education's *Higher Education in Postwar Japan*. 1964 White Paper (published in English translation as Monumento Nipponica Monograph no. 22, Sophia University).

7. Average annual tuition in national and public upper-secondary schools ran between 10,000 and 13,000 yen from 1970 to 1975 (or roughly $40 in 1976 dollars). Tuition in the private upper-secondary schools was of course higher; it rose from 46,000 to 79,000 yen from 1970 to 1974 and then jumped to 113,000 yen in 1975.

8. According to a 1974 survey, in day universities the proportions of student expenditures earned were as follows: national, 23 percent; public, 28 percent; private, 19 percent. Only in the private institutions did expenditures exceed income. Scholarships provided 10.5 percent of the expenditures in national day universities but only 2.8 percent in the private day universities. Mombushō, *Gakusei Seihatsu Chōsa Kōhō* [Ministry of Education, University Life Survey] (Tokyo, 1974), p. 10.

9. Turning these figures around to ask how youth from the poorest versus better situated homes responded, we get the following results for proportions specifying cost burdens and inappropriate course types:

	Cost Burden	Course Inappropriate
Fathers in independent enterprise with net incomes		
Under 500,000 yen (1966, $1,390)	29%	19
Over 1 million yen (1966, $2,780)	10	15
Employee fathers earning per annum		
Under 500,000 yen	52	14
Over 1 million yen	3	5

The sharper contrast among sons of employee fathers may well arise because these incomes are inherently better indicators of "permanent" incomes, with less transitory or random components; also, they are more accurately reported.

Chapter 9

1. This is the same as the marginal external interest cost at the appropriate points on an *S* curve like that in figure 8.1, 8.2, or 8.3.
2. There is an extensive technical literature on the "present value" versus the "rate of return" rule, but this need not concern us here. For most purposes these are equivalent, provided (and the proviso is sometimes critical) that they are properly applied.
3. On these concepts and some of their applications see the papers by various authors in Bowman (1958).
4. For fathers aged 50 in Tokyo and Osaka it was 950,000 yen a year, or 79,000 yen a month, compared with projected secondary-school geometric means of 81,000 yen a month in urban areas. For other fathers it was 73,000 yen a month compared with a rural student estimate of the same amount. Since these geographic classifications are not quite matched, the student estimates are somewhat the higher, but not substantially so.

Chapter 11

1. Perceptions of entrepreneurial prestige among rural Japanese boys are discussed in Lewis (1968).
2. Birthrates were exceptionally high just after the war. The cohort of young people who were part of that baby-boom are having small families, and births in those families are not so concentrated in time. For discussions of demographic cohort effects at each and all levels of schooling as compared with effects of the spread of higher education on employment situations in the United States, see Smith and Welch (1980).
3. In fact there were, of course, relatively high nonresponse rates on perceptions of direct-entry first jobs among youth fully expecting to go on to higher education and taking examinations for that purpose. Similarly, there were higher nonresponse rates among the terminal students with respect to perceptions of job options that might be available and attractive to them (or their classmates) if they were to enter the labor market after graduation from a university.
4. There are several reasons why students found the employment status question comparatively easy to answer, but especially important is the fact that even a working adult, when asked what he does, will tend to respond by stating with what firm or agency he works. For younger men especially, that often is the

most meaningful answer, since what a man will be doing can and frequently does change considerably over time, even without any shift in his employment status or in the particular organization with which he is affiliated.

5. For a more detailed discussion see Tomoda (1968*a*).

Chapter 12

1. In this case the percentages are taken against all respondents, including the very few who failed to circle any of the five responses (the opinionnaire is item 34 of the student questionnaire, which is reproduced as appendix A). In most cases the nonresponses were around 1 percent, and even those circling "can't say" were in most instances few.

2. See also Mincer (1958, 1962) and Bowman (1965, 1966, 1968).

3. Becker does not deal directly with institutional constraints, however, For a discussion of the economics of specialization and specialized training in contrast to the "specific" component in human capital see Bowman (1965, 1971).

4. Exactly such matters were of course involved in the debates over company schools and conditions for "recognized" status of intraenterprise training programs in Japan at the time of the Industrial Training Act of 1958 and in the years that immediately followed.

5. This fact is well understood by both businessmen and individuals, though it would not be stated in quite these terms. The young man knows it when he decides against a "dead-end" job with high immediate pay in favor of a lower paying job that opens up future career opportunities. The small businessman advertises that he will allow time for the pursuit of further studies by young workers he employs. Most sophisticated in his awareness will of course be the executive of a large corporation who is assessing his options in personnel policy. The theoretical formulation of this phenomenon was laid out by Becker (1962, 1964) with reference to "general" and "specific" human capital, but it applies also to the sharing of human-investment costs and returns by employer and employee in a life-commitment system.

6. Even taking work in English only, literature on the life-commitment system is extensive. See especially Marsh and Mannari (1972, 1975), Taira (1970), and various articles in Okochi, Karsh, and Levine (eds., 1974). Also, from somewhat different perspectives, see Cole (1971, 1976) and Dore (1974).

7. A further advantage of factor analysis on attitude questionnaires is the contribution it can make in illuminating ways in which respondents may have perceived the items used, which is not always what may have been in the minds of the researchers.

8. The scale values ran from 1 for strong agreement to 5 for strong disagreement.

9. All zero-order correlations between scores on the various indexes were close to zero, as they should be, with one exception: among students there was a significant positive correlation between MOB and VALED. This correlation was not just a matter of the index construction; it was also evidenced on correlations between initial factor scores, which were not removed by the orthogonal rotation.

Chapter 13

1. An important exception is work by Myers (1972) concerning decisions with respect to study abroad and return migration among young men from less developed nations. Freeman (1971) has also given some attention to expectational data.

2. Sano (1966) was well aware of this paradox.

3. For related comments on "assortative mating" between firms and employees see Kuratani (1973). Important here also is the learning by employers about the capabilities of their employees, which is related to recent developments in the "economics of information" and the educational "screening" hypothesis, but has not yet received the attention it deserves.

4. This does not mean that the decision theory is undermined, but that the year-to-year links between the timing of postschool investments of individuals in themselves and the sequence of observed earnings are attenuated.

5. On this see especially Mincer (1974), Bowman (1968, 1974*a*), and Rosen (1977).

6. This is setting obsolescence aside, or assuming "costless" learning sufficient to neutralize obsolescence at work.

7. The net contribution of schooling (undiscounted) would be area $A + B$ *minus* the costs of the schooling incurred before the point of entry to the labor market, taken as the origin in figure 13.1. Call those costs C. Then the undiscounted net total becomes $B + J - C$, and the postschool proportion of this is $(J - A)/(B + J - C)$ instead of $(J - A)/(B + J)$. Another way of looking at these relationships is to compare the gross J with the gross $A + B$.

8. Exogenous growth effects would require modification of Y_m^* to rise through time, but it would also raise Y_m to progressively higher values over time.

9. Some of the findings were included in Bowman (1970*a*).

10. If the expected discounted net value is negative, the option will not be taken up; hence, the magnitude of the negative value is irrelevant in this model.

11. Some of the evidence is discussed in Bowman (1976).

Chapter 14

1. Koh (1977, p. 6) cited evidence on this matter from the 1974 White Paper on Labor (Ministry of Labor 1975) and, especially, from the overview of a number of surveys of small enterprises by Kiyonari (1970). Kiyonari concluded, among other things, that since the late sixties relatively younger men have been leaving wage employment to go into self-employment, "as they found entrepreneurship more attractive in terms of financial rewards and the opportunity to use one's ability more fully." Also, he cited evidence that "small and medium size firms in the 60's were no longer characterized by low productivity and low wages because of structural changes and technological advances."

2. Nevertheless, with their usual adaptability, Japanese firms sometimes created fictional seniority to attract qualified young men away from their initial employers, thus maintaining the form of the life-commitment system but circumventing its constraints in the interest of economic efficiency. See Levine (1958, chapters 3,4, and 5) and the summary chapter of Okochi, Karsh, and Levine (eds., 1974).

3. For all industries taken together, entry wages from upper-secondary schools are still somewhat higher in big firms than in small ones, but this contrast reflects industry differences in types of jobs and of upper-secondary graduates, in location and living costs, in urban sophistication, in expectations of continued or temporary affiliation, in chances of moving from wage to entrepreneurial roles, and in sex composition of the newly hired working force, among other complex matters.

4. The ensuing demographic trough eases these adjustment problems somewhat, though it does not eliminate the disadvantage of being a member of an exceptionally large cohort. For an illuminating discussion of this problem with reference to the United States see Smith and Welch (1978).

5. As stated earlier, the *juku* are private preparatory and remedial classes that are often, though not always, conducted by teachers in their homes after school hours. The *yobiko* are university preparatory schools that supplement the regular schools as examination cram programs for initial university aspirants and for *rōnin*.

6. The lower success rates among the general- and the technical-course graduates reflect the fact that the students in these courses were applying to institutions that were different from those to which university applicants from other curricula were seeking admission, although we cannot make any direct comparisons in this respect between the destinations sought by the graduates of general and technical courses.

7. Taking these figures all together, it is all the more remarkable that *rōnin* proportions of university entrants remained virtually unchanged.

8. Recent econometric studies in the United States provide some evidence on this point. For a more intensive study with more limited coverage but with evidence directly applicable to this question see Hyde (1976).

9. For an insightful brief discussion of the shifting forces that have been at play in recent decisions about higher education in Japan see Cummings (1976*a,b*). Among the many recent discussions of changes and policies in higher education see also (in addition to official documents) Kitamura and Cummings (1972), Kobayashi (1971), Teichler (1972), and Pempel (1971, 1973).

10. The economics of these problems is immensely complex. See the seminal modern contribution in neoclassical economics by Coase (1960).

11. An analogous attempt to force hierarchical restructuring of public education in California exacerbated the disorders in that state, where disruptions were the most serious in the United States. Also, one of the results of the California policy has been an exaggeration of the perverse relations between a student's family income and the amount of subsidy he receives from the state.

12. Whether these special subsidies to national universities were ever justified in a general societal perspective could be questioned.

13. See Nerlove (1972), for example.

14. Paradoxically, schools reforms intended to relax examination pressures and to create and maintain a democratic environment in the schools have contributed to quite contrary developments in the recent evolution of the *juku* system. For an excellent discussion see Rohlen (1980). A related analysis of the prospects for an increasingly "inherited meritocracy"is presented in Dore (1975).

15. On both of these points see Noda (1975).

Appendix C

1. Examinations have been less narrowly academic than is commonly supposed, however. There have been pressures in Japan toward tightening and narrowing the range and nature of the fields covered.

References

Abegglen, James C. 1958. *The Japanese Factory*. New York: Free Press.

Amano, Ikuo. 1972. *Kongo no Daigaku Shingakushasū no Dōkō* [The Trend in University Entrance]. Pamphlet, Nihon Rikuruto Senta [Japan Recruit Center], June.

______. 1978. *Kyūsei Senmon Gakkō* [Outgoing Professional Schools]. Tokyo: Nippon Keizai Shinbunsha Press.

Anderson, C. Arnold. 1975. "Expanding Educational Opportunities: Conceptualization and Measurement." *Higher Education* 4:393-408.

Arai, Ikuo (ed.). 1979. *Raningu Sosaieti* [The Learning Society]. Gendai no Esupuri, no. 146, Tokyo: Shibundo Publishing Co.

Aso, Makoto. 1965. "Kōki Chūtōkyōiku ni okero Gakkōkaiso no Jisshōteki Kenkyū" [A Study of the School Stratification System of the Senior General-Course High Schools]. *Kyōikugaku Kenkyū* [Japanese Journal of Educational Research] 32, no. 4: 237-48.

Aso, Makoto, Nobuo Nakanishi, and Yasumasa Tomoda (eds.). 1980. *Shūshoku: Daigakusei no Senshoku Kōdō* [College Students and Their Occupational Selections]. Tokyo: Yūhikaku Publishing Co.

Aso, Makoto, and Morikazu Ushiogi (eds.). 1977. *Gakureki Kōyōron: Gakureki Shakai kara Gakuryoku Shakai e no Michi* [Uses of School Backgrounds: The Way from Diploma Society to Attainment Society]. Tokyo: Yūhikaku Publishing Co.

______. 1979. "Kōtōgakkō Kyōiku no Hatten to Kōtōgakkō Kenkyū no Tenkai" [A Review of Sociological Studies of Secondary Schools from 1945 to 1978]. *Kyōiku Shakaigau Kenkyū* [Journal of Educational Sociology], no. 34, pp. 64-78.

Austin, Lewis (ed.). 1976. *Japan: The Paradox of Progress*. New Haven: Yale University Press.

Azumi, Koya. 1969. *Higher Education and Business Recruitment in Japan*. New York: Teachers College Press.

Basmann, Robert L. 1963. "The Causal Interpretation of Non-triangular Systems of Economic Relations." *Econometrica* 31: 439-48.

______. 1965. "A Note on the Statistical Testability of 'Explicit Causal Chains' against the Class of 'Interdependent Models.'" *Journal of the American Statistical Association* 60: 1080-93.

Becker, Gary S. 1962. "Investment in Human Capital: A Theoretical Analysis." *Journal of Political Economy* 70, no. 5, part 2: S9-S49.

______. 1964 (2d ed. 1975). *Human Capital*. New York: National Bureau of Economic Research.

______. 1965. "A Theory of the Allocation of Time." *Economic Journal* 75:493-517.

______. 1967. *Human Ca;ital and the Personal Distribution of Income: An Analytical Approach* (Woytinsky Lecture no. 1). Ann Arbor: Institute of Public Administration and Department of Economics, University of Michigan.

Bowman, Mary Jean. 1962. "The Land Grant Colleges and Universities in Human Resource Development." *Journal of Economic History* 22 (December):523-46.

______. 1965. "From Guilds to Infant Training Industries." In C. A. Anderson and M. J. Bowman (eds.), *Education and Economic Development.* Chicago: Aldine, pp. 98-129.

______. 1966. "The Costing of Human Resource Development." In E. A. G. Robinson and J. E. Vaizey (eds.), *The Economics of Education.* New York: St. Martin's Press, pp. 421-50.

______. 1968. "The Assessment of Human Investments as Growth Strategy." In *Federal Programs for the Development of Human Resources* (Joint Economic Committee, 90th session). Washington, D. C.: Government Printing Office, pp. 84-99.

______. 1970*a*. "Mass Elites on the Threshold of the 1970's." *Comparative Education* 6:141-60.

______. 1970*b*. "Education and Economic Growth." In R. L. Johns (ed.), *Economic Factors Affecting the Financing of Education in the Decade Ahead.* Gainesville: Florida State University Press.

______. 1972. "Expectations, Uncertainty, and Investments in Human Beings." In C. F. Carter and J. L. Ford (eds.), *Uncertainty and Expectations in Economics.* Oxford: Basil Blackwell.

______. 1974*a*. "Learning and Earning in the Postschool Years." In Fred N. Kerlinger and John B. Carroll (eds.), *Review of Research in Education 2.* Itasca, Ill.: F. E. Peacock Publishers.

______. 1974*b*. "Post-School Learning and Human Resource Accounting." *Review of Income and Wealth*, Income and Wealth Series 20, no. 4 (December):483-500.

______. 1976. "Through Education to Earnings?" *Proceedings of the National Academy of Education* 3:221-92.

______. 1979. "Out-of-School Learning." In Douglas Windham (ed.), *Economic Dimensions of Education.* Washington, D. C.: National Academy of Education.

Bowman, Mary Jean (ed.). 1958. *Expectations, Uncertainty, and Business Behavior.* New York: Social Science Research Council.

Cane, Alan. 1974. "Pay-as-You-Learn Universities on Brink of Bankruptcy." *Times Higher Education Supplement* 18 December p. 11.

Carroll, Adger B., and Loren A. Innen. 1967. "Costs and Returns for Two Years of Post-Secondary Technical Schooling: A Pilot Study." *Journal of Political Economy* 75, no. 6 (December): 862-73.

Chusho-Kigyo-Cho. 1970. *Chusho-Kigyo Keiei Jittai Chōsa* [Association of Small and Medium Enterprises, A Survey of Management of Small and Medium Enterprises]. Tokyo: Chusho-Kigyo-Cho.

Coase, Ronald H. 1960. "The Problem of Social Cost." *Journal of Law and Economics* 3 (October):1-44.

Cole, Robert E. 1971. *Japanese Blue Collar: The Changing Tradition.* Berkeley and Los Angeles: University of California Press.

______. 1976. "Changing Labor Force Characteristics and Their Impact on Japanese Industrial Relations." In Lewis Austin (ed.), *Japan: The Paradox of Progress.* New Haven: Yale University Press, pp. 165-256.

Cummings, William K. 1972. "The Crises of Japanese Higher Education" (a review of Michio Nagai, 1971, *Higher Education in Japan: Its Take-off and Crash* [Tokyo: University of Tokyo Press]). *Minerva* 10, no. 4 (October):631-38.

______. 1975. "Understanding Behavior in Japan's Academic Marketplace." *Journal of Asian Studies* 39, no. 2 (February): 313-40.

______. 1976*a*. The Aftermath of the University Crisis." *Japan Interpreter* 10 (Winter):350-60.

______. 1976*b*. "The Problems and Prospects of Japanese Higher Education." In Lewis Austin (ed.), *Japan: The Paradox of Progress.* New Haven: Yale University Press, pp. 57-87.

______. 1980. *Education and Equality in Japan.* New York: Princeton University Press.
Cummings, William K., Ikuo Amano, and Kazuyuki Kitamura. 1979. *Changes in the Japanese University: A Comparative Perspective.* New York: Praeger Publishers.
Cummings, William K., and Atsushi Naoi. 1974. "Social Background, Education, and Personal Advancement in a Dualistic Employment System." *Developing Economies* 12, no. 3:245-73.
Denison, Edward F. 1967. *Why Growth Rates Differ: Postwar Experience in Nine Western Countries.* Washington, D.C.: Brookings Institution.
Denison, Edward F., and William K. Chung. 1976. *How Japan's Economy Grew So Fast.* Washington, D.C.: Brookings Insitution.
Doeringer, Peter B., and Michael J. Piore. 1971. *Internal Labor Markets and Manpower Analysis.* Lexington, Mass.: D. C. Heath.
Dore, Ronald P. 1974. *British Factory-Japanese Factory.* Berkeley and Los Angeles: University of California Press.
______. 1975. "The Future of Japan's Meritocracy." In Gianni Fodella (ed.), *Social Structures and Economic Dynamics in Japan up to 1980.* Treviso: Longo and Zoppelli, pp. 169-86.
______. 1976. *The Diploma Disease: Education, Qualification and Development.* Berkeley and Los Angeles: University of California Press.
Ehara, Takekazu. 1973. "Kōtōgakkō Sotsugyōsha no Shinro Sentaku ni kansuru Yōin Bunseki: Shingakusha o chushin to shite" [A Multivariate Analysis of High School Graduates' Career Planning], *Kyōikugaku Kenkyū* [Japanese Journal of Educational Research] 40, no. 1:11-22.
Emi, Koichi. 1963. *Government Fiscal Activity and Economic Growth in Japan, 1868-1960.* Institute of Economic Research, Hitotsubashi University, Economic Research Series 6. Tokyo: Kenkyusha Printing Co.
______. 1968. "Economic Development and Educational Investment in the Meiji Era." In UNESCO, *Readings in the Economics of Education.* Paris, pp. 94-106 (abridged from the English language translation by Soda Kichimasa).
Evans, Robert, Jr. 1971. *The Labor Economies of Japan and the United States.* New York: Praeger Publishers.
______. 1975. "Japan's Labor Economy--Prospect for the Future." *Monthly Labor Review* 95, no. 10 (October):3-8.
Fägerlind, Ingemar. 1975. *Formal Education and Adult Earnings.* Stockholm: Almqvist & Wiksell.
Foster, Philip. 1965. *Education and Social Change in Ghana.* Chicago: University of Chicago Press.
Freeman, Richard B. 1971. *The Markets for College Trained Manpower.* Cambridge, Mass.: Harvard University Press.
______. 1976. *The Overeducated American.* New York: Academic Press.
Fukaya, Masashi. 1977. "Shingaku Juku to sono Kinō: Shūdan Mensetsu Chōsa o tegakari to shite" [The Function of "Juku" in the Modern Japanese Education]. *Kyōiku Shakaigaku Kenkyū* [Journal of Educational Sociology], no. 32, pp. 51-64.
Galenson, Walter, with the collaboration of Konosuke Odaka. 1976. "The Japanese Labor Market." In Hugh Patrick and Henry Rosovsky (eds.), *Asia's New Giant.* Washington, D.C.: Brookings Institution, pp. 587-672.
Glazer, Nathan. 1976. "Social and Cultural Factors in Japanese Economic Growth." In Hugh Patrick and Henry Rosovsky (eds.), *Asia's New Giant.* Washington, D.C.: Brookings Institution, pp. 897-924.
Goto, Seiya. 1961. "Rōnin ni kansuru Ichi Kōsatsu" [An Essay on the *Rōnin*]. *Kyōiku Shakaigaku Kenkyū* [Journal of Educational Sociology], no. 16, pp. 86-98.
Griliches, Zvi. 1975. *Estimating Returns to Schooling: Some Econometric Problems.* Presidential address, meeting of the Econometric Society, Toronto, 1975. (Mimeograph. Cambridge, Mass.: Harvard University).

Griliches, Zvi, and W. H. Mason. 1972. "Education, Income, and Ability." *Journal of Political Economy* 80, no. 3, part 2 (May/June):S75-S103.

Hägerstrand, Torsten. 1965. "Quantitative Techniques for Analysis of the Spread of Information and Technology." In C. A. Anderson and M. J. Bowman (eds.), *Education and Economic Development*. Chicago: Aldine, pp. 244-80.

______. 1968. *Innovation Diffusion as a Spatial Process*, translated by Allan Pred. Chicago: University of Chicago Press.

Hara, Kimi. 1963. "Nippon ni okeru Daigaku Nyūshi no Shakaiteki Haikei" [The Social Background and the University Admissions System in Japan]. *Kyōikugaku Kenkyū* [Japanese Journal of Educational Researc] 30, no. 2:103-8.

Harada, Akira. 1969. "Gakureki to Chiiki Ido" [School Career and Migration'. *Kyōiku Shakaigaku Kenkyū* [Journal of Educational Sociology], no. 24, pp. 113-25.

Harker, Bruce Rogers. 1971. "Education Communication, and Agricultural Change: A Study of Japanese Farmers." Ph.D. dissertation, University of Chicago.

Harvey, Valerien. 1967. "Economic Aspects of Teachers' Salaries." Ph.D. dissertation, University of Chicago.

Hashimoto, Masanori. 1979. "Bonus Payments, On-the-Job Training, and Lifetime Employment in Japan." *Journal of Political Economy* 87, no. 5, part 1 (October):1086-1104.

Hashizume, Sadao (ed.). 1976. *Gakureki Hencho to sono Kozai* [The Merits and Demerits of Diploma Emphasis]. Tokyo: Daiichi Hōki Publishing Co.

Hata, Masaharu. 1977. "Kōtōgakkō Kakusa to Kyōiku Kikai no Kōzō [School Hierarchy and the Structure of Educational Opportunity]. *Kyōiku Shakaigaku Kenkyū* [Journal of Educational Sociology], no. 32, pp. 67-79.

Hiratsuka, Masunori. 1957. "Some Important Moments in the History of Modern Japanese Education" (summary of a lecture given in the United States and in England, 1955-56). *Bulletin of the Research Institute of Comparative Education and Culture* no. 1, pp. 96-102.

Hosoya, Toshio (ed.). 1973. *Gakkō Kyōiku no Kihonmondai* [Fundamental Issues of School Education]. Tokyo: Hyoronsha Publishing Co.

Hyde, William D. (IV). 1976. *Metropolitan Vocational Proprietary Schools*. Lexington, Mass.: D. C. Heath.

Ichikawa, Shogo. 1972. "Gakko towa Nanika: Yakuwari-Kinō no Saikentō" [The Function of the School Reconsidered]. *Kyōiku Shakaigaku Kenkyū* [Journal of Educational Sociology], no. 27, pp. 4-18.

Ikeda, Hideo. 1969*a*. "College Aspirations and Career Perspectives among Japanese Senior Secondary Students." *Comparative Education* 5, no. 2 (June): 177-87.

______. 1969*b*. "Kyōiku Asupireishon to Shokugyō Keireki no Mitōshi ni kansuru Chōsa Kenkyu" [Some Analyses of Educational Aspirations and Career Perspectives among Japanese Senior-Secondary Students]. *Shakaigaku Hyōron* [Japanese Sociological Review] 20, no. 2: 21-36.

______. 1976. "Gakureki Shikōsei to Kōtō Kyōiku" [Students' Preferences for Senior-Secondary Curriculum and Their Course Selectivity in Relation to College Aspirations]. *Kyōiku Shakaigaku Kenkyū* [Journal of Educational Sociology], no. 26, pp. 38-52.

Inoue, Keichi. 1976. "From Labour Surplus to Labour Shortage Economy: The Case of Japan." *International Labour Review* 113, no. 2 (March/April): 217-25.

Ishi, No. 1974. "Shingakuritsu to Sotsugyōritsu" [Entrance Rates and Retention Rates]. *Institute for Democratic Education* (Tokyo), no. 151 (September), pp. 54-55.

Iwai, Tatsuya. 1961. "Sangyō Kōzō no Henka to Chūto Kyōiku" [Changes in Industrial Structure and Secondary Education]. *Kyōiku Shakaigaku Kenkyū* [Journal of Educational Sociology], no. 16, pp. 2-23.
Kadowaki, Atsushi. 1978. *Gendai no Shussekan* [Modern Outlooks on Success in Life]. Tokyo: Nippon Keizai Shinbunsha Press.
Kaja, Moto (ed.). 1970. *Kyoiku to Keizai* [Education and Economy]. Tokyo: Daiichi Hōki Publishing Co.
Kanamori, H. 1972. "What Accounts for Japan's High Rate of Growth?" *Review of Income and Wealth* 18 (June):155-72.
Kaneko, Yoshio. 1970. "Employment and Wages." *Developing Economies* 8 (December):454-55.
Keizai Kikakucho Kokumin Seikatsu Kyoku (ed.). 1978. *Nipponjin no Kyōikukan to Shokugyōkan: Seikatsu Yōkyu no Jittai to Akusesibiliti* [Japanese Views of Education and Occupation: Present Status of Living Needs and Educational and Occupational Accessibilities]. Tokyo: Ōkurashō Insatsu Kyoku Publishing Bureau.
Keizai Shingikai (ed.). 1963. *Keizai Hatten ni okeru Jinteki Nōryoku Kaihatsu no Kadai to Taisaku* [The Tasks and Counterpolicy of Human Resource Development in Economic Growth]. Tokyo: Ōkurashō Insatsu Kyoku Publishing Bureau.
Kikuchi, Jozi. 1967. "Gendai Nihon ni okeru Chūto Kyōiku Kikai" [Access to Secondary Education in Modern Japan]. *Kyōiku Shakaigaku Kenkyū* [Journal of Educational Sociology], no. 22, pp. 126-47.
Kitamura, Kazuyuki, and William K. Cummings. 1972. "The 'Big Bang' Theory and Japanese University Reform." *Comparative Education Review* 16, no. 2 (June):303-24.
Kiyonari, Tadao. 1970. *Nihon Chusho-Kigyo no Kozo Hendo* [Structural Changes in the Small-Medium Enterprise Sector of Japan]. Tokyo: Shinhyoron.
Kobayashi, Tetsuya. 1971. "Changing Policies in Higher Education--the Japanese Case." *World Yearbook of Education 1971-2*. London: Evans.
Koh, Tsu Koon. 1977. "Education, Entrepreneurial Formation, and Entrepreneurial Behavior in Japan." Ph.D. dissertation, University of Chicago.
Kondo, Motoo, Yoshiyuki Nogaki, Akira Harada, and Masato Takahata. 1963. "Shingaku Jumbikyōiku no Kenkyū" [A Study of Out-of School Education in Preparation for Entrance Examinations]. *Kyōiku Shakaigaku Kenkyū* [Journal of Educational Sociology], no. 18, pp. 239-55.
Kono, Shigeo (ed.). 1975. *Gendai no Gakkō*. Tokyo: Daiichi Hōki Publishing Co.
Kono, Shigeo, and Ikuo Arai (eds.). 1976. *Gendai Gakkō no Kōzō* [Structure of Modern Schools]. Tokyo: University of Tokyo Press.
______. 1978. *Gendai Kyōiku no Kōzō to Kadai* [Structure and Tasks of Modern Education]. Tokyo: Gyōsei Publishing Co.
Kuratani, Masatoshi. 1973. "Specific Training, Employment Stability, and Earnings Distribution in Japan." Ph.D. dissertation, Columbia University.
Levine, Solomon B. 1958. *Industrial Relations in Postwar Japan*. Urbana: University of Illinois Press.
Lewis, David M. 1968. "The Perception of Entrepreneurial Prestige by Rural Japanese Boys." *Rural Sociology* 33, no. 1 (March): 71-79.
Linder, Staffan B. 1970. *The Harried Leisure Class*. New York: Columbia University Press.
Lipset, Seymour M., Reinhard Bendix, and F. Theodore Malm. 1962. "Job Plans and Entry into the Labor Market." In Sigmund Nosow and William F. Form (eds.), *Man, Work, and Society*. New York: Basic Books.

Mainichi Shinbun Shakaibu. 1977. *Shingaku Juku Ripouto: Ranjuku Jidai* [The Report of Private Preparatory Schools for the Entrance Examination at Full Maturity]. Tokyo: Simile Publishing Co.

Marsh, Robert M., and Hiroshi Mannari. 1971. "Lifetime Commitment in Japan: Roles, Norms, and Values." *American Journal of Sociology* 76, no. 5 (March):795-812.

______. 1972. "A New Look at 'Lifetime Commitment' in Japanese Industry." *Economic Development and Cultural Change* 20, no. 4: 611-30.

______. 1975. *Modernization and the Japanese Factory*. Princeton, N.J.: Princeton University Press.

Matsubara, Haruo. 1971. *Gendai no Seinen* [Modern Youth]. Tokyo: Chuokoron Publishing Co.

______. 1978. *Nippon no Seishonen: Seishonen Kyōiku no Teisho* [Japanese Youth: Introduction to Youth Education]. Tokyo: Tokyoshoseki Publishing Co.

Matsubara, Haruo, Hitoshi Takahashi, Kiyoshi Takeuchi, and Fumie Kumagai. 1979. *Nichibei Kōkōsei Hikaku Chōsa* [Comparative Survey of Japanese and American High School Students]. Japan Institute for the Youth.

Matsui, Shigeo. 1971. "The Problem of the Comprehensive Secondary School in Japan." *International Review of Education* 17, no. 1:27-38.

Minami, R. 1972. "Transformation of the Labor Market in Postwar Japan." *Hitotsubashi Journal of Economics* 13 (June):57-72.

Mincer, Jacob. 1958. "Investment in Human Capital and Personal Income Distribution." *Journal of Political Economy* 66, no. 4 (August):281-302.

______. 1952. "On the Job Training: Costs, Returns, and Some Implications." *Journal of Political Economy* 70, no. 5, part 2:S50-79.

______. 1970. "The Distribution of Labor Incomes: A Survey with Special Reference to the Human Capital Approach." *Journal of Economic Literature* 8:1-26.

______. 1974. *Schooling, Experience, and Earnings*. New York: National Bureau of Economic Research.

Ministry of Labor. 1975. White Paper on Labor, 1974. Tokyo.

Miyachi, Seiya. 1978. *Chūto Kyōiku to Shokugyō Seikatsu: Gakkō to Shakai no Kakawari o kangaeru* [Secondary Education and Work Life: A Study of the Relations between School and Society]. Tokyo: Kawashimashoten Publishing Co.

Modigliani, F., and K. J. Cohen. 1961. *The Role of Anticipations and Plans in Economic Behavior and Their Use in Economic Analysis and Forecasting. University of Illinois Bulletin.*

Mombushō. 1977. *Daijin Kanbō Chōsa Tōkeika Zenkoku Gakushū Juku tō no Jittai* [Ministry of Education, Bureau of Statistics, Conditions of the *Juku* in the Nation].

Nagai, Michio. 1971. *Higher Education in Japan: Its Take-off and Crash,* translated by Jerry Dusenbury. Tokyo: University of Tokyo Press.

______. 1979. Foreword to William K. Cummings, Ikuo Amano, and Kazuyuki Kitamura (eds.). *Changes in the Japanese University*. New York: Praeger.

Nakayama, Ichiro. 1965. "The Modernization of Industrial Relations in Japan." In Japan Institute of Labor, *The Changing Pattern of Industrial Relations*. Tokyo, pp. 86-87.

Naoi, Atsushi, and Hidenori Fujita. 1978. "Kyōiku Tassei Katei to sono Chii Keisei Kōka" [The Effects of the Educational Achievement Process on Status Attainment]. *Kyōiku Shakaigaku Kenkyū* [Journal of Educational Sociology], no. 33, pp. 91-105.

National Institute for Educational Resarch. 1977. *Modernization of Education in Japan* (World Bank project). Tokyo, April.

Nerlove, Marc. 1972. "On Tuition and the Costs of Higher Education: Prolegomena to a Conceptual Framework." *Journal of Political Economy* 80, no. 3, part 2 (May/June):178-218.
Noda, Kazuo. 1975. "Big Business Organization." In Ezra F. Vogel (ed.), *Modern Japanese Organization and Decision Making.* Berkeley and Los Angeles: University of California Press, 18-42.
OECD (ed.). 1971. *Reviews of National Policies for Education: Japan.* Paris: OECD.
Okamoto, Hideaki. 1970*a*. "Manpower at the Enterprise Level, I." *Japan Labor Bulletin*, 1 October, pp. 5-8.
______. 1970*b*. "Manpower at the Enterprise Level, II." *Japan Labor Bulletin,* 1 November, pp. 7-10.
______. 1971. "The Roles of State and Enterprise in Development of Skills at Work or On-the-Job in Japanese History." (Paper read at the Conference on Manpower Problems in East and Southeast Asia, Singapore, May.)
Okochi, Kazuo, Bernard Karsh, and Solomon B. Levine (eds.). 1974. *Workers and Employers in Japan: The Japanese Employment Relations System.* Princeton, N.J.: Princeton University Press.
Ono, Hiroshi. 1970. "Sengo Nippon no Koyō to Chūsotsu Shūshokusha no Dōkō" [An Analysis of the Placement and Working Conditions of Lower-Secondary-School Graduates in the Labor Market of Postwar Japan]. *Kyōiku Shakaigaku Kenkyū* [Journal of Educational Sociology], no. 25, pp. 196-208.
Passin, Herbert. 1965. *Society and Education in Japan.* New York: Bureau of Publications, Teachers College, Columbia University; and East Asian Institute, Columbia University.
______. 1970. *Japanese Education: A Bibliography of Materials in the English Language.* New York: Teachers College Press.
Patrick, Hugh (ed.). 1976. *Japanese Industrialization and its Social Consequences.* Berkeley and Los Angeles: University of California Press.
Patrick, Hugh, and Henry Rosovsky (eds.). 1976. *Asia's New Giant: How the Japanese Economy Works.* Washington, D.C.: Brookings Institution.
Pedersen, George. 1973. *The Itinerant Schoolmaster.* Chicago: Midwest Administration Center.
Pempel, T. J. 1971. "Evaluating Japan's Mass Higher Education." *Japan Quarterly* 18, no. 4 (October):450-54.
______. 1973. "The Politics of Enrollment Expansion in Japanese Universities." *Journal of Asian Studies* 33, no. 1 (November): 67-86.
Reid, Margaret G. 1934. *The Economics of Household Production.* New York: John Wiley.
Rohlen, Thomas P. 1977. "Is Japanese Education Becoming Less Egalitarian? Notes on High School Stratification and Reform." *Journal of Japanese Studies* 3, no. 1:37-70.
______. 1979. "Permanent Employment Faces Recession, Slow Growth, and an Aging Work Force." *Journal of Japanese Studies* 5, no. 2:235-72.
______. 1980. "The Juku Phenomenon: An Exploratory Essay." *Journal of Japanese Studies* 6, no. 2:207-42.
Rosen, Sherwin. 1972. "Learning and Experience in the Labor Market." *Journal of Human Resources* 7:326-42.
______. 1977. "Human Capital: A Survey of Empirical Research." In Ronald E. Ehrenberg (ed.), *Research in Labor Economics* 1:3-38. Greenwich, Conn.: JAI Press.
Rosen, Sherwin, and Robert Willis. 1979. "Education and Self-Selection." *Journal of Political Economy* 87, no. 5, part 2: S7-36.
Sano, Yohko. 1966. "An Analysis of Industrial Wage Differentials." *Keio Daigaku Keizaigaku Kenkyū* [Keio University's Economic Studies], no. 4, pp. 29-43.
Schultz, Theodore W. 1961. "Investment in Human Capital." *American Economic Review*, March, pp. 1-17.

Sewell, William H., and Robert M. Hauser. 1975. *Education, Occupation, and Earnings: Achievement in the Early Career.* New York: Academic Press.

Shackle, G. L. S. 1952. *Expectations in Economics.* 2d ed. Cambridge: Cambridge University Press.

______. 1955. *Uncertainty in Economics.* Cambridge: Cambridge University Press.

______. 1961. *Decision, Order, and Time in Economics.* Cambridge: Cambridge University Press.

Shibanuma, Susumu (ed.). 1976. *Shogaikoku no Kyōiku no Genjyō to Kadai: Waga Kuni no Kyōiku no Shiten ni tatte* [Present Status and Tasks of Education in European Countries: Seen from a Viewpoint of Japanese Education]. Tokyo: Gyōsei Publishing Co.

Shimada, Haruo. 1974. *The Structure of Earnings and Investments in Human Resources: A Comparison between the United States and Japan.* Ph.D. dissertation, University of Wisconsin, Madison.

Shimbori, Michiya. 1965. *Nippon no Daigaku Kyōjo Shijō* [Academic Marketplace in Japan]. Tokyo: Toyōkan Publishing Co.

______. 1966. *Gakureki: Jitsuryokushugi o Kobamu mono* [Credentials: Obstruction in Meritocracy]. Tokyo: Daiyamondo Publishing Co.

______. 1969. *Gakubatsu* [School Cliques]. Tokyo: Fukumura Publishing Co.

______. 1976. *Gendai Nippon no Kyōiku Byōri* [Educational Pathology in Contemporary Japan]. Tokyo: Gyōsei Publishing Co.

Shimizu, Yoshihiro. 1957. *Shiken* [Entrance Examinations]. Tokyo: Iwanamishoten Publishing Co.

______. 1970. *Kyōiku Kaikaku no Tenbō* [Perspectives in Educational Reforms]. Tokyo: University of Tokyo Press.

______. 1977. *Gendai Kyōiku no Kadai* [Tasks of Modern Education]. Tokyo: University of Tokyo Press.

______. 1978. *Shimizu Yoshihiro Chosaku Senshū*, Jen Gokan [Shimizu Yoshihiro's Selected Works, in a series of 5 volumes]. Tokyo: Daiichi Hōki Publishing Co.

Smith, James P., and Finis Welch. 1980. "The Overeducated American? A Review Article." *Proceedings of the National Academy of Education*, in press.

Sumiya, Michio. 1967. "The Function and Social Structure of Education: Schools and Japanese Society." *Journal of Social and Political Ideas in Japan* 5, nos. 2-3:117-38.

Tachibanaki, Toshiaki. 1975. "Wage Determinations in Japanese Manufacturing Industries--Structural Change and Wage Differentials." *International Economic Review* 16, no. 3 (October):562-86.

______. 1976. "Quality Change in Labor Input: Japanese Manufacturing." *Review of Economics and Statistics* 58, no. 3 (August): 293-99.

Taira, Koji. 1970. *Economic Development and the Labor Market in Japan.* New York: Columbia University Press.

Teichler, Ulrich. 1972. "Some Aspects of Higher Education in Japan." *Kokusai Bunka Shinkokai Bulletin on Japanese Culture*, no. 114 (June/July), pp. 1-20.

______. 1976. *Das Deilemma der modernen Bildungsgesellschaft: Japans Hochschulen unter den Zwangen der Statuszuteiling.* Stuttgart: Klett.

Todd, Edward S. 1969. *Some Economic Implications of Secondary School Curricula.* Ph.D. dissertation, University of Chicago.

Tominaga, Kenichi. 1969. "Trend Analysis of Social Stratification and Social Mobility in Contemporary Japan." *Developing Economies* 7 (December):471-98.

Tominaga, Kenichi (ed.). 1979. *Nippon no Kaisō Kōzō* [The Structure of Social Classes in Japan]. Tokyo: University of Tokyo Press.

Tomoda, Yasumasa. 1968*a*. "Occupational Aspirations of Japanese High School Students." *International Journal of Educational Sciences* 2:217-25.

______. 1968*b* "Daigaku Nyūgakusha no Chiriteki Idō to Chiikibetsu Haishutsuritsu" [A study of the Geographical Distribution of College Entrants]. *Kyōikugaku Kenkyū* [Japanese Journal of Educational Research] 35, no. 4:294-304.

______. 1970. "Todōfukenbetsu Daigaku Shingakuritsu Kakusa to sono Kitei Yōin" [Self-Determinants of Regional Differences in College Enrollment Rates of Forty-Six Prefectures in Japan]. *Kyōiku Shakaigaku Kenkyū* [Journal of Educational Sociology], 25, pp. 185-195.

Ushiogi, Morikazu. 1971*a* "Kōtō Kyōiku no Kokusai Hikaku: Kōtō Kyōiku Sotsugyōsha no Shūgyo Kōzō no Hikaku Kenkyū" [An International Comparison of Higher Education: The Occupational Structures of Higher-Education Graduates]. *Kyōiku Shakaigaku Kenkyū* [Journal of Educational Sociology], no. 26, pp. 2-16.

______. 1971*b* "A Comparative Study of the Occupational Structure of University Graduates." *Developing Economies* 9 (September): 350-68.

______. 1975*a*. "Kyōiku to Kaisō Idō ni kansuru Simulation Bunseki" [Simulation Analysis of Education and Social Mobility]. *Nagoya Daigaku Kyōikugakubu Kenkyū Kiyō* [Bulletin of the Faculty of Education, Nagoya University] 22:49-70.

______. 1975*b*. "Jinkō Hendō ka no Kōkō Zōsetsu Taisaku" [Policy-making and the Democratic Swell in Secondary School-Age Population]. *Nagoya Daigaku Kyōikugakubu Kenkyū Kiyō* [Bulletin of the Faculty of Education, Nagoya University] 21:51-67.

______. 1975*c*. "Shinro Kketei Katei no Pasu Kaiseki" [Path Analysis Applied to the Educational Selection Process: Factors in Admission to Secondary Schools]. *Kyōiku Shakaigaku Kenkyū* [Journal of Educational Sociology], no. 30, pp. 75-86

______. 1976. "The Impact of Educational Expansion on the Labor Market." Typescript.

______. 1978. *Gakureki Shakai no Tenkan* [Transformation of Credential Society]. Tokyo: University of Tokyo Press.

Ushiogi, Morikazu (ed.). 1979. *Kōkō Kyōiku Gimuka no Kanōsei ni kansuru Kisoteki Kenkyū* [Possibilities of Compulsory Upper-Secondary Education in Japan: A Report of the Toyota Foundation]. Nagoya: Nagoya Daigaku Kyōikugakubu, Kyōiku Shakaigaku Kenkyū Shitsu [Department of Educational Sociology, Nagoya University].

Vogel, Ezra F. 1962. "Entrance Examinations and Emotional Disturbances in Japan's 'New Middle Class.'" In Robert J. Smith and Richard K. Beardsley (eds.), *Japanese Culture: Its Development and Characteristics*. Chicago: Aldine.

Walsh, J. R. 1935. "The Capital Concept Applied to Man." *Quarterly Journal of Economics* 49 (February):255-85.

Wang, Bee-Lan Chan. 1975. *Educational Selection, Achievement, and Decision-making in West Malaysia*. Ph.D. dissertation, University of Chicago.

Watanabe, Tsunehiko. 1965. "Economic Aspects of Dualism in the Industrial Development of Japan." *Economic Development and Cultural Change* 13, no. 3 (April):293-312.

Welch, Finis, and Iva Maclennan. 1976. "The U.S. Census Occupational Taxonomy: How Much Information Does It Contain?" Santa Monica: Rand Publication R-1849-HEW.

Wold, Herman. 1960. "A Generalization of Causal Chain Models." *Econometrica* 28:443-63.

Yamamoto, G. K., and Tsuyoshi Ishida (eds.). 1971. *Selected Readings on Modern Japanese Culture*. San Francisco: McCutchan.

Yano, Takashi (ed.). 1979. *Dare ga Kyōiku o ninaubeki ka: Kodomo to Katei-Gakkō-Chiiki no Yakuwari* [On Whose Shoulders Should Education Be Carried: The Roles of Children, Home, School, and the Community]. Nishi Nippon Shinbun Press.

Yasuda, Saburo. 1971. *Shakai Idō* [Social Mobility]. Tokyo: University of Tokyo Press.

Yoshino, M. Y. 1968. *Japan's Managerial System: Tradition and Innovation.* Cambridge, Mass.: Massachusetts Institute of Technology Press.

Zabalza, Antoni, Philip Turnbull, and Gareth Williams. 1979. *The Economics of Teacher Supply.* Cambridge: Cambridge University Press.

Index